Kentucky Kitchens

TELEPHONE PIONEERS
c/o Chrissy Robey
502-926-8555

MEIER '89

Telephone
of Pioneers
America

ANSWERING THE CALL OF THOSE IN NEED

This cookbook is a collection of our favorite recipes which are
not necessarily original recipes.

Published by
Favorite Recipes Press
P. O. Box 305142
Nashville, Tennessee 37230

ISBN: 0-87197-263-8
Library of Congress Number: 89-37026

Manufactured in the United States of America

EXPRESSION
OF
APPRECIATION

A collection of recipes from telephone employees and friends seems like an easy thing to assemble, until you volunteer to do it.

I want to take this space to thank and gratefully acknowledge all the people who contributed in so many ways to make this cookbook a success.

I especially want to thank the Pioneer Life Members (retired employees). They sent recipes from Pikeville to Paducah, and really got busy when I called for help.

I also want to thank Wanda Wiegand (Chapter Administrator) for her support and assistance.

A special thanks goes to Laura Meier for drawing the pictures for the chapter openers, and to Jan Anderson for her beautiful cover design.

My deepest gratitude goes to Jeanie Walker, Carmen Stilger, Janet Arnold, Margaret Taylor, and Barbara Struck for their hours of work.

Last but not least, a hug for my husband, Frank Fendley, who contributed his recipes; gathered recipes from everyone in his office; typed, sorted, and put up with me.

Dana Fendley

Dana Fendley
Cookbook Chairperson

THE
TELEPHONE
PIONEER STORY

The Telephone Pioneers of America is the world's largest voluntary association of industrial employees. It is composed of men and women in the United States and Canada who have served 15 or more years in the telephone industry.

It was established in 1911 by men and women who were dedicated pioneers of the telephone industry.

The purpose of the Telephone Pioneers is to provide a means of friendly association and fellowship for employees in the telephone industry, both active and retired; to foster among them a continuing fellowship and spirit of mutual helpfulness; and to participate in activities that are of service to the community.

The Pioneer motto is *Fellowship, Loyalty and Service* — a motto which unifies the great diversity and individual interests and talents.

It is through the Pioneer program that these words really come to life. For here is the interaction of people — enjoying each other's friendly companionship, working and learning together, being of service to members and to the local community, and bringing experience and time-honored tradition to the challenges of a fast changing world.

The Pioneers sell cookbooks to raise money for community service projects. In the 1988 Pioneer year, over $81,000.00 was raised and donated in Kentucky to these projects:

Special Olympics	$ 5,455.75
Youth Services	$ 6,805.16
Needy Families	$ 5,022.39
Child Victims Trust Fund	$13,381.19
Needy Children	$ 6,029.69
Camp Bluebird	$ 7,526.44
Drug Abuse	$ 3,504.50
Visual	$ 2,011.50
Hearing	$ 1,264.46

Pioneers do more than give money to community projects. They may be the drivers of the Ronald McDonald House van, the ones who rebuilt your headstart center, the donors that made the Red Cross blood drive a success, and the huggers who cuddled your Special Olympian. Did your youngster come home with a "Just Say No to Drugs" message? Pioneers have been hard at work getting that lesson out to their communities. And you can be pretty sure no walkathon, telethon, or bowlathon happens in North America without Pioneer participation.

Pioneers are proud of their organization and welcome this opportunity to share their story with you.

TELEPHONE PIONEERS
OF
AMERICA

Kentucky Chapter No. 32

Councils

A. T. & T.	Louisville Central-West
Big Sandy	Louisville South-East
Blue Grass	Pennyrile
Capital	Purchase

Life Member Clubs

Big Sandy	Lexington
Bowling Green	Louisville
Capital	Madisonville
Daniel Boone	Owensboro
Hopkinsville	Paducah
Winchester	

TABLE OF CONTENTS

FAVORITE RECIPE FINDER

RECIPE TITLE	PAGE

The Stephen Foster Story is played in an open air theater at "My Old Kentucky Home" in Bardstown, Kentucky.

Kentucky Favorites

MY OLD KENTUCKY HOME

KENTUCKY FAVORITES

ELEPHANT STEW

1 elephant
Brown gravy

2 rabbits (optional)

Cut elephant into bite-sized pieces; allow about 2 months for this step. Combine with brown gravy to cover in elephant pot over kerosene fire. Cook at 465 degrees for 4 weeks. Add rabbits only if needed for unexpected guests, as not everyone likes to find a hare in his stew. Yield: 3800 servings.

Henry and Martha Hooper

RECIPE FOR PRESERVING A HUSBAND

Be careful of your selection. Do not choose too young. When once selected give your entire thought to preparation for domestic use. Some insist on keeping them in a pickle. Others constantly put them in hot water. This makes them sour, hard and sometimes bitter. Even poor varieties may be made sweet, tender and good by garnishing them with patience, well sweetened with love and seasoned with kisses. Wrap them in a mantle of charity. Keep warm with a steady fire of domestic decoration and serve with peaches and cream. Prepared in this manner they will keep for years.

Virginia Hodges

SUMMER RECIPE

Wild flowers
1 large grassy field
6 children, various sizes
2 or 3 small frisky dogs

1 shallow unpolluted brook
Small pebbles
Deep blue sky
Hot sun

Spread the flowers across the grassy field. Mix the children and dogs into the field, stirring constantly. Pour the brook over the pebbles. Top with deep blue sky. Bake in hot sun. Remove children from field. Cool in shallow water in bathtub.

Patti Reece

RECIPE FOR LIFE

1 cup good thoughts
1 cup consideration for
  others
1 cup kind deeds
3 cups forgiveness

2 cups well beaten faults
Tears of joy, sorrow and
  sympathy
4 cups prayer and faith

Mix good thoughts, consideration, kind deeds, forgiveness and well beaten faults. Add tears of joy, sorrow and sympathy for others. Fold in prayer and faith to lighten other ingredients and raise the texture to great heights of Christian living. Pour all this into your family life. Bake well with the heat of human kindness. Serve with a smile.

Patti Reece

KENTUCKY MINT JULEP

This is a Derby Day tradition.

Boiling water
Sugar
Mint leaves

Crushed ice
100-proof Kentucky
  Bourbon

Combine 1 part boiling water and 2 parts sugar in pitcher. Stir until sugar is dissolved. Place 3 or 4 mint leaves in bottom of glass. Add crushed ice. Press ice to bruise mint leaves. Pour mixture of 2 parts bourbon and 1 part sugar syrup over ice. Garnish with a sprig of mint.

BEER CHEESE

16 ounces sharp Cheddar
  cheese
16 ounces mild Cheddar
  cheese
1 clove of garlic, minced
1 teaspoon salt

1 teaspoon dry mustard
4 drops of Tabasco sauce
3 tablespoons
  Worcestershire sauce
1 12-ounce can beer

Shred cheeses finely in food processor. Combine cheeses with next 5 ingredients in mixer bowl; beat until smooth. Add beer gradually, beating until well blended. Chill in airtight container. Let stand at room temperature for 30 minutes. Beat with mixer just before serving. Serve with crackers. Yield: 12 to 16 servings.

BENEDICTINE

*This recipe is an original Kentucky Favorite from
Jennie Carter Benedict, caterer, cookbook writer
and owner of Benedict's Restaurant.*

1 large cucumber
1 small onion, grated
8 ounces cream cheese,
  softened
1/4 teaspoon salt

1 tablespoon mayonnaise
1 or 2 drops of green food
  coloring
Sour cream

Peel and shred cucumber. Drain cucumber and onion well. Beat cream cheese, salt, mayonnaise and food coloring in mixer bowl until well blended. Add cucumber and onion; mix well. Add enough sour cream to make of dipping consistency. May omit sour cream to use as sandwich filling. Yield: 12 to 24 servings.

BREAD AND BUTTER PICKLES

1 gallon medium
  cucumbers
6 to 12 large onions
2 green bell peppers,
  chopped
1/2 cup coarse salt

5 cups vinegar
5 cups sugar
1 1/2 teaspoons turmeric
2 teaspoons mustard seed
1 1/2 teaspoons celery seed
1/2 teaspoon ground cloves

Slice unpeeled cucumbers very thinly. Slice onions very thinly. Combine cucumbers, onions and green pepper in large bowl. Sprinkle with salt. Chill, covered with weighted lid, in refrigerator for 3 hours. Drain well. Rinse with cold water; drain well. Combine vinegar, sugar, turmeric, mustard and celery seed and cloves in very large saucepan. Bring to a boil; reduce heat. Add vegetables gradually, stirring very little. Scald vegetables in liquid; do not boil. Pack pickles into hot sterilized jars. Add hot liquid, leaving 1/2-inch headspace; seal with 2-piece lids. Chill before serving. May substitute allspice for turmeric.
Yield: 10 to 12 quarts.

HALL'S SWEET AND SOUR SLAW

2 heads cabbage
1/2 cup onion
1/2 cup carrots
1/3 cup celery

1/3 cup sugar
2 tablespoons salt
1/3 cup vinegar
1/3 cup oil

Process cabbage, onion, carrots and celery in food processor until coarsely shredded. Toss vegetables in salad bowl. Mix sugar, salt, vinegar and oil in small bowl. Pour over vegetables; toss lightly. Chill in refrigerator.
Yield: 8 to 12 servings.

BURGOO

Burgoo is a hearty soup made from chicken, mutton, beef and a variety of vegetables. No two cooks prepare it the same way. Most keep their recipes secret. Tradition says that Burgoo came from Wales and found its way to the Kentucky frontiers through Virginia.

2 pounds beef
2 pounds pork
2 pounds veal
2 pounds lamb
4 pounds chicken
8 quarts cold water
1 1/2 pounds potatoes
1 1/2 pounds onions
1 1/2 pounds carrots
2 green bell peppers

2 cups chopped cabbage
4 cups tomato purée
3 cups whole kernel corn
2 cups chopped okra
2 cups lima beans
1 cup chopped celery
Salt and pepper to taste
Tabasco sauce to taste
1 cup chopped parsley

Combine beef, pork, veal, lamb, chicken and water in very large soup pot. Bring to a boil; reduce heat. Simmer until meat is tender enough to fall from bones. Remove meat; cool slightly. Remove bones; chop meat. Return meat to broth. Chop potatoes, onions, carrots and peppers. Add to pot with cabbage, tomato purée, corn, okra, lima beans and celery. Simmer until thickened, stirring occasionally. Season with salt, pepper and Tabasco sauce. Stir in parsley just before serving.
Yield: 48 servings.

RIB CAFE-STYLE BARBECUE CHICKEN

3 2½-pound chickens
2 tablespoons vinegar
3½ cups tomato sauce
1 cup catsup
1 bay leaf
Juice of 1 lemon
¼ cup finely chopped
　onion
1½ teaspoons red pepper

1 teaspoon salt
1 teaspoon black pepper
¼ cup red wine vinegar
1 teaspoon pickling spice
½ teaspoon oregano
½ teaspoon garlic powder
1 teaspoon celery seed
¼ cup packed brown
　sugar

Cut chickens into quarters. Arrange in baking dishes. Bake at 350 degrees for 45 minutes or until brown. Drain and cool to room temperature. Combine remaining ingredients in saucepan. Bring to a boil; reduce heat. Simmer for 20 minutes, stirring frequently. Remove bay leaf. Place chicken skin side up on grill over hot coals. Grill for several minutes. Baste generously with sauce. Turn chicken; baste generously with sauce. Grill for 10 minutes or until chicken is slightly charred. Yield: 12 servings.

Barbara Struck

HOT BARBECUE

1½ pounds ground chuck
2 tablespoons butter
½ cup chopped onion
¼ to ½ teaspoon cayenne
2 tablespoons vinegar
2 tablespoons
　Worcestershire sauce

1 teaspoon paprika
1 teaspoon chili powder
¾ cup catsup
¾ cup water
1 tablespoon salt
½ teaspoon pepper
Sandwich buns

Cook ground chuck in butter in skillet until brown and crumbly. Push ground beef to side of skillet. Add onion. Sauté until golden. Mix ground chuck and onion together. Add cayenne, vinegar, Worcestershire sauce, paprika, chili powder, catsup, water, salt and pepper; mix well. Simmer for 30 minutes or until thickened, stirring frequently. Serve on heated buns. Garnish with relish, pickles or onions. Yield: 6 to 8 servings.

Jean W. Willis

SLIDERS

This is a re-created recipe of the famous little square hamburgers that taste best at 3:00 AM. If you punch holes in them they even look like the real thing.

1/4 **cup instant minced onion**
1/4 **cup hot water**
2 1/4 **to** 2 1/2 **pounds ground round**
1 **3-ounce jar strained beef baby food**

2/3 **cup canned beef broth**
Oil
Salt and pepper to taste
10 **hot dog buns**
40 **dill pickle slices**

Soak onion in water in covered bowl for 15 minutes. Combine ground round, baby food and broth in bowl; mix well. Divide mixture into 1/4 cup portions. Pat each into 3-inch square patty in sandwich-size plastic bag. Heat 1/2 teaspoon oil for each patty in large skillet over high heat. Add patties; do not crowd. Cook until brown. Turn patties over; season with salt and pepper. Steam buns or microwave until soft. Cut each bun into halves; split halves. Place 2 pickle slices, 1 teaspoon onion and 1 patty on each bun half. Yield: 20 sandwiches.

COUNTRY HAM

Country ham is sugar-cured, smoked and aged.
An 18-month old ham is best.

1 **country ham**
1 1/2 **gallons water**
1/2 **cup whole cloves**
1 **cup packed brown sugar**
1 **cup vinegar**

1 **cup packed brown sugar**
1 **cup cornmeal**
1 **tablespoon ground cloves**
1 **teaspoon cinnamon**

Soak ham in 1 1/2 gallons water overnight. Sprinkle 1/4 cup whole cloves in roasting pan. Place ham in pan. Sprinkle remaining cloves over ham. Add 1-inch water. Add mixture of 1 cup brown sugar and vinegar. Bake at 375 degrees for 1 hour. Reduce temperature to 275 degrees. Bake for 20 minutes per pound. Bone and trim ham as desired. Place ham in shallow roasting pan. Combine 1 cup brown sugar, cornmeal, ground cloves and cinnamon in bowl. Sprinkle over ham. Increase oven temperature to 375 degrees. Bake until brown. Slice as desired.

RED EYE GRAVY

Country ham slices
1/4 cup water
1/4 cup coffee

1/2 teaspoon Kitchen
Bouquet

Brown ham slices in skillet. Remove to warm platter. Keep warm. Brown ham drippings; drain excess grease. Add water and coffee, stirring to deglaze skillet. Bring to a boil. Add Kitchen Bouquet for darker gravy. Pour over fried ham slices.

CAPTAIN'S COUNTRY HAM STERNWHEELS WITH BELLE'S RED EYE

*This 4-generation family recipe from Katie Tivnan was served at the inaugural reception for Dr. Harvey Sloan, Mayor of Louisville. This recipe appeared in **The Courier Journal** and the **Inaugural Souvenir Cookbook**.*

6 medium-thick slices
  Kentucky country ham
Freshly ground pepper to
  taste
4 cups self-rising flour
4 teaspoons baking
  powder
2 1/2 cups buttermilk

1/2 teaspoon soda
1 cup shortening
1 cup self-rising flour
Pan drippings
1 teaspoon paprika
1 cup hot coffee
1 cup hot water

Remove rinds from ham slices. Render grease from rinds in skillet over low heat. Remove rinds. Reserve drippings. Cut ham into chunks. Put through medium blade of food grinder. Place in skillet. Cook over medium heat for 20 minutes turning frequently with spatula. Season with pepper. Remove from skillet; drain on paper towels. Reserve drippings in skillet. Sift 4 cups flour and baking powder into large bowl. Make well in center. Crumble shortening into mixture with fingers. Pour mixture of buttermilk and soda into well. Knead in bowl until mixed. Sprinkle 1 cup flour on board. Turn dough onto floured board; knead lightly. Press to desired thickness. Roll lightly with floured rolling pin; cut with biscuit cutter. Press indentation in center of each biscuit with small floured glass such as whiskey jigger. Do not cut through. Pinch dough to form 6 to 8 spokes from outer edge to center indentation on each biscuit. Press ham into center indentation and between spokes. Place on greased baking sheet. Bake at 375 degrees for 15 minutes or until brown. Combine drippings, paprika, coffee and water in skillet. Simmer for 5 minutes. Remove from heat. Pour into gravy boat. Arrange sternwheels on platter with gravy boat in center. Yield: 30 to 36 sternwheels.

Mrs. Dan J. Tivnan, Jr.

DEEP-FRIED FROG LEGS

12 frog legs
Salt and pepper to taste
1 cup flour

2 eggs, beaten
1/4 cup milk
Oil for frying

Season frog legs with salt and pepper. Beat eggs and milk in bowl. Dip frog legs into mixture; coat with flour. Repeat. Heat 1/2-inch oil in heavy skillet. Fry frog legs until golden brown and tender. Serve immediately. Yield: 2 to 4 servings.

FRANKS IN BLANKETS

8 frankfurters
2 slices sharp Cheddar
  cheese

8 slices bacon
8 frankfurter buns, split

Split frankfurters lengthwise. Cut each slice cheese into 4 strips. Place 1 strip cheese in each frankfurter. Wrap each with 1 strip bacon; bacon should not overlap. Fasten bacon with toothpicks. Cook in skillet over medium-low heat, turning frankfurters frequently to cook bacon evenly. Remove toothpicks. Place frankfurters in toasted buns. Serve immediately. Yield: 8 servings.

Peggy Posante

★ Reduce cholesterol by substituting 3 egg whites for 2 whole eggs in recipes. It is the yolk that contains the cholesterol.

HOT BROWN

This recipe has been changed and duplicated for years in Louisville, but this is the one that is now served at the Brown Hotel.

1/2 cup melted butter
1/2 cup flour
3/4 cup half and half
3/4 cup heavy cream
1/3 cup grated Romano cheese
1/4 cup grated Parmesan cheese

1/2 cup Sherry
2 egg yolks, well beaten
4 toast points
2 slices cooked turkey breast
4 slices crisp-fried bacon

Blend butter and flour in saucepan. Cook until mixture is dry and golden brown, stirring constantly. Stir in half and half and cream. Cook until thickened, stirring constantly. Add Romano and Parmesan cheeses. Cook until cheeses melt, stirring constantly. Bring Sherry to a boil in small saucepan for 30 seconds. Add to sauce. Cook until smooth, stirring constantly. Remove from heat. Strain sauce into bowl. Stir a small amount of hot mixture into egg yolks; stir egg yolks into hot mixture. Place 2 toast points in each of 2 ovenproof dishes. Top with turkey slices and hot brown sauce. Broil until sauce is lightly browned. Top with 2 crossed slices bacon. Garnish with additional Parmesan cheese. Yield: 2 servings.

CORN FRITTERS

2 cups whole kernel corn
1 1/4 cups self-rising flour
2 egg yolks
1 teaspoon sugar

Paprika to taste
2 egg whites, stiffly beaten
Oil for frying

Drain corn, reserving 1/2 cup liquid. Combine flour, egg yolks, corn, reserved liquid, sugar and paprika in bowl; mix well. Fold in egg whites gently. Drop by tablespoonfuls into hot oil in heavy skillet. Cook until brown, turning once. Serve hot with maple syrup or garnished with sprinkle of confectioners' sugar. May substitute crushed pineapple for corn.
Yield: 8 to 10 servings.

PLEASANT HILL EGGPLANT

1 large eggplant
1/2 medium onion, chopped
2 tablespoons butter
3 tablespoons chopped parsley
1 can cream of mushroom soup

Dash of Worcestershire sauce
Salt and pepper to taste
Butter crackers, crushed
Butter

Cut top from eggplant. Scoop out pulp, leaving 1/2-inch thick shell; reserve shell. Cook eggplant pulp in a small amount of water in saucepan until tender; drain and chop coarsely. Sauté onion in 2 tablespoons butter in skillet until tender. Add parsley; mix well. Stir in cooked eggplant, soup, Worcestershire sauce, salt and pepper. Add enough cracker crumbs to make of stuffing consistency. Spoon into eggplant shell. Sprinkle with additional cracker crumbs; dot with butter. Bake at 375 degrees for 30 to 35 minutes. Yield: 6 servings.

SPINACH CASSEROLE

1 10-ounce package frozen spinach
1 tablespoon chopped onion
1/4 cup butter
1/4 cup flour
1 cup milk
1 teaspoon sugar
Salt and white pepper to taste

3 tablespoons chopped onion
1/4 cup butter
3/4 cup chopped mushrooms
4 eggs, well beaten
1 cup chopped crisp-fried bacon
1/2 cup shredded Cheddar cheese

Cook spinach using package directions; drain well. Sauté 1 tablespoon onion in 1/4 cup butter in skillet until tender. Add flour; mix well. Stir in milk gradually. Cook until thickened, stirring constantly. Add sugar, salt and pepper. Stir in spinach. Sauté 3 tablespoons onion in 1/4 cup butter in skillet until tender. Add mushrooms. Sauté for 1 minute longer. Add eggs and bacon. Cook until eggs are set, stirring frequently. Combine spinach mixture with egg mixture in baking dish. Top with cheese. Broil until cheese melts. Serve hot. Yield: 6 to 8 servings.

NASHVILLE HOUSE FRIED BISCUITS

2²/₃ packages dry yeast
¹/₂ cup warm water
4 cups milk
¹/₄ cup sugar

¹/₂ cup shortening
2 tablespoons salt
7 to 9 cups flour
Oil for deep frying

Dissolve yeast in warm water in large bowl. Add milk, sugar, shortening, salt and enough flour to make stiff dough. Let rise, covered, until doubled in bulk. Knead on floured surface until smooth and elastic. Shape into biscuits. Deep-fry in 350 to 365 degree oil until brown. Biscuits may be frozen individually and stored in plastic bags. Let thaw and rise; do not allow to rise too high. Oil should be slightly hotter than 350 degrees but if too hot, the biscuits will be soggy in center. Yield: 7 dozen.

Barbara Struck

BOONE TAVERN CORNSTICKS

¹/₂ cup flour
2 cups white cornmeal
¹/₂ teaspoon salt
1 teaspoon baking powder

¹/₂ teaspoon soda
2 cups buttermilk
2 eggs, well beaten
¹/₄ cup melted lard

Sift flour, cornmeal, salt and baking powder into bowl. Add mixture of soda and buttermilk; mix well. Add eggs and lard, mixing well after each addition. Place greased cornstick pan in 450 to 500-degree oven until pan smokes. Pour batter into prepared pan. Bake at 450 degrees for 18 minutes or until brown. It is important to heat the greased pan before filling with batter to give cornsticks crisp outsides. Yield: 12 cornsticks.

Barbara Struck

HUSH PUPPIES

2 cups cornmeal
2 teaspoons baking
   powder
1 teaspoon salt
Finely chopped onion to
   taste

²/₃ cup milk
1 egg, slightly beaten
Oil for deep frying

Combine cornmeal, baking powder and salt in bowl; mix well. Add onion; mix well. Stir in milk and egg. Shape into golf ball-sized balls. Deep-fry in hot oil until brown. Hush puppies taste best when deep-fried in oil in which fish has been cooked. Yield: 16 hush puppies.

CINNAMON ROLLS

These are just like rolls from the shop in the mall.

2 packages dry yeast
1/2 teaspoon sugar
1/2 cup 105 to 115-degree water
3 cups flour
1/3 cup sugar
1 teaspoon salt
1 cup milk, scalded
1/3 cup oil
2 eggs, at room temperature

1 to 2 cups flour
1/2 cup butter, softened
1 cup packed brown sugar
1/2 cup sugar
2 tablespoons cinnamon
1 cup sifted confectioners' sugar
1 teaspoon vanilla extract
2 to 3 tablespoons warm milk

Dissolve yeast and 1/2 teaspoon sugar in water. Combine 3 cups flour, 1/3 cup sugar and salt in mixer bowl; mix well. Cool milk to 110 degrees. Add to flour mixture with oil, eggs and yeast; beat until smooth. Beat in about 1 1/2 cups flour gradually until dough pulls from side of bowl. Knead on floured surface for 8 to 10 minutes or until smooth and elastic. Place in greased bowl, turning to coat surface. Let rise, covered, for 1 hour or until doubled in bulk. Combine butter, brown sugar, 1/2 cup sugar and cinnamon in mixer bowl; mix until smooth. Roll dough into 8x10-inch rectangle on floured surface. Spread with brown sugar mixture; roll as for jelly roll. Cut into fourteen 1 1/2-inch slices. Grease two 9-inch baking pans. Place 1 roll in center of each pan. Arrange 6 rolls around each center roll. Let rise, covered, for 30 to 40 minutes or until doubled in bulk. Bake at 350 degrees for 25 to 30 minutes or until brown. Remove to wire racks to cool. Blend confectioners' sugar, vanilla and enough warm milk to make of drizzling consistency in small bowl. Drizzle over cooled rolls. May be wrapped tightly and frozen for up to 1 month. Thaw in wrapping at room temperature. Yield: 14 rolls.

HOT FRUIT BAKE

1 20-ounce can sliced
  pineapple
1 17-ounce can apricots
1 16-ounce can peaches
1 15-ounce can spiced
  apple rings

1 16-ounce can pears
1/2 cup butter
1/2 cup sugar
2 tablespoons cornstarch
1 cup dry Sherry

Drain fruit. Layer pineapple, apricots, peaches, apple rings and pears in glass baking dish. Melt butter in saucepan. Add sugar and cornstarch; mix well. Stir in Sherry gradually. Cook over low heat until thickened, stirring constantly. Pour over fruit. Chill, covered, overnight. Bake, uncovered, at 350 degrees for 30 to 40 minutes. Serve as breakfast side dish.
Yield: 6 to 8 servings.

Ruth Dye

KENTUCKY MOUNTAIN PUDDING

1 egg
3/4 cup sugar
3 tablespoons (heaping)
  flour
1 1/2 teaspoons baking
  powder

1/8 teaspoon salt
1 teaspoon vanilla extract
1/2 cup chopped apples
1/2 cup chopped pecans
Vanilla ice cream

Beat egg and sugar in mixer bowl until light and fluffy. Sift in flour, baking powder and salt; mix well. Stir in vanilla. Fold in apples and pecans. Pour into greased baking dish. Bake at 350 degrees for 25 minutes. Serve warm with ice cream.
Yield: 4 to 6 servings.

Christy Michelle Lewis

CHOCOLATE CHIP PECAN PIE

2 eggs, slightly beaten
1/2 cup melted margarine
1 cup sugar
1/2 cup flour
1 teaspoon vanilla extract
1 cup semisweet
  chocolate chips
1 cup chopped pecans
1 unbaked 9-inch pie shell

    Combine eggs, margarine and sugar in bowl; mix well. Add flour and vanilla; mix well. Fold in chocolate chips and pecans. Pour into pie shell. Bake at 350 degrees for 45 minutes. Yield: 8 servings.

Dorothy O'Neal

KENTUCKY PIE

1/2 cup sugar
1/2 cup packed brown
  sugar
1/2 cup flour
2 eggs, slightly beaten
1 cup melted butter
1 teaspoon vanilla extract
1 cup chopped walnuts
1 cup semisweet
  chocolate chips
1 frozen 9-inch pie shell

    Combine sugar, brown sugar and flour in bowl; mix well. Add eggs, butter and vanilla; mix well. Fold in walnuts and chocolate chips. Pour into frozen pie shell. Bake at 325 degrees for 1 hour. Serve warm with whipped cream. Yield: 8 servings.

Barbara Struck

★ It isn't what you have in your pocket that makes you thankful, it is what you have in your heart.

OLD TALBOTT TAVERN PIE

3/4 **cup sugar**
1/2 **cup flour**
1/4 **teaspoon salt**
1 1/4 **cups water**
2 **egg yolks**
1/2 **cup fresh orange juice**

1 **tablespoon grated**
  orange rind
2 **tablespoons lemon juice**
1 **baked 9-inch pie shell**
1 **recipe meringue**
3/4 **cup sweetened coconut**

Combine 3/4 cup sugar, flour and 1/4 teaspoon salt in top of double boiler; mix well. Stir in water gradually until blended. Cook over direct heat for 5 minutes, stirring constantly. Stir a small amount of hot mixture into egg yolks; stir egg yolks into hot mixture. Place top of double boiler over rapidly boiling water. Cook for 5 minutes, stirring constantly. Remove from heat. Add orange juice, orange rind and lemon juice; mix well. Chill in refrigerator. Pour chilled filling into baked pie shell. Spread meringue over filling, sealing to edge. Sprinkle with coconut. Yield: 8 servings.

Meringue

2 **egg whites**
1/2 **cup sugar**

Salt to taste
2 **tablespoons water**

Combine egg whites, 1/2 cup sugar, salt to taste and water in top of double boiler. Beat with rotary beater until smooth. Bring water to a rapid boil. Beat for 1 minute longer. Remove from heat. Beat until stiff peaks form.

Trudie Gadjen

★ For high meringue, add 1/2 teaspoon baking powder
  to room temperature egg whites before beating.

Basketball is King in Kentucky. We either play it or talk it 12 months a year.

Appetizers,
Beverages and Soups

BASKETBALL

APPETIZERS

ASPARAGUS ROLLS

1 loaf sandwich bread
Mayonnaise
Parmesan cheese

Cooked asparagus spears
Melted butter

    Cut crust from bread slices; flatten bread with rolling pin. Spread each slice with mayonnaise; sprinkle with cheese. Place 2 or more asparagus spears on each slice; bring opposite corners of slice together, fastening with pick. Brush with melted butter. Place on baking sheet. Bake at 375 degrees for 20 minutes or until golden brown.

Maxine Beavin

CHEESE HORS D'OEUVRES

4 ounces Cheddar cheese,
  shredded
1/2 cup chopped ripe
  olives

1/2 cup mayonnaise
Chopped onion to taste
1 loaf party rye bread

    Combine cheese, olives, mayonnaise and onion in bowl; mix well. Spread on slices of party rye bread. Place on baking sheet. Broil until cheese bubbles. Serve warm.
Yield: 20 appetizers.

Dot Berry

CHEESE COOKIES

1 cup flour
1/2 cup butter, softened
1 5-ounce jar Old English
  cheese spread, softened

1/8 teaspoon red pepper
1/2 teaspoon salt
1/8 teaspoon paprika
Pecan halves

    Place flour and butter in bowl. Cut in butter until crumbly. Add cheese, red pepper, salt and paprika; mix well. Shape into balls; place on greased baking sheet. Press pecan half into center of each to flatten. Bake at 350 degrees for 12 to 15 minutes or until brown. Yield: 30 appetizers.

Clara Nance

SESAME AND CHEDDAR STICKS

1¹/₂ cups flour
2 teaspoons sesame seed
¹/₂ teaspoon salt
4 ounces sharp Cheddar
  cheese, shredded

¹/₂ cup butter, softened
3 tablespoons
  Worcestershire sauce
2 teaspoons cold water

Combine flour, sesame seed and salt in bowl; mix well. Cut in cheese and butter until crumbly. Add mixture of Worcestershire sauce and water; mix well. Shape into ball. Roll to ¹/₄-inch thickness on floured surface. Cut into 3¹/₂-inch strips. Place strips on baking sheet. Bake at 450 degrees for 6 to 8 minutes or until golden brown. Remove to wire rack to cool. Yield: 6 dozen.

Trudie Gadjen

SLAP STICKS

¹/₄ cup butter
3 teaspoons minced onion
  flakes
²/₃ cup shredded sharp
  cheese

1 teaspoon celery seed
Dash of salt
2 cups buttermilk baking
  mix
²/₃ cup milk

Melt butter in 9x13-inch shallow baking pan. Sprinkle 2 teaspoons onion flakes over butter. Mix remaining 1 teaspoon onion, cheese, celery seed, salt and baking mix in bowl. Add milk; mix well. Dough will be soft. Stir vigorously about 30 strokes. Knead lightly on floured surface. Roll into 6x10-inch rectangle. Cut into 1x3-inch strips. Arrange in prepared baking pan, turning to coat both sides with butter mixture. Bake at 425 degrees for 15 minutes or until golden brown. Yield: 20 sticks.

Trudie Gadjen

★ Learn from the mistakes of others; you can't live long enough to make them all yourself.

DEVILED BISCUITS

1   10-count package
    refrigerator biscuits
1/4 cup margarine

1   4 1/2-ounce can deviled
    ham
1/4 cup Parmesan cheese

Cut each biscuit into quarters. Arrange on baking sheet. Heat margarine and deviled ham in saucepan, stirring to mix well. Pour ham mixture over biscuits, coating well. Sprinkle with cheese. Bake at 400 degrees for 15 minutes or until golden brown. Serve as hot snack or as bread with a salad. Yield: 40 biscuits.

Gwen Mills

BAKED CHICKEN NUGGETS

7 or 8 boned chicken
  breasts
2 cups bread crumbs
1 cup Parmesan cheese

1 1/2 teaspoons salt
4 teaspoons thyme
4 teaspoons basil
1 cup melted butter

Cut chicken into 1 1/2-inch pieces. Combine bread crumbs, cheese, salt, thyme and basil in bowl; mix well. Dip chicken into butter; coat with bread crumb mixture. Place in single layer on baking sheet. Bake at 400 degrees for 20 minutes or until tender and brown. Yield: 14 to 16 appetizers.

Trudie Gadjen

PARTY CHICKEN LIVERS

1 pound chicken livers
1/4 cup white wine
10 to 12 slices bacon

3 tablespoons Dijon
  mustard
3/4 cup cracker crumbs

Trim chicken livers. Marinate in wine in bowl for 10 minutes; drain. Cut bacon slices into halves. Microwave bacon for 3 to 4 minutes or parboil in boiling water for 1 minute. Drain on paper towels. Coat chicken livers lightly with mustard; wrap each with bacon, securing with pick. Place in buttered baking dish. Sprinkle with cracker crumbs. Bake at 425 degrees for 20 to 25 minutes or until bacon is crisp. Drain on paper towels. Yield: 6 servings.

Wilma Allen

RUMAKI

12 chicken livers
12 water chestnuts
12 slices bacon
1/4 cup lemon juice
1/4 cup soy sauce
1/4 cup oil
3 tablespoons catsup
1 teaspoon liquid garlic
1/2 teaspoon pepper
1/2 cup packed brown
   sugar

Cut chicken livers, water chestnuts and bacon slices into halves. Wrap each liver half and water chestnut half together with 1/2 bacon slice, securing with pick. Place in shallow dish. Combine lemon juice, soy sauce, oil, catsup, garlic and pepper in bowl; mix well. Pour over chicken livers. Marinate in refrigerator overnight, turning occasionally. Coat each appetizer with brown sugar. Place on rack in baking pan. Bake at 450 degrees for 10 minutes. Turn appetizers over. Bake for 15 minutes longer. Yield: 2 dozen appetizers.

Peggy Posante

MICROWAVE RUMAKI

8 ounces chicken livers
1 1/2 tablespoons honey
1 tablespoon soy sauce
2 tablespoons oil
1/2 clove of garlic, pressed
1   5-ounce can water
   chestnuts, drained
Bacon slices

Rinse chicken livers under cold running water; drain on paper towels. Cut into halves; place in bowl. Combine honey, soy sauce, oil and garlic in small bowl; mix well. Pour over livers. Let stand for 30 minutes, turning livers occasionally. Drain on paper towels. Place 1 water chestnut and 1 liver piece together; wrap with bacon and secure with toothpick. Place 6 appetizers at a time on paper plate lined with three thicknesses of paper towel. Cover with double thickness of paper towel. Microwave on High for 5 minutes or until bacon is crisp, turning plate once. Serve hot. Yield: 1 1/2 dozen.

Mary Cook

RANCH BUFFALO WINGS

24 chicken wing drumettes
1/2 cup melted butter
1/4 cup (or less) hot pepper
  sauce
3 tablespoons vinegar

2 packages ranch salad
  dressing mix
1/2 teaspoon paprika
Celery sticks

Dip chicken into mixture of butter, hot pepper sauce and vinegar. Place in baking pan; sprinkle with 1 package salad dressing mix. Bake at 350 degrees for 25 to 30 minutes or until brown. Sprinkle with paprika. Prepare 1 package salad dressing mix using package directions. Serve dressing as dip for chicken and celery sticks. Yield: 24 appetizers.

Juyne Bushart

MARINATED CHICKEN WINGS

1 cup catsup
1/4 cup honey
1/4 cup soy sauce

1/4 cup lemon juice
1 1/2 to 2 pounds chicken
  wings

Combine catsup, honey, soy sauce and lemon juice in bowl; mix well. Remove tips from wings; discard. Cut wings into 2 pieces. Place in shallow dish; pour marinade over top. Marinate in refrigerator for several hours to overnight. Drain, reserving marinade. Place wings in shallow baking pan. Bake at 275 degrees for 1 hour or until lightly browned, basting occasionally with marinade. Yield: 2 to 2 1/2 dozen.

Donna Hearn

CRAB MEAT MORNAY

1 bunch green onions,
  finely chopped
1/2 cup chopped parsley
1/2 cup butter
2 cups evaporated milk
1/2 pound sharp Cheddar
  cheese, shredded
Salt and red pepper to
  taste

1 pound crab meat, flaked
1 small green bell pepper,
  finely chopped
1   4-ounce can chopped
  pimentos, drained
1   2 1/2-ounce can
  chopped mushrooms,
  drained

Sauté green onions and parsley in butter in skillet. Add evaporated milk. Cook until thickened, stirring constantly. Add cheese, salt and pepper; mix well. Add crab meat, green pepper, pimentos and mushrooms; mix well. May thicken with a small amount of flour if necessary. Heat to serving temperature. Serve with crackers. Yield: 8 cups.

Sandy Adams

CRAB-STUFFED CHERRY TOMATOES

1 6-ounce package frozen crab meat, thawed	1 tablespoon finely chopped parsley
1 pint cherry tomatoes	1/2 teaspoon dry mustard
1/4 cup mayonnaise	Pinch of salt

Flake crab meat; drain on paper towels. Cut thin slice from tops and bottoms of tomatoes. Remove pulp; drain shells on paper towels. Mix crab meat, mayonnaise, parsley, mustard and salt in bowl. Stuff tomatoes with crab mixture. Chill for 30 minutes or longer. Garnish with parsley or watercress. Yield: 24 servings.

Juyne Bushart

FANCY DEVILED EGGS

1 6-ounce package frozen crab meat, thawed	1 tablespoon finely chopped onion
8 hard-boiled eggs	3/4 teaspoon dillweed
1/2 cup mayonnaise	1/2 teaspoon grated lemon rind
1 tablespoon Dijon mustard	
2 to 3 teaspoons capers	1/2 teaspoon pepper

Flake crab meat; drain. Cut eggs into halves lengthwise. Mash egg yolks in large bowl. Chill egg whites, covered, in refrigerator. Combine egg yolks with mayonnaise, mustard, capers, onion, dillweed, lemon rind and pepper; mix well. Stir in crab meat. Chill, covered, for 2 hours or longer. Fill egg whites with crab mixture just before serving. Garnish with pimento strips and parsley. Yield: 16 egg halves.

Juyne Bushart

RAINBOW DEVILED EGGS

6 hard-boiled eggs
1 cup tuna
1/2 teaspoon salt
1/2 teaspoon dry mustard

1 teaspoon lime juice
Dash of pepper
1/4 cup mayonnaise

Cut eggs into halves lengthwise. Mash yolks in bowl. Add tuna, seasonings and mayonnaise. Fill egg whites with tuna mixture. Chill until serving time. Yield: 12 egg halves.

Thelma Pearson

HAM AND CHEESE APPETIZERS

1 cup melted margarine
2 tablespoons lemon juice
2 tablespoons prepared
  mustard
2 tablespoons poppy seed
2 tablespoons
  Worcestershire sauce

1 medium onion, finely
  chopped
4 packages rolls
1 16-ounce package
  sliced boiled ham
1 pound Swiss cheese
  slices

Mix first 6 ingredients in bowl. Remove rolls from foil pans; cut into 2 layers. Spread cut surfaces with margarine mixture. Layer ham and cheese on bottom layer; cover with tops. Return to pans; cover with foil. Bake at 450 degrees for 20 to 25 minutes or until heated through. Cut into serving portions.
Yield: 4 dozen appetizers.

Juyne Bushart

HOT DOG WRAP-UPS

1 package hot dogs
1 8-ounce can pineapple
  chunks

8 ounces sliced bacon
1 cup packed brown sugar

Cut hot dogs into 1-inch pieces. Drain pineapple. Cut bacon slices into halves. Wrap each hot dog piece and 1 pineapple chunk together with 1/2 bacon slice, securing with pick. Place in 9x13-inch baking dish. Sprinkle with brown sugar. Bake at 375 degrees for 20 minutes or until brown. Yield: 3 dozen.

Cindy Ray Hill

MICROWAVE COCKTAIL WIENERS

1 pound wieners   **1½ cups barbecue sauce**

Cut wieners into bite-sized pieces. Combine wieners and barbecue sauce in 1½-quart glass casserole; mix until wieners are coated with sauce. Microwave, covered, on High for 6 minutes, stirring once. Serve hot with toothpicks. Yield: 10 servings.

Peggy Posante

COCKTAIL MEATBALLS

1 pound ground beef
½ cup dry bread crumbs
⅓ cup finely chopped onion
¼ cup milk
1 egg, slightly beaten
1 tablespoon finely chopped parsley

1 teaspoon salt
½ teaspoon Worcestershire sauce
⅛ teaspoon pepper
¼ cup oil
1 12-ounce bottle of chili sauce
1 10-ounce jar grape jelly

Combine first 9 ingredients in bowl; mix well. Shape into 1-inch balls. Cook meatballs in hot oil in large skillet until brown; drain well. Place in bowl. Heat chili sauce and jelly in skillet until jelly is melted, stirring constantly. Add meatballs. Simmer for 30 minutes, stirring occasionally. Yield: 5 dozen meatballs.

Frank Fendley

DERBY MEATBALLS

2 pounds ground beef
1 egg, slightly beaten
1 onion, chopped
1 teaspoon salt

1 8-ounce bottle of chili sauce
½ cup grape jelly

Combine ground beef, egg, onion and salt in bowl; mix well. Shape into small meatballs. Place in saucepan with mixture of chili sauce and jelly. Simmer for 1½ hours, stirring occasionally. Yield: 8 dozen meatballs.

Patsy Leffler

MUSHROOM MEATBALLS

1 can cream of mushroom
  soup
1/2 cup water
1 pound ground beef
1/2 cup bread crumbs
2 tablespoons finely
  chopped onion

1 tablespoon chopped
  parsley
1 egg, slightly beaten
1/4 teaspoon salt
1 tablespoon shortening

Blend mushroom soup and water in bowl. Combine 1/4 cup soup mixture and ground beef in large bowl; mix well. Add bread crumbs, onion, parsley, egg and salt; mix well. Shape into 1 1/2-inch meatballs. Brown in hot shortening in skillet; drain. Add remaining soup mixture. Simmer, covered, for 15 minutes, stirring occasionally. Yield: 4 servings.

Donna Hearn

TAMALE BALLS

1 pound ground beef
1 pound ground pork
1 1/2 cups cornmeal
3/4 cup tomato juice
1/2 cup flour
4 cloves of garlic, finely
  chopped

1 tablespoon chili powder
2 teaspoons salt
5 cups tomato juice
1 tablespoon chili powder
2 teaspoons salt

Combine ground beef, ground pork, cornmeal, 3/4 cup tomato juice, flour, garlic, 1 tablespoon chili powder and 2 teaspoons salt in bowl; mix well. Shape into small balls. Combine remaining 5 cups tomato juice, 1 tablespoon chili powder and 2 teaspoons salt in saucepan; mix well. Add meatballs. Simmer for 2 hours, stirring occasionally. Yield: 100 meatballs.

Donna Browning

MEXICAN SKINS

3 baked potatoes
Bart's Famous Chili
Monterey Jack cheese,
   shredded

Jalapeño peppers,
   chopped

Bake potatoes. Cut into halves; scoop out most of pulp. Deep-fry skins in hot oil until brown. Fill with Bart's Famous Chili; sprinkle with cheese and peppers. Place on baking sheet. Broil until cheese melts. Yield: 6 potato skins.

Bart's Famous Chili

1 1/4 pounds ground chuck
1 cup finely chopped onion
1 teaspoon finely chopped
   garlic
1 tablespoon beef base
1 tablespoon chili powder

1/2 teaspoon cumin
1 teaspoon oregano
2 cups water
6 ounces pinto beans
6 ounces stewed tomatoes
6 ounces tomato paste

Cook ground beef, onion, garlic and beef base in skillet until ground beef is brown and crumbly. Add chili powder, cumin, oregano, water, beans, tomatoes and tomato paste; mix well. Simmer for 20 to 30 minutes, stirring frequently.

Ladonna Darnell

GLORIA'S STUFFED MUSHROOMS

1 1/2 pounds mushrooms
3 tablespoons Parmesan
   cheese
Garlic salt to taste
1 tablespoon chopped
   parsley

1 small onion, grated
1 cup fresh bread crumbs
2 tablespoons melted
   margarine
1/4 cup oil
Salt and pepper to taste

Clean mushrooms. Dry with paper towel. Remove and discard stems. Combine cheese, garlic salt, parsley, onion, bread crumbs, margarine, oil, salt and pepper in bowl; mix well. Stuff mushroom caps with mixture. Place on baking sheet. Bake at 350 degrees for 20 minutes or until stuffing is brown. Yield: 12 servings.

Mary E. Quinker

RANCH NACHOS

1   8 to 10-ounce package
   tortilla chips
3/4 cup prepared ranch
   salad dressing

6 ounces sharp Cheddar
   cheese, shredded
1/4 cup sliced green onions

Arrange chips in shallow baking dish. Pour salad dressing over chips. Sprinkle with cheese and green onions. Bake at 350 degrees for 8 minutes or until cheese is melted. May also top with sliced ripe olives, jalapeño peppers or finely chopped bell peppers. Yield: 4 servings.

Juyne Bushart

MINI PIZZAS

1 pound ground beef
1 pound hot pork sausage
1/2 teaspoon garlic salt
1/2 teaspoon steak sauce

1 teaspoon oregano
1 pound Velveeta cheese
2 loaves party rye bread

Brown ground beef and sausage in skillet, stirring until crumbly; drain. Add seasonings; mix well. Cut cheese into cubes. Add to ground beef mixture. Heat until cheese is melted, stirring frequently. Spread mixture on bread slices; place on baking sheet. Bake at 400 degrees for 10 minutes or until bread is lightly toasted. May be frozen before baking. May vary the seasoning by adding 1 teaspoon cayenne pepper. Yield: 40 servings.

Bernidea Fort, Mary E. Quinker

CREAM CHEESE OLIVE BALLS

8 ounces cream cheese
1   6-ounce jar stuffed
   olives

Finely chopped pecans

Shape ball of softened cream cheese around each olive; roll in pecans. Place on baking sheet. Chill, covered, overnight. Slice each ball into halves. Serve with crackers. Yield: 4 servings.

Jayne Roberts

OLIVE PUFFS

1/2 cup margarine, softened
2 cups shredded sharp
  Cheddar cheese
1 cup self-rising flour
1 teaspoon paprika
48 stuffed olives, drained

Cream margarine and cheese in bowl until well mixed. Add flour and paprika; mix well. Chill dough for 20 minutes. Dry olives with paper towels. Shape 1/2 teaspoon dough around each olive; place on baking sheet. Chill, covered, overnight. Bake at 400 degrees for 10 to 12 minutes or until lightly browned. Yield: 48 appetizers.

Yocianne Everett

ONION PUFFS

1/2 cup water
1/4 cup butter
1 envelope dry onion soup
  mix
2 teaspoons caraway seed
1 teaspoon dry mustard
1/2 cup flour
1 cup shredded Swiss
  cheese
2 eggs, slightly beaten

Combine water, butter, soup mix, caraway seed and mustard in saucepan. Bring to a boil, stirring frequently. Reduce heat to low. Add flour all at once. Stir vigorously for about 30 seconds or until mixture forms ball. Remove from heat. Beat in cheese and eggs until cheese is melted and mixture is smooth. Drop by teaspoonfuls 2 inches apart onto large greased baking sheet. Bake at 375 degrees for 15 minutes or until puffed and golden brown. Turn off oven. Leave onion puffs in oven for 10 minutes longer. Serve warm. Yield: 24 onion puffs.

Juyne Bushart

★ Keep an assortment of finger foods in the freezer. A few of each can be thawed or heated in the microwave for unexpected company munchies.

SALMON SQUARES

1 16-ounce can red salmon
Milk
1½ cups soft bread
  crumbs
1 egg, slightly beaten
2 tablespoons lemon juice
1 teaspoon chopped onion
¼ teaspoon salt
⅛ teaspoon pepper
½ cup sour cream
¼ cup mayonnaise
Dillseed

Drain salmon, reserving liquid. Add enough milk to liquid to measure ¾ cup. Flake and bone salmon. Combine salmon, liquid, bread crumbs, egg, lemon juice, onion, salt and pepper in bowl; mix well. Spoon into buttered 8x8-inch baking dish. Bake at 350 degrees for 1 hour. Mix sour cream and mayonnaise in small bowl; spread over baked salmon. Sprinkle with dillseed. Cut into squares. Yield: 4 servings.

Trudie Gadjen

SEAFOOD PUFFS

1 cup sifted flour
½ teaspoon salt
1 cup water
½ cup butter
4 eggs
1 can or 1 package frozen
  crab meat, thawed
1 can shrimp
1 cup mushroom soup
¼ cup finely chopped
  green bell pepper
1 2-ounce jar chopped
  pimento, drained
¼ teaspoon salt
Cayenne pepper to taste
3 tablespoons Sherry
1 cup buttered bread
  crumbs

Mix flour and ½ teaspoon salt in bowl. Heat water and butter in saucepan until butter melts. Add flour mixture all at once; stir vigorously until mixture leaves side of pan. Add eggs 1 at a time, mixing well after each addition. Drop by teaspoonfuls 1 inch apart onto greased baking sheet. Bake at 400 degrees for 15 to 25 minutes or until golden brown. Cool on wire rack. Combine crab meat, shrimp, soup, green pepper, pimento, remaining ¼ teaspoon salt, cayenne pepper, Sherry and bread crumbs in bowl; mix well. Split cooled puffs; fill with mixture. Place on baking sheet. Bake at 350 degrees for 8 to 10 minutes or until heated through. Yield: 50 puffs.

Barbara C. Hendrick

EASY SAUSAGE BALLS

3 cups buttermilk baking
  mix
1/2 cup milk

1   8-ounce jar Cheese
    Whiz
1 pound sausage

Combine baking mix and milk in bowl; mix well. Add Cheese Whiz and sausage; mix well. Drop by spoonfuls onto baking sheet. Bake at 425 degrees for 15 minutes or until brown. Drain. Yield: 48 servings.

Melinda Miller

AUNT SARA'S HAM AND SAUSAGE BALLS

1 pound mild pork sausage
2 pounds cooked country
  ham, minced
2 cups bread crumbs

2 eggs, slightly beaten
2 cups (about) milk
Brown Sugar Sauce

Bring sausage to room temperature. Combine sausage, ham, bread crumbs and eggs in bowl. Add enough milk to make of desired consistency; mix well. Shape into small balls on baking sheet. Bake at 350 degrees for 20 minutes or until brown. Drain. Serve with Brown Sugar Sauce. May also pour Brown Sugar Sauce over balls to serve. Yield: 160 appetizers.

Brown Sugar Sauce

2 cups packed brown
  sugar
1 cup white vinegar

1 cup water
1 tablespoon prepared
  mustard

Combine brown sugar, vinegar, water and mustard in saucepan. Heat until brown sugar dissolves, stirring constantly. Serve with ham and sausage balls.

Barbara Struck

SAUSAGE BALLS

1 pound hot or mild
  sausage
10 ounces sharp Cheddar
  cheese, shredded

3 cups buttermilk baking
  mix

Combine sausage, cheese and baking mix in bowl; mix well. Shape into small balls. Place on baking sheet. Bake at 350 degrees for 25 to 30 minutes or until brown. Drain. May add milk or water and beef bouillon granules for variation. May be frozen and reheated. Yield: 80 sausage balls.

Aggie Burks, Paula Goodlett
Betty Krueger, Carmen Stilger
Barbara Struck, Pat Wilhelm

SAUSAGE ROLL

1 pound hot sausage
2 cups flour
1 tablespoon baking
  powder

1/2 teaspoon salt
5 tablespoons shortening
2/3 cup milk

Bring sausage to room temperature. Mix flour, baking powder and salt in bowl. Cut in shortening until crumbly. Add milk; mix well. Divide dough into 2 portions. Roll each to 1/2-inch thickness on floured surface. Spread softened sausage over dough. Roll as for jelly roll. Freeze until easy to slice. Cut into 1/4-inch slices. Place on baking sheet. Bake at 400 degrees for 30 minutes or until brown. Serve with hot mustard.
Yield: 48 servings.

Marty Hill

★ Save paper towel rolls to store cords for appliances. Tuck cord inside and label roll with appliance the cord fits — no more "fishing" for the right cord and cords don't tangle.

SHRIMP EGG ROLLS

12 ounces cooked shrimp,
finely chopped
2 cups shredded Chinese
celery cabbage
8 to 10 water chestnuts,
shredded
2 stalks celery, finely
chopped
2 tablespoons oil
1 cup bean sprouts
1 teaspoon salt
1 tablespoon soy sauce
1 teaspoon sugar
6 to 8 egg roll wrappers
1 egg, slightly beaten
2 cups oil for deep frying

Stir-fry shrimp, cabbage, water chestnuts and celery in 2 tablespoons hot oil in wok for 2 to 3 minutes or until tender-crisp. Add bean sprouts. Stir in salt, soy sauce and sugar; mix well. Spoon mixture onto egg roll wrappers. Fold ends; roll to enclose filling. Brush with egg to seal. Deep-fry several at a time in 2 cups hot oil in skillet until brown and crisp. Yield: 6 or 8 egg rolls.

Joan Echsner

TINY TUNA PIZZAS

1 7-ounce can oil-pack
tuna
1/4 cup chili sauce
1 teaspoon finely chopped
onion
1/4 teaspoon salt
1/8 teaspoon oregano
1 small loaf party rye bread
Parmesan cheese

Combine tuna, chili sauce, onion, salt and oregano in bowl; mix well. Spread on bread slices. Place on baking sheet. Sprinkle with cheese. Bake at 425 degrees for 4 minutes or until heated through. Serve hot. Yield: 20 servings.

Dot Berry

★ A little dry mustard rubbed into hands after peeling onions will remove the odor.

WACKY WATER CHESTNUTS

1 pound sliced bacon
1 8-ounce can water
  chestnuts
1¼ cups catsup

1¼ cups sugar
2½ tablespoons
  Worcestershire sauce

Cut bacon slices and water chestnuts into halves. Wrap water chestnuts with bacon slice; secure with pick. Place on baking sheet. Bake at 400 degrees for 30 minutes; drain. Combine catsup, sugar and Worcestershire sauce in saucepan. Bring to a boil, stirring until sugar is dissolved. Combine sauce and water chestnuts in baking dish. Bake at 375 degrees for 20 minutes. Serve hot in chafing dish. Yield: 10 servings.

Janis R. Boud

ZUCCHINI APPETIZERS

1 cup buttermilk baking
  mix
½ cup finely chopped
  onion
½ cup Parmesan cheese
½ teaspoon salt
½ teaspoon seasoned salt
½ teaspoon oregano

¾ teaspoon garlic salt
2 tablespoons chopped
  parsley
Pepper to taste
¼ cup oil
4 eggs, slightly beaten
3 cups thinly sliced
  zucchini

Combine baking mix, onion, cheese, salt, seasoned salt, oregano, garlic salt, parsley, pepper, oil and eggs in bowl; mix well. Stir in zucchini. Spread in greased 9x13-inch baking dish. Bake at 350 degrees for 25 to 30 minutes or until golden brown. Cut into 1-inch squares. Zucchini may be shredded rather than sliced. Yield: 117 appetizers.

Betty Krueger, Sue Skelton

AVOCADO DIP

1 large avocado, peeled
1/2 cup mayonnaise
1 teaspoon chili sauce
1 clove of garlic, crushed

2 tablespoons minced
  onion
1 tablespoon lemon juice
1 tomato, peeled, chopped

Coarsely chop avocado. Combine mayonnaise, chili sauce, garlic, onion, lemon juice and tomato in bowl; mix well. Fold in avocado gently. Add salt to taste. Chill for several hours before serving. Yield: 2 cups.

Todd Gonnah

BEEFY HERB DIP

8 ounces cream cheese,
  softened
1 cup sour cream
4 envelopes instant beef
  broth
1 clove of garlic, minced
1/8 teaspoon sage

2 tablespoons chopped
  parsley
2 tablespoons freeze-dried
  chives
1/8 teaspoon crushed
  rosemary leaves
Hot pepper sauce to taste

Beat cream cheese, sour cream and beef broth in bowl until smooth. Add garlic, sage, parsley, chives, rosemary and hot pepper sauce; mix well. Chill for 1 hour before serving. Serve with fresh vegetables. Yield: 2 cups.

Linda Broyles

DRIED BEEF DIP

8 ounces cream cheese,
  softened
1/3 cup sour cream
1/2 cup chopped green bell
  pepper
1/2 cup chopped celery

2 tablespoons chopped
  ripe olives
2 tablespoons chopped
  onion
1 2-ounce jar dried beef,
  shredded

Blend cream cheese and sour cream in bowl. Add remaining ingredients; mix well. Chill for several hours before serving. Serve with assorted crackers or vegetables. Yield: 3 cups.

Gwen Mills

CHIPPED BEEF DIP

4 ounces chipped beef
16 ounces cream cheese,
  softened
Freeze-dried chives to
  taste

1½ teaspoons garlic
  powder
2 teaspoons onion powder
2 teaspoons MSG

    Process chipped beef in blender container until finely chopped. Combine remaining ingredients in bowl; mix well. Add chipped beef; mix well. Shape into ball. Yield: 2½ cups.

Bernadette Mills

BEEFY HAM DIP

1 2-ounce jar dried beef
1 onion
1 3-ounce can deviled
  ham

½ cup mayonnaise
16 ounces cream cheese,
  softened
Garlic powder to taste

    Combine beef and onion in food processor container. Process with steel blade until chopped. Add ham, mayonnaise, cream cheese and garlic powder. Process until smooth. Add additional mayonnaise if necessary to make of desired consistency. Serve with fresh vegetables. Yield: 3 cups.

Dollie D. Billiter

HOT BROCCOLI AND CHEESE DIP

2 10-ounce packages
  frozen chopped broccoli
1 cup chopped onion
¼ cup butter
1 6-ounce roll garlic
  cheese, chopped

1 4-ounce can mushroom
  stems and pieces, drained
1 can cream of mushroom
  soup
1 15-ounce bag corn
  chips

    Cook broccoli in a small amount of water in saucepan just until thawed; drain. Sauté onion in butter in skillet. Add cheese, stirring constantly until melted. Stir in mushrooms, soup and broccoli. Thin with a small amount of milk if necessary. Spoon into chafing dish. Serve hot with corn chips. Yield: 1½ quarts.

Juyne Bushart

RO-TEL CHEESE DIP

1 10-ounce can Ro-Tel
tomatoes

2 pounds Velveeta cheese

Pour tomatoes into blender container. Process for 2 minutes or until finely chopped. Cut cheese into small cubes; place in Crock•Pot. Add tomatoes. Cook on High for 15 minutes. Stir with wooden spoon. Cook for 15 minutes longer. Reduce temperature to Low. Serve in Crock•Pot. Yield: 3 cups.

Peggy Posante

CLAM DIP

8 ounces cream cheese,
softened
1 6-ounce can minced
clams

1 onion, grated
¼ teaspoon
Worcestershire sauce

Blend cream cheese with a small amount of clam juice in small bowl. Add onion, Worcestershire sauce and clams; mix well. Chill until serving time. Serve with crackers or potato chips. Yield: 2 cups.

Mary Cook

CRAB DIP

1 6-ounce can crab meat,
drained
16 ounces cream cheese,
softened
1 onion, grated

½ cup mayonnaise
1 cup catsup
2 tablespoons horseradish
Tabasco sauce to taste

Combine crab meat, cream cheese, onion and mayonnaise in bowl; mix well. Spoon into serving dish. Combine catsup, horseradish and Tabasco sauce in small bowl; mix well. Pour over crab meat mixture. Serve with party crackers. Yield: 4 cups.

Walt Forbey

CRAB AND SHRIMP DIP

1 6-ounce can crab meat, drained
8 ounces cream cheese, softened
Lettuce leaves
1 8-ounce bottle of shrimp sauce
1 4-ounce can shrimp, drained

Combine crab meat and cream cheese in bowl; mix well. Shape into brick. Place on lettuce-lined serving platter. Pour shrimp sauce over top. Sprinkle shrimp over sauce. Garnish with cherry tomatoes and sprigs of parsley. Chill for several hours before serving. Yield: 10 servings.

Juyne Bushart

DILL DIP

1 cup sour cream
1 cup mayonnaise
1 teaspoon dillweed
1 teaspoon seasoned salt
2 green onions, chopped

Combine sour cream, mayonnaise, dillweed, salt and onions in bowl; mix well. Chill for 6 hours before serving. Serve with carrots, celery and radishes. May serve with cauliflower and broccoli flowerets cooked in a small amount of boiling salted water for 2 minutes or until tender-crisp, then drained and chilled. Yield: 3 cups.

Wilma Allen

FRUIT DIP

8 ounces cream cheese, softened
1 13-ounce jar marshmallow creme

Beat cream cheese and marshmallow creme in mixer bowl until smooth. Serve with fresh fruit. Yield: 3 cups.

Betty Schweinhart

FRESH FRUIT DIP

1 cup sour cream
1/2 teaspoon cinnamon
1/2 teaspoon nutmeg
Dash of cloves

1 teaspoon vanilla extract
1/2 teaspoon rum extract
2 tablespoons sugar

Combine all ingredients in bowl; mix well. Chill until serving time. Serve with fresh fruit. Yield: 1 cup.

Sandy Adams

LOW-CALORIE DIP

1 tablespoon minced onion
1 tablespoon lemon juice
1 tablespoon instant
   bouillon
Dash of garlic powder
Dash of Tabasco sauce

1 teaspoon
   Worcestershire sauce
6 ounces cream-style
   cottage cheese
1   4-ounce can pimentos
1/8 teaspoon salt

Combine onion, lemon juice, bouillon, garlic powder, Tabasco sauce, Worcestershire sauce, cottage cheese, pimentos and salt in blender container. Purée until smooth. Pour into serving dish. Serve with fresh vegetables. Yield: 1 1/2 cups.

Marge Houseworth

HERB MAYONNAISE DIP

1 cup mayonnaise
1/2 cup sour cream
1/2 teaspoon lemon juice
1/2 teaspoon
   Worcestershire sauce
1 tablespoon chopped
   onion

1 tablespoon chopped
   chives
1/4 teaspoon salt
Dash of garlic salt
1/4 teaspoon paprika
1/8 teaspoon curry powder

Combine mayonnaise, sour cream, lemon juice, Worcestershire sauce, onion, chives, salt, garlic salt, paprika and curry powder in bowl; mix well. Serve with fresh vegetables. Yield: 1 1/2 cups.

Nancy Lockard

TACO PLATE

16 ounces cream cheese, softened
2 cups sour cream
1 envelope taco seasoning mix
1 cup finely chopped onion
2 cups shredded lettuce
2 cups chopped tomato
2 cups shredded Cheddar cheese
Tortilla chips

Mix cream cheese, sour cream and taco seasoning mix in bowl. Spread on large round platter. Sprinkle layers of onion, lettuce, tomato and Cheddar cheese over cream cheese layer. Serve with tortilla chips. Yield: 24 servings.

Cindy Rayhill

NACHO DIP

1 pound ground beef
1 onion, chopped
2 15-ounce cans refried beans
1 4-ounce can green chilies, drained
2 cups shredded Cheddar cheese
2 cups shredded Monterey Jack cheese
2 8-ounce bottles of taco sauce
2 cups sour cream
1 12-ounce can pitted ripe olives, drained
Tortilla chips

Brown ground beef with onion in skillet, stirring until ground beef is crumbly; drain. Spread refried beans in bottom of 9x13-inch baking dish. Layer ground beef mixture, chilies and half the cheeses over bean layer. Pour taco sauce over top. Sprinkle with remaining cheeses. Bake at 350 degrees for 15 minutes or until bubbly. Spread with sour cream; sprinkle with olives. Serve with tortilla chips. Yield: 12 servings.

Bernidea Fort

TEX-MEX DIP

2 10-ounce cans bean dip
3 medium avocados
2 tablespoons lemon juice
1/2 teaspoon salt
1/4 teaspoon pepper
1 cup sour cream
1/2 cup mayonnaise
1 envelope taco
  seasoning mix
1 cup chopped green
  onions
2 cups chopped tomatoes
3 3-ounce cans pitted
  ripe olives, drained
1 8-ounce package
  shredded Cheddar cheese
Tortilla chips

Spread bean dip in bottom of 9x13-inch dish. Mash avocados in bowl. Add lemon juice, salt and pepper; mix well. Spread over bean layer. Combine sour cream, mayonnaise and taco seasoning mix in bowl; mix well. Spread over avocado layer. Layer onions, tomatoes and olives over top. Sprinkle with cheese. Serve with tortilla chips. Yield: 12 servings.

Sandy McGill

LAYERED TACO DIP

1/2 head lettuce, shredded
2 tomatoes, chopped
2 10-ounce cans bean dip
1 cup shredded Cheddar
  cheese
1 cup sour cream
3 green onions, sliced
1 avocado, sliced
1 6-ounce can pitted ripe
  olives, drained
Tortilla chips

Arrange lettuce on large serving platter. Layer tomatoes, bean dip, cheese, sour cream, onions, avocado and olives over lettuce. Serve with tortilla chips. Yield: 12 servings.

Yocianne Everett

TACO SALAD DIP

8 ounces cream cheese, softened
8 ounces sour cream
1 envelope taco seasoning mix
Shredded lettuce
Chopped tomatoes
4 to 6 ounces Cheddar cheese, shredded
1 8-ounce bottle of taco sauce
Tortilla chips

Mix cream cheese, sour cream and taco seasoning mix in mixer bowl. Chill, covered, overnight. Spread cream cheese mixture in bottom of 8x8-inch dish. Layer lettuce, tomatoes and Cheddar cheese over top. Drizzle with taco sauce. Serve with tortilla chips. Recipe may be doubled and served in 9x13-inch dish. Yield: 6 servings.

Mary B. Mason

SPICY TACO SALAD DIP

8 ounces cream cheese, softened
16 ounces sour cream
1 envelope taco seasoning mix
1 8-ounce bottle of mild taco sauce
8 ounces hot pepper cheese, shredded
8 ounces Cheddar cheese, shredded
Shredded lettuce
Chopped tomatoes

Mix cream cheese, sour cream and taco seasoning mix in bowl. Spread on 13-inch round serving plate. Chill for 30 minutes. Pour taco sauce over top. Layer with cheeses, lettuce and tomatoes. Yield: 12 servings.

Jean Geary

SOMBRERO DIP

1 pound ground beef
1/2 cup chopped onion
1/2 cup hot catsup
2 8-ounce cans kidney beans, mashed
1/2 teaspoon salt
1 tablespoon chili powder
Chopped onions
Stuffed green olives
Shredded Cheddar cheese
Tortilla chips

Brown ground beef and ½ cup onion in skillet, stirring until ground beef is crumbly and onion is tender; drain. Add catsup, beans, salt and chili powder; mix well. Heat to serving temperature. Spoon into fondue pot or Crock•Pot. Keep warm on Low. Garnish with chopped onions, chopped stuffed green olives and shredded Cheddar cheese. Serve with tortilla chips.
Yield: 20 servings.

Celesta Wilson

NACHOS AND TACO DIP

2 pounds ground beef
1 envelope taco
  seasoning mix
2 cups sour cream
1 cup shredded Cheddar
  cheese
1 head lettuce, shredded

2 green bell peppers,
  chopped
1 onion, chopped
1 pint cherry tomatoes,
  chopped
1 24-ounce package
  nacho chips

Brown ground beef and half the taco seasoning mix in skillet, stirring until ground beef is crumbly; drain. Layer sour cream, remaining taco seasoning mix, Cheddar cheese, lettuce, green peppers, onion and tomatoes in large serving dish. Serve with nacho chips. Yield: 24 servings.

Shirley Smith

ORIENTAL DIP

4 teaspoons soy sauce
1 teaspoon ginger
1 teaspoon vinegar

2 tablespoons finely
  chopped onion
1 cup mayonnaise

Combine soy sauce, ginger, vinegar and onion in bowl; mix well. Add mayonnaise; mix well. Serve with fresh vegetables. May store in refrigerator for 2 to 3 weeks. Yield: 1¼ cups.

Mrs. Robert Klausing

SOUR CREAM RANCH DIP

1 envelope ranch salad
dressing mix
1 envelope green onion
dip mix

2 cups mayonnaise
2 cups sour cream
1 4-ounce can chopped
ripe olives, drained

Combine all ingredients in bowl; mix well. Chill, covered, overnight. Serve with fresh vegetables. Yield: 1 quart.

Rebecca Ray

SPINACH DIP

1 package Knorr's
vegetable soup mix
1 8-ounce can chopped
water chestnuts
8 ounces cream cheese,
softened

1/4 cup (about) mayonnaise
1 10-ounce package frozen
chopped spinach, thawed
Rye bread slices

Combine vegetable soup mix, drained water chestnuts and cream cheese in bowl; mix well. Add enough mayonnaise to make of dipping consistency. Drain and squeeze spinach dry. Add to cream cheese mixture; mix well. Spread on rye bread slices. Yield: 3 cups.

Betty Krueger

BRAUNSCHWEIGER SPREAD

1 small onion, chopped
16 ounces braunschweiger
1 tablespoon
Worcestershire sauce

6 ounces cream cheese,
softened
1 tablespoon milk

Combine onion, braunschweiger, Worcestershire sauce and 3 ounces cream cheese in bowl; mix well. Press into plastic wrap-lined bowl. Chill for several hours. Unmold onto serving plate. Blend remaining 3 ounces cream cheese and milk in small bowl. Spread over top and side of braunschweiger mold. A margarine container may be used to mold braunschweiger mixture. Serve with assorted crackers. Yield: 3 cups.

Claudia S. Geurin

CHIPPED BEEF BALL

2   2-ounce packages
   chipped beef, chopped
16 ounces cream cheese,
   softened
2 tablespoons MSG

1 tablespoon chopped
   onion
2 tablespoons
   Worcestershire sauce

Combine half the chipped beef, cream cheese, MSG, onion and Worcestershire sauce in bowl; mix well. Shape into ball. Roll ball in remaining chipped beef to coat well. May add 1 to 4 teaspoons horseradish, 1/4 cup sour cream and 1/4 cup grated Parmesan cheese. Yield: 1 chipped beef ball.

Nancy Lockard, Anna Lee Pruitt
Barbara Struck

RANCH CHEESE BALL

1 cup shredded Cheddar
   cheese
6 ounces cream cheese
1 package ranch salad
   dressing mix

1/2 cup mayonnaise
1/2 cup milk
5 ounces sliced almonds,
   toasted

Let Cheddar cheese and cream cheese stand at room temperature for 1 hour. Combine salad dressing mix, mayonnaise and milk in mixer bowl; mix well. Add cream cheese; beat until smooth. Fold in Cheddar cheese. Chill, covered, in freezer for 30 minutes. Shape into ball; roll in almonds to coat.
Yield: 1 cheese ball.

Juyne Bushart

★ Cheese balls should be served at room temperature for improved flavor and easier spreading.

LIGHT AND FLUFFY CHEESE BALL

16 ounces cream cheese
1 8-ounce jar Old English
cheese
1 tablespoon MSG
1 tablespoon minced onion
1 tablespoon Parmesan
cheese
1/2 cup crushed pecans

Combine softened cream cheese, Old English cheese, MSG, onion and Parmesan cheese in bowl; mix well. Chill for 1 hour. Shape into ball; roll in pecans to coat well. Serve with crackers. Yield: 1 cheese ball.

Ann Schmitt

PINEAPPLE CHEESE BALL

16 ounces cream cheese,
softened
1/4 cup crushed pineapple,
well drained
1/4 teaspoon seasoning salt
2 tablespoons chopped
green bell pepper
2 tablespoons chopped
green onion
1 cup chopped pecans

Combine cream cheese, pineapple, seasoning salt, green pepper and onion in mixer bowl; mix well. Shape into ball; roll in pecans to coat well. May add additional 2 tablespoons green pepper, 2 tablespoons green onion and 3/4 cup pineapple if desired. Yield: 1 cheese ball.

Patsy Akers, Carmen Stilger

SHRIMP CHEESE BALL

2 6-ounce cans shrimp,
drained
16 ounces cream cheese,
softened
2 tablespoons minced
onion
Dash of Tabasco sauce
Dash of Worcestershire
sauce
Salt and pepper to taste
1 12-ounce bottle of
cocktail sauce

Combine first 6 ingredients in bowl; mix well. Chill for several hours to overnight. Shape into ball just before serving; place on serving plate. Pour cocktail sauce over ball. Serve with crackers. Yield: 1 cheese ball.

Monica Kayse

THREE-CHEESE BALL

1 10-ounce package
   sharp Cheddar cheese
8 ounces cream cheese,
   softened
4 ounces bleu cheese,
   crumbled
1 teaspoon grated onion

1/2 teaspoon
   Worcestershire sauce
1/2 teaspoon red pepper
   sauce
1/4 teaspoon dry mustard
1 cup pecan halves

Combine Cheddar cheese, cream cheese and bleu cheese in bowl; mix well. Add onion, Worcestershire sauce, red pepper sauce and mustard; mix well. Shape into ball. Press pecan halves on outside of ball. Chill, covered, for several hours to overnight. Yield: 1 cheese ball.

DEVILED HAM SPREAD

2 4-ounce cans deviled
   ham
1 4-ounce jar pimento
   spread
1/2 cup mayonnaise

4 teaspoons parsley flakes
Several drops of Tabasco
   sauce
1/4 cup finely chopped
   pecans

Combine ham, pimento spread, mayonnaise, parsley flakes, Tabasco sauce and pecans in bowl; mix well. Serve with assorted crackers. Yield: 2 cups.

Betty Schweinhart

PIMENTO CHEESE SALAD SPREAD

16 ounces cream cheese,
   softened
1 2-ounce jar pimento
1 egg, beaten

1 tablespoon vinegar
1 tablespoon sugar
2 tablespoons milk
1 cup chopped pecans

Beat cream cheese and pimento in mixer bowl until well mixed. Combine egg, vinegar, sugar and milk in saucepan. Cook over medium heat until thickened, stirring constantly. Cool. Add to cream cheese mixture; beat until creamy. Fold in pecans. Serve with crackers or bread. Yield: 4 cups.

Erma S. Messer

FANCY CHICKEN LOG

16 ounces cream cheese, softened
1 tablespoon steak sauce
1/2 teaspoon curry powder
1/4 cup chopped celery
1/3 cup chopped parsley
1 1/2 cups minced cooked chicken
1/4 cup chopped toasted almonds

Mix cream cheese, steak sauce and curry powder in bowl. Stir in celery, 2 tablespoons parsley and chicken. Chill remaining parsley. Shape mixture into 9-inch log. Wrap with plastic wrap. Chill for 4 hours. Combine remaining parsley and almonds. Roll log in mixture to coat well; place on serving plate. Serve with crackers. Yield: 1 log.

Jayne Roberts

SALMON LOG

1   16-ounce can red sockeye salmon
8 ounces cream cheese, softened
2 teaspoons chopped onion
1 tablespoon lemon juice
1/4 teaspoon salt
1/2 cup chopped pecans
3 tablespoons chopped parsley

Combine salmon, cream cheese, onion, lemon juice and salt in bowl; mix well. Chill for several hours or until firm. Shape into log. Combine pecans and parsley in small bowl. Roll log in mixture to coat well. Chill for several hours. Serve with crackers. Yield: 1 log.

Alma Brite

SALMON SPREAD

2   15-ounce cans red salmon
16 ounces cream cheese, softened
2 tablespoons lemon juice
4 teaspoons minced onion
2 teaspoons prepared horseradish
2 teaspoons celery seed
1/2 teaspoon salt
Coarsely ground black pepper to taste
1 cup finely chopped pecans
Fresh parsley

Drain salmon; bone and flake. Combine cream cheese, lemon juice, onion, horseradish, celery seed, salt and pepper in bowl; mix well. Stir in salmon gently. Spoon mixture into well-oiled 5-cup mold. Chill for several hours to overnight. Unmold onto serving platter. Press pecans into surface. Garnish with sprigs of parsley. Serve with assorted crackers.
Yield: 16 servings.

Trudie Gadjen

SALMON ROLL

1 16-ounce can pink salmon, drained, flaked
8 ounces cream cheese, softened
1 tablespoon lemon juice
1/2 teaspoon onion powder
1/4 teaspoon salt
1 teaspoon horseradish
3 tablespoons parsley flakes
1/2 cup chopped pecans

Combine salmon, cream cheese, lemon juice, onion powder, salt, horseradish and 1 1/2 teaspoons parsley in bowl; mix well. Chill until firm. Shape into roll. Combine remaining parsley flakes and pecans. Coat roll with mixture. Chill overnight. Serve with crackers. Yield: 1 roll.

Celesta Wilson

AUNT NELLIE'S SHRIMP SPREAD

8 ounces cream cheese, softened
2 tablespoons mayonnaise-type salad dressing
Dash of garlic powder
Several drops of Worcestershire sauce
Several drops of Tabasco sauce
3/4 cup shredded Cheddar cheese
1 4-ounce can shrimp
1 12-ounce bottle of cocktail sauce

Combine cream cheese, salad dressing, garlic powder, Worcestershire sauce, Tabasco sauce, cheese and shrimp in bowl; mix well. Shape into log; place on serving plate. Pour cocktail sauce over top. Serve with crackers. Yield: 1 log.

Barbara Struck

RANCH SNACK CRACKERS

1 package ranch salad
   dressing mix
3/4 cup oil
1/4 teaspoon lemon pepper

1/2 teaspoon dillweed
1/4 teaspoon garlic powder
16 ounces oyster crackers

Blend salad dressing mix and oil in bowl. Add lemon pepper, dillweed and garlic powder. Pour over crackers in large baking dish. Bake at 250 degrees for 15 to 20 minutes, stirring frequently. May substitute mini Ritz crackers for oyster crackers.

Maxine Beavin, Aggie Burks
Juyne Bushart, LaDonna Darnell
Marlene Fowler, Barbara Struck

GRANOLA

7 cups oats
3/4 cup sesame seed
3/4 cups wheat germ
2 cups coconut

1 cup oil
1 cup honey
1 cup sunflower seed
1 teaspoon vanilla extract

Combine all ingredients in large bowl; mix well. Spread on 2 large baking sheets. Bake at 200 degrees for 4 to 5 hours, stirring occasionally. Yield: 1 recipe.

Cindy Jones

GRANOLA SNACK

6 cups oats
1/2 cup coconut
3/4 cup wheat germ
1 cup chopped pecans

2/3 cup oil
1 1/2 teaspoons vanilla
   extract
2/3 cup honey

Combine oats, coconut, wheat germ and pecans in large bowl; mix well. Combine oil, vanilla and honey in small bowl; mix well. Stir into dry ingredients. Spread in 9x13-inch baking dish. Mixture will be loose. Bake at 300 degrees for 30 minutes, stirring every 10 minutes. Cool completely. Store in airtight container. Yield: 8 cups.

Patricia J. Tudor

PARTY MIX

1/2 cup margarine
11/2 teaspoons seasoned
  salt
4 teaspoons
  Worcestershire sauce
3/4 cup pretzel sticks
2 cups bite-size crispy rice
  squares cereal

2 cups bite-size crispy
  corn squares cereal
2 cups bite-size crispy
  wheat squares cereal
1/2 cup raisins
1 12-ounce can salted
  peanuts

    Melt margarine in 9x13-inch pan. Stir in seasoned salt and Worcestershire sauce. Add pretzels, cereals, raisins and peanuts; toss until all pieces are coated well. Bake at 250 degrees for 45 minutes, stirring every 15 minutes. Cool completely. Store in airtight container. Yield: 9 cups.

Trudie Gadjen

CHEERIOS PARTY MIX

6 ounces pretzel sticks
6 ounces Rice Chex cereal
6 ounces Wheat Chex
  cereal
6 ounces Cheerios
2 cups salted mixed nuts

2 cups butter
1/4 cup Worcestershire
  sauce
1 tablespoon garlic salt
1 tablespoon celery salt

    Combine pretzels, cereals and mixed nuts in large roasting pan. Combine butter, Worcestershire sauce, garlic salt and celery salt in saucepan. Heat over low heat until butter is melted, stirring constantly. Pour over cereal mixture; mix well. Bake at 250 degrees for 1 hour, stirring occasionally. Cool on paper towels. Store in airtight containers. Yield: 5 cups.

Trudie Gadjen, Jean Schmidt

POPCORN BALLS

1 cup packed brown sugar
1/2 cup molasses
1/4 cup water
1 1/2 teaspoons vinegar

1 tablespoon butter
1 cup popcorn, popped
2 cups salted peanuts

Combine sugar, molasses and water in saucepan. Cook, uncovered, over high heat to 250 to 268 degrees on candy thermometer, hard-ball stage, stirring constantly. Add vinegar and butter, stirring until butter is melted. Combine popcorn and peanuts in large bowl. Pour sugar mixture over top; toss to coat well. Shape into balls; place on baking sheet. Bake at 300 degrees for several minutes. Remove immediately from baking sheet; cool completely. Store in airtight container. Yield: 2 to 3 dozen.

Mary Cook

QUICK SNACK

1/2 cup margarine
1 6-ounce package chocolate chips
1 cup peanut butter

1 17-ounce package Rice Chex cereal
1 pound confectioners' sugar

Melt margarine, chocolate chips and peanut butter in saucepan, stirring constantly. Place cereal in large bowl. Pour chocolate mixture over top, stirring until cereal is well coated. Add confectioners' sugar; mix well. Store in airtight container. Yield: 1 recipe.

Pat Cole

★ To keep popcorn balls from sticking to the hands, dip hands in cold water.

BEVERAGES

JOHN'S BANANA PUNCH

1½ to 2 cups sugar
4 cups water
4 bananas, mashed
2 cups orange juice

1 46-ounce can
    pineapple juice
4 liters ginger ale, chilled

Bring sugar and water to a boil in saucepan, stirring to dissolve sugar. Cool. Mix bananas, orange juice and pineapple juice in large bowl. Stir in sugar syrup. Pour into freezer containers. Freeze until firm. Thaw until slushy. Spoon into glasses or pour into punch bowl. Add ginger ale. Yield: 2 gallons.

Barbara Struck

BANANA SLUSH PUNCH

5 bananas, mashed
1 12-ounce can frozen
    orange juice concentrate,
    thawed
1 6-ounce can frozen
    lemonade concentrate,
    thawed

2 to 3 cups sugar
1 46-ounce can
    pineapple juice
4 quarts club soda, chilled

Combine bananas with orange juice and lemonade concentrates in 1-gallon container; mix well. Sprinkle with sugar. Add pineapple juice, stirring to dissolve sugar. Add enough water to fill container. Freeze until slushy. Place in 2-gallon punch bowl. Add club soda. May substitute ginger ale or lemon-lime soda for club soda and reduce sugar to taste. Yield: 2 gallons.

Gail Gardner

★ For crushed ice, freeze water in plastic quart or ½ gallon milk carton. To use, take the carton to solid concrete, and slam it on all four sides, open, and have crushed ice.

CHRISTMAS PUNCH

Juice of 6 large oranges
Juice of 4 large lemons
1/2 to 3/4 cup sugar

1 pint raspberry sherbet
1 pint pineapple sherbet
2 quarts club soda

Combine orange juice, lemon juice and sugar in punch bowl. Stir until sugar is dissolved. Add raspberry sherbet; mix well. Add pineapple sherbet; mix well. Stir in club soda. Yield: 1 gallon.

Trudie Gadjen

MY CHRISTMAS PUNCH

1 6-ounce package
 strawberry gelatin
1 6-ounce package
 cherry gelatin
1 6-ounce package
 orange gelatin
12 cups boiling water
1 46-ounce can apple juice

1 46-ounce can orange
 juice
1 46-ounce can pineapple
 juice
2 12-ounce cans frozen
 lemonade concentrate
1 1/2 cups sugar
1 quart ginger ale, chilled

Dissolve gelatins in boiling water in large container. Cool. Add juices, lemonade concentrate and sugar to taste; mix well. Pour 1 quart into ring mold. Freeze until firm. Unmold. Place in punch bowl. Add remaining punch. Add ginger ale just before serving. Yield: 75 servings.

Patsy Dumont

FRUIT PUNCH

3 envelopes cherry drink
 mix
2 cups sugar
2 quarts water

1 quart ginger ale, chilled
1 46-ounce can pineapple
 juice, chilled

Stir drink mix and sugar into water in large container until dissolved. Pour into freezer trays. Freeze until firm. Mix with ginger ale and pineapple juice in punch bowl just before serving. Yield: 5 quarts.

Debbie Rigdon

SUMMER LIME COOLER

1   6-ounce can frozen
   limeade concentrate,
   thawed

¹/₄ cup sugar
4 cups crushed ice

Combine limeade concentrate, sugar and ice in blender container. Process at medium speed until smooth. Serve immediately or store in freezer. Yield: 6 servings.

Brenda Owens

ORANGE JULIUS

1   6-ounce can frozen
   orange juice concentrate,
   thawed
1¹/₂ cups water

¹/₃ cup nonfat dry milk
   powder
¹/₂ cup sugar
8 to 10 ice cubes

Combine orange juice, water, milk powder, sugar and ice cubes in blender container. Process for 30 seconds or until smooth. Serve immediately. Yield: 3 servings.

Yocianne Everett

MOCK FROZEN PEACH DAIQUIRI

1 cup juice-pack canned
   peaches
2 tablespoons frozen pink
   lemonade concentrate

1 tablespoon fresh lemon
   juice
1 egg white
1 cup crushed ice

Chill peaches in covered container in freezer until very cold. Combine with pink lemonade concentrate, lemon juice, egg white and ice in blender container. Purée until smooth. Pour into glasses. Yield: 2¹/₂ cups.

Wellness Committee

POLLY'S PUNCH

1 12-ounce can frozen
orange juice concentrate
1 6-ounce can frozen
lemon juice concentrate
1 46-ounce can pineapple
juice
3 cups sugar
1 quart hot tea
3 cups water
1 bottle of maraschino
cherries
1 liter ginger ale

Prepare orange juice and lemon juice concentrates using package directions. Combine with pineapple juice in 2-gallon container. Add sugar, hot tea, water and cherries. Combine with ginger ale in punch bowl at serving time. Yield: 7 quarts.

Rhoda Bailey

CONNIE'S PUNCH

1 46-ounce can pineapple
juice
2 cups sugar
2 envelopes unsweetened
lemonade drink mix
2 liters ginger ale, chilled

Combine juice, sugar and lemonade mix in 1-gallon container. Add enough water to measure 1 gallon; mix well. Freeze. Thaw for 6 hours or until slushy. Combine with ginger ale in punch bowl at serving time. Yield: 50 servings.

Della Mundy

PINK PUNCH

2 3-ounce packages
cherry gelatin
2 cups sugar
1 quart boiling water
2 quarts cold water
1 12-ounce can frozen
orange juice concentrate
1 12-ounce can frozen
lemonade concentrate
1 46-ounce can pineapple
juice, chilled
2 bottles of ginger ale,
chilled

Dissolve gelatin and sugar in boiling water in large container. Stir in cold water, frozen juice concentrates and pineapple juice. Pour into punch bowl. Add ginger ale just before serving. Yield: 50 servings.

Brenda Owens

FRUITED TEA

5 tea bags
2 quarts boiling water
3/4 cup white grape juice

1 cup lemon juice
1 1/2 cups sugar

Steep tea in boiling water in large container for 5 minutes. Remove tea bags. Add juice and sugar, stirring until sugar dissolves. Let stand until cool. Chill in refrigerator. Yield: 10 cups.

Debbie Windhorst

SPICY TOMATO JUICE

6 quarts tomato juice
1 tablespoon salt
1 tablespoon celery salt

1 tablespoon garlic salt
1 tablespoon onion salt
1/3 cup sugar

Combine all ingredients in saucepan; mix well. Bring to a boil. Simmer until of desired consistency. Yield: 6 quarts.

Yocianne Everett

PARTY PUNCH

2 small envelopes orange
drink mix
1 46-ounce can
pineapple juice, chilled

3 10-ounce bottles of
7-Up, chilled
1/2 gallon orange sherbet
1/2 gallon vanilla ice cream

Prepare drink mix in pitcher using package directions. Pour into punch bowl. Add juice and 7-Up. Float scoops of sherbet and ice cream in punch. Yield: 50 servings.

Dollie D. Billiter

PINEAPPLE PUNCH

1/2 gallon sherbet
1 2-liter bottle of ginger
ale, chilled

1 small can crushed
pineapple

Soften sherbet in punch bowl for 1 hour. Add ginger ale and pineapple; mix well. Yield: 20 servings.

Janet Arnold

TROPICAL PINEAPPLE PUNCH

1 cup sugar
2 small packages
  lemon-lime drink mix
2 cups hot water
1 46-ounce can pineapple
  juice, chilled

1 2-liter bottle of lemon-
  lime soda, chilled
1/2 gallon pineapple
  sherbet

Combine sugar, drink mix and hot water in large bowl. Stir until sugar and drink mix are dissolved. Cool. Combine with pineapple juice and soda in punch bowl; mix well. Spoon in sherbet. Yield: 22 cups.

Wanda Wiegand

PINK SMOOTHIE

1 cup cranberry juice,
  chilled

1/4 cup orange juice, chilled
1 cup vanilla ice cream

Combine cranberry juice, orange juice and ice cream in blender container. Process until smooth. Serve immediately. Yield: 2 cups.

Lucy Davis

BOURBON SLUSH

2 small tea bags
1 cup boiling water
1/2 cup sugar
31/2 cups water
1/2 cup Bourbon

1 6-ounce can frozen
  orange juice concentrate,
  thawed
1/3 cup thawed frozen
  lemonade concentrate

Steep tea bags in boiling water in saucepan. Remove tea bags. Stir in sugar until dissolved. Combine tea, 31/2 cups water, Bourbon, orange juice concentrate and lemonade concentrate in large freezer container. Freeze for 24 to 48 hours. Scoop into glasses with ice cream scoop. Garnish as desired.
Yield: 8 to 10 cups.

Philip C. Wettig

AMARETTO

1 cup sugar
1/2 cup water

1 teaspoon almond extract
3 cups vodka

Combine sugar and water in saucepan. Boil until sugar dissolves. Mix with almond extract and vodka in glass container. Add food coloring if desired. Let stand, covered, for 3 days to age. Yield: 4 cups.

EGGNOG

4 egg yolks
1 cup sugar
1 small can cream, chilled
1 quart milk, chilled
1 teaspoon vanilla extract

4 egg whites
6 tablespoons Bourbon or
   rum
Nutmeg

Beat egg yolks and sugar in bowl until thick and lemon-colored. Add cream, milk and vanilla; mix well. Place in freezer until well chilled. Beat egg whites in mixer bowl until stiff peaks form. Fold gently into milk mixture. Pour into chilled serving glasses. Add 1 tablespoon Bourbon or rum to each glass. Garnish with a sprinkle of nutmeg. Yield: 6 servings.

George Nelson

CHOCOLATE EGGNOG

3 quarts eggnog, chilled
1 1/4 cups chocolate syrup
1/4 cup rum
1 1/2 cups whipping cream

3 tablespoons sugar
1 tablespoon baking cocoa
1 ounce semisweet
   chocolate, shaved

Combine eggnog, chocolate syrup and rum in large punch bowl. Beat whipping cream, sugar and cocoa in small mixer bowl at high speed until soft peaks form. Spoon onto eggnog. Sprinkle with shaved chocolate. Yield: 24 servings.

Mary Cook

TROPICAL CHAMPAGNE PUNCH

1 46-ounce can Hawaiian
  Punch
¼ cup sugar (optional)

½ cup Brandy
1 fifth of champagne,
  chilled

Combine Hawaiian Punch and sugar in large pitcher; stir until sugar dissolves. Add Brandy; mix well. Chill until serving time. Stir in Champagne just before serving. Add ice. Garnish with orange slices and strawberries. Yield: 20 servings.

Donna Oldham

FLORIDA FLING

1 quart freshly squeezed
  orange juice, chilled

1 fifth of Champagne,
  chilled

Pour orange juice into large pitcher. Add Champagne just before serving; mix well. Pour into tall stemmed glasses.
Yield: 10 servings.

Beverly Perkins

STRAWBERRY DAIQUIRI

1 10-ounce package
  frozen strawberries
6 ounces rum

1 12-ounce can frozen
  limeade concentrate
5 cups crushed ice

Combine all ingredients in blender container. Process until smooth. Serve immediately or store in freezer. Yield: 8 cups.

Brenda Owens

KAHLUA

1 quart water
10 teaspoons instant
  coffee powder
2½ cups sugar

1 fifth of vodka
1 tablespoon vanilla
  extract

Combine water, coffee powder and sugar in saucepan. Simmer for 1 hour. Cool. Combine with vodka and vanilla in 2-quart container. Yield: 2 quarts.

PARTY KAHLUA

4 cups sugar
4 cups water
¾ cup instant coffee
  powder

1 pint Brandy
1 fifth of vodka
8 teaspoons vanilla extract

Combine sugar and water in saucepan. Cook over medium-high heat until sugar dissolves, stirring constantly. Bring to a boil. Boil for 3 minutes. Blend coffee powder with a small amount of syrup in large saucepan. Add remaining syrup. Bring to a full boil. Combine with Brandy, vodka and vanilla in 1-gallon container. Let stand for 4 to 6 weeks. Yield: 3 quarts.

Joan Echsner

PIÑA COLADA

¾ cup light rum
1 cup unsweetened
  pineapple juice

½ cup cream of coconut
¼ cup whipping cream
2 cups crushed ice

Combine rum, pineapple juice, cream of coconut, whipping cream and ice in blender container. Process until smooth. Pour over additional crushed ice in glasses. Garnish with pineapple spears. Yield: 6 servings.

Ed Jamison

SANGRIA

½ cup lemon juice
½ cup orange juice
½ cup sugar
⁴⁄₅ quart dry red wine

1   7-ounce bottle of club
  soda, chilled
½ cup mixed fruit
Ice cubes

Combine lemon juice, orange juice, sugar, wine, club soda and fruit in pitcher; mix well. Pour over ice cubes in tall glasses. I use oranges and pineapple. Yield: 6 cups.

Tony Williams

JUYNE'S SPARKLER

Boone's Farm Strawberry Hill Wine

Low-calorie orange or lemon-lime soda

Chill wine and soda. Mix equal parts in pitcher. Makes a refreshing, bubbly "lite" wine cooler.

Juyne Bushart

WHISKEY SOUR PUNCH

1 small orange
3   6-ounce cans frozen lemonade concentrate, thawed
3 cups orange juice, chilled

1   32-ounce bottle of club soda, chilled
2 trays ice cubes
1 fifth of Bourbon

Cut orange into thin slices. Discard end pieces. Flute edges of slices with small sharp knife; set aside. Combine lemonade concentrate, orange juice, club soda, ice cubes and Bourbon in punch bowl; mix well. Garnish with orange slices. Yield: 25 servings.

Sandy Adams

HOT APPLE CIDER

1 cup water
1/3 to 2/3 cup sugar
1/4 cup whole cloves
1 teaspoon chopped candied ginger

1 cinnamon stick, broken
2 cups apple cider
1 cup orange juice
2 tablespoons lemon juice

Bring water and sugar to a boil in saucepan. Boil for 10 minutes. Place cloves, ginger and cinnamon in cheesecloth bag or tea ball. Let stand in sugar syrup for 1 hour. Stir in apple cider, orange juice and lemon juice. Heat to the boiling point. Remove spices. Serve hot or cold. May substitute apple juice for apple cider. Yield: 8 servings.

Trudie Gadjen

HOT CRANBERRY CIDER

3 quarts apple cider
1 quart cranberry juice
  cocktail
1/4 cup sugar
3 oranges
16 whole cloves

6 cinnamon sticks
1 teaspoon whole allspice
2 cups rum
1 teaspoon bitters
  (optional)
1/4 cup sugar (optional)

Combine cider, cranberry juice and 1/4 cup sugar in 30-cup percolator. Pierce oranges with fork. Place oranges, cloves, cinnamon and allspice in coffee basket. Perk as for coffee. Add rum, bitters and 1/4 cup sugar. Yield: 32 servings.

Phyllis Atherton

HOT GRAPE PUNCH

2 tea bags
1 cup boiling water
1 cup sugar
1 cup orange juice

1/2 cup lemon juice
1   24-ounce bottle of
    grape juice
5 cups hot water

Steep tea bags in boiling water in large container. Remove tea bags. Stir in sugar until dissolved. Combine with orange juice, lemon juice, grape juice and hot water in punch bowl; mix well. Serve with cookies or cake. Yield: 12 servings.

Chrissy Robey

LOW-CALORIE SPICED DRINK

2 quarts apple juice
1 quart orange juice
2 cinnamon sticks

1 tablespoon whole cloves
3 to 4 packets artificial
  sweetener

Combine apple juice, orange juice, cinnamon and cloves in large saucepan. Heat to serving temperature; remove from heat. Stir in artificial sweetener. Strain into mugs. Yield: 3 quarts.

Chrissy Robey

HOT SPICED PERCOLATOR PUNCH

2¼ cups pineapple juice
1¾ cups water
2 cups cranberry juice
1 tablespoon whole cloves
3 cinnamon sticks, broken

1½ teaspoons whole
  allspice
½ cup packed brown
  sugar
¼ teaspoon salt

Pour pineapple juice, water and cranberry juice into 8-cup percolator. Place cloves, cinnamon, allspice, sugar and salt in basket. Perk for 10 minutes. Yield: 8 to 10 servings.

Barbara C. Hendrick

HOT WINE PUNCH

Red wine
Cranapple juice
Whole cloves
Cinnamon sticks

Orange slices
Lemon slices
Sugar to taste

Combine desired amounts of wine and cranapple juice in saucepan. Place cloves and cinnamon in cheesecloth bag or tea ball. Add to juice in pan. Add unpeeled orange and lemon slices. Bring to a simmer. Simmer for 15 minutes. Add sugar; stir until dissolved. May store in glass bottle in refrigerator. Reheat just to serving temperature; do not boil.

Kris Russell

RUM COFFEE

Ground coffee
Orange rind
Cinnamon stick
2 or 3 whole cloves
Water

Rum
Brown sugar
Whipped cream
Nutmeg

Combine coffee, orange rind, cinnamon and cloves in basket of percolator. Place water in percolator. Perk coffee. Place 1 ounce rum and 1 teaspoon brown sugar in each coffee cup. Add hot coffee. Top with whipped cream and nutmeg.

Linda Ford

HOT BUTTERED RUM

1 pound brown sugar
1 pound confectioners'
sugar
1 pound butter
1 quart vanilla ice cream
1 teaspoon allspice

1 teaspoon cinnamon
1 teaspoon nutmeg
Rum
Brandy
Nutmeg

Combine brown sugar, confectioners' sugar, butter, ice cream, allspice, cinnamon and nutmeg in saucepan. Heat over very low heat until mixture is consistency of thin cake batter, stirring constantly. Cool. Place in freezer container. Freeze, covered, until firm. Place 2 teaspoons frozen mixture in mug. Add 1 1/2 ounces each of rum and Brandy. Fill mug with hot water. Stir to melt frozen mixture. Sprinkle with nutmeg. Yield: 50 servings.

Ann Zimmerman

HOT CRANBERRY TEA

3 cups cranberries
3 1/2 quarts water
12 whole cloves
4 cinnamon sticks

Juice of 2 lemons
Juice of 2 oranges
2 cups sugar

Combine cranberries, water, cloves and cinnamon in large saucepan. Bring to a boil, stirring frequently; reduce heat. Simmer, covered, for 12 minutes. Strain through several thicknesses of cheesecloth, squeezing gently. Return to saucepan. Add lemon juice, orange juice and sugar. Stir until sugar dissolves. Serve hot. Yield: 3 1/2 quarts.

Juyne Bushart

★ For <u>fresh</u> coffee, always open the can only long enough to place coffee in coffeepot, place lid on tightly and store in refrigerator — the freshness lasts until the last tablespoon is used.

SPICED HOT TEA

20 whole cloves
20 whole allspice
5 quarts boiling water
2½ cups sugar

1 family-size tea bag
2 cinnamon sticks
Juice of 3 oranges
Juice of 5 lemons

Place cloves and allspice in cheesecloth bag. Combine with water and sugar in saucepan. Bring to a boil. Boil for 10 to 12 minutes. Remove spice bag. Add tea bag and cinnamon sticks. Steep for 5 minutes. Remove tea bag and cinnamon. Add orange and lemon juices; mix well. Heat to serving temperature; do not boil. Yield: 22 cups.

SPARKLING TEA PUNCH FOR 50

1½ cups water
4 cups sugar
6 cups pineapple juice, chilled
4 cups orange juice, chilled

1 cup lemon juice
½ gallon weak tea, chilled
1 large bottle of ginger ale, chilled
Fresh mint

Combine water and sugar in saucepan. Cook until sugar is dissolved, stirring frequently. Cool. Combine with juices and tea in large container. Add ginger ale just before serving. Serve over ice in tall glasses. Yield: 50 servings.

Ladonna Darnell

CROCK•POT WASSAIL

2 quarts apple juice
1 pint cranberry juice
¾ cup sugar
1 teaspoon aromatic bitters
2 cinnamon sticks

1 teaspoon whole allspice
1 small orange, peeled
Whole cloves
1 cup rum (optional)

Pour apple juice, cranberry juice, sugar, bitters, cinnamon and allspice into Crock•Pot. Stud orange with cloves. Add to juice mixture. Add rum. Cook on High for 1 hour. Simmer on Low for 4 to 8 hours. Serve warm. May substitute apple cider for apple juice. Yield: 12 cups.

Dennis Bryan

SOUPS

FRESH STRAWBERRY SOUP

2 pints strawberries,
  cut into halves
1 tablespoon cornstarch

1 cup orange juice
1 cup Burgundy
1/2 cup sugar

Process strawberry halves in blender or food processor container until puréed. Combine cornstarch and 1/4 cup orange juice in saucepan; mix well. Add remaining orange juice, Burgundy and sugar; mix well. Bring to a boil. Cook until thickened, stirring constantly. Remove from heat. Combine with puréed strawberries in large bowl. Chill in refrigerator. Ladle into soup bowls. Garnish with sour cream and a whole strawberry.
Yield: 6 servings.

Ladonna Darnell

COLD PEACH SOUP

1 1/2 pounds peaches,
  peeled, sliced
16 ounces sour cream
1 cup fresh orange juice
1 cup pineapple juice

1/2 cup dry Sherry
1 tablespoon fresh lemon
  juice
2 tablespoons sugar

Process peaches in food processor container until smooth. Add sour cream, orange juice, pineapple juice, Sherry and lemon juice; process until smooth. Press through sieve into large bowl. Stir in sugar. Chill in refrigerator. Ladle soup into bowls. Yield: 6 servings.

Ladonna Darnell

★ Serve cold soups in bowls nestled into larger bowls of crushed ice for an icy soup on a hot day.

BEAN SOUP

1 pound dried Great
  Northern beans
1 cup chopped celery
1/2 cup chopped onion
1 ham bone
8 cups water

1 cup chopped carrots
1 cup chopped potatoes
1 16-ounce can tomatoes
1/4 cup catsup
Tabasco sauce to taste
Salt and pepper to taste

Combine beans, celery, onion, ham bone and water in soup pot. Bring to a boil. Reduce heat. Simmer until beans are tender, stirring occasionally. Add carrots, potatoes, tomatoes and catsup; mix well. Cook until vegetables are tender, adding more water if necessary. Season with Tabasco sauce, salt and pepper. Yield: 6 servings.

Janet Arnold

CARROT CREAM SOUP

1 cup chopped onion
1 clove of garlic, minced
1/4 cup butter
6 cups chicken broth
10 carrots, peeled,
  chopped

5 potatoes, peeled,
  chopped
1/2 teaspoon salt
1/2 teaspoon sugar
1/2 teaspoon white pepper
1 cup half and half

Sauté onion and garlic in butter in saucepan until tender. Add broth, carrots, potatoes, salt, sugar and pepper; mix well. Bring to a boil; reduce heat. Simmer for 1 hour or until vegetables are tender. Pour soup into blender container; process until smooth. Return soup to saucepan. Heat to serving temperature. Stir in half and half just before serving. Yield: 8 servings.

Sidney Hanks

★ Fried bacon allowed to become cold, then grated or crumbled finely over the top of a vegetable salad or soup gives it a delicious flavor.

CREAM OF CAULIFLOWER SOUP

Flowerets of 1 head
  cauliflower
1 onion, chopped
3 cups chicken broth
2 tablespoons butter

2 tablespoons flour
1 cup cream
Salt, pepper and nutmeg
  to taste

Combine cauliflower, onion and broth in saucepan. Bring to a boil. Boil for 15 minutes. Remove cauliflower and onion to blender container; purée until smooth. Reserve broth. Combine butter and flour in soup pot. Cook for 2 minutes, stirring constantly. Add broth gradually. Cook until thickened, stirring constantly. Stir in cauliflower purée. Add cream; mix well. Add seasonings. Heat to serving temperature. Yield: 6 servings.

Janice R. Boud

MICROWAVE CHEDDAR CHEESE SOUP

2 tablespoons butter
2 tablespoons chopped
  onion
1/3 cup flour
1 1/4 teaspoons dry mustard
1/4 teaspoon garlic powder
1/4 teaspoon paprika
3 cups milk
3 tablespoons chicken-
  seasoned stock base

2 teaspoons
  Worcestershire sauce
1 1/2 cups thinly sliced
  celery
3 cups milk
2 1/2 cups shredded
  Cheddar cheese

Combine butter and onion in 4-quart glass bowl. Microwave, uncovered, on High for 1 minute; mix well. Microwave for 3 minutes longer or until onion is tender. Add flour, dry mustard, garlic powder and paprika; mix well. Stir in 3 cups milk gradually. Add stock base, Worcestershire sauce and celery. Microwave, uncovered, on High for 10 minutes or until slightly thickened, stirring occasionally. Stir in remaining 3 cups milk and cheese. Microwave on High for 8 minutes or until heated to serving temperature or to 160 degrees on temperature probe, stirring occasionally. Ladle into soup bowls. Garnish with bell pepper, pimento, toasted almonds or bacon. Yield: 8 servings.

Wilma Allen

CHICKEN NOODLE SOUP

1   2 to 3-pound chicken
3 quarts water
1½ cups chopped onion
2½ cups chopped celery
1 teaspoon salt
1 bay leaf
1 teaspoon thyme

2 tablespoons dried
   parsley
1 teaspoon marjoram
2 cups chopped carrots
8 cups tomatoes
3 cups egg noodles
1 teaspoon pepper

Combine chicken, water, ½ cup onion, ½ cup celery, salt and bay leaf in soup pot. Bring to a boil; reduce heat. Cook, covered, until chicken is tender. Remove chicken from pot. Cool slightly. Remove meat from bones. Skim surface of broth. Return chicken to soup pot. Add remaining 1 cup onion, remaining 2 cups celery, thyme, parsley, marjoram, carrots and tomatoes. Simmer until vegetables are tender. Remove bay leaf. Add noodles. Simmer for 10 to 15 minutes or until noodles are tender. Add pepper and additional salt to taste. Yield: 12 servings.

Dena Sue Montgomery

NEW ENGLAND CLAM CHOWDER

8 ounces bacon, finely
   chopped
1 large onion, minced
1 carrot, minced
¾ cup minced celery
½ teaspoon thyme
½ teaspoon dillweed

½ teaspoon white pepper
¼ cup flour
4 cups fish stock
1 bay leaf
3 cups diced potatoes
2 cups chopped clams
1 cup whipping cream

Cook bacon in stockpot until crisp. Add onion, carrot and celery. Sauté for 5 to 8 minutes or until tender. Add thyme, dillweed and pepper; mix well. Cook for 2 minutes longer. Stir in flour. Cook for 5 minutes over medium heat, stirring constantly. Bring fish stock to a boil in saucepan. Pour over vegetable mixture; mix well. Add bay leaf. Simmer for 10 minutes or until thickened, stirring frequently. Add potatoes; mix well. Cook until tender. Mash about ½ cup potatoes with spoon in stockpot. Stir in clams and cream. Remove bay leaf. Heat to serving temperature. Do not boil. Add salt and pepper to taste. Yield: 8 servings.

Wanda Wiegand

CORN AND TOMATO SOUP

12 ears of corn
2 heads cabbage, chopped

2 cups water
2 gallons ripe tomatoes

Cut corn from cobs; do not scrape. Combine corn and cabbage with water in large saucepan. Bring to a boil; reduce heat. Simmer over low heat for 20 minutes. Scald tomatoes. Peel and chop. Add to soup. Simmer for 20 minutes. Ladle into hot sterilized jars, leaving 1/2-inch headspace. Seal with 2-piece lids. Yield: 10 quarts.

Ida Thompson

EGG DROP SOUP

6 13-ounce cans chicken
  broth
4 1/2 tablespoons cornstarch
1/3 cup cold water
3/4 teaspoon sugar

3/4 teaspoon salt
1/4 teaspoon pepper
3 eggs, well beaten
1 1/2 cups chopped green
  onions with tops

Bring broth to a boil in saucepan; reduce heat. Stir in mixture of cornstarch and water. Cook until thickened, stirring constantly. Stir in seasonings; reduce heat. Add eggs gradually to broth, stirring to separate eggs into threads. Remove from heat. Stir in green onions. Serve immediately. Yield: 12 servings.

Bea Senn

BROCCOLI AND HAM SOUP

1 cup finely chopped ham
2 cloves of garlic, minced
2 tablespoons oil
1 10-ounce package
  frozen chopped broccoli

1 cup canned tomatoes
1/2 teaspoon nutmeg
5 cups canned bouillon
1 1/2 cups macaroni
Salt and pepper to taste

Sauté ham and garlic in oil in saucepan until brown. Stir in next 4 ingredients. Bring to a boil; reduce heat. Simmer for 20 minutes. Add macaroni. Cook for 5 to 10 minutes longer or until macaroni is tender. Season with salt and pepper. Garnish with Parmesan cheese. Yield: 6 servings.

Lucy Davis

MICROWAVE SPLIT PEA SOUP

1 pound dried split peas
1 ham bone
8 cups boiling water
1 small onion, sliced
5 peppercorns

1/2 cup chopped peeled
    potato
1 cup chopped cooked ham
1/3 cup sliced carrot
Salt and pepper to taste

Combine split peas, ham bone, water, onion and pepper-corns in 4-quart glass bowl. Microwave, tightly covered, on High for 25 minutes or until peas are tender, stirring once. Remove ham bone; cut off ham. Add to soup. Add carrot, potato and chopped ham. Microwave, covered, on High for 15 to 20 minutes or until vegetables are tender-crisp. Add salt and pepper. Yield: 8 to 10 servings.

Cindy Jones

MINESTRONE SOUP

2 to 3 pounds beef shanks
16 cups water
1 tablespoon salt
2 cups chopped cabbage
1 20-ounce can chick-
    peas
1 16-ounce can tomatoes
2 cups sliced carrots

1 10-ounce package
    frozen peas
1 cup sliced celery
1 cup broken spaghetti
1 bay leaf
1 to 2 tablespoons salt
1/2 teaspoon pepper

Combine beef shanks, water and 1 tablespoon salt in soup pot. Bring to a boil; reduce heat. Simmer, covered, for 2 1/2 to 3 hours or until beef is tender. Remove beef shanks from pot. Cool slightly. Remove beef from bone. Return beef to soup. Add cabbage, chick-peas, tomatoes, carrots, peas, celery, spaghetti, bay leaf, remaining salt and pepper; mix well. Simmer for 30 to 45 minutes or until vegetables are tender. Remove bay leaf. Garnish with parsley sprigs. Yield: 6 servings.

Cindy Jones

CHEESE AND POTATO SOUP

3 cups potato flakes
2 cups water
1/2 cup chopped celery
1/2 cup chopped carrots
1/4 cup chopped onion
1 teaspoon parsley
2 chicken bouillon cubes

1/2 teaspoon salt
1/2 teaspoon pepper
1 1/2 cups milk
2 tablespoons flour
8 ounces Velveeta cheese,
   cubed

Combine potato flakes, water, celery, carrots, onion, parsley, bouillon cubes, salt and pepper in stockpot. Bring to a boil; reduce heat. Simmer for 2 1/2 hours. Add milk, flour and Velveeta. Simmer for 30 minutes longer or until thickened, stirring frequently. Yield: 6 to 8 servings.

Roy Dobbs

MICROWAVE FRENCH ONION SOUP

2 tablespoons butter
3 medium onions, thinly
   sliced
3 cans condensed beef
   broth

2 1/4 cups water
Salt to taste
6 to 8 slices French bread,
   toasted
Parmesan cheese

Combine butter and onions in 3-quart glass bowl. Microwave, covered, on High for 8 minutes or until onions are transparent, stirring once. Stir in broth and water. Microwave, covered, on High for 8 to 10 minutes or until onions are tender. Add salt. Ladle into soup bowls. Add 1 bread slice to each bowl; sprinkle with Parmesan cheese. Yield: 6 to 8 servings.

Mary Cook

★ For a quick hearty soup prepare any cream soup according to directions on can, add any leftover vegetables you may have and serve with a sprinkle of cheese.

MICROWAVE CREAM OF POTATO-ONION SOUP

4 medium potatoes, peeled
2 medium onions
3/4 teaspoon salt
1/4 cup water
3 tablespoons butter
2 tablespoons flour

3 cups milk
2 tablespoons minced
  parsley
1/2 teaspoon celery salt
White pepper to taste

    Chop potatoes and onions. Place in 3-quart glass casserole. Add salt and water. Microwave, covered, on High for 10 to 12 minutes or until tender, stirring once. Purée in blender or food processor container. Microwave butter in glass casserole on High for 30 seconds or until melted. Blend in flour. Stir in milk gradually. Add puréed vegetables and seasonings; mix well. Microwave, uncovered, on High for 5 minutes or until heated to serving temperature, stirring occasionally. Yield: 6 servings.

Cindy Jones

SPINACH AND POTATO BISQUE

2 cups fresh spinach
4 cups chicken broth
6 green onions, sliced
2 cups mashed potatoes

2 cups half and half
1/2 teaspoon Tabasco
  sauce
1/2 teaspoon pepper

    Stem and chop spinach. Bring broth to a boil in stockpot; reduce heat. Add spinach and green onions. Simmer for 3 to 5 minutes. Process broth mixture 1/4 at a time in blender container until smooth. Return mixture to stockpot. Whisk in mashed potatoes until smooth. Add half and half, Tabasco sauce and pepper; mix well. Heat to serving temperature. Ladle into soup bowls. Garnish with a twist of lemon. Yield: 6 servings.

Pamela Simms

FIJI CREAM OF PUMPKIN SOUP

2 tablespoons grated onion
2 tablespoons butter
2 cups chicken broth
1/4 cup potato flakes
1 teaspoon salt

1/4 teaspoon white pepper
1/8 teaspoon nutmeg
1 2/3 cups evaporated milk
1 cup cooked pumpkin

Sauté onion in butter in saucepan. Add broth. Bring to a boil. Remove from heat. Stir in potato flakes and seasonings. Beat until smooth. Add evaporated milk and pumpkin; mix well. Simmer for 15 minutes, stirring frequently. Ladle into serving bowls. Garnish with sour cream. Yield: 4 servings.

Patti Roby

POLISH SAUSAGE SOUP

1 Polish sausage ring, finely chopped
1 large onion, chopped
2 potatoes, finely chopped
1½ cups finely chopped celery
1 can whole kernel corn
1 can kidney beans
2 cans tomato purée
3 cups water
2 or 3 jalapeño peppers, chopped (optional)

Combine sausage, onion, potatoes, celery, corn, beans, tomato purée and water in saucepan. Bring to a boil; reduce heat. Simmer until sausage and potatoes are cooked and soup has thickened to desired consistency. Season with salt to taste. Add jalapeño peppers if desired. Yield: 4 servings.

Roy White

MICROWAVE CREAMY TOMATO SOUP

¼ cup butter
1 tablespoon finely chopped onion
3 tablespoons flour
2 tablespoons sugar
1 teaspoon salt
Pepper to taste
1 16-ounce can tomato juice
2 cups milk

Combine butter and onion in 2-quart glass casserole. Microwave on High for 2 minutes or until butter in melted. Add flour, sugar, salt and pepper; mix well. Stir in tomato juice gradually. Microwave on High for 4 minutes or until heated through, stirring once. Stir in milk gradually. Microwave on Medium-High for 8 to 10 minutes or just to the simmering point, stirring every 2 minutes. Ladle into soup bowls. Garnish with croutons or oyster crackers. Yield: 6 servings.

Wilma Allen

TOMATO AND CELERY SOUP

1 onion, chopped
1/2 cup chopped celery
2 tablespoons butter
1 can tomato soup
1 soup can water

1 tablespoon lemon juice
1 teaspoon sugar
1 teaspoon minced parsley
1/8 teaspoon pepper
1/4 teaspoon salt

Sauté onion and celery in butter in saucepan until tender. Add remaining ingredients; mix well. Simmer for 5 minutes. Pour into serving bowls. Garnish with shredded cheese and additional parsley. Yield: 2 servings.

Sally Trent

TUNA AND CHEDDAR CHOWDER

1/4 cup thinly sliced green
   onions
1 tablespoon butter
1 can Cheddar cheese
   soup

1/2 soup can milk
1/2 soup can water
2 teaspoons lemon juice
1   7-ounce can tuna,
   drained

Sauté onion in butter in saucepan until tender. Add soup; mix well. Stir in milk, water and lemon juice; mix well. Add tuna. Heat to serving temperature, stirring frequently. Yield: 2 servings.

Gail Gardner

BASIC CREAMED VEGETABLE SOUP

2 tablespoons flour
3 tablespoons butter,
   softened
1 cup chicken broth
1 cup milk

1/2 cup cream
2 to 3 tablespoons Sherry
Worcestershire sauce to
   taste
1 cup cooked vegetables

Process flour, butter and broth in blender container until smooth. Add milk, cream, Sherry and Worcestershire sauce. Blend for 2 to 3 seconds longer. Add vegetables and salt and pepper to taste; blend until puréed. Pour into saucepan. Heat just to serving temperature; do not boil. Serve with croutons and shredded cheese. Yield: 4 to 6 servings.

Patricia J. Tudor

OLD-FASHIONED VEGETABLE SOUP

2¹/₂ pounds beef shanks
1 tablespoon salt
¹/₈ teaspoon thyme
6 peppercorns
1 bay leaf
2 whole allspice
2 beef bouillon cubes
6 cups hot water

2 cups chopped potatoes
2 stalks celery, sliced
2 carrots, sliced
¹/₂ cup chopped onion
1 16-ounce can tomatoes
1 12-ounce can whole
   kernel corn, drained

Combine beef shanks, salt, thyme, peppercorns, bay leaf, allspice, bouillon cubes and hot water in stockpot. Simmer, covered, for 3 hours or until meat is tender. Remove beef shanks, peppercorns and bay leaf. Cut beef from bone; return beef to broth. Add potatoes, celery, carrots, onion, tomatoes and corn. Simmer, covered, for 30 minutes or until vegetables are tender. May use any combination of vegetables, such as parsnips, turnips, cabbage, green beans or lima beans. Broth can be prepared ahead and frozen for up to 3 weeks.
Yield: 6 to 8 servings.

Mary Cook

PURÉE OF VEGETABLE SOUP

2 cups chopped potatoes
¹/₂ cup chopped celery
1 cup chopped onion
1 cup peas
1 cup green beans

1 cup lima beans
1 cup sliced carrots
4 cups milk
2 cups chicken broth
Salt and pepper to taste

Cook potatoes, celery, onion, peas, green beans, lima beans and carrots in small amount of water in saucepan until tender; drain. Purée vegetables in blender container until smooth. Heat milk and chicken broth in saucepan. Add vegetables; mix well. Heat just to serving temperature; do not boil. Strain soup before serving. Season with salt and pepper.
Yield: 8 servings.

Beverly Perkins

WON TON SOUP

1/2 cup prawns
1/2 cup ground pork
2 tablespoons water
  chestnuts
2 tablespoons bamboo
  shoots
1/2 teaspoon salt
1 teaspoon cornstarch
24 won ton wrappers

1 egg white, lightly beaten
8 cups chicken broth
1/2 cup sliced bamboo
  shoots
1/4 cup sliced water
  chestnuts
2 cups chopped bok choy
1/4 cup chopped green
  onions

Combine prawns, pork, 2 tablespoons water chestnuts and 2 tablespoons bamboo shoots in food processor container. Process until smooth. Add salt and cornstarch; mix until smooth. Place 1 heaping teaspoon of filling on each won ton wrapper. Fold and roll wrappers to enclose filling, sealing with egg white. Boil in several inches of water in large saucepan for 2 minutes. Rinse in cold water; drain. Bring chicken broth to a boil in saucepan; reduce heat. Add 1/2 cup bamboo shoots and 1/4 cup water chestnuts and won tons. Simmer for 5 minutes. Add bok choy and green onions. Simmer for 1 minute longer. Serve immediately. Yield: 8 servings.

Juyne Bushart

★ Save even small amounts of leftover vegetables and rice. Keep a container in the freezer to collect these leftovers until a suitable amount accumulates, then have a hearty (and interesting) soup supper.

Kentucky has many beautiful lakes and fishing holes. Some of the most popular are in western Kentucky, near Paducah.

Salads

KENTUCKY LAKE

FRUIT SALADS

LOW-CAL AMBROSIA

1 package unflavored
  gelatin
1 can diet soda
1 6-ounce can frozen
  orange juice concentrate

1 teaspoon coconut
  extract
2 cups crushed pineapple
3 apples, chopped

Soften gelatin in diet soda in saucepan. Heat until gelatin in dissolves, stirring frequently. Combine with orange juice concentrate in bowl; mix well. Add coconut extract, pineapple and apples; mix well. Chill for 1 hour to 1 week. Yield: 15 servings.

Shirley Smith

MOLDED AMBROSIA

1 cup graham cracker
  crumbs
1/2 cup melted butter
1 9-ounce can crushed
  pineapple
1 3-ounce package
  orange gelatin

1/3 cup sugar
1 cup boiling water
1 cup sour cream
1/2 teaspoon vanilla extract
1 cup chopped mandarin
  oranges
1/2 cup flaked coconut

Combine graham cracker crumbs and butter in bowl; mix well. Reserve 1/3 cup. Press remaining mixture into 8x8-inch serving dish. Chill in refrigerator. Drain pineapple, reserving syrup. Stir gelatin and sugar into boiling water in bowl until dissolved. Stir in reserved pineapple syrup. Chill until partially set. Add sour cream and vanilla; beat until fluffy. Fold in pineapple, oranges and coconut. Spoon over crumb crust in serving dish. Sprinkle top with reserved crumbs. Chill until set.
Yield: 12 servings.

Virginia Emmitt

APRICOT SALAD

2 3-ounce packages
  apricot gelatin
2/3 cup sugar
2/3 cup water
2 4³/4-ounce jars baby
  food apricots
1 20-ounce can crushed
  pineapple

1 14-ounce can
  sweetened condensed
  milk
8 ounces cream cheese,
  softened
1 cup chopped pecans

Combine gelatin, sugar and water in saucepan. Bring to a boil, stirring until gelatin and sugar are dissolved. Remove from heat. Add apricots and pineapple; mix well. Let stand until cool. Combine condensed milk and cream cheese in bowl; mix well. Stir in gelatin mixture and pecans. Pour into 9-cup mold. Chill until firm. Unmold onto serving plate. Yield: 20 servings.

Patricia J. Tudor

BLUEBERRY SALAD

2 3-ounce packages
  blackberry gelatin
2 cups boiling water
1 15-ounce can
  blueberries
1 8-ounce can crushed
  pineapple

8 ounces cream cheese,
  softened
1/2 cup sugar
1 cup sour cream
1/2 teaspoon vanilla extract
1/2 cup chopped pecans

Dissolve gelatin in boiling water in bowl. Drain blueberries and pineapple, reserving syrup. Add enough water to reserved syrup to measure 1 cup. Add to gelatin. Stir in blueberries and pineapple. Pour into shallow 2-quart serving dish. Chill, covered, until set. Combine cream cheese, sugar, sour cream and vanilla in bowl; mix well. Spread over salad. Sprinkle with pecans. Yield: 12 servings.

Bernice J. Mills, Judy Roberts

CHERRY COLA SALAD

1 can unsweetened red pie
  cherries
2 3-ounce packages
  cherry gelatin

3/4 cup (scant) sugar
1 20-ounce can crushed
  pineapple
1 8-ounce bottle of cola

Heat cherries in saucepan almost to the boiling point. Stir in gelatin and sugar until dissolved. Add undrained pineapple; mix well. Stir in cola. Pour into serving dish. Chill until set. Yield: 12 servings.

Jewell Hundley

CHERRY SALAD

3 cups red cherries
2 cups water
1/2 cup sugar
1 6-ounce package
  cherry gelatin

1 8-ounce can crushed
  pineapple, drained
1/2 cup chopped pecans

Combine cherries, water and sugar in saucepan. Simmer until cherries are tender, stirring frequently. Remove from heat. Stir in gelatin until dissolved. Add pineapple and pecans; mix well. Pour into mold. Chill until set. Unmold onto serving plate. Yield: 12 servings.

Mrs. Richard Hargrove

CHERRY CREAM SALAD

1 14-ounce can
  sweetened condensed
  milk
8 ounces cream cheese

1 can cherry pie filling
16 ounces whipped
  topping
1/2 cup chopped pecans

Combine condensed milk and softened cream cheese in bowl; blend well. Stir in cherry pie filling. Add whipped topping and pecans; mix well. Pour into serving dish. Chill for several hours to several days. Yield: 12 servings.

Betty Gillihan

CRANBERRY FREEZE

1 6-ounce can whole
  berry cranberry sauce
1/2 cup whipped topping

1 8-ounce can crushed
  pineapple, drained
1/4 cup chopped pecans

Combine cranberry sauce, whipped topping, pineapple and pecans in bowl; mix well. Spoon into shallow dish. Freeze until firm. Let stand at room temperature for several minutes before serving. Cut into squares; place on lettuce-lined salad plates. Yield: 6 servings.

Sandi Tipton Clark

EASY WHIPPED TOPPING SALAD

8 ounces whipped topping
1 3-ounce package
  strawberry gelatin

1 8-ounce can crushed
  pineapple, drained
8 ounces cottage cheese

Combine whipped topping, dry strawberry gelatin, pineapple and cottage cheese in bowl; mix well. Chill until serving time. May add 1 cup miniature marshmallows, 1 can pineapple tidbits and 1/2 cup chopped pecans. Yield: 8 servings.

Martha S. Harper, Molly Hisel

FALL FRUIT SALAD

3 tablespoons lemon juice
3 tablespoons honey
1 1/2 teaspoons oil
1/4 teaspoon ginger
Sections of 4 oranges

4 pears, coarsely chopped
1 cup raisins
2 red apples, coarsely
  chopped

Combine lemon juice, honey, oil and ginger in large bowl; mix well. Add oranges, pears, raisins and apples; toss to mix. Chill until serving time. Yield: 10 servings.

Dana Fendley

FROZEN FRUIT SALAD

1 can peach or cherry pie
  filling
1 14-ounce can
  sweetened condensed
  milk
1 8-ounce can crushed
  pineapple
16 ounces whipped
  topping
1 cup chopped nuts

Combine pie filling, condensed milk and pineapple in bowl; mix well. Fold in whipped topping and nuts gently. Spoon mixture into 9x13-inch serving dish. Freeze for 2 hours or longer. Cut into squares. Yield: 12 servings.

Helen Lovan

GELATIN FRUIT SALAD

1 6-ounce package
  strawberry gelatin
1 20-ounce can crushed
  pineapple
8 ounces cream cheese,
  softened
1/2 cup chopped nuts
1 16-ounce can whole
  berry cranberry sauce
1 12-ounce can Milnot

Combine gelatin and pineapple in saucepan. Simmer until gelatin dissolves, stirring constantly. Add cream cheese; mix well. Remove from heat. Add nuts and cranberry sauce; mix well. Chill until partially set. Stir in Milnot. Pour into 8-cup mold. Chill until firm. Unmold onto serving plate. May omit cream cheese, substitute orange juice for Milnot and add chopped celery and grated orange rind. Yield: 10 servings.

Oma King Kelly

TANGY FRUIT SALAD

1 20-ounce can peaches
1 20-ounce can pears
1 20-ounce can pineapple
  chunks
2 apples, chopped
Sections of 2 oranges,
  chopped
4 bananas, sliced
2 tablespoons orange
  breakfast drink mix
1 6-ounce package
  vanilla instant pudding
  mix

Drain and chop canned fruit, reserving juice. Combine canned fruit, apples, oranges and bananas in large bowl. Blend reserved juice with orange drink mix and pudding mix in bowl. Add to fruit. Chill until serving time. Yield: 20 servings.

Evelyn McClure

CHRISTMAS FRUIT BOWL

1   3-ounce package lime gelatin
1   3-ounce package cherry gelatin
8 ounces whipping cream
Sugar to taste
8 ounces seedless grapes cut into halves
3 apples, chopped
Sections of 2 grapefruit
Sections of 3 oranges
1   16-ounce can peaches
1   8-ounce can pears
1   16-ounce can pineapple chunks
1 cup chopped pecans

Prepare each gelatin according to package directions using 1¹/₂ cups boiling water for each flavor. Pour into separate 8x9-inch dishes. Chill until firm. Whip cream in small bowl, adding sugar. Chill in refrigerator. Combine fresh fruit in bowl. Drain canned fruit; chop peaches and pears. Add to fresh fruit. Add pecans. Cut gelatin into squares. Fold gelatin and whipped cream into fruit mixture gently. Chill for 30 minutes. Yield: 20 servings.

Charlene P. Atkinson

FRUIT SALAD AND COOKED DRESSING

1   16-ounce can pineapple chunks
¹/₂ cup sugar
3 tablespoons flour
2 eggs, beaten
1 tablespoon butter
1 tablespoon lemon juice
3 bananas, sliced
3 apples, chopped
1 cup seedless grapes
1 jar maraschino cherries, drained

Drain pineapple, reserving 1 cup juice. Combine reserved juice with next 4 ingredients in double boiler. Cook until thickened, stirring constantly. Cool. Add lemon juice. Mix fruit in serving bowl. Chill in refrigerator. Pour dressing over fruit. Garnish with nuts and additional cherries. Yield: 10 servings.

Dorothy Luckett

TROPICAL FRUIT SALAD

1   3-ounce package peach
    gelatin
1 cup boiling water
1   15-ounce can tropical
    fruit

8 ounces whipped topping
2 bananas, sliced

Dissolve gelatin in boiling water in bowl. Drain fruit, reserving liquid. Add enough water to fruit liquid to measure 1 cup. Stir into gelatin. Chill for 1½ hours or until partially set. Add whipped topping, drained fruit and bananas; mix well. Pour into mold. Chill until firm. Unmold onto serving plate. Yield: 6 servings.

Shirley Smith

YOGURT FRUIT SALAD

8 ounces lemon yogurt
8 ounces plain yogurt
8 ounces whipped topping

4 to 5 cups assorted
    chopped fruit
1 cup chopped pecans

Combine lemon yogurt, plain yogurt and whipped topping in bowl; mix well. Add fruit. Stir in pecans. Spoon into 8x12-inch dish. Freeze, covered, until firm. Thaw slightly in refrigerator; cut into squares. May use bananas, pineapple, cantaloupe, blueberries, grapes or mandarin oranges. Yield: 12 servings.

Bea Senn

HEAVENLY FIVE-CUP SALAD

1 cup drained mandarin
    oranges
1 cup drained
    pineapple chunks

1 cup miniature
    marshmallows
1 cup flaked coconut
1 cup sour cream

Combine mandarin oranges, pineapple, marshmallows and coconut in bowl; toss to mix. Stir in sour cream. Chill, covered, for several hours to overnight. May use pineapple tidbits instead of chunks or add 1 cup nuts. Yield: 6 servings.

Melinda Carey, Paula Goodlett
Monica Kayse, Shirley Smith

GELATIN AND SOUR CREAM SALAD

1   3-ounce package
    orange gelatin
1   8-ounce can crushed
    pineapple

8 ounces sour cream
8 ounces whipped topping
1 cup chopped pecans

Combine dry gelatin and pineapple in bowl; mix well. Fold in sour cream, whipped topping and pecans gently. Chill overnight. Yield: 4 servings.

Laverne Hollingsworth

MILLIONAIRE SALAD

8 ounces cream cheese,
    softened
2 tablespoons sugar
1   16-ounce can crushed
    pineapple
2 cups cooked rice
1 cup chopped pecans

1 tablespoon mayonnaise-
    type salad dressing
1   10-ounce package
    miniature marshmallows
1 cup whipping cream,
    whipped

Combine cream cheese and sugar in bowl; mix well. Add pineapple, rice, pecans, salad dressing and marshmallows; mix well. Fold in whipped cream gently. Yield: 10 servings.

Virginia Stith

ORANGE SHERBET SALAD

1   6-ounce package
    orange gelatin
1 cup boiling water
1 pint orange sherbet
1 envelope whipped
    topping mix

1   20-ounce can crushed
    pineapple
1 cup miniature
    marshmallows
1   11-ounce can mandarin
    oranges, drained

Dissolve gelatin in boiling water in bowl. Spoon in softened sherbet; mix well. Chill for 5 minutes. Prepare whipped topping using package directions. Chill in refrigerator. Add pineapple, marshmallows and oranges. Fold in whipped topping gently. Chill until set. Yield: 12 servings.

Georgia B. Flora

MANDARIN DUET SALAD

2 3-ounce packages
  orange gelatin
2 cups boiling water or
  fruit juice

1 pint orange sherbet,
  softened
1 11-ounce can mandarin
  oranges, drained

Dissolve gelatin in boiling water in bowl. Add sherbet; stir until melted. Stir in oranges. Pour into 1½-quart ring mold. Chill until firm. Unmold onto salad plate. May fill center with mixed fruit salad. Yield: 6 servings.

Margaret Taylor

MANDARIN ORANGE SALAD

60 Ritz crackers, crushed
1 cup melted butter
½ cup sugar
6 ounces frozen
  unsweetened orange
  juice concentrate, thawed

1 14-ounce can
  sweetened condensed
  milk
8 ounces whipped topping
2 11-ounce cans
  mandarin oranges, drained

Combine cracker crumbs, butter and sugar in bowl; mix well. Reserve ½ cup mixture for topping. Press remaining mixture into 9x13-inch dish. Combine orange juice concentrate and condensed milk in bowl; mix well. Fold in whipped topping and mandarin oranges. Spoon gently over crumb crust. Top with reserved crumbs. Chill or freeze until serving time.
Yield: 12 servings.

Virginia Emmitt

ORANGE SALAD

16 ounces cottage cheese
1 can crushed pineapple
1 can mandarin oranges,
  drained

1 can coconut
1 6-ounce package
  orange gelatin
Whipped topping

Combine first 4 ingredients in bowl; mix well. Sprinkle with orange gelatin. Fold in whipped topping gently. Chill until serving time. Yield: 12 servings.

Molly Hisel

ORANGE AND PEAR SALAD

1 15-ounce can pears
1 3-ounce package
  orange gelatin
3 ounces cream cheese,
  softened
8 ounces whipping cream,
  whipped

Drain pears, reserving juice. Bring juice to a boil in saucepan. Stir in gelatin until dissolved. Chill until partially set. Purée pears and cream cheese in blender container. Add to gelatin; mix well. Fold in whipped cream gently. Pour into mold. Chill until firm. Unmold onto serving plate. Yield: 10 servings.

Norma Hamilton

SARAH'S PEACH SALAD

2 3-ounce packages
  peach gelatin
3½ cups boiling water
4 cups chopped canned
  peaches
1 cup peach syrup
½ cup sugar
2 tablespoons flour
1 egg, beaten
3 ounces cream cheese,
  softened
1 cup whipping cream,
  whipped
1 cup chopped nuts
½ cup miniature
  marshmallows
½ cup shredded Cheddar
  cheese

Dissolve gelatin in boiling water in bowl. Chill until partially set. Fold in peaches gently. Chill until firm. Combine peach syrup, sugar, flour and egg in top of double boiler; mix well. Cook over simmering water until thickened, stirring constantly. Fold in cream cheese gently. Cool. Fold in whipped cream, nuts and marshmallows gently. Spread over gelatin. Sprinkle with Cheddar cheese. Chill for several hours. Yield: 10 to 12 servings.

Sarah Watson

PINEAPPLE SALAD

1 14-ounce can
   sweetened condensed
   milk
¼ cup lemon juice

1 20-ounce can crushed
   pineapple, drained
Whipped topping

Combine condensed milk and lemon juice in bowl; mix well. Stir in pineapple. Fold in whipped topping gently. Chill until serving time. Yield: 12 servings.

Molly Hisel

INDIVIDUAL FROZEN PINEAPPLE SALADS

8 ounces cream cheese,
   softened
¼ cup sugar
¼ cup packed brown
   sugar

1 15-ounce can crushed
   pineapple, drained
2 cups pineapple yogurt
½ cup finely chopped
   pecans

Combine cream cheese, sugar and brown sugar in bowl; beat well. Add pineapple and yogurt; mix well. Spoon into paper-lined muffin cups. Sprinkle with pecans. Freeze, covered, until firm. Remove from freezer 10 minutes before serving.
Yield: 8 servings.

Rhonda Austin

PINK CLOUD

1 20-ounce can juice-
   pack crushed pineapple
2 tablespoons sugar
1 3-ounce package
   strawberry gelatin

16 ounces small curd
   cottage cheese
9 ounces whipped topping

Combine pineapple and sugar in saucepan. Heat to boiling point. Remove from heat. Stir in gelatin until dissolved. Cool to room temperature. Add cottage cheese; mix well. Fold in whipped topping gently. Place in 2½-quart bowl. Chill for several hours to overnight. Yield: 6 servings.

Calene Budell, Monica Kayse

STRAWBERRY SALAD

2　3-ounce packages
　strawberry gelatin
1 cup boiling water
1 to 2　10-ounce
　packages frozen
　strawberries
3 bananas, mashed or
　sliced

1　8 to 16-ounce can
　crushed pineapple,
　drained
1/2 to 1 cup nuts
8 ounces sour cream
1 can coconut (optional)

　　Dissolve gelatin in boiling water in bowl. Add frozen straw-berries, stirring until thawed. Add bananas, pineapple and nuts; mix well. Pour half the mixture into glass dish. Chill in refrigerator until firm. Spread sour cream over congealed mixture. Sprinkle with coconut. Pour remaining mixture over sour cream. Chill until firm. May add 8 ounces cream cheese to sour cream if desired. Yield: 9 servings.

Joyce Alexander, Mary Hemingway
Betty Krueger, Kris Russell

STRAWBERRY GELATIN SALAD

1　6-ounce package
　strawberry gelatin
16 ounces whipped
　topping
16 ounces cottage cheese

1 can crushed pineapple,
　drained
1/2 to 1 cup chopped
　pecans

　　Combine dry gelatin and whipped topping in bowl; mix well. Add cottage cheese, pineapple and pecans; mix well. Chill until serving time. Yield: 8 servings.

Carmen Stilger

STRAWBERRY PRETZEL SALAD

1 to 2 cups crushed
   pretzel sticks
3/4 cup melted butter
1/4 to 1/2 cup sugar
8 ounces cream cheese,
   softened
1 cup sugar
8 ounces whipped topping

1　6-ounce package
   strawberry gelatin
2 cups boiling water
1　16-ounce can crushed
   pineapple (optional)
2　10-ounce packages
   frozen strawberries

Combine pretzel crumbs, butter and 1/4 to 1/2 cup sugar in bowl; mix well. Press into 9x13-inch baking dish. Bake at 350 degrees for 12 minutes. Cool. Combine cream cheese, 1 cup sugar and whipped topping in mixer bowl; beat well. Spread in baked crust. Chill until firm. Dissolve gelatin in boiling water in bowl. Add pineapple with juice and frozen strawberries. Stir until strawberries thaw. Spread over cream cheese layer. Chill until firm. May use 2 cups pineapple juice instead of pineapple. Yield: 12 servings.

Bernidea Fort, Richard Grant
Johnnie Harper, Marty Hill
Grace Murphy, Jane Wallace

WALDORF SALAD

1/2 cup mayonnaise
1 tablespoon sugar
1 tablespoon lemon juice
1/8 teaspoon salt

3 medium apples, chopped
1 cup sliced celery
1/2 cup chopped walnuts

Combine mayonnaise, sugar, lemon juice and salt in bowl; mix well. Add apples, celery and walnuts; toss to mix. Chill, covered, until serving time. Yield: 6 servings.

Debbie Anderson

WATERGATE SALAD

1   8 to 20-ounce can
crushed pineapple
1   3-ounce package
pistachio instant
pudding mix

1/2 to 11/2 cups miniature
marshmallows
1/2 cup chopped pecans
8 to 16 ounces whipped
topping

Drain pineapple, reserving juice. Combine pudding mix and reserved juice in bowl. Add pineapple, marshmallows and pecans; mix well. Fold in whipped topping gently. Chill until serving time. May add 1/2 cup chopped nuts. Yield: 6 servings.

Martha S. Harper, Molly Hisel
Patricia J. Tudor

ZIPPY GELATIN SALAD

2 tablespoons cinnamon
red hots candies
1 cup boiling water
1   3-ounce package
raspberry gelatin

1 envelope unflavored
gelatin
2 cups unsweetened
applesauce

Dissolve cinnamon candies in boiling water in bowl. Stir in raspberry gelatin until dissolved. Sprinkle unflavored gelatin over applesauce to soften. Stir into raspberry gelatin mixture. Chill until firm. Garnish with chopped nuts. Yield: 6 servings.

Norma Gray

★ Use well-washed but unpeeled fresh fruit whenever possible. The extra fiber and other nutritional benefits promote good health.

MAIN DISH SALADS

TOSSED TACO SALAD

1 pound ground chuck
1 envelope taco seasoning
  mix
1 head lettuce, shredded
1   15-ounce can kidney
  beans, drained, rinsed
2 to 3 tomatoes, chopped
1 onion, chopped

1 to 2 cups shredded
  Cheddar cheese
1 cup mayonnaise
1/2 cup taco sauce
2 teaspoons chili powder
1   8-ounce package
  tortilla chips, crushed

Brown ground chuck in skillet, stirring until crumbly; drain. Add seasoning mix using package directions. Cool. Combine lettuce, beans, tomatoes, onion, Cheddar cheese and ground chuck in large salad bowl; toss well. Mix mayonnaise, taco sauce and chili powder in small bowl. Sprinkle tortilla chips over top of salad; drizzle with mayonnaise mixture. Serve immediately. May substitute chili hot beans for kidney beans or 1 bottle of Catalina salad dressing mix for mayonnaise mixture. Serve with additional taco sauce if desired. Yield: 4 servings.

Janis Arnett, Carmen Stilger

TACO SALAD

Lettuce, chopped
Tomatoes, chopped
Shredded Cheddar cheese
Sour cream

1 to 2   15-ounce cans chili
  with beans
2 tablespoons taco sauce
Nacho chips

Layer lettuce, tomatoes and cheese on individual salad plates. Top with sour cream. Heat chili and taco sauce to serving temperature in saucepan. Spoon over salad. Serve with nacho chips. May substitute mixture of 1 pound ground beef, 1 envelope taco seasoning mix and 1 15-ounce can kidney beans for chili with beans. May also use nacho chips as first layer of salad.

Bernidea Fort

SUPPER SALAD

1/3 cup oil
3 tablespoons cider
  vinegar
3 tablespoons chopped
  parsley
3 tablespoons chopped
  green onion
1/2 teaspoon salt

Pepper to taste
5 medium pototoes,
  cooked, sliced
1 16-ounce can green
  beans, drained
2 cups cooked ham strips
1/2 cup thinly sliced
  radishes

Mix oil, vinegar, parsley, onion, salt and pepper in small bowl. Layer warm potato slices and vinegar mixture in salad bowl. Let stand, covered, for 30 minutes. Add beans, ham and radishes; toss gently. May be prepared day ahead. Chill, covered, overnight. Add radishes just before serving.
Yield: 4 servings.

Joyce Alexander

CALIFORNIA CHICKEN SALAD

1/2 cup butter
2 cups mayonnaise
1/4 cup minced parsley
1/2 teaspoon curry powder
1/4 teaspoon minced garlic
Pinch of marjoram
Salt to taste
Pepper to taste

4 cups shredded cooked
  chicken breasts
2 cups sliced seedless
  green grapes
1/2 cup toasted slivered
  almonds
Lettuce leaves
Paprika to taste

Melt butter in saucepan. Remove from heat; cool to room temperature. Combine mayonnaise, parsley, curry powder, garlic, marjoram, salt and pepper in bowl; mix well. Stir in melted butter gently. Combine chicken, grapes and almonds in large bowl; toss well. Arrange on lettuce-lined salad plate. Spoon mayonnaise mixture over top; sprinkle with paprika.
Yield: 4 servings.

Ladonna Darnell

CHICKEN SALAD

3 to 4 ounces chopped
 cooked chicken
Small bunch of green
 grapes, sliced
1/8 cup slivered almonds

1 stalk celery, chopped
2 to 3 tablespoons
 mayonnaise
Salt to taste

Combine chicken, grapes, almonds, celery, mayonnaise and salt in bowl; mix well. Serve as salad or as sandwich spread. Yield: 2 servings.

Peggy Graviss

KENTUCKY TURKEY SALAD

4 cups chopped smoked
 turkey
1 cup finely chopped celery
1/2 cup slivered almonds
1 cup mayonnaise

1/2 cup whipping cream,
 whipped
Salt to taste
1 tablespoon fresh lemon
 juice

Combine turkey, celery, almonds, mayonnaise, whipped cream and salt in large bowl; mix well. Add additional mayonnaise if desired. Drizzle lemon juice over top. Serve as a sandwich spread. Yield: 10 sandwiches.

Beverly Perkins

TURKEY SALAD

4 cups chopped cooked
 turkey
1/2 cup finely chopped
 celery
1/2 cup shredded carrots
1/2 cup sweet pickle salad
 cubes

11/2 cups mayonnaise-type
 salad dressing
1 tablespoon sugar
Salt to taste
Pepper to taste

Combine turkey, celery, carrots, pickle cubes, salad dressing, sugar, salt and pepper in large salad bowl; toss well. Chill until serving time. May substitute sweet pickle relish for sweet pickle salad cubes. Yield: 4 servings.

Grady Peacock

JAVA SALAD

1 8-ounce bottle of Green
  Goddess salad dressing
2 cups hot cooked rice
1/4 cup raisins
1 tablespoon minced onion
2 6-ounce cans tuna,
  flaked
2/3 cup diagonally sliced
  celery
1/4 cup chopped green bell
  pepper
1/4 cup tomato chutney
1/4 cup chopped parsley
1 4-ounce can pimentos,
  chopped
1/4 cup cashews

Mix salad dressing and rice in salad bowl. Add raisins and onion; mix well. Chill, covered, for several hours. Add tuna, celery, green pepper, chutney, parsley, pimentos and cashews; toss lightly. Chill for several hours before serving.
Yield: 8 servings.

Gwen Mills

JUAN TORRES' SEAFOOD SALAD

6 tomatoes
1 green bell pepper
1 purple onion
4 cloves of garlic
1 shallot
8 ounces halibut
8 ounces shrimp
8 ounces scallops
8 ounces crab meat
8 ounces clams
1/3 cup chopped fresh
  cilantro
1/3 cup chopped watercress
Juice of 2 limes
Tabasco sauce to taste
Salt to taste
White pepper to taste

Chop tomatoes, green pepper and onion. Mince garlic and shallot. Cut halibut into 1/2-inch pieces. Steam halibut, shrimp, scallops, crab meat and clams for 60 seconds. Combine with tomatoes, green pepper, onion, garlic, shallot, cilantro, watercress, lime juice, Tabasco sauce, salt and pepper in large bowl; mix well. Marinate in refrigerator for 24 hours. Drain in colander for 5 minutes before serving. Yield: 12 servings.

J. Bruce Stitt

SHRIMP SALAD

1 cup chopped celery
1/2 cup chopped pecans
3 hard-boiled eggs,
  grated
1/4 cup finely chopped
  onion
1/4 cup chopped green bell
  pepper

1 tablespoon lemon juice
1/4 cup chopped sweet
  pickles
3 packages frozen salad-
  size shrimp, thawed
Salt to taste
Pepper to taste
1/2 cup mayonnaise

Combine celery, pecans, eggs, onion, green pepper, lemon juice, pickles, shrimp, salt and pepper in large salad bowl; toss well. Add mayonnaise; mix well. Chill until serving time. Yield: 6 servings.

Chrissy Robey

CREAMY ITALIAN PASTA SALAD

1 cup mayonnaise
2 tablespoons red wine
  vinegar
1 clove of garlic, minced
1 teaspoon basil
1 teaspoon salt
1/4 teaspoon pepper

1 1/2 cups spiral macaroni,
  cooked, drained
1 cup quartered cherry
  tomatoes
1/2 cup chopped green bell
  pepper
1/2 cup sliced ripe olives

Combine mayonnaise, vinegar, garlic, basil, salt and pepper in salad bowl; mix well. Stir in macaroni, tomatoes, green pepper and olives. Chill, covered, until serving time. Yield: 3 cups.

Debbie Anderson

★ Cook pasta for salads just until tender then rinse under cold running water and drain well to prevent gumminess.

MACARONI SALAD

1 cup mayonnaise
2 tablespoons vinegar
1 tablespoon prepared
  mustard
1 teaspoon sugar
1 teaspoon salt
1/4 teaspoon pepper

8 ounces elbow macaroni,
  cooked, drained
1 cup sliced celery
1 cup chopped green or
  red bell pepper
1/4 cup chopped onion

Combine mayonnaise, vinegar, mustard, sugar, salt and pepper in salad bowl; mix well. Add macaroni, celery, pepper and onion; stir well. Chill, covered, until serving time. Yield: 5 cups.

Debbie Anderson

PASTA SALAD

16 ounces macaroni
  spirals or shells
1/2 cup (or more) Italian
  salad dressing
1 cup chopped green bell
  pepper

1 cup chopped onion
1 cup chopped tomato
1 cup chopped cucumber
2 tablespoons Salad
  Supreme seasoning

Cook macaroni using package directions; drain. Cool completely. Place in salad bowl. Add salad dressing, green pepper, onion, tomato, cucumber and seasoning; mix well. Chill for several hours before serving. Yield: 4 servings.

Cindy Rayhill

★ Substitute colored vegetable pastas for plain pasta
  to add variety in color and flavor.

SPAGHETTI SALAD

1 package spaghetti
1/2 head cabbage, chopped
1/2 bunch of celery,
  chopped
3 small onions, chopped
1 2-ounce can pimento,
  drained
1 1/2 tablespoons prepared
  mustard
2/3 cup water
2/3 cup sugar
2/3 cup vinegar
2 tablespoons cornstarch
1 teaspoon salt

Cook spaghetti using package directions. Rinse and drain. Combine with cabbage, celery, onions and pimento in salad bowl; mix well. Combine mustard, water, sugar, vinegar, cornstarch and salt in saucepan. Bring to a boil, stirring constantly. Cook until mixture thickens, stirring constantly. Pour over spaghetti mixture. Chill for 8 hours to 2 weeks in airtight container. Yield: 8 servings.

Celesta Wilson

SUMMER PASTA SALAD

1/2 cup sliced almonds
8 ounces bow-tie noodles,
  cooked
2 11-ounce cans
  mandarin oranges,
  drained
1 large apple, sliced
3 cups chopped cooked
  turkey
2 stalks celery, chopped
1 cup mayonnaise
2 tablespoons whipping
  cream
2 tablespoons fresh lemon
  juice
1 tablespoon sugar
Romaine lettuce leaves

Place almonds in small baking pan. Bake at 300 degrees for 10 minutes or just until lightly browned. Combine noodles, oranges, apple, turkey and celery in large salad bowl; mix well. Mix mayonnaise, cream, lemon juice and sugar in small bowl. Pour over noodle mixture; toss lightly to coat. Chill for 1 hour. Spoon onto lettuce-lined salad plates. Sprinkle with toasted almonds. Yield: 8 servings.

Dana Fendley

VEGETABLE SALADS

THREE-BEAN SALAD

1 cup sugar
1 cup tarragon vinegar
1/2 cup salad oil
1 teaspoon celery seed
1 teaspoon mustard seed
1/4 teaspoon salt
1　16-ounce can green
　beans, drained

1　16-ounce can kidney
　beans, drained
1　16-ounce can wax
　beans, drained
1 onion, sliced
1 green bell pepper, sliced

Combine sugar, vinegar, oil, celery seed, mustard seed and salt in saucepan. Bring to a boil. Cook for 5 minutes. Combine beans, onion and green pepper in bowl. Pour warm dressing over vegetables. Cool. Marinate in airtight container in refrigerator for 4 hours to overnight. May add celery, pimentos or lima beans. May substitute mayonnaise-type salad dressing for vinegar dressing. Yield: 8 to 10 servings.

Cheryl Hardimon, Martha S. Harper
Kathy Yurt

BROCCOLI SALAD

1 bunch broccoli, chopped
3 to 6 hard-boiled eggs,
　chopped
1　6-ounce can black
　olives, sliced

1 small red onion, chopped
3/4 to 1 cup mayonnaise
2 to 4 tablespoons sugar
2 tablespoons vinegar

Combine broccoli, eggs, olives, mushrooms, onion and water chestnuts in salad bowl. Stir in almonds; mix well. Toss with mixture of mayonnaise, sugar and vinegar. Chill until serving time. May add raisins, sunflower seed, crumbled bacon, mandarin oranges, mushrooms, water chestnuts, almonds or celery. May mix ranch-style dressing mix with mayonnaise for dressing. Yield: 6 servings.

Cheryl Barnes, Patsy Ford
Mrs. Michael C. Starke, Kathy Yurt

CABBAGE AND PINEAPPLE SALAD

2 cups shredded cabbage
1 cup pineapple tidbits

Mayonnaise to taste

Chill cabbage in refrigerator in bowl until crisp. Stir in pineapple. Toss with mayonnaise. Chill, covered, in refrigerator until serving time. Yield: 4 servings.

Sue Skelton

CABBAGE SALAD

2 cups mayonnaise-type
  salad dressing
1/4 to 1/2 cup Parmesan
  cheese
1/3 cup sugar
12 to 16 ounces bacon,
  crisp-fried

1 head cabbage, chopped
1 medium onion, chopped
Flowerets of 1 head
  cauliflower

Combine salad dressing, Parmesan cheese and sugar in small bowl; mix well. Crumble bacon into salad bowl. Add cabbage, onion and cauliflower; mix lightly. Add dressing; toss lightly. Chill in refrigerator overnight. Toss again before serving. Yield: 12 servings.

Patti Reece

CARROT AND RAISIN SALAD

1 tablespoon honey
6 tablespoons mayonnaise
1/4 cup milk
1 tablespoon fresh lemon
  juice

1/4 teaspoon salt
3 cups shredded carrots
1 cup raisins

Blend honey, mayonnaise, milk, lemon juice and salt in bowl until smooth. Combine carrots and raisins in salad bowl; mix lightly. Add dressing; toss lightly. Chill in refrigerator until serving time. For lower calorie salad use sugar substitute for honey and decrease the amount of mayonnaise. May add pineapple. Yield: 6 servings.

Karen Estes, Clara Nance

COPPER PENNIES

1 can tomato soup
1 cup sugar
3/4 cup vinegar
1 tablespoon salt
1 teaspoon pepper
1 cup oil
1 teaspoon paprika

1 tablespoon mustard
1 tablespoon
   Worcestershire sauce
3 pounds carrots, sliced
1 onion, chopped
1 green bell pepper,
   chopped

Combine soup, sugar, vinegar, salt, pepper, oil, paprika, mustard and Worcestershire sauce in blender container; process until smooth. Cook carrots in salted water in saucepan until tender-crisp; drain. Cool. Layer carrots, onion and green pepper in salad bowl. Pour marinade over vegetable layers. Marinate in covered container in refrigerator for 12 hours to 1 week. Yield: 15 servings.

Betty Ragan

CAULIFLOWER AND BROCCOLI TOSS

3/4 to 1 cup mayonnaise
1/2 envelope buttermilk
   salad dressing mix
2 tablespoons sugar
2 tablespoons vinegar
1 bunch green onions,
   chopped

Flowerets of 1 head
   cauliflower
Flowerets of 1 bunch
   broccoli

Blend mayonnaise, buttermilk dressing mix, sugar and vinegar in bowl until smooth. Combine green onions, cauliflower and broccoli in salad bowl; mix lightly. Add dressing; mix well. Chill, covered, in refrigerator overnight. May add celery if desired. May add chopped hard-boiled eggs and chopped American cheese at serving time. May substitute dressing of 1/4 cup sour cream, 2 tablespoons sugar, 1/2 cup mayonnaise-type salad dressing, 1 tablespoon lemon juice, 1/2 teaspoon Tabasco sauce, 1/2 teaspoon Worcestershire sauce and 2 tablespoons Italian salad dressing. Yield: 6 to 8 servings.

Patsy Akers, Mary Sermersheim

SHOE PEG CORN SALAD

3/4 cup oil
1/2 cup sugar
1/2 cup vinegar
1 teaspoon salt
1 teaspoon pepper
1 can small green peas, drained
1 can Shoe Peg corn, drained
1 can French-style green beans, drained
1 medium onion, finely chopped
1 green bell pepper chopped
1 small jar pimentos

Combine oil, sugar, vinegar, salt and pepper in saucepan. Bring to a boil. Cook until sugar is dissolved, stirring constantly. Combine peas, corn, beans, onion, green pepper and pimentos in salad bowl; mix lightly. Pour hot dressing over vegetables; toss lightly. Marinate, covered, in refrigerator overnight. Drain half the marinade from salad just before serving. Yield: 6 to 8 servings.

Betty Krueger

BARBARA'S CUCUMBER SALAD

1/2 cup cottage cheese
1/4 cup mayonnaise-type salad dressing
1/2 cup sour cream
2 tablespoons chopped celery
2 tablespoons chopped green onion tops
2 tablespoons chopped green bell pepper
3/4 cup thinly sliced cucumbers
1/2 teaspoon salt
Paprika to taste

Combine cottage cheese and salad dressing in blender container; process until smooth. Add sour cream; process until smooth. Combine with celery, green onion tops, green pepper and cucumbers in salad bowl; mix well. Season with salt and paprika. Chill in refrigerator for 2 hours. May chop cucumbers and serve as dip. Yield: 4 servings.

Bea Senn

GELATIN AND CUCUMBER SALAD

1 3-ounce package
   lemon gelatin
1/2 cup boiling water
1 cup mayonnaise

1 cup cottage cheese
1 cup chopped nuts
1 small onion, grated
2 cucumbers, chopped

Dissolve gelatin in boiling water in bowl. Add remaining ingredients; mix well. Pour mixture into mold. Chill until set. Unmold onto serving plate. Yield: 6 to 8 servings.

Debbie Windhorst

GREEK SALAD

1/3 cup olive oil
1/4 cup wine vinegar
1 teaspoon salt
1 teaspoon oregano
1 small head lettuce
1 small cucumber, sliced

1 bunch radishes, sliced
3 green onions, cut into
   1-inch pieces
2 tomatoes, cut into wedges
12 green olives
Feta cheese, crumbled

Blend olive oil, vinegar, salt and oregano in bowl until smooth. Combine vegetables and olives in salad bowl; mix lightly. Pour dressing over salad; toss lightly. Top with feta cheese. Garnish with anchovies. Yield: 6 to 8 servings.

Gwen Bond

CRISP MARINATED SALAD

1 cup sugar
3/4 cup white vinegar
1 teaspoon salt
Pepper to taste
1 16-ounce can French-
   style green beans, drained
1 1/2 cups chopped celery

1 16-ounce can small
   green peas, drained
1 16-ounce can bean
   sprouts, drained
1 8-ounce can water
   chestnuts, drained
3 green onions, sliced

Blend first 4 ingredients in bowl until well mixed. Combine vegetables in salad bowl; mix well. Pour dressing over vegetables. Marinate in refrigerator for 8 hours to 3 weeks. May add 3 tablespoons oil to dressing. Yield: 6 to 8 servings.

Dot Berry, Kathleen S. McDougal

SEVEN-LAYER SALAD

1 10-ounce package
  frozen green peas
1 head lettuce, chopped
1 cup chopped green bell
  pepper
1 cup chopped green
  onions or red onion
1 cup chopped celery

1 1/2 cups sour cream
1/2 cup mayonnaise
9 slices crisp-fried
  bacon, crumbled
4 ounces shredded
  Cheddar cheese
  or Parmesan cheese

Cook peas using package directions; drain. Cool. Layer lettuce, green pepper, green onions, celery and peas in 9x12-inch dish. Spread with mixture of sour cream and salad dressing. Top with crumbled bacon and cheese. Chill, covered, until serving time. May add water chestnuts with vegetables. May add sliced boiled eggs and croutons to top. Yield: 6 to 8 servings.

Marjorie Basil, Patti Reece
Jean Wice

MANDARIN SALAD

1/4 cup sliced almonds
1 1/2 tablespoons sugar
1/4 cup oil
2 tablespoons sugar
2 tablespoons white
  vinegar
1 tablespoon chopped
  parsley
1/2 teaspoon salt

Pepper to taste
Tabasco sauce to taste
1/2 head lettuce
2 stalks celery, chopped
2 green onions, thinly
  sliced
1 11-ounce can mandarin
  oranges

Combine almonds and 1 1/2 tablespoons sugar in small saucepan. Cook over low heat until sugar melts and almonds are coated. Cool; break almonds apart. Shake oil, 2 tablespoons sugar, vinegar, parsley, salt, pepper and Tabasco sauce in covered jar. Tear lettuce into bite-sized pieces. Place lettuce, celery, onions and oranges in plastic bag. Pour dressing into bag. Close bag tightly; shake until well coated. Add almonds; shake again. Arrange salad on serving plates. Yield: 4 to 6 servings.

Frank Fendley

MARINATED VEGETABLES

2/3 cup oil
2 cups sugar
1 1/3 cups vinegar
2 large cans peas, drained
2 large cans Shoe Peg
    corn, drained

2 cans French-style green
    beans, drained
2 cups chopped onion
2 cups chopped green bell
    pepper
1 1/3 cups chopped celery

Combine oil, sugar and vinegar in saucepan. Bring to a boil, stirring constantly; remove from heat. Combine peas, corn, beans, onion, green pepper and celery in salad bowl; toss lightly. Pour hot vinegar mixture over vegetables; mix well. Chill for 24 hours before serving. Yield: 16 servings.

Helen Courtney

TWENTY-FOUR HOUR SALAD

1 cup sugar
1/2 cup vinegar
1/4 cup oil
1/4 teaspoon salt
1   16-ounce can French-
    style green beans,
    drained
1 small onion, chopped

1   16-ounce can medium
    peas, drained
1   4-ounce jar pimentos,
    drained, chopped
1 medium green bell
    pepper, chopped
4 stalks celery, chopped

Combine sugar, vinegar, oil and salt in small bowl; mix well. Combine beans, onion, peas, pimentos, green pepper and celery in salad bowl; mix well. Pour vinegar mixture over vegetables; mix well. Marinate in refrigerator for 24 hours to 4 weeks, stirring occasionally. Drain well before serving.
Yield: 8 servings.

Mae Pate

MEXICAN SALAD

1/2 head lettuce, coarsely
  chopped
1   16-ounce can small
  green peas, drained
5 green onions, chopped

1   28-ounce can tomatoes
1   16-ounce jar hot taco
  sauce
Salt and pepper to taste

Combine lettuce, peas, onions, undrained tomatoes, taco sauce, salt and pepper in salad bowl; toss gently. Chill for 2 hours or longer. Toss before serving. May substitute fresh tomatoes for canned tomatoes. Yield: 6 servings.

Charlene P. Atkinson

STUFFED HEAD LETTUCE

1 small firm head iceberg
  lettuce
4 ounces bleu cheese
8 ounces cream cheese,
  softened

Milk
2 tablespoons chopped
  chives
1 pimento, chopped

Hollow out lettuce from stem end to make shell. Combine bleu cheese and cream cheese in bowl; mix well. Add enough milk to make of desired consistency; beat until smooth. Add chives and pimento. Spoon into lettuce shell. Chill for 2 hours or longer. Cut crosswise into 1-inch slices. Place on salad plates. Serve with favorite dressing. Yield: 4 to 6 servings.

Gwen Mills

★ Lettuces come in many colors, flavors and textures. Try your favorite lettuce salad with a new different lettuce — or even two.

GERMAN POTATO SALAD

6 medium potatoes
2 to 3 stalks celery,
  chopped
1 green bell pepper,
  chopped
2 hard-boiled eggs,
  chopped
4 slices bacon

1 medium onion, chopped
Bacon drippings
2 tablespoons flour
1/4 cup vinegar
1/4 cup water
1/4 cup sugar
Salt and pepper to taste

Cook potatoes in skins in water to cover in saucepan until tender. Cool. Peel and slice potatoes. Place in large salad bowl. Add celery, green pepper and eggs; toss gently. Fry bacon in skillet until crisp; partially drain skillet. Sauté onion in remaining bacon drippings in skillet. Crumble bacon; stir into onion. Add flour, vinegar, water, sugar, salt and pepper; mix well. Cook until thickened, stirring constantly. Add additional water if necessary. Pour over salad; mix gently. Yield: 6 servings.

Juyne Bushart

POTATO SALAD

5 medium potatoes
5 tablespoons mayonnaise
4 1/2 teaspoons prepared
  mustard
1 teaspoon vinegar
1 teaspoon sugar
2 tablespoons milk
1 medium onion, chopped

1 green bell pepper,
  chopped
1/2 cup sweet pickle relish
2 hard-boiled eggs,
  chopped
Salt to taste
Paprika to taste

Cook potatoes in water to cover in large saucepan until tender; cool. Peel and chop potatoes. Combine mayonnaise, mustard, vinegar, sugar and milk in saucepan. Cook until smooth, stirring constantly. Cool. Combine onion, green pepper, relish, eggs and potatoes in salad bowl; toss gently. Pour mayonnaise mixture over top; mix well. Add salt; mix well. Sprinkle with paprika. Garnish with sprigs of parsley. Yield: 6 servings.

Jewel Owens

SAUERKRAUT SALAD

1 cup vinegar
1 cup sugar
1 large can sauerkraut,
  drained
2 cans whole kernel
  corn, drained

1 1/2 cups chopped celery
1 small green bell pepper,
  chopped
1 small onion, chopped
1 cup slivered almonds

Heat vinegar and sugar in saucepan until sugar dissolves, stirring constantly. Combine sauerkraut, corn, celery, green pepper, onion and almonds in large salad bowl; mix well. Pour hot vinegar over top; mix well. Chill until serving time.
Yield: 6 servings.

Sharron Hakola

SAUERKRAUT AND PIMENTO SALAD

1 32-ounce can
  sauerkraut, drained
1 2-ounce jar pimento,
  chopped
1 green bell pepper, finely
  chopped

1 onion, finely chopped
1 cup chopped celery
1 1/2 cups sugar
1 1/3 cups water
2/3 cup cider vinegar
1/2 cup oil

Mix sauerkraut, pimento, green pepper, onion and celery in large salad bowl. Heat sugar, water and vinegar in saucepan until sugar is dissolved, stirring constantly. Cool. Stir in oil. Pour over vegetables; mix well. Chill, covered, for several hours to overnight. Drain before serving. Yield: 8 servings.

Dollie D. Billiter

★ Rinse sauerkraut under cold running water and drain well to remove excess salt.

APPLE SLAW

2 cups shredded cabbage
2 large red delicious
  apples, shredded
1/3 cup shredded carrot
1/4 cup currants
1/4 cup unsweetened
  applesauce

1/4 cup reduced-calorie
  mayonnaise
1/4 teaspoon celery seed
1/8 teaspoon pepper
1/4 cup oat bran

Combine cabbage, apples, carrot, currants, applesauce, mayonnaise, celery seed and pepper in salad bowl; mix well. Chill, covered, for 2 hours or longer. Sprinkle with oat bran at serving time. Yield: 6 servings.

Wellness Committee

CHINESE SLAW

1 to 2 cans seasoned
  green beans, rinsed,
  drained
1 can tiny peas, drained
1 can Chinese vegetables,
  drained
1 onion, thinly sliced
1 cup chopped celery

1 can water chestnuts,
  sliced
1 green bell pepper, finely
  chopped
1 cup sugar
3/4 cup vinegar
Salt and pepper to taste

Combine beans, peas, Chinese vegetables, onion, celery, water chestnuts, green pepper, sugar, vinegar, salt and pepper in large salad bowl; mix well. Chill until serving time. Flavor improves when prepared day ahead. Yield: 6 servings.

Dorothy Meyers

AUNT MAY'S MUSTARD SLAW

2 eggs, well beaten
1 cup sugar
1/2 cup vinegar
1 teaspoon dry mustard
Salt and pepper to taste
1 head cabbage, shredded

Combine eggs, sugar, vinegar, mustard, salt and pepper in saucepan; mix well. Cook until thickened, stirring constantly. Cool. Pour over cabbage in salad bowl; toss well.
Yield: 8 servings.

Bea Senn

TWENTY-FOUR HOUR CABBAGE SLAW

1 head cabbage, shredded
1 white onion, chopped
2 stalks celery, chopped
3/4 cup shredded carrot
1 1/2 cups sugar
1 teaspoon dry mustard
1 teaspoon salt
2/3 cup oil
1 cup vinegar

Combine cabbage, onion, celery and carrot in salad bowl; mix well. Combine sugar, mustard, salt, oil and vinegar in saucepan. Bring to a boil, stirring constantly. Pour over vegetables; mix well. Chill, covered, for 24 hours before serving.
Yield: 8 servings.

Mary J. Abell

SLIM SLAW

1 medium head cabbage
1 cucumber, peeled
1 green bell pepper
2 slices onion
20 to 24 packets artificial sweetener
1 1/2 cups vinegar
1/4 cup oil
2 tablespoons Mrs. Dash seasoning
3 to 4 radishes, sliced

Chop cabbage, cucumber, green pepper and onion one at a time in food processor container. Combine with artificial sweetener, vinegar, oil and seasoning in large salad bowl; mix well. Chill for several hours. Add radishes just before serving.
Yield: 12 servings.

Diane Wilkes

GERMAN COLESLAW

1 medium green bell pepper, chopped
1 medium head cabbage, shredded
1 2-ounce jar pimento, drained
2 medium onions, chopped
1 cup sugar
1 cup oil
2/3 cup white vinegar
1 teaspoon salt

Combine green pepper, cabbage, pimento and onions in salad bowl; mix well. Combine sugar, oil, vinegar and salt in saucepan; mix well. Bring to a boil, stirring constantly. Pour over slaw; toss well. Chill, covered, for 24 hours to 1 week.
Yield: 8 servings.

Marjorie Basil

SPINACH SALAD

Spinach leaves, rinsed, drained
2 ounces Gorgonzola cheese, crumbled
3 tablespoons chopped walnuts
3 tablespoons oil
1 tablespoon wine vinegar
1/2 teaspoon salt
Freshly ground pepper to taste

Chop enough spinach leaves for 4 servings in salad bowl. Sprinkle with cheese and walnuts. Combine oil, vinegar, salt and pepper in small jar. Cover tightly; shake well to mix. Pour over salad; toss lightly. Yield: 4 servings.

Wanda Wiegand

★ The smallest spinach leaves are the most tender for salads. Use the larger leaves in cooked dishes.

ORIENTAL SPINACH SALAD

1/3 cup sugar
1 onion, minced
1 cup oil
1/4 cup vinegar
3 tablespoons
   Worcestershire sauce
1/2 cup catsup
1 package spinach, rinsed,
   drained

1 can bean sprouts,
   drained
1 can water chestnuts,
   sliced
3 hard-boiled eggs,
   chopped
5 to 6 slices bacon, crisp-
   fried, crumbled

Combine sugar, onion, oil, vinegar, Worcestershire sauce and catsup in bowl; mix well. Combine spinach, bean sprouts, water chestnuts, eggs and bacon in salad bowl. Add dressing; toss lightly. Yield: 4 servings.

Peggy Noel

EASY TOMATO ASPIC

1 can Mexican-style
   stewed tomatoes
1 package unflavored
   gelatin

1   3-ounce package lemon
   gelatin
1 cup boiling water

Sprinkle tomatoes with unflavored gelatin. Dissolve lemon gelatin in boiling water in bowl. Add tomato mixture. Pour into blender container. Process until tomatoes are chopped. Pour into mold. Chill until firm. Unmold onto serving plate. Serve with dressing or cottage cheese. Yield: 4 servings.

Robbie Lowery

★ Fresh tomatoes may be frozen for use in cooking. Wash well, remove core and pack into freezer containers or freezer bags.

BLEU CHEESE SALAD DRESSING

4 ounces bleu cheese
1/4 cup oil
2 tablespoons vinegar
3/4 cup sour cream
1/4 cup mayonnaise

1 teaspoon chopped
    chives
Pinch of sugar
Dash of Worcestershire
    sauce

Crumble bleu cheese into bowl. Add oil, vinegar, sour cream, mayonnaise, chives, sugar and Worcestershire sauce; mix well. Chill, covered, until serving time. Yield: 2 cups.

Monica Kayse

DELICIOUS FRENCH DRESSING

2 1/2 cups sugar
1 teaspoon salt
1 teaspoon paprika
1 tablespoon grated onion

1 cup catsup
3 cups oil
1 cup vinegar
1 teaspoon celery seed

Combine sugar, salt, paprika, onion, catsup, oil, vinegar and celery seed in blender container; process until smooth. Store in airtight container in refrigerator. Yield: 6 cups.

Pat Conn

HONEY MUSTARD DRESSING

4 cups light mayonnaise
1/2 cup oil
3/4 cup honey
1/4 cup mustard

1/4 cup cider vinegar
Onion salt to taste
Cayenne pepper to taste

Combine mayonnaise, oil, honey, mustard, vinegar and salt and pepper in large bowl; mix well. Store in covered container in refrigerator. Yield: 6 cups.

Ladonna Darnell

HONEY LIME DRESSING

1 cup sugar
1/2 cup honey
2 tablespoons dry mustard
1 tablespoon ground
  ginger
1/3 cup lime juice
1/3 cup water
2 cups corn oil

Combine sugar, honey, dry mustard, ginger, lime juice and water in blender container; process until smooth. Add corn oil in fine stream, blending constantly. This dressing is excellent on fresh fruit. Yield: 4 cups.

Donna Oldham

ITALIAN SALAD DRESSING

1 cup olive oil
1/4 cup fresh lemon juice
1/4 cup herb vinegar
1/2 teaspoon dry mustard
1 teaspoon grated onion
1/2 teaspoon paprika
1/2 teaspoon oregano
1 1/2 teaspoons thyme
2 cloves of garlic, crushed
1 teaspoon salt (optional)
1 teaspoon sugar
  (optional)

Combine olive oil, lemon juice, vinegar, dry mustard, onion, paprika, oregano, thyme and garlic in covered jar. Add salt and sugar. Shake thoroughly. Let stand for several hours to blend flavors. May substitute safflower oil for olive oil, or use 1/2 cup of each oil. Store at room temperature if olive oil is used.
Yield: 1 1/2 cups.

Betty Jo Daniel

★ For healthy and nutritious garden salad dressings, use reduced-calorie brands or prepare your own dressing by combining 1/4 cup vinegar, 2 tablespoons water, 1 package dry Italian salad dressing mix, 2/3 cup corn, sunflower or safflower oil and one 8-ounce container of plain low-fat yogurt in shaker jar; shake until well mixed.

COTTAGE CHEESE SALAD DRESSING

1 pint sour cream
8 ounces cottage cheese
1/2 cup mayonnaise

1 cucumber, ground
1 tablespoon Durkee's
Famous Sauce

Combine sour cream, cottage cheese, mayonnaise, cucumber and Durkee's sauce in bowl; mix well. Serve on salad of your choice. Store, covered, in refrigerator. Yield: 4 cups.

Patsy Leffler

MITZIE'S SALAD DRESSING

6 tablespoons olive oil
2 1/2 tablespoons fresh
   lemon juice
1 teaspoon sugar
1 teaspoon salt

1/2 teaspoon Dijon
   mustard
1 small clove of garlic,
   crushed
1/4 to 1/2 teaspoon pepper

Combine olive oil, lemon juice, sugar, salt, mustard, garlic and pepper in covered container; shake well. May store up to 3 weeks in refrigerator. Use only fresh lemon juice. Yield: 1/2 cup.

Mitzie Black

MOM'S SALAD DRESSING

1 egg
1/2 cup sugar
1 tablespoon flour
1/2 teaspoon salt

1/2 cup vinegar
1/2 tablespoon celery seed
1 cup mayonnaise-type
   salad dressing

Beat egg in mixer bowl. Add sugar, flour and salt; mix well. Add vinegar gradually, mixing well. Pour into saucepan. Cook over medium heat until thickened, stirring constantly. Remove from heat. Add celery seed. Cool. Stir in salad dressing. This is an excellent tangy dressing for slaw, deviled eggs or potato salad. Yield: 1 3/4 cups.

Margaret Downs

SWEET CELERY SEED DRESSING

1   14-ounce can
   sweetened condensed
   milk
1/3 cup oil
1/3 cup cider vinegar

1 teaspoon celery seed
3/4 teaspoon dry mustard
1/2 teaspoon salt
1/4 teaspoon pepper

Combine condensed milk, oil, vinegar, celery seed, dry mustard, salt and pepper in mixing bowl. Beat until well mixed. This dressing is especially good with cabbage slaw, lettuce salads and fruit salads. Yield: 2 1/2 cups.

Dollie D. Billiter

POPPY SEED DRESSING

3/4 cup sugar
1 teaspoon dry mustard
1 teaspoon salt
1/3 cup vinegar

1 tablespoon onion juice
1 cup oil
1 1/2 tablespoons poppy
   seed

Combine sugar, dry mustard, salt, vinegar and onion juice in bowl; mix well. Add oil in fine stream, beating constantly until thick. Add poppy seed; mix well. Serve with fruit salads. Store in refrigerator. Yield: 2 cups.

Joyce Johnson

ROQUEFORT DRESSING

1 cup mayonnaise
1 cup sour cream
1 large package Roquefort
   cheese

4 or 5 dashes Tabasco
   sauce
1 teaspoon salt
1 teaspoon pepper

Combine mayonnaise, sour cream, Roquefort cheese, Tabasco sauce, salt and pepper in mixer bowl. Beat until smooth. Chill, covered, in refrigerator container. Serve over favorite green salad. Yield: 3 cups.

Dot Berry

SLAW DRESSING

1 egg
¹/₄ cup sugar

¹/₄ cup vinegar
¹/₄ cup water

Beat egg and sugar in saucepan. Add vinegar and water. Bring to a boil over medium heat, stirring constantly. Cook until thickened, stirring constantly. Remove from heat. Cool. Pour over cabbage slaw. Yield: ³/₄ cup.

Peggy Posante

THOUSAND ISLAND DRESSING

¹/₂ cup catsup
¹/₄ teaspoon onion salt
1 tablespoon finely grated
  onion
1 teaspoon
  Worcestershire sauce

2 tablespoons sweet
  pickle relish
3 hard-boiled eggs,
  chopped
1 cup mayonnaise

Combine catsup, onion salt, onion, Worcestershire sauce and pickle relish in bowl; mix well. Add eggs and mayonnaise; mix well. Yield: 2 cups.

Dollie D. Billiter

THOUSAND ISLAND OLIVE DRESSING

1 cup mayonnaise
¹/₄ cup catsup
2 tablespoons vinegar
1 teaspoon paprika
¹/₂ cup sliced olives

2 tablespoons parsley
  flakes
1 small onion
3 hard-boiled eggs

Combine mayonnaise, catsup, vinegar, paprika, olives and parsley in small bowl; mix well. Cut onion and eggs into slivers. Add to dressing; mix well. Chill until serving time. Yield: 2¹/₂ cups.

Carol Young

TANGY THOUSAND ISLAND DRESSING

1 cup mayonnaise
2 tablespoons chili sauce
2 tablespoons chopped
  stuffed olives
2 teaspoons minced chives

2 hard-boiled eggs, finely
  chopped
1/2 teaspoon paprika
Salt and pepper to taste

Combine mayonnaise, chili sauce, olives and chives in small mixer bowl. Add eggs; mix well. Add paprika, salt and pepper. Chill in covered container. Yield: 1 1/2 cups.

Joanie Echsner

WESTERN DRESSING MIX

2 tablespoons salt
2 teaspoons MSG
2 teaspoons parsley flakes
1 teaspoon garlic powder

1 teaspoon pepper
1/2 teaspoon onion powder
1 cup mayonnaise
1 cup buttermilk

Combine first 6 ingredients in airtight container; shake to mix. Store until ready to use. Combine 3 1/2 teaspoons mixture with mayonnaise and buttermilk in small bowl; mix well. Store in refrigerator. Yield: 2 cups.

Gwen Mills

WHIPPED FRUIT SALAD DRESSING

1 egg yolk
1/2 cup sugar
1 tablespoon flour
1/2 cup pineapple juice

1/4 cup lemon juice
1 cup whipping cream,
  whipped

Beat egg yolk in mixer bowl until thick. Add mixture of sugar and flour; mix well. Add fruit juices gradually, beating constantly. Pour into double boiler. Cook until thickened, stirring constantly. Cool completely. Fold in whipped cream. Store in covered container in refrigerator. Yield: 2 cups.

Marge O'Daniel

This is a scene from Shakertown, near Pleasant Hill, Kentucky. The Shakers hung everything up when they were finished with it, including chairs.

Main Dishes

SHAKERTOWN

MEATS

BEEF WELLINGTON

1 3-pound fillet of beef
Salt and pepper to taste
Oil
1/4 cup finely chopped
   mushrooms
1 tablespoon butter

1 tablespoon Brandy
1 recipe Quick Puff Pastry
1 cup Chopped Chicken
   Liver
1 egg, beaten

Trim fat from beef; season with salt and pepper. Place on rack in roasting pan; brush with oil. Bake at 400 degrees for 30 minutes for rare. Cool to room temperature. Sauté mushrooms in butter in skillet for 1 minute, stirring occasionally. Add Brandy. Cook until liquid evaporates. Add Chopped Chicken Liver; mix well. Spread mixture over beef. Roll Quick Puff Pastry less than 1/4 inch thick on floured surface. Place fillet liver side down on pastry. Wrap pastry around beef. Moisten edge with water and overlap to seal; trim ends. Place liver side up on greased baking. Brush with beaten egg. Cut decorative designs from scraps of pastry; place on top. Brush with egg. Bake at 450 degrees for 25 minutes or until pastry is golden brown. Let stand in warm place for 10 minutes before carving. Place on serving platter. Garnish with mushroom caps. Yield: 6 servings.

Quick Puff Pastry

2 cups flour
1 teaspoon salt

3/4 cup butter, softened
6 tablespoons water

Combine flour and salt in bowl. Cut in butter until crumbly. Add water; mix lightly until moistened. Knead dough lightly on floured surface.

Chopped Chicken Liver

1/2 pound chicken livers
1 onion, sliced
6 tablespoons chicken fat

2 hard-boiled eggs
Salt and pepper to taste

Remove any fat from chicken livers. Sauté chicken livers and onion in 4 tablespoons chicken fat until liver is cooked through but still pink in center. Process in food processor container with eggs, salt, pepper and remaining 2 tablespoons chicken fat until smooth. May use for sandwich spread. May substitute margarine for chicken fat.

Sally Trent

STANDING PRIME RIB AU JUS

1   4 to 6-pound beef rib   Salt and pepper to taste
    roast   Garlic to taste

Let roast stand at room temperature for 1½ hours before cooking. Rub roast with salt, pepper and garlic. Place fat side up in shallow baking pan. Roast at 375 degrees for 1 hour. Turn off heat. Let roast stand in oven; do not open oven door. Set oven temperature to 375 degrees. Reheat roast for 30 to 40 minutes. Roast will be brown and crisp on outside and rare inside.
Yield: 10 to 12 servings.

Donald W. Noel

TEXAS BARBECUED BRISKET

1   5 to 6-pound beef   Onion salt and celery salt
    brisket   to taste
5 ounces liquid smoke   1 cup barbecue sauce
5 ounces Worcestershire   5 tablespoons brown sugar
    sauce   5 tablespoons light corn
Garlic salt to taste   syrup

Place beef brisket in roasting pan. Pour liquid smoke and Worcestershire sauce over beef. Turn to coat both sides. Sprinkle with garlic salt, onion salt and celery salt. Chill, covered with aluminum foil, in refrigerator for 8 to 24 hours. Bake, covered, at 300 degrees for 3 hours. Combine barbecue sauce, brown sugar and corn syrup in bowl; mix well. Spread over beef. Bake for 1 hour longer. Slice brisket cross grain. Serve with pan drippings. May bake day before serving and reheat.
Yield: 10 to 12 servings.

Betty Donovan

BARBECUED BEEF BRISKET

1½ tablespoons
  seasoning salt
1½ tablespoons pepper
1½ teaspoons paprika
1   6-pound beef brisket
2 cups oil

2 cups cider vinegar
½ cup Worcestershire
  sauce
2 bay leaves, crumbled
1 recipe Barbecue Sauce

Combine seasoning salt, pepper and paprika in small bowl; mix well. Rub into beef brisket. Place brisket in a shallow container. Combine oil, vinegar, Worcestershire sauce and bay leaves in bowl; mix well. Pour over beef brisket. Chill, covered, in refrigerator for 8 hours to overnight, turning occasionally. Drain, reserving marinade. Rake hot coals to one end of grill. Place brisket on rack at opposite end of grill. Cook, with grill closed, for 2½ to 3 hours, basting with reserved marinade every 30 minutes and turning occasionally. Brush both sides with Barbecue Sauce. Cook for 30 minutes to 1 hour longer or until tender, basting top of brisket with Barbecue Sauce. Serve with remaining sauce. Yield: 14 servings.

Barbecue Sauce

4 cups catsup
1 cup cider vinegar
1 cup Worcestershire
  sauce
1 medium onion, chopped
½ cup margarine

2 tablespoons seasoning
  salt
2 tablespoons brown sugar
1 tablespoon chili powder
1 tablespoon pepper
1 bay leaf

Combine all ingredients in saucepan. Bring to a boil, stirring occasionally. Remove bay leaf. Yield: 6 ⅔ cups.

Mary B. Mason

BARBECUED ROAST

1   5-pound beef roast
1 bottle of chili sauce
1 bottle of barbecue sauce
1/2 cup catsup
1 cup water
1 tablespoon dark vinegar

2 teaspoons dry mustard
2 tablespoons sugar
2 tablespoons chili powder
1 teaspoon salt
1 onion, chopped

Cook beef roast in water to 1/2 its depth in saucepan until tender. Combine remaining ingredients in large bowl; mix well. Shred roast into bowl. Marinate, covered, overnight in refrigerator. Pour into Crock•Pot. Cook on Low for 2 to 3 hours. Yield: 10 to 12 servings.

Terri Arnold

ROAST BEEF

1 beef roast
1 bottle of chili sauce
1 cup water

1/4 cup butter
1 clove of garlic, minced
Parmesan cheese

Place beef roast in roasting pan. Pour chili sauce and water over roast. Dot with butter; sprinkle with garlic and cheese. Bake, covered, at 350 degrees for 3 hours or until tender. May substitute garlic salt for garlic.

John and April Heldreth

★ Lean cuts of beef such as rump and round usually require longer cooking times than fatter cuts but the number of servings per pound is greater.

ITALIAN ROAST

1 4-pound beef chuck roast
1 teaspoon salt
1 teaspoon pepper
1/2 cup cinnamon
1 tablespoon oil
1 green bell pepper, finely chopped
3 stalks celery, finely chopped
1 onion, finely chopped
1/4 cup margarine
1 16-ounce can tomato sauce
1 15-ounce can tomato sauce with tomato bits
1 12-ounce can tomato paste
1 package rigatoni noodles

Sprinkle roast on both sides with salt, pepper and cinnamon. Brown on both sides in hot oil in skillet. Remove to large saucepan. Sauté green pepper, celery and onion in margarine in skillet; drain. Add to roast. Add tomato sauces with 1 sauce can of water for each; mix well. Simmer, covered, for 1 hour. Cut roast into bite-sized pieces; discard fat. Return roast to saucepan. Simmer for 2 hours longer. Cook rigatoni using package directions; drain. Add to roast. Simmer over very low heat for 30 minutes, stirring frequently. Yield: 6 to 8 servings.

Georgia Dobbs

STEAK ORIENTAL

1/2 cup soy sauce
1/4 cup packed brown sugar
1/2 teaspoon ginger
2 cloves of garlic, minced
1/2 teaspoon pepper
2 tablespoons oil
1 5 to 7-pound pot roast, 2-inches thick

Combine soy sauce, brown sugar, ginger, garlic, pepper and oil in jar. Cover tightly; shake well to mix. Pour over roast in shallow baking dish. Chill, covered, in refrigerator for 2 to 3 days, turning occasionally. Drain. Place steak on rack in broiler pan. Broil for 8 minutes on each side. Cut into very thin slices. Yield: 12 servings.

Ethel Cottrell

BEEF POT ROAST WITH VEGETABLES

1   3 to 3¹/₂-pound beef
     chuck or rump roast
1 tablespoon oil
2¹/₂ cups water
2 teaspoons salt
¹/₄ teaspoon pepper
1 bay leaf
4 medium onions, sliced

3 stalks celery, coarsely
     chopped
6 medium carrots,
     coarsely chopped
4 medium potatoes, cut
     into halves
3 tablespoons flour
¹/₄ cup water

Brown roast on both sides in hot oil in large skillet. Add 2¹/₂ cups water, salt, pepper, bay leaf, 1 sliced onion and 1 chopped stalk celery. Simmer, covered, for 2 to 2¹/₂ hours or until beef is tender. Add remaining vegetables. Simmer for 45 minutes to 1 hour or until vegetables are tender. Remove beef and vegetables to hot serving dish. Discard bay leaf. Mix flour with ¹/₄ cup water. Stir into pan drippings. Cook until thickened, stirring constantly. Serve with pot roast. May substitute 1 cup red wine for part of cooking water. Yield: 6 servings.

Pamela Simms

SWEET AND SOUR BRISKET

1   3-pound beef brisket
1 onion, sliced
1 clove of garlic, minced
6 tablespoons brown sugar
¹/₄ cup vinegar

¹/₂ cup catsup
¹/₂ cup water
1¹/₂ teaspoons salt
Pepper to taste

Place beef brisket in baking dish. Spread onion slices over top. Combine garlic, brown sugar, vinegar, catsup, water, salt and pepper in bowl; mix well. Pour over brisket. Bake, covered with foil, at 300 degrees for 2 to 3 hours or until fork-tender. Serve leftovers for sandwiches. Yield: 5 servings.

Kris Russell

ED'S BARBECUED STEAK

1/2 cup A-1 steak sauce
1/2 cup Worcestershire
  sauce
1/4 cup melted butter
1 teaspoon soy sauce

1 teaspoon Louisiana hot
  sauce
Salt and pepper to taste
Rib eye steaks

Combine steak sauce, Worcestershire sauce, butter, soy sauce, hot sauce, salt and pepper in bowl; mix well. Place steaks in shallow dish. Pour sauce over steaks. Marinate in refrigerator for 1 hour or longer, turning occasionally. Drain, reserving marinade. Grill steaks over hot coals to desired degree of doneness, basting with reserved marinade.

Alice Ritchey

FLANK STEAK

1/2 cup soy sauce
3 tablespoons oil
3 tablespoons honey

3/4 teaspoon ginger
1 clove of garlic, crushed
1 flank steak

Combine soy sauce, oil, honey, ginger and garlic in bowl; mix well. Pour over steak in shallow dish. Marinate, covered, in refrigerator overnight, turning steak occasionally. Grill steak over hot coals until rare. Cut diagonally cross grain.

Sue Skelton

MARINATED FLANK STEAK

2 flank steaks
1/4 to 1/3 cup oil
1/2 to 2/3 cup soy sauce
1 to 2 teaspoons ginger
1 to 2 teaspoons dry
  mustard

1 to 2 teaspoons garlic
  powder
1/2 cup packed brown
  sugar
3/4 cup chopped green
  onions

Score steaks; place in shallow dish. Combine oil, soy sauce, ginger, dry mustard, garlic powder, brown sugar and green onions in bowl; mix well. Pour over steaks. Marinate, covered, in refrigerator overnight. Drain, reserving marinade. Grill steaks over hot coals to desired degree of doneness, basting with

reserved marinade. Cut into 1-inch strips for serving. May omit brown sugar and add 2 tablespoons Kitchen Bouquet.
Yield: 2 servings.

Ruth Dye, Jayne Roberts

JAMAICAN FLANK STEAK

2 flank steaks	4 cloves of garlic, minced
1 cup soy sauce	Salt and pepper to taste
1/4 cup Tabasco sauce	1 recipe Tomato Salsa
1 lime, sliced	

Place steaks in shallow dish. Combine soy sauce, Tabasco sauce, lime, garlic, salt and pepper in bowl; mix well. Pour over steaks. Marinate, covered, in refrigerator for several hours to overnight, turning occasionally. Drain. Grill steaks over hot coals to desired degree of doneness. Cut into very thin slices cross grain. Serve hot or at room temperature with Tomato Salsa.
Yield: 6 to 8 servings.

Tomato Salsa

3 or 4 tomatoes, peeled, seeded, chopped	1 tablespoon chopped cilantro
1 small onion, minced	1/2 teaspoon oregano
Juice of 1 lime	2 cloves of garlic, minced

Combine tomatoes, onion, lime juice, cilantro, oregano and garlic in serving bowl; mix well.

Wanda Wiegand

★ When broiling in the oven, add water to broiler pan to reduce clean up time.

CRACKED PEPPER STEAK

2 8 to 12-ounce ribeye
  steaks, 1¹/₂ inches thick
¹/₄ teaspoon garlic powder
Salt to taste
¹/₄ cup chopped green
  onions

¹/₄ cup butter
1 teaspoon cracked black
  pepper

Sprinkle steaks with garlic powder and salt; set aside. Sauté green onions in butter in large skillet until tender. Remove onions; set aside. Sprinkle ¹/₂ teaspoon cracked black pepper into skillet. Add steaks. Cook over medium heat for 5 to 7 minutes. Sprinkle remaining ¹/₂ teaspoon pepper on top of steaks; turn steaks. Cook for 5 to 7 minutes longer or to desired degree of doneness. Remove to serving platter; sprinkle with sautéed onions. Yield: 2 servings.

Patricia J. Tudor

GREEN PEPPER STEAK

1 pound beef chuck or
  round steak
¹/₄ cup soy sauce
1 clove of garlic, minced
1¹/₂ teaspoons grated
  fresh ginger
¹/₄ cup oil
1 cup thinly sliced green
  onions

1 cup green or red bell
  peppers, cut into 1-inch
  squares
2 stalks celery, thinly
  sliced
1 tablespoon cornstarch
1 cup water
2 tomatoes, cut into
  wedges

Cut beef cross grain into ¹/₈-inch strips. Combine beef, soy sauce, garlic and ginger in bowl; toss to coat. Marinate while preparing vegetables; drain. Heat oil in large skillet or wok. Stir-fry beef over high heat until brown. Simmer, covered, over low heat for 30 to 40 minutes or until tender if necessary. Return heat to high. Add vegetables. Stir-fry for 10 minutes or until vegetables are tender-crisp. Mix cornstarch with water. Add to pepper steak. Cook until thickened, stirring constantly. Add tomatoes. Cook until heated through. Yield: 4 servings.

Linda Berg, Patia Lee Hanlin
Alice Ritchey

HAWAIIAN PEPPER STEAK

1 1/2 pounds beef sirloin
  steak
2 teaspoons MSG
1/4 cup oil
1 can beef broth
1/2 teaspoon sugar
1/4 teaspoon dry mustard
1 1/2 tablespoons soy sauce
1 onion, finely chopped

1 green bell pepper, finely
  chopped
1 tablespoon cornstarch
2 tablespoons pineapple
  juice
1 small can pineapple
  chunks
4 servings cooked rice

Cut steak into thin strips; sprinkle with 1 teaspoon MSG. Brown in hot oil in large skillet. Add next 4 ingredients. Simmer for 15 to 20 minutes, stirring frequently. Add onion, green pepper and remaining 1 teaspoon MSG. Cook for 5 minutes. Blend cornstarch with pineapple juice in small bowl. Add to pepper steak gradually, stirring until thickened. Add pineapple. Simmer for 3 to 5 minutes or until heated through. Serve over rice. Yield: 4 servings.

Frank Fendley

PEPPER STEAK

2 thin slices gingerroot
2 cloves of garlic, crushed
1 to 2 tablespoons peanut
  oil
1/2 pound round steak, cut
  into thin strips
2 green bell peppers,
  thinly sliced

1/2 teaspoon sugar
1/2 can bean sprouts
1 beef bouillon cube
1 cup water
2 tablespoons cornstarch
Soy sauce to taste
2 or 3 tomatoes, quartered
2 green onions, sliced

Sauté gingerroot and garlic in hot oil in wok. Remove and discard. Stir-fry steak in oil until brown. Push to 1 side of wok. Add green peppers and sugar. Stir-fry for 1 to 2 minutes. Remove from heat. Cool, covered, for 1 to 2 minutes. Return to heat. Add bean sprouts. Stir-fry for 1 minute. Combine bouillon, water, cornstarch and soy sauce in bowl; mix until smooth. Add to wok. Cook until thickened, stirring constantly. Add tomatoes. Cook for 1 to 2 minutes or until heated through. Sprinkle with green onions. Serve over rice or chow mein noodles. Yield: 2 servings.

Joan Echsner

ROULADE

8 6-ounce thinly sliced
  round steaks
8 teaspoons mustard
Salt and pepper to taste
8 slices bacon
2 onions, cut into wedges

2 large dill pickles, cut into
  quarters
Shortening
2 cups water
Flour

Pound steak with meat mallet until very thin. Spread each with 1 teaspoon mustard; sprinkle with salt and pepper. Place 1 piece of bacon, onion and pickle on each steak. Roll to enclose, securing with string. Brown beef rolls on all sides in hot shortening in skillet. Reduce heat; drain. Add water. Simmer, covered, for 45 minutes to 1 hour or until tender, stirring occasionally. Remove string; place roulades on warm platter. Add flour to pan juices, stirring until thickened. Spoon over roulades. Yield: 8 servings.

Linda Berg

SWISS STEAK

2 to 2¹/₂ pounds round
  steak
¹/₄ cup flour
2 tablespoons oil
1 teaspoon salt
¹/₈ teaspoon pepper
1 onion, sliced

1 4-ounce can
  mushrooms
1 can cream of tomato
  soup
1 10-ounce package
  frozen peas

Cut steak into 6 pieces. Coat with flour. Brown on both sides in hot oil in skillet. Sprinkle with salt and pepper. Add onion, mushrooms and soup. Simmer, covered, for 1 hour and 30 minutes, stirring occasionally. Add peas. Cook for 30 minutes longer or until peas and steak are tender. May also bake at 350 degrees for same amount of cooking time. Yield: 6 servings.

Wilma Allen

SIRLOIN TIP GOULASH

1 pound sirloin tip steak
1/4 cup flour
Pepper to taste
2 tablespoons oil
1 onion, sliced
2 cloves of garlic, minced
3 tomatoes, chopped
1 6-ounce can tomato
   paste
1 cup water
2 tablespoons brown sugar
1 tablespoon paprika
1 teaspoon salt
1/4 teaspoon marjoram
1 cup mushroom halves
Hot cooked egg noodles
   with poppy seed

Cut steak into 1-inch cubes. Coat in mixture of flour and pepper. Brown steak on all sides in hot oil in skillet. Add onion and garlic. Cook until onion is tender, stirring frequently. Combine next 7 ingredients and pepper to taste in bowl; mix well. Add to steak; mix well. Spoon into 2-quart casserole. Bake, covered, at 350 degrees for 1 1/2 hours. Add mushrooms. Bake, covered, for 8 to 10 minutes longer or until steak is tender. Serve over egg noodles. Garnish with chopped parsley. May substitute one 28-ounce can tomatoes for fresh tomatoes. Yield: 4 servings.

Margaret Taylor

MICROWAVE BEEF GOULASH

2 tablespoons oil
2 onions, chopped
1 clove of garlic, minced
1 teaspoon paprika
2 pounds beef stew meat,
   cut into 3/4-inch cubes
4 medium potatoes,
   peeled, chopped
4 medium tomatoes,
   peeled, chopped
1 green bell pepper,
   chopped
1/2 teaspoon caraway seed
4 cups beef broth
Salt and pepper to taste
Sour cream

Combine oil, onions and garlic in 4-quart glass casserole. Microwave on High for 2 to 3 minutes or until onion is transparent. Add next 7 ingredients. Microwave, covered, on High for 5 minutes. Microwave, on Medium for 45 to 60 minutes or until beef in fork-tender, stirring once. Sprinkle with salt and pepper. Let stand, covered, for 5 minutes. Ladle into soup bowls. Top with sour cream. Yield: 8 servings.

Cindy Jones

BEEF SHISH KABOB

3 pounds round or sirloin
  steak
Whole fresh mushrooms
Juice of 1½ lemons
3 tablespoons oil
1 medium onion, grated
1 teaspoon salt
¼ teaspoon ginger
2 teaspoons
  Worcestershire sauce
1 bay leaf, crushed
1 clove of garlic, crushed
½ teaspoon dry mustard
2 green bell peppers,
  coarsely chopped
2 large onions, coarsely
  chopped
2 cans whole white
  potatoes

Cut steak into cubes. Stem mushrooms. Place steak and mushrooms in bowl. Combine lemon juice, oil, grated onion, salt, ginger, Worcestershire sauce, bay leaf, garlic and dry mustard in bowl; mix well. Pour over steak. Marinate, covered, in refrigerator for 4 hours to overnight. Drain. Thread beef, mushrooms, peppers, onions, and potatoes alternately on skewers. Grill over hot coals for 15 to 20 minutes or to desired degree of doneness, turning frequently. Yield: 8 servings.

Marylucy Caron

ITALIAN SPAGHETTI SAUCE

5 pounds rolled rump beef
2 cups butter
2 46-ounce cans tomato
  juice
2 large cans mushrooms
1 clove of garlic, minced
1 dried red pepper

Cut beef into 1-inch cubes. Brown on all sides in butter in large skillet. Add tomato juice, mushrooms, garlic and pepper. Simmer, covered, for 4 hours or until beef is tender. Use 4 cups sauce to one 8-ounce box spaghetti. Garnish with shredded Swiss cheese. This is an old family recipe dating back to Civil War days. Yield: 6 to 8 quarts.

Mrs. Michael Starke

MICROWAVE OVEN BEEF STEW

2 pounds beef bottom
  round steak
1/2 cup flour
2 cups 1/2-inch carrot slices
6 to 8 small onions
2 medium potatoes, cut
  into quarters
2 bay leaves

1/2 teaspoon marjoram
1 teaspoon salt
1/4 teaspoon pepper
1 can tomato soup
1 can consommé
1 1/2 cups water
1   10-ounce package
  frozen peas

Cut round steak into 3/4-inch cubes. Coat steak cubes with flour; place in 3-quart glass casserole. Add carrots, onions, potatoes and seasonings. Add soup, consommé and water; mix well. Microwave, covered, on High for 5 minutes. Stir until well mixed. Microwave, covered, on Medium for 40 to 50 minutes or until steak and vegetables are almost tender. Stir in peas. Microwave for 10 minutes longer. Let stand, covered, for 10 minutes. Remove bay leaves. Serve over biscuits.
Yield: 4 to 6 servings.

Pamela Simms

BEEF STEW

1 1/2 cups cubed cooked
  beef
2 tablespoons margarine
1 cup chopped onion
1 clove of garlic, minced
1   15-ounce can beef
  gravy

2 cooked carrots, coarsely
  chopped
2 cooked potatoes, cubed
1/2 teaspoon salt
Dash of pepper

Brown beef in hot margarine in skillet. Add onion and garlic. Sauté until onion is tender, stirring occasionally. Add gravy, vegetables and seasonings. Heat to serving temperature, stirring occasionally. Yield: 4 servings.

Zora Logsdon

OLD-FASHIONED BEEF STEW

1½ pounds cubed stew
   beef
Salt and pepper to taste
2 tablespoons flour
Oil
1½ cups water
2 large potatoes, cubed
2 medium onions, cut into
   quarters
2 large carrots, sliced
1 8-ounce can peas,
   drained
1 6-ounce can tomato
   paste
½ teaspoon garlic powder
1 tablespoon vinegar
Thyme to taste
1 bay leaf

Sprinkle beef with salt and pepper. Coat with flour. Brown on all sides in hot oil in skillet. Add water. Simmer for 2 hours. Cook potatoes, onions and carrots in water to cover in saucepan until tender; drain. Combine with beef in greased baking dish. Add tomato paste, garlic powder, vinegar, thyme and bay leaf to beef drippings in skillet. Add water if necessary to make a sauce-like consistency. Bring to a boil. Pour over vegetables and beef. Bake at 350 degrees for 45 minutes. Yield: 4 to 6 servings.

Darlene Evans

MICROWAVE EASY BEEF STEW SUPREME

2 pounds beef round steak
1 8-ounce bottle of Italian
   salad dressing
2 medium onions
4 potatoes
4 carrots
2 cans tomato soup
4 bay leaves
½ teaspoon salt
⅛ teaspoon pepper

Cut round steak into ½-inch cubes; place in bowl. Add salad dressing. Marinate overnight in refrigerator. Drain steak cubes. Place in 4-quart glass casserole. Cut onions, potatoes and carrots into quarters. Add to steak. Pour undiluted soup over top. Add bay leaves, salt and pepper. Microwave, covered, on Medium for 60 minutes or until steak and vegetables are tender, stirring twice. Remove bay leaves. Yield: 6 to 8 servings.

Mary Cook

TENDERLOIN CASSEROLE

1 pound beef tenderloin,
  cubed
Flour
2 tablespoons oil
1 cup finely chopped
  celery
2 onions, finely chopped

1 can cream of chicken
  soup
1 can cream of mushroom
  soup
1 soup can water
1/2 cup rice
1/2 teaspoon salt

Coat beef with flour. Brown beef on all sides in hot oil in skillet. Add celery and onions. Sauté until vegetables are tender. Add soups, water, rice and salt; mix well. Pour into casserole. Bake, covered, at 350 degrees for 1 1/2 hours or until beef is tender, stirring frequently. Yield: 4 to 6 servings.

Gwen Mills

VEAL PARMESAN

1 package breaded veal
  cutlets
1 large jar spaghetti sauce
2 cups shredded
  mozzarella cheese

3 tablespoons Parmesan
  cheese

Place veal cutlets in 9x13-inch baking dish. Bake at 350 degrees for 10 minutes. Cover with spaghetti sauce; sprinkle with cheeses. Bake for 10 to 15 minutes longer or until cheese melts. Serve with tossed salad and garlic bread. Yield: 6 servings.

Wanda Trimble

BARBECUED BOLOGNA ROLL

1   15-pound bologna
  roll

1 large bottle of hickory
  smoked barbecue sauce

Place skewers in each end of bologna roll. Grill over hot coals for 20 minutes, rotating and basting with barbecue sauce. Yield: 30 to 40 servings.

Frank Hayden

CABBAGE ROLLS WITH TOMATO GRAVY

2 heads cabbage
3 pounds ground chuck
1/4 cup rice
Salt and pepper to taste
2 eggs, beaten

2 large cans tomato sauce
2 tablespoons bacon
drippings
2 tablespoons flour
1 can tomato soup

Remove core from each head of cabbage. Place cabbages in boiling water in saucepan. Cook until 20 leaves can be removed; drain. Combine ground chuck, rice, salt, pepper and eggs in bowl; mix well. Spoon mixture onto cabbage leaves; roll each to enclose filling. Fasten with pick. Chop remaining cabbage; place in 2 large saucepans. Add water to half the depth of cabbage. Arrange cabbage rolls in single layer on chopped cabbage. Spread tomato sauce over rolls. Simmer, covered, for 2 hours. Combine bacon drippings and flour in skillet; mix well. Cook until brown, stirring constantly. Add soup gradually, stirring until thickened. Place cabbage rolls on serving dish. Spread tomato gravy over top. Yield: 20 servings.

Nancy Lockard

RITA'S GOOD CHILI

3 pounds ground chuck
1 medium onion, chopped
1 container Bloomer's chili
meat
1   16-ounce can tomatoes
1   8-ounce can tomato
purée

1 can mushrooms
2 packages Bloomer's chili
powder
1 to 2 tablespoons salt
1 to 2 tablespoons pepper
4 tablespoons basil
8 to 16 ounces spaghetti

Cook ground chuck with onion in large skillet until brown and crumbly, stirring frequently; drain. Add chili meat; mix in with fork. Add tomatoes, tomato purée, mushrooms, chili powder and salt and pepper. Sprinkle basil over top. Simmer for 30 minutes. Cook spaghetti according to package directions; drain. Add chili to spaghetti and toss to mix or place spaghetti on plates and ladle chili over top. Yield: 6 to 8 servings.

Rita Long

CHILI

1 pound ground beef
2 tablespoons oil
4 cloves of garlic, minced
3 tablespoons chili powder
1 teaspoon salt
1/2 teaspoon cumin
1/4 teaspoon oregano
1/2 teaspoon red pepper
11/2 teaspoons sugar
41/2 teaspoons paprika
41/2 teaspoons flour
41/2 teaspoons cornmeal
1 can tomatoes
2 cups water
1 can chili beans

Brown ground beef in hot oil in skillet, stirring until crumbly; drain. Add garlic, chili powder, salt, cumin, oregano, red pepper, sugar, paprika, flour and cornmeal; mix well. Cook for several minutes, stirring constantly. Add tomatoes and water. Simmer for 10 minutes, stirring frequently. Add beans. Simmer for several minutes or until of serving temperature, stirring occasionally. Yield: 10 servings.

Linda Wigginton

TOM'S WORLD FAMOUS CHILI

11/2 pounds lean ground
beef
1 onion, chopped
1 clove of garlic, minced
Pepper to taste
1/2 teaspoon salt
21/3 cups water
11/2 16-ounce cans whole
tomatoes, chopped
2 16-ounce cans kidney
beans
1 15-ounce can tomato
sauce
3 tablespoons chili powder
1/2 cup (scant) catsup
Hot pepper sauce to taste
2 ounces spaghetti

Brown ground beef with onion in large skillet, stirring until ground beef is crumbly; drain. Add garlic, pepper, salt and water; mix well. Add undrained tomatoes and kidney beans, tomato sauce, chili powder, catsup and hot pepper sauce. Simmer for 11/2 to 2 hours, stirring occasionally. Add additional water if necessary for desired consistency. Break spaghetti into 11/2-inch pieces. Cook using package directions; drain. Add to chili just before serving; mix well. This has been made and served to hundreds at school functions many times. Yield: 10 servings.

Tom Anderson

DANNY'S CHILI

2 pounds ground beef
1 package chili seasoning
  mix
4 medium tomatoes,
  coarsely chopped
1 can tomato sauce
1 1/2 bunches green
  onions, chopped
1/2 green bell pepper,
  chopped

2 to 3 cloves of garlic,
  minced
1 can kidney beans
3/4 to 1 teaspoon cayenne
  pepper
Salt to taste
1/2 small package spaghetti

Brown ground beef in saucepan, stirring until crumbly; drain. Add chili mix, tomatoes, tomato sauce, onions, green pepper, garlic, kidney beans, cayenne pepper and salt; mix well. Simmer for 2 minutes, stirring occasionally. Cook spaghetti according to package directions using salted water; drain. Add to chili; mix well. Yield: 6 to 8 servings.

Danny Bond

MICROWAVE CHILI

1 1/2 pounds ground chuck
1 medium onion, chopped
1 medium green bell
  pepper, chopped
1/4 teaspoon garlic juice
1 16-ounce can tomatoes

1 15-ounce can chili
beans
1 8-ounce can tomato
sauce
1 tablespoon chili powder
1/4 teaspoon oregano

Crumble ground chuck into 4-quart glass casserole. Microwave on High for 4 1/2 minutes; drain. Add onion and green pepper; mix well. Microwave, covered, for 5 minutes or until vegetables are tender. Add garlic juice, tomatoes, chili beans, tomato sauce, chili powder and oregano; mix well. Microwave, covered, on High for 5 minutes; mix well. Microwave, uncovered, on Medium for 25 minutes, stirring once. May serve over hot cooked spaghetti or stir cooked spaghetti into hot chili.
Yield: 6 to 8 servings.

Peggy Posante

BROCCOLI HAMBURGER CASSEROLE

1 pound ground beef
1 package egg noodles, cooked
1 10-ounce package frozen broccoli, cooked
1 package dry onion soup mix
1 can cream of mushroom soup
Bread crumbs
Shredded Cheddar cheese
Parsley flakes

Brown ground beef in skillet, stirring until crumbly; drain. Combine ground beef, egg noodles, broccoli, onion soup mix and mushroom soup in casserole; mix well. Top with mixture of bread crumbs, Cheddar cheese and parsley flakes. Bake at 300 degrees for 20 to 30 minutes. Broil until topping is brown. Yield: 8 to 10 servings.

Janet Milburn

BEEF AND CABBAGE CASSEROLE

1 pound ground beef
1 onion, chopped
1 15-ounce can tomato sauce
$1/8$ teaspoon cinnamon
$1/8$ teaspoon cloves
1 teaspoon salt
4 cups shredded cabbage

Brown ground beef with onion in skillet, stirring until ground beef is crumbly; drain. Add tomato sauce, cinnamon, cloves and salt; mix well. Layer cabbage and ground beef $1/2$ at a time in 12x12-inch casserole. Bake at 350 degrees for 45 minutes. Yield: 4 servings.

Carol Young

★ The easier something is to prepare, the less a husband likes it.

CHOW MEIN CASSEROLE

1 pound ground beef
2 onions, chopped
1 can cream of mushroom
  soup
1 can cream of chicken
  soup
1½ cups warm water

½ cup rice
1 tablespoon soy sauce
1 2-ounce can
  mushrooms, drained
1 8-ounce can sliced
  water chestnuts, drained
Chow mein noodles

Brown ground beef with onions in skillet, stirring until ground beef is crumbly; drain. Add mushroom soup, chicken soup, water, rice, soy sauce, mushrooms and water chestnuts; mix well. Pour into casserole. Bake, covered, at 350 degrees for 30 minutes. Remove cover. Bake for 30 minutes. Sprinkle with chow mein noodles. Bake for 3 to 4 minutes longer.
Yield: 6 servings.

Patsy Ford

COMPANY BEEF CASSEROLE

1 pound ground beef
1 onion, chopped
2 cups tomatoes
1 tablespoon steak sauce
1 tablespoon catsup
¼ cup chopped green bell
  pepper

2 tablespoons chopped
  parsley
6 ounces spaghetti
1 can cream of mushroom
  soup
1 cup shredded Cheddar
  cheese

Brown ground beef with onion in skillet, stirring until ground beef is crumbly; drain. Add tomatoes, steak sauce, catsup, green pepper and parsley. Simmer for 30 minutes, stirring frequently. Cook spaghetti using package directions; drain. Combine spaghetti, meat sauce and soup in casserole; mix well. Top with cheese. Bake at 350 degrees for 30 minutes or until hot and bubbly. Yield: 6 servings.

Donna Hearn

CRUNCHY BEEF CASSEROLE

1 7-ounce package elbow macaroni
1 pound ground beef
1 can cream of mushroom soup
1 14-ounce can tomatoes, chopped

3/4 cup shredded Cheddar cheese
1/4 cup chopped green bell pepper
3/4 teaspoon seasoned salt
1 3-ounce can French fried onions

Cook macaroni using package directions; drain. Brown ground beef in large skillet, stirring until crumbly; drain. Add macaroni, mushroom soup, tomatoes, cheese, green pepper and seasoned salt; mix well. Layer half the ground beef mixture in 2-quart casserole sprayed with nonstick cooking spray. Sprinkle with half the fried onions; top with remaining ground beef mixture. Bake, covered, at 350 degrees for 30 minutes. Sprinkle with remaining onions. Bake, uncovered, for 5 minutes longer. Yield: 4 to 6 servings.

Patricia J. Tudor

HAMBURGER AND CORN CASSEROLE

1 1/2 pounds ground beef
1 onion, chopped
1 12-ounce can whole kernel corn, drained
1 can cream of chicken soup
1 can cream of mushroom soup
1 cup sour cream

1/4 cup chopped pimento
3/4 teaspoon salt
1/4 teaspoon pepper
3 cups medium noodles, cooked
1 cup bread crumbs
3 tablespoons melted butter

Brown ground beef in large skillet, stirring until crumbly. Add onions. Cook just until tender; drain. Add corn, chicken soup, mushroom soup, sour cream, pimento, salt, pepper and noodles; mix well. Pour into 2-quart casserole. Mix bread crumbs with melted butter in bowl. Sprinkle over top of mixture. Bake at 350 degrees for 30 minutes. Yield: 8 to 10 servings.

Betty Schweinhart

MARILYN'S HAMBURGER CASSEROLE

1½ pounds ground beef
1 onion, chopped
Garlic to taste
2 dashes of cinnamon
1 8-ounce can tomato
   sauce
1 8-ounce package
   macaroni
2 tablespoons margarine

Salt to taste
2 eggs, beaten
3 tablespoons margarine
⅓ cup flour
2 cups milk
⅓ cup Parmesan cheese
Nutmeg
Butter

Brown ground beef with onion and garlic in skillet, stirring until ground beef is crumbly; drain. Add cinnamon and tomato sauce; mix well. Set aside. Cook macaroni using package directions; drain. Add 2 tablespoons margarine, salt and eggs; mix well. Set aside. Melt 3 tablespoons margarine in saucepan. Stir in flour until smooth. Add milk and salt. Cook until thickened, stirring constantly. Add cheese and nutmeg; mix well. Layer half the noodles, all the ground beef mixture, half the cheese sauce, remaining noodles and remaining cheese sauce in buttered casserole. Dot with butter; sprinkle with additional nutmeg. Bake at 375 degrees for 1 hour. Yield: 8 to 10 servings.

Donna Browning

GROUND BEEF AND NOODLE CASSEROLE

8 ounces fine noodles
2 cups chopped onions
2 tablespoons shortening
2 pounds ground beef
1 4-ounce can sliced
   mushrooms, drained
1 can cream of chicken
   soup
1¼ cups milk

2 teaspoons salt
¼ teaspoon pepper
¼ cup soy sauce
1 teaspoon
   Worcestershire sauce
8 ounces Cheddar cheese,
   shredded
1 5-ounce can chow mein
   noodles

Cook noodles using package directions; drain. Sauté onions in hot shortening in large skillet for 5 minutes or until tender. Add ground beef. Cook until brown and crumbly; drain. Add mushrooms, soup, milk, salt, pepper, soy sauce and Worcestershire sauce; mix well. Place noodles in 3-quart casserole.

Spread ground beef mixture over top. Sprinkle with cheese. Bake at 350 degrees for 15 minutes. Sprinkle with chow mein noodles. Bake for 10 minutes longer. Yield: 8 to 10 servings.

Chrissy Robey

MICROWAVE GROUND BEEF CASSEROLE

1¹/₂ pounds ground beef
¹/₄ cup chopped onion
Pepper to taste

1 can cream of mushroom
soup
Tater Tots

Crumble ground beef into 2-quart glass casserole. Microwave on High for 8 minutes or until cooked through; drain. Add onion and pepper. Spoon soup over top. Microwave for 5 minutes or until bubbly. Brown Tater Tots using package directions. Arrange over casserole. May be prepared conventionally by browning ground beef in skillet, combining with onion, pepper and soup in casserole and baking at 400 degrees for 20 minutes. Top with Tater Tots and bake until brown. Yield: 6 servings.

Sue Settle

HAMBURGER TREAT

1 pound ground beef
¹/₄ teaspoon garlic salt
¹/₄ teaspoon pepper
1 teaspoon salt
1 tablespoon sugar
2 6-ounce cans tomato
sauce

1 6 to 8-ounce package
noodles
3 to 6 ounces cream
cheese, softened
1 cup sour cream
1 onion, chopped
¹/₂ cup Parmesan cheese

Brown ground beef in skillet, stirring until crumbly; drain. Add garlic salt, pepper, salt, sugar and tomato sauce. Simmer, covered, for 15 minutes, stirring frequently. Cook noodles using package directions; drain. Add cream cheese; mix well. Mix sour cream and onion in small bowl. Layer half the noodle mixture, all the ground beef mixture, all the sour cream mixture and remaining noodle mixture in 2-quart baking dish. Sprinkle with Parmesan cheese. Bake at 350 degrees for 30 minutes. May add chopped green bell pepper and oregano. Yield: 6 to 8 servings.

Virginia Hodges, Dorothy Luckett

ITALIAN HOT DISH

1¼ pounds ground chuck
1 onion, chopped
½ green bell pepper,
  chopped
1 tablespoon Italian
  seasoning
½ teaspoon salt
½ teaspoon pepper
1 12-ounce package egg
  noodles
1 can mixed vegetables,
  drained
1 cup tomato juice
Parmesan cheese

Brown ground chuck with onion and green pepper in skillet, stirring until ground chuck is crumbly; drain. Add Italian seasoning, salt and pepper; mix well. Cook noodles using package directions; drain. Combine noodles, ground beef mixture and mixed vegetables in large baking dish; mix well. Pour tomato juice over top; sprinkle with Parmesan cheese. Bake at 300 degrees for 30 minutes. Yield: 8 servings.

Dollie D. Billiter

PENNSYLVANIA DUTCH CASSEROLE

1 pound ground chuck
1 onion, chopped
¼ teaspoon salt
¼ teaspoon pepper
¼ teaspoon crushed red
  pepper (optional)
1 15-ounce can shredded
  sauerkraut
1 can water
1 small package medium
  noodles

Brown ground chuck with onion, salt, pepper and red pepper in large skillet, stirring until ground chuck is crumbly; drain. Add sauerkraut, water and noodles. Simmer until noodles are tender, stirring occasionally. Place in casserole. Bake at 350 degrees for 30 minutes. May top with buttered bread crumbs before baking. May reduce water to ½ can and microwave on High until heated through. Yield: 4 to 6 servings.

Larry Cougenour

154

BEEFY CHEESE AND NOODLE CASSEROLE

1 onion, chopped
2 tablespoons oil
2 pounds ground beef
1 large jar meatless
  spaghetti sauce
8 to 10 shakes Beau
  Monde seasoning

1 teaspoon chili powder
1   16-ounce package wide
  noodles
1 pound sharp Cheddar
  cheese, shredded

Sauté onions in oil in skillet until golden brown. Add ground beef. Cook until brown, stirring until crumbly; drain. Add spaghetti sauce and seasonings; mix well. Simmer for 30 minutes. Cook noodles using package directions; drain. Layer noodles, meat sauce and cheese ½ at a time in 4-quart casserole. Bake at 325 degrees for 1 hour or until brown. Yield: 8 to 10 servings.

Mildred Van Hoose

PIZZA CASSEROLE

2 pounds ground beef
1 pound hot sausage
1 onion, chopped
1 package extra wide egg
  noodles
2 jars sausage pizza sauce

1 package sliced
  pepperoni
1 jar sliced mushrooms
2 cups shredded
  mozzarella cheese

Brown ground beef and sausage with onion in skillet, stirring until ground beef is crumbly; drain. Cook noodles using package directions; drain. Combine ground beef mixture, noodles, pizza sauce, pepperoni and mushrooms in large bowl; mix well. Pour into casserole. Top with cheese. Bake at 350 degrees for 15 minutes. Yield: 12 servings.

Dollie D. Billiter

GROUND BEEF AND POTATO CASSEROLE

1 pound ground round
1 onion, chopped
1   8-ounce can tomato
   sauce

2 potatoes, peeled, sliced
1 teaspoon garlic salt
2 eggs, beaten
1 cup plain yogurt

Brown ground beef with onion in skillet, stirring until ground beef is crumbly; drain. Add tomato sauce, potatoes and garlic salt. Cook for 5 minutes, stirring frequently. Pour into casserole. Mix eggs and yogurt in bowl. Spread over ground beef mixture. Bake at 350 degrees for 1 hour. Yield: 6 servings.

Alice Baker

FOUR-CHEESE LASAGNA

3/4 cup chopped onion
2 cloves of garlic, minced
2 tablespoons oil
3/4 pound ground beef
3 1/2 cups chopped
   tomatoes
1   6-ounce can tomato
   paste
1 large can tomato sauce
2 teaspoons salt
1/4 teaspoon pepper

2 teaspoons oregano
Basil to taste
12 ounces lasagna noodles
1 cup small curd cottage
   cheese
3/4 cup Parmesan cheese
2 cups shredded Cheddar
   cheese
8 ounces mozzarella
   cheese, shredded

Sauté onion and garlic in hot oil in skillet until onion is tender. Add ground beef. Cook until brown, stirring until crumbly; drain. Add tomatoes, tomato paste, tomato sauce, salt, pepper, oregano and basil. Simmer for 2 hours or until sauce is thick, stirring frequently. Cook lasagna noodles in salted water for 15 minutes or until tender. Rinse in cool water until cool enough to handle; drain. Layer noodles, meat sauce, cottage cheese, Parmesan cheese, Cheddar cheese and mozzarella cheese 1/3 at a time in greased 9x13-inch baking dish. Bake at 340 degrees for 40 minutes. Yield: 10 servings.

Brenda Collins

LASAGNA

1¹/₂ pounds ground beef
2 tablespoons olive oil
3   6-ounce cans tomato
  paste
3 cups water
¹/₂ cup minced onion
1 clove of garlic, minced
2 tablespoons chopped
  parsley
1 tablespoon salt
¹/₄ teaspoon pepper
3 bay leaves
¹/₂ teaspoon oregano
1   16-ounce package
  lasagna noodles
¹/₂ cup Parmesan cheese
1 to 1¹/₂ pounds ricotta or
  cottage cheese
³/₄ to 1 pound mozzarella
  cheese, sliced

Brown ground beef in hot olive oil in skillet, stirring until crumbly; drain. Add next 9 ingredients; mix well. Simmer for 4 to 5 hours, stirring occasionally; remove bay leaves. Cook lasagna noodles using package directions; drain. Alternate layers of noodles, ground beef sauce, Parmesan cheese and ricotta cheese in 9x13-inch baking dish. Top with layer of mozzarella cheese. Bake at 350 degrees for 30 minutes or until mozzarella cheese is bubbly. Let stand for 15 minutes before serving. Yield: 16 servings.

Betty Jo Daniel

EASY LASAGNA

1 pound ground beef
2 cups cottage cheese
¹/₂ cup Parmesan cheese
2 eggs, beaten
1 teaspoon salt
¹/₂ teaspoon pepper
1 jar mushrooms, drained
1 large jar spaghetti sauce
1   16-ounce package
  lasagna noodles
1 pound mozzarella
  cheese, sliced

Brown ground beef in skillet, stirring until crumbly; drain. Combine next 6 ingredients in bowl; mix well. Layer half the spaghetti sauce, lasagna noodles, cottage cheese mixture, ground beef and mozzarella cheese in 9x13-inch baking dish. Repeat layers, ending with lasagna noodles and spaghetti sauce. Bake, covered with foil, at 350 degrees for 20 minutes. Remove foil. Bake for 20 minutes longer. Let stand for 15 minutes before serving. Yield: 8 servings.

Donna Browning, Cathy Hamilton

MANICOTTI

1 box jumbo pasta shells
2 pounds cottage cheese
2 eggs, beaten
2 teaspoons parsley flakes
1 teaspoon salt
1/2 teaspoon pepper

3 cups shredded
  mozzarella cheese
1 jar chunky garden
  vegetables spaghetti
  sauce

Cook pasta shells in salted water just until tender; drain. Rinse in cold water; drain. Combine cottage cheese, eggs, parsley flakes, salt, pepper and 2 cups mozzarella cheese in bowl; mix well. Pour half the spaghetti sauce into 9x13-inch baking dish. Stuff pasta shells with cottage cheese mixture; place in sauce. Pour remaining sauce over shells. Sprinkle with remaining 1 cup mozzarella cheese. Bake at 325 degrees for 30 minutes. Let stand for 15 minutes before serving.
Yield: 6 servings.

Lila Mae White

JIFFY PORCUPINES

1 pound ground beef
2/3 cup quick cooking rice
1/2 cup chopped onion
1 teaspoon salt
1/4 teaspoon pepper

2 tablespoons oil
1   15-ounce can tomato
  sauce
1/4 cup water

Combine ground beef, rice, onion, salt and pepper in bowl; mix well. Shape into 1-inch meatballs. Brown meatballs lightly on all sides in hot oil in 10-inch skillet; drain. Add mixture of tomato sauce and water. Simmer, covered, for 20 minutes, stirring occasionally. Yield: 4 servings.

Paula Goodlett

LIMA BEANS AND MEATBALLS

1   10-ounce package
  frozen lima beans
2 to 3 slices bread
1/4 cup milk
1 teaspoons salt
1/4 teaspoon pepper
1 egg, beaten
1 clove of garlic, minced

1 pound ground beef
1 tablespoon melted butter
1/2 cup water
1/2 teaspoon salt
1/4 teaspoon pepper
3 tablespoons melted
  butter
1 cup sour cream

Cook lima beans using package directions until tender; drain. Soak bread in milk in bowl. Combine 1 teaspoon salt, 1/4 teaspoon pepper, egg, garlic and ground beef in large bowl; mix well. Squeeze excess moisture from bread. Add to ground beef mixture; mix well. Shape into walnut-sized balls. Brown meatballs on all sides in 1 tablespoon butter in skillet; place in 2-quart casserole. Pour water into pan drippings; mix well. Pour over meatballs. Season lima beans with remaining 1/2 teaspoon salt, 1/4 teaspoon pepper and 3 tablespoons butter; add to meatballs. Bake, covered, at 350 degrees for 30 minutes. Spoon sour cream over top. Bake, uncovered, for 5 minutes longer.
Yield: 4 to 6 servings.

Shirley Fitzpatrick

MICROWAVE ITALIAN MEATBALLS

1 pound ground chuck
1 egg
1 medium onion, chopped
1/4 cup chopped green bell
  pepper
1/4 cup Parmesan cheese

1 teaspoon parsley flakes
1/4 teaspoon basil
1/4 teaspoon oregano
1/8 teaspoon garlic juice
1   16-ounce can tomato
  sauce

Combine ground chuck, egg, onion, green pepper and Parmesan cheese in bowl; mix well. Shape into 20 meatballs; place in 2-quart glass casserole. Microwave on High for 7 minutes; drain. Combine seasonings and tomato sauce in bowl; mix well. Pour over meatballs. Microwave on High for 8 minutes, stirring once. Serve over favorite pasta. Yield: 20 meatballs.

Peggy Posante

MEATBALL STEW

1½ pounds ground beef
½ cup chopped onion
½ cup fresh bread crumbs
1 clove of garlic, crushed
1 egg, beaten
1½ teaspoons salt
¼ teaspoon pepper
2 tablespoons oil
1 cup water
1 16-ounce can tomatoes
½ cup red wine

1 tablespoon beef stock
  base
½ teaspoon marjoram
½ teaspoon thyme
8 ounces mushrooms,
  sliced
3 medium zucchini, cut
  into 1-inch pieces
2 tablespoons cornstarch
¼ cup water

Combine ground beef, onion, bread crumbs, garlic, egg, salt and pepper in bowl; mix well. Shape into meatballs. Brown on all sides in hot oil in large skillet; drain. Remove meatballs to bowl. Combine 1 cup water, undrained tomatoes, wine, stock base, marjoram and thyme in skillet; mix well. Bring to a boil. Add meatballs. Reduce heat. Simmer, covered, for 25 minutes. Add mushrooms and zucchini. Simmer for 15 minutes or until zucchini is tender. Add mixture of cornstarch and ¼ cup water gradually. Cook for 1 minute, stirring constantly. Yield: 4 to 5 servings.

Janice R. Boud

SWEDISH MEATBALLS

3 slices bread, crumbled
⅓ cup milk
1 pound ground beef
1 small onion, minced
½ teaspoon salt
¼ teaspoon pepper

Dash of nutmeg
2 tablespoons oil
1 envelope brown gravy
  mix
1¼ cups water
½ cup mayonnaise

Soak bread in milk in large bowl. Add ground beef, onion, salt, pepper and nutmeg; mix well. Shape into 1-inch meatballs. Chill in refrigerator. Brown meatballs on all sides in hot oil in large skillet. Prepare brown gravy according to package directions using 1¼ cups water. Blend in mayonnaise. Add to meatballs. Bring to serving temperature. Serve with hot egg noodles. Yield: 8 servings.

Joseph B. Snodgrass

MICROWAVE SWEDISH MEATBALLS

1 cup milk
1/2 cup dry bread crumbs
8 ounces lean ground beef
8 ounces lean ground pork
1 egg, slightly beaten
1 small onion, chopped
1 tablespoon
  Worcestershire sauce
1/2 teaspoon salt

1/4 teaspoon pepper
1/8 teaspoon cloves
2 tablespoons oil
1/4 cup flour
1/2 teaspoon instant beef
  bouillon
1/2 cup hot water
1/2 cup cream

Pour milk over crumbs in medium bowl. Let stand for 10 minutes. Add next 8 ingredients; mix well with fork. Shape into 1-inch balls. Preheat microwave browning dish on High for 5 minutes. Add oil and meatballs. Microwave on High for 4 minutes, turning meatballs once. Remove meatballs. Blend flour into drippings. Dissolve bouillon in hot water. Stir bouillon and cream into flour mixture gradually. Add meatballs. Microwave, covered, on Medium for 6 minutes or until sauce is thickened and meatballs are cooked through. Let stand for 5 minutes. Yield: 4 servings.

Donna Lea

HAMBURGER DRESSING ROLL

1 1/2 pounds ground beef
1 cup bread or cracker
  crumbs
2 eggs, beaten
Salt and pepper to taste
Bread crumbs

Chopped celery
Chopped onion
Sage
3 to 4 teaspoons bouillon
  granules
1 cup water

Combine ground beef, 1 cup crumbs, eggs, salt and pepper in bowl; mix well. Flatten and spread to resemble pizza crust on large sheet of aluminum foil. Combine enough bread crumbs, celery, onion and sage with bouillon and water to make dressing in bowl; mix well. Spread over top of ground beef mixture. Roll as for jelly roll; press ends together, securing with picks if necessary. Place in baking pan. Bake at 350 degrees for 1 hour or to desired degree of doneness. May substitute sausage for ground beef. Yield: 6 to 8 servings.

Helen Yaeger

MEAT LOAF

1½ to 2 pounds ground
  beef
1 egg, beaten
1 cup fresh bread crumbs
1 medium onion, chopped
1¼ teaspoons salt
¼ teaspoon pepper
1 can tomato sauce
2 tablespoons prepared
  mustard
2 tablespoons brown sugar
2 tablespoons vinegar
1 cup water

Combine ground beef, egg, bread crumbs, onion, salt, pepper and ½ can tomato sauce in bowl; mix well. Shape into loaf. Place in baking dish. Bake at 300 degrees for 20 minutes; drain. Combine remaining tomato sauce, mustard, brown sugar, vinegar and water in saucepan; mix well. Bring to a boil. Pour over meat loaf. Bake for 30 minutes longer, basting 3 to 4 times. Yield: 6 to 8 servings.

Mary T. Hyams

HAMBURGER CORN PONE PIE

1 pound ground beef
½ cup chopped onion
1 tablespoon shortening
2 teaspoons chili powder
¾ teaspoon salt
1 cup canned tomatoes
1 cup red kidney beans
1 cup corn bread batter

Brown ground beef with onion in hot shortening in skillet, stirring until ground beef is crumbly; drain. Add chili powder, salt and tomatoes. Simmer for 15 minutes. Add beans; mix well. Pour into casserole; top with corn bread batter. Bake at 425 degrees for 20 minutes or until corn bread is brown and crisp. Yield: 6 servings.

Izola Croft

MICROWAVE SHEPHERD'S PIE

1 pound lean ground beef
2 slices soft white bread,
  coarsely crumbled
2/3 cup milk
1 egg, slightly beaten
1/4 cup finely chopped
  onion

1 tablespoon
  Worcestershire sauce
1 teaspoon salt
3 cups hot mashed
  potatoes
1 cup finely chopped
  American cheese

Combine ground beef, bread crumbs, milk, egg, onion, Worcestershire sauce and salt in medium bowl; mix well. Pat evenly into 9-inch glass pie plate. Microwave on Medium-High for 7 minutes; drain. Spread potatoes over ground beef layer. Sprinkle cheese over top. Microwave on Medium-High for 5 minutes or until cheese is melted. Let stand for 3 minutes. Yield: 4 to 5 servings.

Tony Williams

MICROWAVE SALISBURY STEAK

1 1/2 pounds lean ground
  beef
1 envelope brown gravy
  mix

1 cup water
1 small onion, thinly sliced
1 teaspoon salt
1/4 teaspoon pepper

Shape ground beef into four or five 1/2-inch thick patties. Preheat microwave browning dish on High for 4 minutes. Add patties. Microwave on High for 4 minutes, turning patties once. Add gravy mix, water and onion. Microwave, covered, on High for 6 to 8 minutes or to desired degree of doneness. Season with salt and pepper. Yield: 4 to 5 servings.

Sour Cream Salisbury Steak—Add 1/2 cup sour cream and 1 2-ounce jar well-drained mushrooms during final 2 minutes of cooking.

Tasty Herbed Salisbury Steak—Add 1 to 2 teaspoons parsley, basil or thyme with gravy mix.

Saucy Salisbury Steak—Add 1/4 cup catsup and 2 teaspoons Worcestershire sauce with gravy mix.

Tony Williams

TACO PIE

1 8 or 9-inch pie shell
1 pound ground beef
2 envelopes taco
   seasoning mix

1 can refried beans
1 cup shredded Cheddar
   cheese

Bake pie shell at 350 degrees until lightly browned. Brown ground beef in skillet, stirring until crumbly; drain. Prepare taco seasoning mix using package directions. Spread refried beans in pie shell. Spoon in ground beef and half the taco sauce. Sprinkle with cheese. Bake at 350 degrees for 15 to 20 minutes or until cheese is melted. Serve with remaining taco sauce. Garnish with shredded lettuce, chopped tomato, chopped onion, shredded cheese, pickle and taco chips. Yield: 4 to 6 servings.

Sue Settle

POPOVER TACO

1 pound ground beef
1 large onion, finely
   chopped
1 envelope taco
   seasoning mix
1 15-ounce can tomato
   sauce
$1/2$ cup water
1 16-ounce can refried
   beans

1 4-ounce can chopped
   green chilies
1 cup shredded Monterey
   Jack cheese
1 cup milk
2 eggs, beaten
1 tablespoon oil
1 cup sifted flour

Brown ground beef with onion in skillet, stirring until ground beef is crumbly; drain. Stir in taco seasoning mix, tomato sauce and water; mix well. Simmer for 10 minutes, stirring frequently. Spread refried beans in greased 9x13-inch baking dish. Layer half the chilies, all the ground beef and remaining chilies over beans. Sprinkle with cheese. Mix milk, eggs, oil and flour in small bowl until smooth. Pour over mixture. Bake at 400 degrees for 30 minutes or until golden brown. Cut into squares.
Yield: 8 servings.

Patricia J. Tudor

PIRASHKE

1 cup milk
2 eggs, beaten
1 package dry yeast
1 tablespoon sugar
1 teaspoon salt
1/2 cup melted butter

Flour
1 1/2 pounds ground beef
1 onion, chopped
1 teaspoon cumin
2 hard-boiled eggs
Oil for deep frying

Combine milk, eggs, yeast, sugar, salt and butter in large bowl; mix well. Add enough flour to make a soft dough. Let rise. Roll to 1/4-inch thickness on floured surface. Cut into 3-inch triangles. Brown ground beef with onion and cumin in skillet, stirring until ground beef is crumbly; drain. Chop hard-boiled eggs; add to ground beef mixture; mix well. Spoon 1 tablespoon ground beef mixture onto each triangle of dough. Fold to enclose filling, pressing edges to seal. Deep-fry in hot oil until golden brown on all sides; drain.

Lloyd Hall

RUNZAS

1 2-loaf recipe for yeast
   dough
1 medium head cabbage,
   chopped

2 medium onions, chopped
3 pounds ground beef
Salt and pepper to taste

Let dough rise. Cook cabbage, onions and ground beef in large skillet until ground beef is brown and vegetables are tender, stirring to crumble beef; drain. Add salt and pepper. Roll dough to 1/4-inch thickness on floured surface. Cut into triangles. Spoon ground beef mixture onto triangle. Fold to enclose filling, sealing edges. Place on baking sheet. Let rise again. Bake at 350 degrees until golden brown.

Dianna Zimmer

SPAGHETTI CASSEROLE

8 ounces spaghetti
Sliced American cheese
1½ pounds ground beef
1 small jar homestyle
   spaghetti sauce
1 small package shredded
   Cheddar cheese
1 small can French fried
   onions

Cook spaghetti using package directions; drain. Spread in 9x13-inch baking dish. Layer with American cheese. Brown ground beef in skillet, stirring until crumbly; drain. Spread over cheese slices. Top with spaghetti sauce. Sprinkle with Cheddar cheese and fried onions. Bake at 350 degrees for 30 minutes. Yield: 10 servings.

Ethel Shephard

ITALIAN SPAGHETTI AND MEATBALLS

1 pound ground beef
1 egg, beaten
1 medium onion, chopped
4 cloves of garlic, minced
¾ cup bread crumbs
Salt to taste
¼ cup oil
2 packages spaghetti
2   4-ounce cans tomato
   sauce
½ teaspoon oregano

Combine ground beef, egg, onion, garlic, bread crumbs and salt in bowl; mix well. Shape into walnut-sized balls. Brown meatballs on all sides in hot oil in skillet; drain. Cook spaghetti using package directions; drain. Combine spaghetti, meatballs, tomato sauce and oregano in saucepan. Simmer for 15 to 20 minutes, stirring frequently. Yield: 10 servings.

Louise Chambers

★ Keep spaghetti sauce in your pantry or freezer for emergencies; you can always produce a company meal in minutes.

SPAGHETTI AND SAUCE

2½ pounds ground beef
3 stalks celery, chopped
1 onion, chopped
1 green bell pepper,
  chopped
Salt and pepper to taste
2 16-ounce cans tomatoes

2 cans tomato sauce
1 bay leaf
Garlic to taste
1 to 2 envelopes spaghetti
  sauce mix
16 ounces spaghetti

Brown ground beef in skillet, stirring until crumbly; drain. Add celery, onion and green pepper. Cook until vegetables are tender, stirring frequently. Add salt, pepper, tomatoes, tomato sauce, bay leaf, garlic and spaghetti sauce mix; mix well. Simmer for 4 to 5 hours, stirring occasionally. Remove bay leaf. Cook spaghetti using package directions; drain. Spoon sauce over hot spaghetti. Yield: 12 servings.

June Brewer

ITALIAN MEAT SAUCE

½ cup sliced onion
2 tablespoons olive oil
2 to 3 pounds ground beef
2 cloves of garlic, minced
2 8-ounce cans
  seasoned tomato sauce
1 3-ounce can sliced
  mushrooms

2 16-ounce cans
  tomatoes
¼ cup chopped parsley
1½ teaspoons oregano
1 teaspoon MSG
¼ teaspoon thyme
1 bay leaf
1 cup water

Sauté onion in olive oil in skillet until almost tender. Add ground beef and garlic. Brown lightly, stirring until crumbly; drain. Add tomato sauce, mushrooms, tomatoes, parsley, oregano, MSG, thyme, bay leaf and water; mix well. Simmer for 2 to 2½ hours or until sauce is thickened, stirring occasionally. Remove bay leaf. Serve over hot spaghetti with Parmesan cheese. Yield: 6 servings.

Billie Y. Weatherington

SPAGHETTI SAUCE BY AGGIE

1 to 2 cans tomato paste
2 cans tomato sauce
1 can tomatoes, crushed
1   4-ounce can
  mushrooms, drained,
  chopped
1 cup chopped celery
1 teaspoon basil
1/2 teaspoon oregano
1 teaspoon chopped
  parsley

1/2 teaspoon rosemary
1 small bay leaf
Salt and pepper to taste
Sugar to taste
1 1/2 pounds ground beef
1 clove of garlic, minced
2 medium green bell
  peppers, chopped
2 medium onions, chopped
2 lean pork chops
1/2 cup dry white wine

Combine first 5 ingredients in large saucepan. Add next 8 seasonings; mix well. Simmer over low heat. Brown ground beef with garlic in skillet, stirring until crumbly. Stir into sauce. Sauté green peppers and onions in pan drippings. Add to sauce. Brown pork chops in skillet. Add to sauce. Simmer for 1 1/2 hours, stirring frequently. Remove pork chops before they cook to pieces. Stir in wine. Simmer for 30 minutes longer. Remove bay leaf. Return pork chops to sauce. Yield: 6 to 8 servings.

Aggie Burks

SPANISH DELIGHT

2 onions, chopped
2 green bell peppers,
  chopped
2 tablespoons oil
1 1/2 pounds ground beef
2 tablespoons chili sauce
2 cans sliced mushrooms

1 can whole kernel corn,
  drained
1 small can tomato paste
1 medium package noodles
1 pound American cheese,
  shredded
1 bottle of sliced olives

Sauté onions and green peppers in hot oil in large skillet. Add ground beef. Cook until brown, stirring until crumbly; drain. Add chili sauce, mushrooms, corn and tomato paste. Simmer for 10 minutes. Cook noodles using package directions; drain. Add to ground beef mixture; mix well. Pour into oiled baking dish. Sprinkle with cheese and sliced olives. Bake at 350 degrees for 20 minutes or until cheese melts. Yield: 6 to 8 servings.

Connie Shelton

SPANISH NOODLES

2 slices bacon, chopped
1½ pounds ground beef
1 small onion, chopped
1 green bell pepper,
  chopped
2 cups noodles

3½ cups canned tomatoes
1 teaspoon
  Worcestershire sauce
2 teaspoons salt
½ teaspoon pepper

Fry bacon in large heavy skillet. Add ground beef, onion and green pepper. Cook until ground beef is brown, stirring until crumbly. Add noodles, tomatoes, Worcestershire sauce and seasonings. Simmer, covered, for 30 minutes or until noodles are tender. Yield: 6 to 8 servings.

Calene Budell, Monica Kayse

EASY HAMBURGER STROGANOFF

1 pound ground beef
1 cup chopped onion
¼ cup margarine
1   4-ounce can sliced
  mushrooms

1 cup sour cream
1 teaspoon
  Worcestershire sauce
Salt and pepper to taste
Cooked noodles

Brown ground beef in skillet, stirring until crumbly; drain. Remove to bowl. Sauté onion in margarine in skillet. Remove to bowl. Add undrained mushrooms to pan drippings. Simmer for 12 minutes. Add ground beef and onions; mix well. Simmer, covered, for 5 minutes. Stir in sour cream, Worcestershire sauce, salt and pepper. Cook for 3 to 5 minutes or until heated through. Serve over hot noodles. Yield: 6 servings.

Nona Marie Besendorf

★ Be sure to drain ground beef well to reduce fat and cholesterol content of the finished recipe.

STUFFED PEPPERS

8 green bell peppers
1 onion, chopped
1 stalk celery, chopped
1/4 cup butter
1 pound ground beef
1 cup minute rice
1 cup chopped canned
  tomatoes
1 8-ounce can tomato
  sauce

Cut green peppers into halves; remove seed and membrane. Parboil in water to cover in saucepan for 5 minutes. Sauté onion and celery in butter in skillet for 4 to 5 minutes or until tender. Add ground beef. Cook until ground beef is no longer pink, stirring until crumbly. Cook rice using package directions. Add rice, tomatoes and tomato sauce to ground beef mixture. Cook until thickened, stirring frequently. Spoon into green pepper halves. Place in baking dish. Spoon any remaining sauce over peppers. Bake at 350 degrees until peppers are tender.
Yield: 16 servings.

Rosaleen Robertson

STUFFED GREEN PEPPERS

4 large green bell peppers
4 cups boiling salted water
1 to 1 1/2 pounds lean
  ground beef
1/4 teaspoon pepper
1/2 teaspoon basil
2 tablespoons chopped
  onion
1/2 cup oats
1 teaspoon salt
1 can tomato rice soup

Cut thin slice from stem end of each green pepper. Remove seed and membrane. Cook in boiling salted water in saucepan for 5 minutes; drain. Combine ground beef, pepper, basil, onion, oats, salt and soup in bowl; mix well. Spoon into green peppers. Place in baking dish. Bake, covered, at 350 degrees for 45 minutes. Remove cover. Bake for 15 minutes longer. Yield: 4 servings.

Dena Sue Montgomery

TATER TOT CASSEROLE

1½ pounds ground beef
1 medium onion, chopped
¾ pound Cheddar cheese,
　shredded

1½ cans celery soup
Salt and pepper to taste
1　2-pound package Tater
　Tots

　　Brown ground beef and onions in skillet, stirring until beef is crumbly; drain. Add cheese, soup, salt and pepper; mix well. Pour into 9x9-inch baking dish. Spread Tater Tots over top. Bake at 350 degrees for 1 hour. Yield: 8 to 10 servings.

Gloria Galloway

HAM AND APRICOTS

1 can apricot halves
1 center-cut ham slice,
　1 inch thick

3 tablespoons brown sugar
¼ teaspoon cloves
½ teaspoon cinnamon

　　Drain apricots, reserving 3 tablespoons liquid. Place ham slice in baking dish. Arrange apricots cut side up over ham. Combine brown sugar, spices and reserved liquid in saucepan. Simmer over low heat until sugar dissolves. Pour over ham. Bake at 350 degrees for 1 hour. Yield: 4 servings.

Ruth Dye

BROCCOLI AND HAM CASSEROLE

8 slices white bread, torn
10 slices sharp cheese
2　10-ounce packages
　frozen broccoli, cooked
2 cups chopped cooked
　ham

6 eggs
3 cups milk
½ teaspoon dry mustard
2 cups shredded sharp
　cheese

　　Layer first 4 ingredients in greased 9x13-inch baking dish. Beat eggs, milk and mustard in bowl until smooth. Pour over layers. Chill overnight. Bring to room temperature. Bake at 350 degrees for 1 hour or until firm. Sprinkle with shredded cheese. Bake until cheese melts. Let stand for 10 minutes before serving. May add chopped onion and bell pepper. Yield: 12 servings.

Barbara Struck, Helen Sundquist

HAM AND CHEESE KABOBS

1 4-ounce can crushed pineapple
1/2 cup packed brown sugar
1 tablespoon cornstarch
1/2 cup canned beef bouillon
1/4 cup vinegar
1 teaspoon soy sauce
1/2 pound cooked ham, cubed
1/2 pound Cheddar cheese, cubed
1 15-ounce can pineapple chunks

Drain crushed pineapple, reserving 1/4 cup juice. Mix brown sugar and cornstarch in saucepan. Add bouillon, vinegar, soy sauce and reserved pineapple juice. Bring to a boil. Boil for 1 minute, stirring constantly. Add crushed pineapple; mix well. Remove from heat; cool. Thread ham, cheese and pineapple chunks onto skewers. Brush with sauce. Place on large baking sheet. Bake at 350 degrees for 10 to 15 minutes or just until cheese begins to melt. Yield: 4 to 6 servings.

Dana Fendley

MAIN COURSE HAM CASSEROLE

1/2 cup butter
1/4 cup flour
2 tablespoons dried onion
1 teaspoon salt
1/2 teaspoon dry mustard
1/4 teaspoon celery seed
2 cups milk
1 cup frozen baby lima beans
1 16-ounce package frozen mixed broccoli, cauliflower and carrots
1 cup cubed cooked ham
8 ounces Cheddar cheese, shredded
Herb-flavored dry stuffing mix

Melt butter in saucepan. Blend in flour. Add onion, salt, mustard, celery seed and milk. Simmer until thickened, stirring constantly. Cook frozen vegetables using package directions; drain. Add vegetables and ham to sauce. Pour into 9x13-inch baking dish. Top with cheese; sprinkle with stuffing mix. Bake at 350 degrees until heated through. Yield: 10 to 12 servings.

Bettie Sue Wallace

COUNTRY HAM CASSEROLE

4 cups milk
1/2 cup butter
6 tablespoons cornstarch
Salt and pepper to taste
3/4 cup butter cracker
  crumbs

2 cups ground country
  ham
2 cups chopped hard-
  boiled eggs
3/4 cup butter cracker
  crumbs

Heat milk in saucepan. Blend in butter and cornstarch. Cook over low heat until thickened, stirring constantly. Season with salt and pepper. Sprinkle 3/4 cup cracker crumbs in greased 9x13-inch baking dish. Layer with ham and chopped eggs. Pour sauce over top. Sprinkle with remaining 3/4 cup crumbs. Bake at 350 degrees for 30 minutes. Yield: 6 servings.

Iris Starke

COUNTRY HAM JAMBALAYA

3 cups water
1 1/2 cups brown rice
Salt to taste
1 onion, chopped
2 green bell peppers,
  chopped
3 stalks celery, chopped
1 tablespoon olive oil
1 teaspoon cayenne

1 teaspoon pepper
2 cups broth
1   14-ounce can
  tomatoes, chopped
1 pound country ham,
  shredded
1 tablespoon thyme
  vinegar

Bring water to a boil in heavy saucepan. Add rice and salt, stirring once. Reduce heat to low. Simmer, tightly covered, for 45 minutes. Sauté onion, green peppers and celery in oil in large saucepan just until vegetables are warm and coated with oil. Add cooked rice, cayenne, pepper, broth and tomatoes. Bring to a boil; reduce heat. Stir in ham and vinegar. Simmer over very low heat for 20 minutes or longer, stirring occasionally. Add water as necessary to keep from sticking; jambalaya should be thick, not soupy. Yield: 6 servings.

Wanda Wiegand

OVEN-FRIED COUNTRY HAM

Country ham

Slice ham 1/4-inch thick. Trim edges. Arrange slices on foil-lined baking sheets. Seal tightly with additional foil. Bake at 250 degrees for 1 hour. May use pan juices for red eye gravy.

Chrissy Robey

HAM AND VEAL LOAF

1 pound ground veal
1 pound ground smoked
  ham
6 tablespoons catsup
1/4 cup minced onion
1/4 cup chopped green bell
  pepper
2 eggs, slightly beaten

1 cup dry bread crumbs
1 can cream of mushroom
  soup
1/4 cup water
1/2 teaspoon salt
Pepper to taste
Mustard Sauce

Combine veal, ham, catsup, onion, green pepper and eggs in bowl; mix well. Add bread crumbs, soup, water, salt and pepper; mix well. Place in 5x9-inch loaf pan. Bake at 350 degrees for 1 hour. Serve hot or cold with Mustard Sauce.
Yield: 6 servings.

Mustard Sauce

1 egg, well beaten
1 tablespoon sugar
1/4 teaspoon salt

3 tablespoons dry mustard
1/2 cup white vinegar
1 tablespoon olive oil

Combine egg, sugar, salt, dry mustard and vinegar in double boiler. Cook over boiling water until thickened, stirring constantly. Cool. Stir in olive oil; mix well. Yield: 1 cup.

Mary J. Thompson

HAM LOAF

2 pounds ham
1 1/2 pounds pork
1 cup cracker crumbs
2 eggs, slightly beaten
1 cup milk

1 cup packed brown sugar
1 tablespoon mustard
1/2 cup vinegar
1/2 cup water

Grind ham and pork together. Combine with cracker crumbs, eggs and milk in bowl; mix well. Shape into loaf in 5x9-inch loaf pan. Combine brown sugar, mustard, vinegar and water in saucepan; mix well. Bring to a boil. Boil for 5 minutes. Bake at 350 degrees for 1 to 1 1/2 hours, brushing frequently with sauce. Yield: 6 servings.

Margaret Taylor

HAWAIIAN SMOKED HAM AND VEGETABLES

1 cup thin cooked ham
  strips
2 tablespoons oil
1 cup sliced canned
  mushrooms
2 cups chopped celery
1 1/2 cups green beans, cut
  into 1-inch pieces
2 1/2 cups chopped
  cauliflower

1/3 cup chopped green
  onions
1 tablespoon cornstarch
1 tablespoon sugar
1 tablespoon soy sauce
1 1/2 cups ham broth
1 egg, well beaten

Sauté ham in oil in skillet for 2 minutes. Add mushrooms, celery, green beans, cauliflower and green onions; mix well. Stir in mixture of cornstarch, sugar, soy sauce and ham broth. Simmer for 10 minutes or until vegetables are tender-crisp and sauce has thickened, stirring frequently. Spoon into serving dish. Pour egg into oiled skillet. Tilt to make a thin layer. Cook until firm; do not stir. Slice into 1/8x1 1/2-inch strips. Sprinkle over ham and vegetables. Yield: 6 servings.

Patti Roby

PORK CHOP CASSEROLE

3/4 to 1 cup uncooked rice
4 to 6 pork chops
1 onion, sliced

1 tomato, sliced
1 green bell pepper, sliced
1 can beef bouillon

Place rice in bottom of baking dish. Brown pork chops on both sides in skillet. Place on rice. Layer onion and tomato over pork chops. Top each pork chop with 1 green pepper ring. Add bouillon. Bake, covered, at 375 degrees for 1 hour. Add water as needed during baking. Yield: 4 to 6 servings.

Clara Nance

CHICKEN-FRIED PORK CHOPS

6 pork chops
2 eggs, well beaten
2 tablespoons milk

1 cup cracker crumbs
1/2 teaspoon salt
1/2 cup water

Dip pork chops in mixture of eggs and milk; coat with cracker crumbs. Brown on both sides in skillet. Add salt and water. Simmer, covered, over low heat for 30 to 45 minutes, turning occasionally. Remove cover. Simmer for 15 minutes longer or until pork chops are very tender. Yield: 6 servings.

Lloyd Hall

DEVILED PORK CHOPS

1 medium red apple
1 tablespoon butter
16 ounces mushrooms,
   sliced
3 tablespoons butter
1/4 teaspoon salt
1/4 teaspoon pepper

4 butterflied pork loin chops
1/2 cup mayonnaise
1 tablespoon chopped
   watercress
1/3 cup soft bread crumbs
1 tablespoon mustard
1/8 teaspoon paprika

Cut apple into wedges. Cook in 1 tablespoon butter in skillet for 5 to 7 minutes or until fork-tender, turning once. Remove to warm platter; keep warm. Sauté mushrooms in 3 tablespoons butter in skillet for 10 minutes. Season with salt and pepper. Remove to warm platter with apples; keep warm. Arrange pork chops on rack in broiler pan. Broil for 10 minutes, turning once. Spread mixture of mayonnaise, watercress, bread crumbs, mustard and paprika on pork chops. Broil for 1 minute longer or until bubbly. Place pork chops on platter with apples and mushrooms. Yield: 4 servings.

Diane Dixon

PORK CHOP DINNER

6 1-inch thick pork chops
3 large potatoes, thinly
   sliced
2 onions, thinly sliced
Salt and pepper to taste

1 teaspoon
   Worcestershire sauce
1 can cream of mushroom
   soup
1 cup milk

Brown pork chops in oiled skillet. Layer potatoes, onions and pork chops in greased baking dish, seasoning each layer with salt and pepper. Cover with mixture of Worcestershire sauce, soup and milk. Bake, covered, at 375 degrees for 45 minutes or until chops are very tender. Bake, uncovered, for 5 minutes longer. Yield: 6 servings.

Shirley Smith

DIXIE PORK CHOPS

8 pork chops
1/2 teaspoon salt
1/2 teaspoon sage
4 tart apples
1/2 cup packed brown
   sugar

2 tablespoons flour
1 cup hot water
1 tablespoon vinegar
1/2 cup raisins

Brown pork chops in greased in skillet. Season with salt and sage. Arrange in baking dish. Reserve drippings in skillet. Core and slice apples into rings. Place rings over pork chops. Sprinkle with brown sugar. Stir flour, water and vinegar into drippings in skillet. Simmer over medium heat until thickened, stirring constantly. Add raisins; mix well. Pour over pork chops. Bake at 350 degrees for 1 hour. Yield: 8 servings.

Bernice Keitner

OVEN PORK CHOPS

4 pork chops
Salt to taste
4 thin slices onion

¼ cup packed brown
   sugar
¼ cup catsup

Season pork chops with salt. Arrange in shallow baking dish. Top each pork chop with 1 onion slice, 1 tablespoon brown sugar and 1 tablespoon catsup. Bake, covered, at 350 degrees for 30 minutes. Bake, uncovered, for 30 minutes longer or until pork chops are tender, basting occasionally with pan drippings. Yield: 4 servings.

Carmen Stilger

PORK CHOP AND POTATO BAKE

6 pork chops
Seasoned salt to taste
1 can cream of celery soup
½ cup milk
½ cup sour cream
¼ teaspoon pepper
½ teaspoon seasoned salt

1 24-ounce package
   frozen hashed brown
   potatoes
1 cup shredded Cheddar
   cheese
1 3-ounce can French-
   fried onions

Brown pork chops in lightly greased skillet. Sprinkle with seasoned salt to taste. Combine soup, milk, sour cream, pepper and ½ teaspoon seasoned salt in large bowl; mix well. Add potatoes, half the cheese and half the onions; mix well. Spoon mixture into 9x13-inch baking dish. Arrange pork chops over potatoes. Bake, covered, at 350 degrees for 40 minutes or until pork chops are tender. Top with remaining cheese and onions. Bake, uncovered, for 5 minutes longer. Yield: 6 servings.

Juyne Bushart, Wanda Wiegand

★ Slash edges of fat on pork chops at 1-inch intervals to keep the meat from curling while it is cooking.

178

SMOTHERED BURRITO

1 can tomatoes
1 8-ounce can tomato
  paste
1 small can spicy tomato
  juice
1 tablespoon salsa
Salt and pepper to taste

Garlic powder to taste
4 to 5 cooked pork chops,
  cut into pieces
Refried beans
Warm flour tortillas
Shredded cheese
Chopped onions

Combine first 7 ingredients in Crock•Pot. Cook until well blended and heated through. Heat refried beans to serving temperature in saucepan. Spread beans on tortillas. Top with small amount of sauce, cheese and onions. Roll tortilla. Arrange on serving dish. Pour remaining sauce over tortillas. Top with additional cheese and onions. Yield: 4 to 8 servings.

Diane Murphy

BOUDIN PIE

1½ pounds pork shoulder
¼ pound beef liver
2 stalks celery
1 green bell pepper,
  chopped
1 onion, chopped
1 teaspoon salt
¼ teaspoon cayenne
¼ teaspoon pepper

¼ teaspoon paprika
1 clove of garlic
1 tablespoon flour
1 tablespoon oil
2 cups cooked white rice
4 green onions, chopped
¼ cup chopped parsley
½ cup red wine
1 recipe 2-crust pie pastry

Chop pork and liver. Combine with next 8 ingredients and water to cover in large saucepan. Bring to a boil; reduce heat. Simmer, covered, for 45 minutes. Remove meat; reserve 1 cup liquid. Discard vegetables. Chop meat coarsely in food processor. Brown flour in hot oil in skillet. Add reserved liquid; mix well. Cook until thickened, stirring constantly. Add chopped meat, rice, green onions and parsley; mix well. Cook until heated through. Remove from heat. Add wine; mix well. Pour into pastry-lined 9-inch pie plate. Top with remaining pastry. Trim edges; cut vents. Bake at 400 degrees for 30 minutes or until brown. Serve with Tabasco sauce. Yield: 6 to 8 servings.

Wanda Wiegand

CANNED PORK MEATLOAF

1 quart Canned Fresh
  Pork, chopped
1/2 cup chopped onion
1 cup chopped potatoes
1 cup bread crumbs

1/2 cup shredded carrots
1 egg, well beaten
1/2 cup chopped celery
Salt to taste

Combine pork, onion, potatoes, bread crumbs, carrots, egg, celery and salt in bowl; mix well. Press into loaf pan. Bake at 350 degrees for 30 minutes or until done. Yield: 6 servings.

Canned Fresh Pork

Pork, cut into 2-inch pieces   Salt

Place pork in baking pan. Cook at 350 degrees for 45 minutes, turning to brown on all sides. Place in hot sterilized quart jars. Add 1 teaspoon salt to each jar. Pour drippings over meat. Seal with 2-piece lids. Process in boiling water bath for 2 hours.

Josie Bratcher

FILIPINO NOODLES WITH PORK

8 ounces thin egg noodles
1 1/2 teaspoons salt
1 clove of garlic, crushed
2 tablespoons oil
1/2 cup chopped onion
1/8 teaspoon pepper
1 pound pork, finely
  chopped
1/4 cup water

3 large tomatoes, sliced
2 teaspoons salt
1/4 cup chopped roasted
  peanuts
2 fried eggs, cut into strips
1/4 cup chopped green
  onions
6 slices lemon

Cook noodles according to package directions, adding 1 1/2 teaspoons salt; drain. Rinse with cold water; drain. Sauté garlic in oil in skillet until soft. Discard garlic. Add onion and pepper to oil. Sauté until tender. Add pork and 1/4 cup water; mix well. Simmer until pork is tender. Add tomatoes and 2 teaspoons salt. Cook until tomatoes are tender. Pour boiling water over noodles to reheat; drain. Stir noodles into pork mixture. Top with peanuts, fried egg strips, green onions and lemon slices. May substitute croutons for peanuts or chicken for pork. Yield: 8 servings.

Patti Roby

PORK STEW

4 pounds pork tenderloin, cubed
Salt and pepper to taste
Garlic powder to taste
1 large onion, chopped
3 stalks celery, chopped
1 large can stewed tomatoes

1 teaspoon cumin
1 tablespoon oregano
1 teaspoon Italian seasoning
2 large zucchini, sliced
2 cups water

Season pork with salt, pepper and garlic powder. Sauté pork and onion in skillet until pork is browned and onion is tender. Add celery, tomatoes, cumin, oregano and Italian seasoning; mix well. Simmer for 5 minutes. Combine zucchini and water in saucepan. Bring to a boil; reduce heat. Simmer for 5 minutes; do not drain. Add pork mixture to zucchini and water; mix well. Simmer for 15 minutes or until pork and vegetables are tender. Yield: 8 to 12 servings.

Betty Krueger

★ Be sure to trim all visible fat from pork before cooking and drain well after cooking. Most pork recipes can be prepared by substituting chicken for pork.

SWEET AND SOUR PORK

1¹/₂ pounds pork shoulder,
  cut into thin strips
2 tablespoons oil
¹/₄ cup water
2 tablespoons cornstarch
¹/₂ teaspoon salt
¹/₄ cup packed brown
  sugar
¹/₄ cup vinegar

1 cup pineapple juice
1 tablespoon soy sauce
³/₄ cup thinly sliced green
  bell pepper
¹/₄ cup sliced onions
1 20-ounce can pineapple
  chunks, drained
2 tablespoons Kitchen
  Bouquet

Brown pork in oil in skillet; reduce heat. Add water. Simmer, covered, for 1 hour. Combine cornstarch, salt, brown sugar, vinegar, pineapple juice and soy sauce in bowl; mix well. Pour over pork. Let stand for 15 minutes. Add green pepper, onions and pineapple chunks. Simmer for 4 to 5 minutes longer. Stir in Kitchen Bouquet. Serve over rice or Chinese noodles. Yield: 4 servings.

Rhonda Cronin

OKINAWA SWEET AND SOUR PORK

1 8-ounce can pineapple
  tidbits
1¹/₂ pounds pork shoulder,
  cubed
1 tablespoon oil
1 teaspoon salt

Pepper to taste
¹/₂ cup barbecue sauce
1 tablespoon cornstarch
2 tablespoons cold water
1 green bell pepper, cut
  into strips

Drain pineapple, reserving syrup. Add enough water to syrup to measure ³/₄ cup. Brown pork in oil in skillet. Season with salt and pepper. Add syrup and barbecue sauce; mix well. Simmer, covered, for 45 minutes or until pork is tender. Stir in mixture of cornstarch and 2 tablespoons cold water. Cook until thickened, stirring constantly. Add pineapple and green pepper; mix well. Heat to serving temperature. Serve over rice or noodles. Yield: 4 servings.

Yocianne Everett

RED CABBAGE WITH APPLES AND GERMAN SAUSAGE

2 tablespoons sugar
1/4 cup bacon drippings
1 small onion, chopped
4 cups shredded red
  cabbage

2 tart apples, sliced
2 tablespoons vinegar
1/2 teaspoon caraway seed
Salt and pepper to taste
6 links German sausage

Brown sugar in bacon drippings in large skillet, stirring constantly. Add onion; mix well. Cook over low heat until onions are slightly brown. Add cabbage, apples, vinegar, caraway seed, salt and pepper. Arrange sausage over top. Simmer for 45 minutes to 1 hour or until tender, adding enough water, stock or red wine to prevent sticking. May use white cabbage, 1/4 cup sugar and 1 tablespoon vinegar if preferred. Yield: 6 servings.

Lillian Muller

GERMAN REUBEN CASSEROLE

6 medium potatoes,
  chopped, cooked
1 16-ounce can
  sauerkraut, drained
1/2 cup Thousand Island
  salad dressing

1 pound smoked sausage,
  sliced
2 tablespoons chopped
  parsley
3/4 cup cubed Swiss
  cheese

Combine potatoes, sauerkraut, salad dressing, sausage, parsley and half the cheese in greased 2-quart baking dish. Bake at 350 degrees for 25 to 30 minutes. Top with remaining cheese. Bake for 5 minutes longer. Yield: 4 servings.

Gladys Miller

★ If you eat one less pat of butter daily for a year, you
  will lose three pounds.

BLACK-EYED PEAS AND SAUSAGE

1/2 pound sausage
2 tablespoons chopped
  onion
1   16-ounce can black-
  eyed peas

1 tablespoon
  Worcestershire sauce

Brown sausage in skillet, stirring until almost done; drain. Add onions; mix well. Cook for 3 minutes longer. Stir in black-eyed peas and Worcestershire sauce. Simmer for 15 minutes. Yield: 4 servings.

Rea W. Yates

POLISH SAUSAGE ALL-IN-ONE-DINNER

2 pounds Polish sausage
4 to 5 medium potatoes
1 medium green bell
  pepper
4 to 6 carrots
1 to 2 onions

1 medium head cabbage
1   16-ounce can French-
  style green beans
1/2 teaspoon salt
1/2 teaspoon pepper
1 cup water

Slice sausage and potatoes. Cut green pepper and carrots into strips. Cut onions and cabbage into quarters. Layer sausage, potatoes, green pepper, carrots, onions and cabbage in large saucepan. Add salt, pepper and water. Bring to a boil; reduce heat. Simmer, covered, for 35 to 45 minutes or until vegetables are tender. Yield: 6 servings.

Ann Schmitt

★ Diet programs can include sausage occasionally if the sausage is cooked well and drained very well.

MY MOM'S HASH

2 pounds pork sausage
2 onions, chopped
2 16-ounce cans kidney
  beans

2 16-ounce cans Shoe
  Peg corn
Salt and pepper to taste

Brown sausage in skillet until partially done, stirring until crumbly. Add onions; mix well. Cook until onions are tender. Add beans, corn, salt and pepper. Simmer for 20 to 30 minutes or to desired consistency, stirring occasionally. Serve over toast or biscuits. May substitute cream-style corn for Shoe Peg corn. Yield: 6 servings.

Thomas Waldrop

SAUSAGE LASAGNA

2 pounds sausage
2 12-ounce cans tomato
  paste
1 12-ounce can tomato
  purée
2 tomato paste cans water
2 teaspoons chili powder
1 teaspoon garlic powder
1 tablespoon onion flakes

2 tablespoons Italian
  seasoning
Salt and pepper to taste
1 16-ounce package
  lasagna noodles
8 ounces cottage cheese
2 6-ounce packages
  sliced mozzarella cheese

Brown sausage in large skillet, stirring until crumbly. Add tomato paste, tomato purée, water, chili powder, garlic powder, onion, Italian seasoning, salt and pepper. Bring to a boil; reduce heat. Simmer, covered, for 15 minutes, stirring occasionally. Cook lasagna noodles according to package directions, using a small amount of oil; drain. Alternate layers of noodles, cottage cheese, cheese slices and sauce in 2-quart baking dish until all ingredients are used. Bake at 350 degrees for 25 to 45 minutes or until hot and bubbly. Let stand for 5 minutes before serving. Undercook noodles slightly for easier handling. Yield: 6 to 8 servings.

Joy Keller

SCRAMBLED EGGS WITH CHEESE

6 eggs, beaten
1 tablespoon butter

4 slices Velveeta cheese
Salt and pepper to taste

Cook eggs in butter in skillet until almost set, stirring frequently. Add cheese, stirring until cheese is melted and eggs are set. Season with salt and pepper. Yield: 3 servings.

Janet Arnold

EGG AND BACON CASSEROLE

1/4 cup butter
4 cups unseasoned
   croutons
2 cups shredded Cheddar
   cheese
2 cups milk

8 eggs, beaten
1/2 teaspoon dry mustard
1   12-ounce package
   bacon, crisp-fried,
   crumbled

Place butter in 7x11-inch baking dish. Melt at 325 degrees for 5 minutes. Tilt dish to coat well. Add croutons; top with cheese. Combine milk, eggs and mustard in bowl; mix well. Pour into prepared dish; sprinkle with bacon. Bake at 325 degrees for 40 to 50 minutes or until eggs are set and cheese is melted. Yield: 6 to 8 servings.

Margaret Blandford

PEG'S EGG SCRAMBLE

8 slices bacon, chopped
2 tablespoons chopped
   onion
1 teaspoon salt
1/4 teaspoon pepper

3 large potatoes, boiled,
   peeled, cubed
6 eggs
1/2 cup shredded Cheddar
   cheese

Cook bacon in skillet until crisp, stirring frequently; drain, reserving 3 tablespoons drippings. Add onion, salt, pepper and potatoes to reserved bacon drippings in skillet. Cook for 5 minutes or until potatoes are golden brown, stirring frequently. Add unbeaten eggs; mix well. Stir in cheese. Cook until eggs are set and cheese is melted, stirring gently. Yield: 4 to 6 servings.

Kris Russell

NEW ZEALAND TOASTIES

Bread slices
Softened butter
1 cup chopped fresh
  mushrooms

2 cups shredded Monterey
  Jack cheese
5 slices bacon, chopped
1 egg

Toast and butter bread. Mix mushrooms, cheese, bacon and egg in bowl. Spread on toast. Place on baking sheet. Bake at 400 degrees until mixture is brown and bubbly. May substitute 1 finely chopped onion for mushrooms. Yield: 8 to 12 servings.

Melanie Bond

CHEESE PUDDING

1 cup crushed saltines
1/4 cup butter
1/4 cup flour
2 cups milk
1/2 teaspoon salt
1/4 teaspoon pepper

8 ounces American
  cheese, shredded
4 hard-boiled eggs, finely
  chopped
1   7-ounce jar pimentos,
  chopped

Sprinkle crushed saltines in greased 8x8-inch baking dish. Melt butter in saucepan. Add flour; mix well. Remove from heat. Add milk gradually, stirring until smooth. Return to heat. Cook until thickened, stirring constantly. Add salt and pepper; mix well. Layer sauce, cheese, eggs and pimentos 1/2 at a time in prepared dish. Top with additional buttered crumbs. Bake at 350 degrees for 25 minutes. Yield: 6 servings.

Dorothy Marshall

★ Cheese is a valuable part of a balanced diet but be
  aware that it is high in fat.

GREEN CHILIES AND RICE CASSEROLE

3 cans cream of chicken
  soup
3 to 4 cups sour cream
1 onion, chopped

2 4-ounce cans chopped
  green chilies
3 cups minute rice, cooked
Shredded Cheddar cheese

Combine soup, sour cream, onion and chilies in bowl; mix well. Fold in rice. Spoon into large baking dish. Top with cheese. Bake at 350 degrees for 30 minutes. Yield: 10 servings.

Linda Geary

NEW ZEALAND MACARONI AND CHEESE

1½ cups macaroni
2 tablespoons butter
2 tablespoons flour
1 cup milk
Salt and pepper to taste
Cayenne pepper to taste

1½ cups shredded
  Monterey Jack cheese
1 onion, grated
Bread crumbs
2 slices crisp-fried bacon
  crumbled

Cook macaroni using package directions; drain. Melt butter in saucepan; stir in flour. Cook for 1 minute, stirring constantly. Add milk gradually; stir until smooth. Cook over medium heat until thickened, stirring constantly. Add seasonings, cheese and onion. Stir until cheese is melted, adding additional milk if necessary. Pour over macaroni; mix well. Spoon into baking dish. Top with bread crumbs and bacon. Bake at 350 degrees for 20 minutes. Yield: 4 servings.

Andrew Both

BAKED MACARONI AND CHEESE

1 cup macaroni, cooked
3 eggs, beaten
3 cups milk
Salt and pepper to taste

Paprika to taste (optional)
8 ounces Cheddar cheese,
  cubed
2 tablespoons margarine

Combine with macaroni, eggs, milk, seasonings and cheese in bowl. Spoon into 2-quart casserole; dot with margarine. Bake at 350 degrees for 40 minutes or until set. Yield: 4 servings.

Patia Lee Hanlin

TEN-MINUTE SKILLET MACARONI

4 slices bacon
1/2 cup chopped onion
1/4 cup chopped green bell
  pepper
1 can cream of celery soup

1 cup shredded American
  cheese
2 tablespoons chopped
  pimentos
4 cups cooked macaroni

Fry bacon in skillet until crisp. Remove bacon to paper towel to drain; crumble. Sauté onion and green pepper in bacon drippings in skillet until tender. Add soup, cheese and pimentos; mix well. Cook until cheese is melted, stirring constantly. Add macaroni and bacon. Heat to serving temperature. Yield: 8 servings.

Joette Calhoun

CHEDDAR JACK QUICHE

1 unbaked 9-inch pie shell
1 cup sliced mushrooms
1/3 cup chopped onion
2 tablespoons margarine
2 tablespoons dry bread
  crumbs
1 cup shredded Swiss
  cheese
1/2 cup shredded sharp
  Cheddar cheese

5 eggs
1/2 cup mayonnaise
1/2 cup whipping cream
2 tablespoons minced
  parsley
1 teaspoon Dijon mustard
1 jalapeño pepper,
  seeded, minced
1/2 teaspoon salt
1/4 teaspoon white pepper

Bake pie shell at 425 degrees for 10 minutes or until lightly browned. Cool. Sauté mushrooms and onion in margarine in skillet until onion is tender and liquid is absorbed. Sprinkle bread crumbs in baked pie shell. Layer cheeses and mushroom mixture over bread crumbs. Combine eggs, mayonnaise, whipping cream, parsley, mustard, jalapeño pepper, salt and white pepper in bowl; mix well. Pour into pie shell. Bake at 375 degrees for 30 minutes or until quiche tests done. Yield: 6 to 8 servings.

Bernidea Fort

QUICHE

1 unbaked 9-inch pie shell
1 cup shredded sharp
  Cheddar cheese
1 cup shredded Swiss
  cheese
1 tablespoon flour
1/4 cup chopped green bell
  pepper

1/4 cup chopped onion
1/2 cup chopped
  mushrooms (optional)
3 eggs, beaten
3/4 cup milk
2 cups chopped cooked
  spinach

Bake pie shell at 350 degrees for 8 minutes. Combine Cheddar cheese, Swiss cheese and flour in large bowl; mix well. Mix green pepper, onion and mushrooms in medium bowl. Add eggs, milk and spinach; mix well. Pour into cheese mixture; mix well. Spoon into pie shell. Bake at 350 degrees for 1 hour. Let stand for 10 minutes before slicing. May substitute other vegetables or meat for spinach. Yield: 6 servings.

Pam Ford

REAL MEN DON'T EAT QUICHE

4 eggs
1 can cream of celery soup
1/2 cup light cream
1 cup shredded Cheddar
  cheese
6 slices crisp-fried bacon
  crumbled

1/2 cup chopped cooked
  spinach
1 unbaked 9-inch pie shell
Nutmeg to taste

Beat eggs in mixer bowl until foamy. Add soup and cream gradually, mixing well. Layer cheese, bacon and spinach in pie shell. Pour soup mixture over top; sprinkle with nutmeg. Bake at 350 degrees for 50 minutes or until center is set. Let stand for 10 minutes before serving. Yield: 6 servings.

Frank Fendley

HAM QUICHE

3 eggs
3/4 cup buttermilk baking
  mix
1/2 cup milk
1　10-ounce package
  frozen broccoli, thawed

1 cup shredded Cheddar
  cheese
1 cup sliced mushrooms
1/4 to 1/2 cup chopped onion
1 cup chopped ham

Combine eggs, baking mix and milk in blender container; process until smooth. Layer broccoli, cheese, mushrooms, onion and ham in buttered quiche pan. Pour egg mixture over top. Bake at 350 degrees for 30 to 35 minutes or until set. Yield: 6 servings.

Brenda Collins

FINLAND RICE AND NUT STEAK

1 cup bread crumbs
1 1/2 cups heavy cream
1/3 cup melted butter
2 cups cooked rice
1 cup ground nuts

1 teaspoon salt
1/4 teaspoon pepper
3 eggs
1 egg yolk

Soak bread crumbs in cream in bowl for 5 minutes. Add butter, rice, nuts, salt, pepper and 3 eggs; mix well. Spoon into buttered 10-inch baking dish. Brush top with egg yolk. Bake at 350 degrees for 1 hour. Cut into 3/4-inch slices. Yield: 9 servings.

Gwen Bond

★ You cannot keep trouble from coming but you need not give it a chair to sit on.

HOLIDAY BREAKFAST

1 pound sausage, cooked,
  crumbled
6 slices bread, cubed
1 cup shredded sharp
  Cheddar cheese

2 cups milk
1 teaspoon salt
1 teaspoon dry mustard
8 eggs, slightly beaten

Combine sausage, bread and cheese in large bowl; mix well. Combine milk, salt, mustard and eggs in bowl; mix well. Pour over sausage mixture; toss lightly. Spoon into greased 9x13-inch baking dish. Chill for 12 hours. Bake at 350 degrees for 35 minutes. Yield: 12 servings.

Jeanne McReynolds

BREAKFAST PIZZA

1 pound pork sausage
1 8-count package
  refrigerator crescent rolls
1 cup frozen hashed
  brown potatoes, thawed
1 cup shredded sharp
  Cheddar cheese

5 eggs
1/4 cup milk
1/2 teaspoon salt
1/4 teaspoon pepper
2 tablespoons Parmesan
  cheese

Brown sausage in skillet, stirring until crumbly; drain. Unroll crescent roll dough. Separate into 8 triangles. Arrange over bottom and up side of 12-inch pizza pan; seal edges. Spoon sausage over crust. Sprinkle with potatoes and cheese. Beat eggs, milk, salt and pepper in mixer bowl until smooth. Pour over top. Sprinkle with Parmesan cheese. Bake at 375 degrees for 25 to 30 minutes or until brown. Yield: 6 to 8 servings.

Patricia J. Tudor

BREAKFAST SOUFFLÉ

1 1/2 pounds pork sausage
3 slices bread
9 eggs, beaten
3 cups milk

1 1/2 teaspoons dry mustard
1 teaspoon salt
1 1/2 cups shredded
  Cheddar cheese

Brown sausage in skillet, stirring until crumbly; drain. Spoon into greased 9x13-inch baking dish. Cut bread into 1/8-inch cubes. Combine eggs, milk, mustard, salt, cheese and bread in bowl; mix well. Spoon over sausage. Chill, covered, overnight. Bake, uncovered, at 350 degrees for 1 hour or until set. Yield: 12 servings.

Kris Russell

SAUSAGE AND EGG BAKE

1 pound sausage
6 to 7 slices bread
1 can sliced mushrooms,
  drained
2 cups shredded Cheddar
  cheese

6 eggs
2 cups milk
1 teaspoon dry mustard
1/2 teaspoon celery seed
1 teaspoon oregano

Brown sausage in skillet, stirring until crumbly; drain. Cut bread into 1/2-inch cubes; place in lightly greased 8x12-inch baking dish. Layer sausage, mushrooms and cheese over bread. Combine remaining ingredients in bowl; mix well. Pour over cheese layer. Chill, covered, for 8 hours to overnight. Bake, uncovered, at 325 degrees for 40 to 45 minutes or until golden brown. Serve immediately. Yield: 6 to 8 servings.

Margaret Blandford

MICROWAVE EGG AND SAUSAGE CASSEROLE

1 pound pork sausage
2 1/4 cups milk
10 eggs
1 1/2 teaspoons dry mustard

1/2 teaspoons salt
1 1/2 cups shredded
  Cheddar cheese
3 slices white bread, cubed

Crumble sausage into large glass bowl. Microwave, covered with plastic wrap, on High for 5 to 6 minutes or until no longer pink, turning bowl once; drain. Add milk, eggs, dry mustard, salt, cheese and bread; mix well. Pour into two 8-inch round glass baking dishes. Microwave 1 dish at a time on Defrost for 15 to 18 minutes, stirring and turning dish every 3 minutes. Microwave on High for 3 minutes. Yield: 8 servings.

Trudie Gadjen

POULTRY

CUTTY'S CHICKENS

1½ cups margarine
2 to 3 tablespoons garlic
  powder
3 to 4 tablespoons
  cayenne pepper
2 to 3 tablespoons black
  pepper
2 cups water
½ cup salt
1 4-ounce bottle of liquid
  smoke

4 cups red cider vinegar
10 chickens, cut into halves
½ cup margarine
½ teaspoon red pepper
2 teaspoons salt
1 teaspoon black pepper
3 tablespoons liquid
  smoke
¼ cup Worcestershire
  sauce
32 ounces catsup

Melt 1½ cups margarine in saucepan. Add garlic powder, cayenne pepper, 2 to 3 tablespoons black pepper and water; mix well. Add ½ cup salt, 4-ounce bottle of liquid smoke and vinegar; mix well. Bring to a boil. Keep warm over low heat. Dip chicken halves into sauce mixture. Place on grill over very hot coals. Grill chicken for 1½ hours or until tender, basting frequently with sauce and turning every 15 minutes or as necessary to insure even cooking and prevent burning. Combine remaining ½ cup margarine, red pepper, 2 teaspoons salt, 1 teaspoon black pepper, 3 tablespoons liquid smoke, Worcestershire sauce and catsup in saucepan; mix well. Bring to a boil. Simmer for 10 minutes, stirring occasionally. Serve as dipping sauce for chicken. Sauce is also good with pork. Yield: 20 servings.

John Randolph "Cutty" Reid

GRILLED CHICKEN

2 whole chickens
Juice of 3 lemons

1 cup melted butter
1 tablespoon salt

Cut chickens into halves. Combine lemon juice, butter and salt in bowl; mix well. Baste chicken halves with sauce. Place on grill over low coals. Grill until tender, basting frequently.
Yield: 4 servings.

Percy L. Wilkerson

BARBECUED CHICKEN

3 tablespoons catsup
2 tablespoons vinegar
1 tablespoon lemon juice
2 tablespoons water
2 tablespoons melted
  butter

3 tablespoons brown sugar
1 teaspoon salt
1 teaspoon chili powder
1 teaspoon paprika
1/2 teaspoon red pepper
1 chicken

Combine catsup, vinegar, lemon juice, water, butter, brown sugar, salt, chili powder, paprika and red pepper in bowl; mix well. Dip chicken into sauce to coat well. Place in 9x13-inch baking dish. Bake at 500 degrees for 15 minutes. Reduce temperature to 300 degrees. Bake for 1 1/4 hours longer.
Yield: 2 servings.

Patricia R. Henson

OVEN BARBECUED CHICKEN

1 3-pound chicken, cut up
1 cup water
1/2 cup catsup
3 tablespoons brown sugar

1 tablespoon
  Worcestershire sauce
1 1/2 teaspoons salt
1/8 teaspoon chili powder

Arrange chicken pieces skin side up in foil-lined 9x13-inch baking dish. Combine water, catsup, brown sugar, Worcestershire sauce, salt and chili powder in bowl; mix well. Pour over chicken. Bake, uncovered, at 400 degrees for 1 hour.
Yield: 4 to 6 servings.

Bettie Sue Wallace

★ Footprints in the sands of time were not made by sitting down.

CHICKEN CACCIATORE

1 tablespoon flour
1 oven cooking bag
1 3-pound chicken, cut up
1 teaspoon salt
1/4 teaspoon pepper
1 teaspoon paprika
1 cup thinly sliced onion
1 cup chopped green bell
  pepper

1 12-ounce can tomatoes
1/4 cup flour
1/4 teaspoon basil
1 teaspoon oregano
1/2 teaspoon garlic powder
1 tablespoon parsley flakes
1 bay leaf
1 1/2 teaspoons sugar
1/2 cup dry red wine

Sprinkle 1 tablespoon flour into oven cooking bag. Place bag in 9x13-inch baking dish. Wash chicken and pat dry. Season with salt and pepper; sprinkle with paprika. Place onion, green pepper and chicken in prepared cooking bag. Drain tomatoes, reserving juice. Arrange tomatoes around chicken. Combine remaining 1/4 cup flour and reserved tomato juice in bowl; mix well. Stir in seasonings, bay leaf, sugar and wine. Pour into cooking bag. Seal bag. Cut six 1/2-inch slits in top of bag. Bake at 350 degrees for 1 hour and 20 minutes. Remove from bag. Discard bay leaf. Serve with hot fluffy rice. Yield: 4 to 6 servings.

Roy Dobbs

CHICKEN CONTINENTAL

4 pounds chicken pieces
Flour
Butter
1 can cream of chicken
  soup
1 teaspoon salt
1/8 teaspoon thyme

1/2 teaspoon celery flakes
2 tablespoons chopped
  onion
1 tablespoon chopped
  parsley
1 1/3 cups water
1 1/3 cups minute rice

Roll chicken in flour to coat. Brown in butter in skillet. Combine next 6 ingredients in saucepan; mix well. Stir in water gradually. Bring to a boil, stirring constantly. Remove from heat; reserve 1/3 cup soup mixture. Pour rice into shallow 2-quart casserole. Stir remaining soup mixture into rice; top with chicken. Pour reserved soup mixture over chicken. Bake, covered, at 375 degrees for 30 minutes. Yield: 6 servings.

Linda Berg

MOIST AND CRISPY CHICKEN

3 cups crispy rice cereal
1 teaspoon paprika
1/2 teaspoon salt

1/4 teaspoon pepper
1 chicken, cut up
1/2 cup mayonnaise

Combine cereal, paprika, salt and pepper in large plastic food bag; shake to mix. Brush chicken with mayonnaise. Place chicken pieces 1 at a time in bag; shake to coat well. Place on rack in broiler pan. Bake at 425 degrees for 40 to 45 minutes or until golden brown and tender. Yield: 4 to 6 servings.

Shirley Smith

FAVORITE BAKED CHICKEN

1 can cream of mushroom
  soup
1 can cream of celery soup
1 can cream of chicken
  soup

1/4 cup melted butter
1/2 cup French dressing
1 cup uncooked rice
6 to 8 chicken pieces,
  skinned

Combine soups, butter and dressing in bowl; mix well. Place rice in 9x13-inch baking dish. Pour 1/3 of the soup mixture over rice. Arrange chicken over rice and soup layers. Spoon remaining soup mixture over chicken. Bake at 325 degrees for 2 1/2 hours. Yield: 3 to 4 servings.

Jean Real

★ Supermarkets now sell packages of chicken parts or combinations of pieces that just meet your requirements without waste.

LAVEINE'S CHICKEN AND DUMPLINGS

**4 to 5 pounds chicken,
  cut up
Salt and pepper to taste
3 cups unsifted flour**

**1/2 teaspoon salt
6 tablespoons shortening
2 tablespoons chicken fat
2/3 cup chicken broth**

Season chicken with salt and pepper to taste. Simmer in water to cover in saucepan until well done. Remove chicken from broth; keep warm. Cool broth. Skim fat from broth, reserving 2 tablespoons. Combine flour, 1/2 teaspoon salt, shortening and reserved chicken fat in bowl; mix well. Add enough broth to make a firm dough. Shape into ball; divide into 4 portions. Roll dough on floured surface to 1/8-inch thick. Cut into 1x2-inch strips; place on waxed paper. Repeat with remaining dough. Bring broth to a boil. Drop dumpling strips into boiling broth one at a time; stir. Reduce heat. Simmer, covered, for 20 minutes.
Yield: 6 to 8 servings.

Billie Y. Weatherington

CHICKEN AND DUMPLINGS

**1 chicken, cut up
2 to 3 bouillon cubes
2 cups flour**

**1/4 teaspoon baking
  powder**

Simmer chicken in water to cover in saucepan until tender. Remove chicken from broth; bone. Add bouillon cubes to broth; stir well. Stir in chicken. Combine flour and baking powder in bowl. Add enough water to make soft dough. Roll dough on floured surface to 1/8-inch thick; cut in squares. Bring broth to a boil. Drop dumplings in boiling broth. Reduce heat. Simmer for 15 to 20 minutes or until tender. Yield: 4 servings.

Helen Yaeger

SLUMGUMS

²/₃ cup flour   ¹/₂ teaspoon salt
1 egg   Chicken broth

Combine flour, egg and salt in bowl; mix well. Knead on floured surface until smooth and elastic. Roll thin. Let stand for 1 hour. Cut into thin strips. Drop into boiling broth in saucepan. Cook over low heat for 30 to 45 minutes. Yield: 4 servings.

Maxine Beavin

ISLAND BROILED CHICKEN

2 chickens, split   1 clove of garlic, minced
1 cup oil   1 teaspoon oregano
¹/₃ cup lemon juice   ¹/₂ teaspoon salt
3 tablespoons soy sauce   ¹/₄ teaspoon pepper

Wash chicken and pat dry. Place in 9x13-inch baking pan. Combine oil, lemon juice, soy sauce, garlic, oregano, salt and pepper in bowl; mix well. Pour over chicken. Marinate in refrigerator for 4 to 5 hours. Place on rack in broiler pan. Broil until golden brown, basting occasionally with marinade. Yield: 4 servings.

Sandi Tipton Clark

LEMON BAKED CHICKEN

1   2¹/₂ to 3-pound   1 clove of garlic, crushed
    chicken, cut up   Salt-free spice/herb blend
1 tablespoon fresh lemon   to taste
    juice   Dash of pepper
1 tablespoon olive oil   Chopped parsley

Arrange chicken in shallow casserole. Combine lemon juice, oil, garlic, and seasonings in bowl; mix well. Pour over chicken. Bake, covered, at 350 degrees for 40 minutes or until tender, basting occasionally. Bake, uncovered, for 10 minutes longer or until browned. Sprinkle with parsley. Yield: 4 servings.

Betty Jo Daniel

CHICKEN POTPIE

1 whole chicken
1/2 cup melted margarine
Salt and pepper to taste
1   16-ounce can mixed
   vegetables
1 can cream of chicken
   soup
Flour
1 onion, chopped

1 teaspoon (heaping)
   chicken bouillon granules
1 stalk celery, chopped
Sage to taste
2 2/3 cups flour
1 teaspoon salt
1 cup shortening
Ice water
Butter

Wash chicken and pat dry; place in baking dish. Drizzle with melted margarine; season with salt and pepper. Bake at 350 degrees for 1 hour. Bone chicken; place chicken in saucepan. Add mixed vegetables and soup; mix well. Cook over medium heat until heated through, stirring frequently. Blend enough flour with a small amount of water to thicken to desired consistency. Stir into saucepan. Add onion, bouillon granules, celery, sage and additional salt and pepper to taste. Combine 2 2/3 cups flour and 1 teaspoon salt in bowl. Cut in shortening until crumbly. Moisten with a small amount of ice water to make consistency of biscuit dough. Divide into 2 portions. Roll each on floured surface. Fit 1 portion into buttered baking dish. Add chicken mixture. Top with remaining dough; dot with butter. Bake at 350 degrees for 1 hour or until golden brown. Yield: 12 servings.

Chrissy Robey

SWEET AND SOUR CHICKEN

1 tablespoon cornstarch
1 tablespoon cold water
1/2 cup sugar
1/2 cup soy sauce
1/4 cup vinegar
1 clove of garlic, minced
1/2 teaspoon MSG

1/2 teaspoon ginger
1/4 teaspoon pepper
1   2 to 2 1/2-pound chicken,
   cut up
1   16-ounce can pineapple
   spears, drained

Combine cornstarch and water in saucepan; mix well. Add sugar, soy sauce, vinegar, garlic, MSG, ginger and pepper; mix well. Cook over medium heat until thickened, stirring constantly.

Brush chicken with glaze; place skin side down in greased shallow baking dish. Bake at 425 degrees for 30 minutes, basting every 10 minutes. Turn chicken skin side up. Bake for 20 minutes. Add pineapple spears. Bake for 10 minutes longer or until tender. Wings will cook more quickly. Yield: 4 to 6 servings.

Jenny Corp

BAKED CHICKEN WITH MUSHROOMS

1/4 **cup flour**
1/2 **teaspoon salt**
1/4 **teaspoon pepper**
1 **teaspoon paprika**
6 **chicken breasts**
1/4 **cup butter**

1 **can cream of chicken soup**
1 **4-ounce can sliced mushrooms**
3 **tablespoons Sauterne**

Combine flour, salt, pepper and paprika in paper bag. Shake chicken breasts 1 at a time in flour mixture to coat. Melt butter in shallow casserole. Arrange chicken skin side down in casserole. Bake at 400 degrees for 30 minutes or until brown on underside. Combine soup, mushrooms and Sauterne in bowl; mix well. Turn chicken; pour wine mixture over top. Bake for 15 minutes longer or until bubbly. Yield: 6 servings.

Helen Lovan

BAKED CHICKEN AND WINE

4 **to 6 chicken breasts**
Butter
1 **can cream of mushroom soup**

1 **can cream of celery soup**
1 **soup can white wine**

Sauté chicken breasts in a small amount of butter in skillet until browned. Arrange chicken in shallow baking dish. Combine mushroom soup, celery soup and wine in bowl; mix well. Pour over chicken. Bake at 350 degrees for 1 to 1 1/2 hours or until tender. Yield: 4 to 6 servings.

Sue Settle

BREADED BAKED CHICKEN BREASTS

2 cups dry bread crumbs
1/2 to 1 teaspoon salt
1/2 to 1 teaspoon pepper
1 to 2 teaspoons garlic
   powder

1/2 teaspoon basil
1/2 teaspoon sage
1/2 cup Parmesan cheese
1/2 cup melted margarine
6 chicken breast filets

Combine crumbs, salt, pepper, garlic powder, basil and sage in bowl; mix well. Combine cheese and melted margarine in small bowl; mix well. Dip chicken filets into margarine mixture; coat with crumb mixture. Roll up; secure with toothpicks. Place in baking pan; sprinkle with remaining crumb mixture. Bake at 350 degrees for 45 minutes. May substitute mixture of cornflake crumbs and stuffing crumbs for bread crumbs. Yield: 6 servings.

Dena Sue Montgomery

CHICKEN CASSEROLE

4 chicken breasts
1 can cream of mushroom
   soup
1/2 cup milk

1 package Uncle Ben's
   wild rice with herbs
1 envelope dry onion soup
   mix

Place chicken breasts in casserole dish. Combine mushroom soup, milk, rice and onion soup mix in bowl; mix well. Pour over chicken. Bake at 350 degrees for 1 hour. Yield: 4 servings.

Barbara Struck

CHICKEN WITH RICE

2/3 to 1 cup minute rice
1 can cream of chicken
   soup

3 or 4 chicken breasts
1/2 envelope dry onion
   soup mix

Combine rice and chicken soup in bowl; mix well. Spread in baking dish. Arrange chicken over rice mixture. Sprinkle with onion soup mix. Bake at 325 degrees for 1 1/2 hours.
Yield: 3 to 4 servings.

Shirley Smith

CHINESE CHICKEN

3 tablespoons soy sauce
1 tablespoon orange juice
  concentrate
1 tablespoon minced fresh
  ginger

1 tablespoon oil
2 scallions, minced
4 chicken breast filets
2 to 3 cups cooked rice
Snow peas

Combine soy sauce, orange juice concentrate, ginger, oil and scallions in bowl; mix well. Add chicken; coat well. Marinate for several minutes. Place chicken on rack in shallow roasting pan. Bake at 450 degrees for 15 minutes. Serve with hot rice and snow peas. Garnish rice with minced green onions.
Yield: 4 servings.

Wanda Wiegand

COUNTRYSIDE CHICKEN

1 cup uncooked rice
1 cup sliced celery
3/4 onion, chopped
2 teaspoons parsley flakes
1/2 teaspoon salt
1/8 teaspoon pepper

1 can cream of mushroom
  soup
3/4 cup mayonnaise-type
  salad dressing
1 1/4 cups water
4 chicken breast filets

Place rice in baking dish. Combine celery, onion, parsley, salt and pepper in bowl; mix well. Spoon over rice. Combine soup and salad dressing in bowl. Add water; mix well. Pour half the soup mixture over the vegetable mixture. Arrange chicken on top. Pour remaining soup mixture over chicken. Bake at 350 degrees for 1 hour. Yield: 4 servings.

Mrs. Vernon (Sandy) Ortenzi

★ Save money by boning chicken breasts yourself. Freeze chicken slightly to make the job easier.

CHICKEN AND CASHEWS

1 cup bouillon
1 to 2 tablespoons
  cornstarch
2 tablespoons soy sauce
2 tablespoons peanut oil
1 clove of garlic
2 chicken breast filets

4 green onions, chopped
8 ounces pea pods
8 ounces mushrooms
1 8-ounce can bamboo
  shoots, drained
1/2 cup cashews

Cut chicken filets into slivers. Combine bouillon, cornstarch and soy sauce in bowl; mix well. Heat oil in wok. Add garlic. Cook until brown; discard garlic. Add chicken. Stir-fry for 1 to 2 minutes; push to side of wok. Add green onions. Stir-fry for 1 minute; push to side of wok. Repeat with pea pods, mushrooms and bamboo shoots. Add soy sauce mixture. Cook until thickened, stirring constantly. Mix all ingredients together; add cashews. Serve over hot cooked rice or chow mein noodles. Yield: 4 servings.

Joan Echsner

HOMEMADE CHICKEN CORDON BLEU

2 chicken breast filets
Salt and pepper to taste
2 slices ham
2 slices Swiss cheese

Flour
1 egg, beaten
Cornflake crumbs
Butter

Flatten chicken filets with meat mallet. Sprinkle with salt and pepper; layer with ham and cheese. Fold over to enclose filling. Dredge in flour; dip into egg. Coat with cornflake crumbs. Cook in a small amount of butter in skillet until brown on both sides. Remove from skillet; place on baking sheet. Bake at 350 degrees until tender. Yield: 2 servings.

Rhonda Austin

CROCK•POT CHICKEN PARISIENNE

6 chicken breasts
Salt, pepper and paprika
   to taste
1 can cream of mushroom
   soup

1/2 cup dry white wine
1   4-ounce can sliced
   mushrooms, drained
1 cup sour cream
1/4 cup flour

Sprinkle chicken breasts lightly with salt, pepper and paprika. Place in Crock•Pot. Combine soup, wine and mushrooms in bowl; mix well. Pour over chicken. Sprinkle with additional paprika. Cook on High for 2 1/2 to 3 1/2 hours (on Low for 6 to 8 hours). Remove chicken 30 minutes before serving. Combine sour cream and flour in bowl; mix well. Spoon into Crock•Pot; mix well. Cook for 30 minutes longer or until heated through. Spoon sauce over chicken. Serve with rice or noodles. Yield: 6 servings.

Robbie Lowery

POULET DIJONNAISE

4 chicken breast filets
Salt and freshly ground
   pepper to taste
2 tablespoons butter

1/4 cup Dijon mustard
1 cup whipping cream

Cut chicken into long thin strips. Sprinkle with salt and pepper. Melt butter in skillet; add chicken. Sauté over medium heat for 5 minutes or until golden brown. Remove to heated dish. Stir mustard into skillet; scraping drippings from bottom of skillet. Add whipping cream, stirring rapidly with wire whisk. Reduce heat to low. Cook until sauce is thick and smooth, stirring frequently. Add chicken; mix gently. Serve over hot rice or spinach noodles. Yield: 4 servings.

Wanda Wiegand

CHICKEN DIVAN

2 chicken breasts
1 10-ounce package
  frozen broccoli, thawed
1 can cream of chicken
  soup
1/4 cup chicken broth

1/2 cup mayonnaise
1/2 teaspoon curry powder
1 teaspoon lemon juice
Bread crumbs
1/2 cup shredded sharp
  Cheddar cheese

Cook chicken in water to cover in saucepan until tender. Remove chicken; reserve 1/4 cup broth. Place broccoli in casserole. Bone chicken; arrange over broccoli. Combine soup, reserved broth, mayonnaise, curry powder and lemon juice in bowl; mix well. Pour over chicken. Sprinkle with crumbs and cheese. Bake at 350 degrees for 30 minutes. Yield: 2 servings.

Ladonna Darnell, Marty Hill

GOURMET CHICKEN BREASTS

1 2-ounce jar dried beef
12 chicken breast filets
12 slices bacon

1 can cream of mushroom
  soup
2 cups sour cream

Layer dried beef in bottom of casserole. Wrap chicken filets with bacon slices. Arrange over dried beef. Combine soup and sour cream in bowl; mix well. Spoon over chicken. Bake at 275 degrees for 3 hours. Garnish with slivered almonds.
Yield: 12 servings.

Linda Broyles, Juyne Bushart
Jane Wallace

CHICKEN PARMIGIANA

8 chicken breast filets
2 eggs, beaten
1 cup Italian-style bread
  crumbs
1/4 cup olive oil

1 15-ounce jar spaghetti
  sauce with meat
1/2 cup Parmesan cheese
1 cup shredded mozzarella
  cheese

Dip chicken into eggs; coat with bread crumbs. Cook chicken in olive oil in skillet until brown on both sides. Pour spaghetti sauce into 7x11-inch baking dish. Place chicken in sauce. Sprinkle with cheeses. Bake at 400 degrees for 15 minutes or until cheese is melted and lightly browned.
Yield: 4 servings.

Patricia J. Tudor

PARMESAN CHICKEN

1 teaspoon Parmesan cheese
1 teaspoon flour

1 chicken breast, skinned
2 teaspoons melted low-calorie margarine

Combine cheese and flour in bowl; mix well. Dredge chicken in cheese mixture to coat. Place in small casserole. Pour melted margarine over top. Bake at 350 degrees for 1 hour.
Yield: 1 serving.

Jean Geary

CHICKEN BREAST WITH PINEAPPLE

4 chicken breast filets
Salt and pepper to taste
Flour
Oil

4 slices pineapple
2 tablespoons margarine
2 tablespoons cornstarch
2 cups pineapple juice

Season chicken with salt and pepper. Dredge in flour to coat. Cook chicken in oil in skillet until tender; drain. Arrange pineapple slices on chicken breasts. Melt margarine in saucepan; stir in cornstarch. Add pineapple juice gradually. Cook until thickened, stirring constantly. Pour over chicken.
Yield: 4 servings.

Sally Trent

ONE-DISH CHICKEN AND POTATO DINNER

4 chicken breasts
Salt to taste
1   16-ounce can tiny peas,
    drained

3 potatoes, sliced
1 tablespoon onion flakes
1 can cream of mushroom
    soup

Place chicken in large casserole. Sprinkle with salt. Add layers of peas, potatoes and onion. Spoon soup over top. Bake, covered, at 375 degrees for 1 hour or until chicken and potatoes are tender. Yield: 4 servings.

Clara Nance

PRINCESS CHICKEN

1 pound chicken breasts
2 tablespoons cornstarch
1 tablespoon soy sauce
1 tablespoon rice wine
2 tablespoons soy sauce
1 tablespoon sugar
1 teaspoon salt
1 teaspoon cornstarch
1 teaspoon sesame oil

1 cup oil
10   1-inch dried hot red
    peppers, stems removed
1 teaspoon Szechuan
    peppercorns
1 teaspoon minced fresh
    gingerroot
1/2 cup chopped roasted
    peanuts

Bone chicken; pound lightly with meat mallet. Cut into 1-inch pieces. Mix 2 tablespoons cornstarch and 1 tablespoon soy sauce in bowl. Add chicken; mix well. Let stand for 30 minutes. Combine rice wine, 2 tablespoons soy sauce, sugar, salt, 1 teaspoon cornstarch and sesame oil in bowl; mix well. Heat oil in wok over high heat for 1 minute. Stir-fry chicken for 2 minutes or until very lightly browned. Remove chicken, draining well over wok. Pour oil from wok, reserving 2 tablespoons. Heat reserved oil in wok over medium heat. Stir-fry red peppers and peppercorns until red peppers turn dark brown. Add gingerroot and cooked chicken. Stir-fry for 1 minute. Add rice wine sauce; mix well. Cook until sauce thickens slightly, stirring constantly. Remove wok from heat. Stir in peanuts. Yield: 6 to 8 servings.

Joan Echsner

CHICKEN AND RICE SOUR CREAM DREAM

1 cup uncooked rice
6 chicken breast filets
3 tablespoons butter
1/4 cup chopped onion
1 small package slivered
  almonds
1 4-ounce can
  mushrooms, drained

1 can cream of mushroom
  soup
1/2 cup chicken broth
3/4 cup sour cream
1 teaspoon salt

Cook rice using package directions. Cut chicken breasts into thirds. Cook chicken in butter in skillet until brown on both sides. Remove chicken. Sauté onion and almonds in pan drippings in skillet. Combine rice, sautéed mixture and mushrooms in 2-quart casserole. Arrange chicken over rice mixture. Combine soup, broth, sour cream and salt in saucepan; mix well. Bring to a simmer, stirring constantly. Pour over chicken. Bake at 400 degrees for 45 minutes. May substitute sautéed fresh mushrooms for canned mushrooms. Yield: 6 servings.

Gayle Sheffer

CHICKEN SALSA

4 chicken breast filets
2 tablespoons oil
1 cup sliced fresh
  mushrooms
1/2 bunch green onions,
  chopped

1 cup heavy cream
3 tablespoons Mexican
  salsa
3 to 4 cups cooked
  spinach noodles
1/4 cup Parmesan cheese

Cut chicken filets into thin strips. Heat oil in large skillet. Add chicken, mushrooms and onions. Cook over high heat until chicken turns opaque. Remove chicken mixture from skillet. Pour cream into skillet. Bring to a rapid boil. Boil rapidly until cream is reduced by half and is very thick, stirring constantly. Remove from heat; add salsa and chicken mixture; mix well. Pour over hot cooked noodles. Sprinkle with Parmesan cheese.
Yield: 4 to 6 servings.

Wanda Wiegand

SMOTHERED CHICKEN BREASTS

4 whole chicken breasts,
  skinned
Garlic salt to taste
1/2 cup butter, sliced
2 cans cream of
  mushroom soup
1/4 cup sour cream
1 large can French-fried
  onions

Arrange chicken in baking dish. Sprinkle with garlic salt. Place small pats of butter on each chicken breast. Spread soup over top. Spoon 1 tablespoon sour cream onto each. Sprinkle with onions. Bake at 350 degrees for 1 1/4 hours.
Yield: 4 to 8 servings.

Wilma Crook

SPICY RUBBED CHICKEN

1 teaspoon thyme
1 teaspoon oregano
1/4 teaspoon cayenne
  pepper
1/4 teaspoon ground
  coriander
1/8 teaspoon allspice
1 1/2 teaspoons salt
4 chicken breast filets
1 tablespoon olive oil

Combine thyme, oregano, cayenne, coriander, allspice and salt in bowl; mix well. Pat spice mixture over chicken; coat completely. Heat oil in large skillet with ovenproof handle. Cook chicken over high heat for 2 minutes or until brown on both sides. Bake at 450 degrees for 10 minutes. Remove to heated serving plate. Serve with baked sweet potatoes and cooked greens.
Yield: 4 servings.

Wanda Wiegand

STIR-FRY CHICKEN

1 pound chicken breast
   filets
2 tablespoons sliced fresh
   ginger
2 teaspoons seasoned salt
1/4 cup packed brown
   sugar
1 teaspoon pepper
1 teaspoon sesame oil
1 tablespoon vegetable oil
3/4 cup sliced onion
2 tablespoons soy sauce
2 tablespoons fresh lemon
   juice

Cut chicken filets into small strips. Place in dish; sprinkle with ginger. Chill in refrigerator for 2 hours. Remove ginger. Add seasoned salt, brown sugar and pepper; mix well. Heat sesame oil and vegetable oil in wok. Add chicken mixture. Stir-fry until 3/4 cooked. Add onion and soy sauce. Stir-fry until chicken is tender. Drizzle with lemon juice; mix gently. Remove from heat.
Yield: 4 servings.

Shirley Smith

SUNSHINE CHICKEN

2 to 3 teaspoons curry
   powder
1/2 teaspoon salt
1/4 teaspoon pepper
6 chicken breast filets
11/2 cups orange juice
1 cup uncooked rice
3/4 cup water
1 tablespoon brown sugar
1 teaspoon dry mustard
3/4 teaspoon salt
Chopped parsley

Combine curry powder, 1/2 teaspoon salt and pepper in bowl; mix well. Press into both sides of chicken filets. Combine orange juice, rice, water, brown sugar, mustard and remaining 3/4 teaspoon salt in large skillet; mix well. Arrange chicken filets over rice mixture. Bring to a boil; reduce heat. Simmer, covered, for 20 minutes. Remove from heat. Let stand, covered, for 5 minutes or until liquid is absorbed. Sprinkle parsley over top.
Yield: 6 servings.

Bernice J. Mills

TRIPLE VEGETABLE CHICKEN

1/2 pound eggplant, cut
  into 2-inch strips
1 1/2 cups sliced
  mushrooms
1 green bell pepper, cut
  into 1-inch cubes
1/4 teaspoon crushed red
  pepper

1 clove of garlic, minced
2 tablespoons olive oil
4 chicken breast filets, cut
  into 1-inch pieces
2 cups vegetable juice
  cocktail
2 tablespoons cornstarch
Hot cooked rice

Sauté eggplant, mushrooms, green pepper, red pepper and garlic in hot oil in skillet until tender-crisp. Add chicken. Cook until chicken is tender, stirring constantly. Reduce heat to low. Stir in vegetable juice and cornstarch. Cook until thickened, stirring constantly. Serve over hot cooked rice. Yield: 5 servings.

Wanda Wiegand

CHINESE RICE

1 cup chopped onion
1 cup chopped green
  onions
1/4 cup oil
3 cups cold cooked rice

2 cups chopped cooked
  chicken breast
4 eggs, slightly beaten
1/4 cup soy sauce

Sauté onion and green onions in oil in skillet until tender. Add rice. Cook until heated through, stirring constantly. Add chicken, eggs and soy sauce. Cook until eggs are set, stirring constantly. Yield: 4 servings.

Bernadette Mills

★ Happiness is like jam; you can't spread even a little without getting some on yourself.

QUICK AND EASY WAR SU GAI

1½ cups buttermilk
  baking mix
1 egg
Milk
Oil for deep frying
1 package chicken breast
  filets, cut into pieces
1½ cups water

1 can chicken broth
2 tablespoons soy sauce
2 to 3 thinly sliced green
  onions
⅓ cup cornstarch
Lettuce, shredded
Slivered almonds

Combine baking mix and egg in bowl; mix well. Add enough milk to make thick batter. Heat oil in deep skillet. Dip chicken into batter. Fry in hot oil until golden brown. Drain on paper towels. Combine water, broth, soy sauce, green onions and cornstarch in microwave dish; mix well. Microwave on High for 10 to 12 minutes or until thickened and clear, stirring every 2 minutes. Place lettuce on dinner plates. Arrange chicken over lettuce; spoon sauce over chicken. Sprinkle with almonds. May also be served over hot cooked rice. Yield: 4 servings.

Sandi Griffie

CHEESY YORKSHIRE CHICKEN

2 tablespoons plus 2
  teaspoons oil
4 chicken breast filets
¾ cup flour
¾ teaspoon baking
  powder
½ teaspoon salt

1 cup evaporated skim milk
2 eggs, beaten
2 ounces Cheddar cheese,
  shredded
2 tablespoons minced
  onion
2 teaspoons parsley flakes

Pour oil into 3-inch deep, 12-inch round casserole. Add chicken; turn to coat well. Bake at 400 degrees for 40 minutes or until tender. Sift flour, baking powder and salt into mixer bowl. Beat in milk and eggs until smooth. Fold in cheese, onion and parsley. Spoon over chicken. Bake for 20 minutes longer or until puffed and browned. Yield: 4 servings.

Jean Geary

CHICKEN CASHEW

2 cups chopped cooked
chicken
1 can cream of mushroom
soup
1 can cream of chicken
soup
1 can cream of celery soup
1 large can mushroom
pieces

1 teaspoon finely chopped
onion
1 tablespoon chopped
celery
1 large can chow mein
noodles
1/4 cup chopped cashews

Combine chicken, soups, mushroom pieces, onion, celery, 2/3 the chow mein noodles and cashews in baking dish; mix well. Sprinkle with remaining noodles and additional cashews if desired. Bake at 375 degrees for 10 minutes. Reduce temperature to 325 degrees. Bake for 30 minutes longer.
Yield: 4 servings.

Jayne Roberts

CHICKEN AND BROCCOLI CASSEROLE

2 10-ounce packages
frozen broccoli
8 chicken thighs, cooked,
chopped
3 cans cream of chicken
soup
1 cup mayonnaise

1 1/2 teaspoons lemon juice
3/4 teaspoon curry powder
1/2 cup shredded sharp
cheese
1 teaspoon melted butter
1/2 cup bread crumbs

Cook broccoli using package directions; drain. Place in buttered casserole. Add chicken. Combine soup, mayonnaise, lemon juice and curry powder in bowl; mix well. Pour over chicken and broccoli layers. Sprinkle with mixture of cheese, butter and bread crumbs. Dot with additional butter. Garnish with paprika. Bake at 325 degrees for 30 to 40 minutes. Yield: 8 servings.

Mrs. Jewell D. Sivels

CRUNCHY CHICKEN CASSEROLE

2 large carrots, sliced
1 cup water
1/4 cup butter
1/4 cup flour
1 can chicken broth
1 cup shredded American
  cheese

4 cups chopped cooked
  chicken
1 2-ounce jar chopped
  pimentos
1/4 cup melted butter
1 cup herb-seasoned
  stuffing mix

Cook carrots in water in covered saucepan for 15 minutes; drain. Melt 1/4 cup butter in 3-quart saucepan. Add flour; mix well. Stir in broth. Cook over medium heat until thickened, stirring constantly; reduce heat. Add cheese; stir until cheese melts. Remove from heat. Add chicken, carrots and pimentos; mix well. Pour into shallow baking dish. Top with mixture of melted butter and stuffing mix. Bake, covered, at 375 degrees for 30 minutes. May substitute peas or a mixture of peas and carrots for carrots. Yield: 8 servings.

Margaret Taylor

STUFFING AND CHICKEN CASSEROLE

2 packages Stove Top
  corn bread stuffing mix
3/4 cup melted margarine
1 1/2 to 2 cups chicken
  broth
3 cups chopped cooked
  chicken
1/2 cup chopped onion

1/2 cup chopped celery
1/2 cup mayonnaise-type
  salad dressing
2 eggs, well beaten
1 1/2 cups milk
1/2 teaspoon salt
Shredded Cheddar cheese

Combine stuffing mix, margarine and broth in bowl; mix well. Press half the mixture over bottom of 9x13-inch baking dish. Combine chicken, onion, celery, salad dressing, eggs, milk and salt in medium bowl; mix well. Spoon into prepared dish. Top with remaining stuffing mixture. Bake at 325 degrees for 35 minutes. Sprinkle with Cheddar cheese. Bake for 10 minutes longer. Yield: 8 servings.

Johnnie Harper

CHICKEN AND ALMOND CASSEROLE

6 chicken breasts, cooked, chopped
1 tablespoon lemon juice
1 tablespoon grated onion
1 can cream of chicken soup
1/2 cup mayonnaise
6 ounces evaporated milk
3/4 cup toasted slivered almonds
Crushed potato chips

Combine chicken, lemon juice, onion, chicken soup, mayonnaise, evaporated milk and almonds in bowl; mix well. Spoon into greased baking dish. Top with crushed potato chips. Bake at 350 degrees for 25 to 30 minutes. Yield: 6 servings.

Laverne Hollingsworth

CHICKEN CASSEROLE

1 can cream of chicken soup
1 can cream of celery soup
1 1/2 cups mayonnaise-type salad dressing
1/2 cup chopped onion
1 chicken, cooked, chopped
1 package stuffing mix
Toasted slivered almonds

Combine soups, salad dressing and onion in saucepan; mix well. Bring to a boil; reduce heat. Add chicken; mix well. Place half the stuffing mix in bottom of 9x13-inch baking dish. Pour chicken mixture into prepared dish. Top with remaining stuffing mix. Sprinkle with slivered almonds. Bake at 350 degrees for 30 minutes. May substitute chicken breasts for whole chicken, canned onion rings for almonds or sour cream for salad dressing. Stuffing may be tossed lightly with 1/2 cup melted butter before layering. Yield: 8 servings.

Jenny Corp, Virginia Hodges
Betty Krueger, Patti Reece

EASY CHICKEN CASSEROLE

4 to 5 potatoes, peeled
3 to 4 chicken breast
   filets, cooked, chopped
1 can cream of mushroom
   soup

1 soup can evaporated
   milk
2 cups shredded cheese

Cook potatoes in a small amount of water until almost tender. Cool slightly; slice. Combine soup and milk in bowl; mix well. Alternate layers of potatoes, chicken, cheese and soup mixture in greased 2-quart baking dish until all ingredients are used. Bake, covered, at 300 degrees for 45 minutes or until potatoes are tender and soup mixture has thickened. May add green bell pepper and onion. Yield: 6 to 8 servings.

Betty Patterson

CHICKEN SUPPER CASSEROLE

3 cups chopped cooked
   chicken
1½ cups chopped celery
¾ cup sliced almonds
1 6-ounce can water
   chestnuts, drained
½ teaspoon salt
3 tablespoons lemon juice

2 tablespoons chopped
   onion
1½ cups mayonnaise
1 can cream of chicken
   soup
¾ cup shredded cheese
1½ cups crushed potato
   chips

Combine chicken, celery, almonds, water chestnuts, salt, lemon juice, onion, mayonnaise and soup in bowl; mix well. Pour into greased baking dish. Top with cheese and potato chips. Bake at 325 degrees for 45 minutes. Yield: 8 servings.

Roberta Walker

POTLUCK CASSEROLE

4 chicken breasts, cooked,
  chopped
1 can cream of chicken
  soup
1 can cream of mushroom
  soup

1 12-ounce can
  evaporated milk
1 16-ounce can mixed
  vegetables, drained
1 package Stove Top
  stuffing mix

Combine chicken, soups, milk and mixed vegetables in bowl. Spoon into 9x13-inch baking dish. Prepare stuffing using package directions. Spread over chicken mixture. Bake at 400 degrees for 45 minutes. Yield: 8 servings.

June B. Rice

SHARON'S WHITE CHILI

1 large jar white beans
2 chicken breasts, cooked,
  shredded
2 cups chicken broth
1 4-ounce can chopped
  green chilies
1 teaspoon salt

1 teaspoon mixed herbs
1/8 teaspoon pepper
1 teaspoon oregano
1 cup cooked rice
1 jar salsa
1 package shredded
  mozzarella cheese

Combine beans, chicken, broth, green chilies, salt, herbs, pepper and oregano in saucepan. Bring to a boil; reduce heat. Simmer for 15 minutes, stirring frequently. Add rice; mix well. Simmer for 5 minutes longer. Ladle into serving bowls. Top with salsa and mozzarella cheese. Yield: 8 servings.

Sharon Amshoff

CHINESE CHICKEN

1/4 cup margarine
1 large package frozen
  green peas, thawed
2 cans cream of chicken
  soup
1 can cream of celery soup
1 large carton sour cream

2 chickens, cooked,
  chopped
1 cup mayonnaise
1 can water chestnuts
1 can chow mein noodles
Butter cracker crumbs

Melt margarine in 9x13-inch baking dish. Add peas. Combine soups, sour cream, chicken, mayonnaise and water chestnuts in saucepan; mix well. Cook until heated through. Pour over peas. Top with chow mein noodles and cracker crumbs. Bake at 350 degrees for 30 minutes or until heated through. Yield: 8 servings.

Robert Casebier

CRESCENT CHICKEN

1 8-count package refrigerator crescent rolls
2 cups chopped cooked chicken

1 cup shredded Cheddar cheese
1 can cream of chicken soup

Separate crescent rolls. Spoon chicken and cheese onto each crescent; roll to enclose filling. Place in 9x13-inch baking dish. Prepare soup using package directions. Pour over rolls. Bake at 350 degrees for 30 minutes. Yield: 8 servings.

Jayne Roberts

SAVORY CHICKEN CRESCENTS

3 ounces cream cheese, softened
2 tablespoons melted margarine
2 cups chopped cooked chicken
2 tablespoons milk
1/4 teaspoon salt
1/4 teaspoon pepper

1 tablespoon minced onion
1 tablespoon minced pimento
1 8-count package refrigerator crescent rolls
1 tablespoon melted margarine
Croutons, crushed

Blend cream cheese and 2 tablespoons melted margarine in bowl. Add chicken, milk, salt, pepper, onion and pimento; mix well. Separate crescent rolls into 4 rectangles on baking sheet; seal perforations. Spoon 1/2 cup mixture onto center of each rectangle. Bring corners together in center; seal. Brush tops with 1 tablespoon melted margarine; top with croutons. Bake at 350 degrees for 25 minutes. Yield: 4 servings.

Pam Ford

CHICKEN AND SAUSAGE GUMBO

12 ounces chorizo sausage
2 tablespoons olive oil
1/4 cup flour
8 cups broth
1   14-ounce can tomatoes, chopped
2 cups chopped onions
1 cup chopped green bell pepper
1 cup chopped celery
2 cups sliced okra
1 tablespoon salt
2 cloves of garlic, mashed
2 teaspoons cayenne
2 teaspoons pepper
3 cups chopped cooked chicken
2 cups fresh oysters
Tabasco sauce
4 cups cooked rice

Brown chorizo in oil in soup pot. Remove sausage from pot. Chop into bite-sized pieces. Add flour to oil and sausage drippings. Heat over very low heat for 20 to 30 minutes or until brown, stirring frequently. Add broth gradually, stirring constantly. Stir tomatoes, onions, green pepper, celery, okra, salt, garlic, cayenne, pepper, chicken and sausage into broth mixture. Bring to a boil, stirring frequently; reduce heat. Simmer for 1 hour or until vegetables are tender and broth is thickened. Add oysters. Simmer for 10 minutes or until oysters are done. Serve with Tabasco sauce in shallow bowl over rice. May substitute any spicy sausage for chorizo. May omit oysters.
Yield: 8 to 10 servings.

Wanda Wiegand

CHICKEN À LA KING

1/2 cup chopped green bell pepper
1/2 cup sliced mushrooms
1/4 cup margarine
3 tablespoons flour
2 1/2 to 3 cups milk
3 cups chopped cooked chicken breast
Pimentos

Sauté green pepper and mushrooms in margarine in skillet until tender. Stir in flour until well mixed. Add milk. Cook over medium heat until thickened, stirring constantly. Add chicken and pimentos. Heat to serving temperature. Serve over toast.
Yield: 4 servings.

Carmen Stilger

STUFFED CHICKEN LEGS

1/2 cup sliced mushrooms
1/4 cup finely chopped
  onion
1/4 cup butter
1 pound Old English
  cheese

1/4 cup flour
1/4 teaspoon paprika
1/4 teaspoon MSG
8 chicken legs

Sauté mushrooms and onion in butter in skillet until tender. Melt cheese in double boiler. Add flour. Cook over boiling water until thickened, stirring constantly. Stir in mushrooms, onion, paprika and MSG. Remove from heat; cool. Cook chicken legs in boiling water to cover in saucepan until tender. Cool slightly. Remove bones from legs, leaving chicken intact. Fill cavity with cheese mixture. Place in greased baking dish. Bake at 350 degrees until heated through. Yield: 8 servings.

Madrid Shaw

MEDITERRANEAN TART

2 tomatoes, peeled,
  seeded, chopped
1 onion, chopped
3 tablespoons unsalted
  butter
1 cup sliced mushrooms
1/2 teaspoon thyme
2 tablespoons flour
1 cup chicken broth
1/2 teaspoon anchovy paste

1 chicken breast, cooked,
  chopped
8 ounces cooked ham,
  chopped
Salt and pepper to taste
16 phyllo sheets
3/4 cup melted butter
Melted butter
1/2 cup shredded cheese

Sauté tomatoes and onion in butter in skillet until tender. Add mushrooms and thyme. Sauté for 3 to 4 minutes longer. Stir in flour and broth. Bring to a boil; reduce heat. Simmer for 5 minutes or until thickened, stirring constantly. Add anchovy paste, chicken, ham, salt and pepper. Layer 8 sheets of phyllo, brushing each with butter in 9x13-inch baking dish. Add chicken mixture and cheese. Top with remaining 8 sheets buttered phyllo. Bake at 300 degrees for 1 hour or until brown. Yield: 8 servings.

Marty Hill

CREAMY AND CRUNCHY CHICKEN-RICE BAKE

1 10-ounce package
  frozen peas
1 8-ounce jar Cheez Whiz
1½ cups hot cooked rice

2 cups chopped cooked
  chicken
1 can French-fried onions

Cook peas using package directions; drain. Combine Cheez Whiz and rice in bowl; mix well. Add chicken, peas and half the French-fried onions; mix lightly. Pour into 1½-quart baking dish. Bake at 350 degrees for 15 minutes. Top with remaining onions. Bake for 5 minutes longer or until onions are brown. Yield: 4 to 6 servings.

Ethel Shephard

CHICKEN AND RICE CASSEROLE

1 package Uncle Ben's
  wild rice mix
4 chicken breasts
1 teaspoon salt
Pepper to taste
¼ cup chopped onion
½ cup margarine

¼ cup flour
1 6-ounce can
  mushrooms
½ cup evaporated milk
2 teaspoons parsley
1 small jar pimentos

Cook rice using package directions. Cook chicken with salt and pepper in water to cover in large saucepan for 45 minutes to 1 hour or until tender; drain, reserving broth. Cool slightly. Bone and chop chicken. Sauté onion in margarine in skillet until tender. Add flour; mix well. Drain mushrooms, reserving liquid. Add enough reserved broth to liquid to measure 1½ cups. Add to flour mixture. Cook over medium heat until thickened, stirring constantly. Stir in milk. Remove from heat. Add rice, chicken, parsley, pimentos and mushrooms; mix well. Pour into 2½-quart baking dish. Bake for 350 degrees 30 minutes. Yield: 6 to 8 servings.

Connie R. Adams

CRUNCHY CHICKEN WITH RICE

3 cups chopped cooked
  chicken
1 cup chopped celery
1/2 cup chopped walnuts
3/4 cup mayonnaise
1 can cream of mushroom
  soup
1/4 cup milk

3 tablespoons lemon juice
3 cups cooked rice
1 small onion, finely
  chopped
Salt and pepper to taste
3 cups crisp rice cereal
1/2 cup margarine

Combine chicken, celery, walnuts, mayonnaise, soup, milk, lemon juice, rice, onion, salt and pepper in 2 1/2-quart baking dish; mix well. Chill overnight. Sauté cereal in margarine in skillet until coated well. Spread over chicken mixture. Bake at 350 degrees until heated through and topping is brown. Yield: 8 servings.

Geneva Duckworth Muntz

HOT CHICKEN AND RICE SALAD

1 cup cooked instant rice
2 cups chopped cooked
  chicken
1 cup chopped celery
1 can cream of chicken
  soup

3/4 cup mayonnaise
1 8-ounce can sliced
  water chestnuts, drained
1 tablespoon minced onion
Crushed cornflakes

Combine rice, chicken, celery, soup, mayonnaise, water chestnuts and onion in bowl; mix well. Pour into greased 9x9-inch baking dish. Top with crushed cornflakes. Bake at 350 degrees for 30 minutes. Yield: 6 servings.

Edna Keys

HOT CHICKEN SALAD

2 cups chopped cooked
  chicken
1 cup chopped celery
2 eggs
1 8-ounce can sliced
  water chestnuts
1 tablespoon chopped
  onion

1/2 cup slivered almonds
1 can cream of mushroom
  soup
1 cup butter cracker
  crumbs
1 cup shredded Cheddar
  cheese

Combine chicken, celery, eggs, water chestnuts, onion, almonds and soup in 9x13-inch baking dish. Bake at 350 degrees for 15 minutes. Top with mixture of cracker crumbs and cheese. Bake for 15 minutes longer or until brown. May add mayonnaise, hard-boiled eggs, green bell pepper, or a combination of mushrooms and cream of chicken soup for variation. May substitute crushed potato chips for cracker crumbs and cheese topping. Yield: 6 to 8 servings.

Patsy Ford, Marlene Fowler
Mrs. Leonard C. Gatewood, Jayne Roberts

SNOW ON THE MOUNTAIN

3 tablespoons butter
3/4 to 1 cup flour
4 cups chicken broth
4 cups half and half
1 1/2 teaspoons salt
1/2 teaspoon pepper

8 cups chopped cooked
  chicken breast
3 to 4 cups fresh sliced
  mushrooms
Cooked rice

Melt butter in saucepan. Add flour; mix well. Stir in chicken broth, half and half, salt and pepper. Cook until thickened, stirring constantly. Add chicken and mushrooms; mix well. Heat to serving temperature; do not boil. Spoon over rice. Serve with various condiments such as chopped tomatoes, green onions, green bell pepper, celery, crushed pineapple, slivered almonds, unsweetened coconut, shredded radishes, chow mein noodles, chopped olives or shredded sharp Cheddar cheese. Yield: 16 servings.

Virginia Hodges

HOT CHICKEN SALAD SOUFFLÉ

2 slices white bread, cubed
2 cups chopped cooked
  chicken
1/4 cup chopped onion
1/2 cup chopped green bell
  pepper
1/2 cup chopped celery
1/2 cup mayonnaise
3/4 teaspoon salt

Pepper to taste
4 slices white bread
2 eggs, well beaten
1 1/2 cups milk
1 can cream of mushroom
  soup
1/2 cup shredded sharp
  cheese

Arrange bread cubes in bottom of greased 8x8-inch baking dish. Combine chicken, onion, green pepper, celery, mayonnaise, salt and pepper in bowl; mix well. Spread over bread cubes in baking dish. Top with bread slices. Pour mixture of eggs and milk over top. Chill overnight. Top with mushroom soup. Bake at 325 degrees for 50 minutes. Sprinkle with cheese. Bake for 10 minutes longer. Yield: 6 servings.

Gwen Mills

CHICKEN SPECTACULAR

1   6-ounce package long
  grain and wild rice mix
2 1/3 cups chicken broth
4 cups chopped cooked
  chicken
2 cups French-style green
  beans

1 can cream of celery soup
1/2 cup mayonnaise
1   8-ounce can water
  chestnuts, drained
2 tablespoons pimento

Cook rice according to package directions using chicken broth. Add chicken, green beans, soup, mayonnaise, water chestnuts and pimento; mix well. Pour into greased 1 1/2-quart baking dish. Bake at 350 degrees for 40 to 50 minutes or until heated through. May also add chopped onion. This recipe may be frozen before baking if desired. Yield: 6 servings.

Janice R. Boud, Roberta Walker

CHICKEN TETRAZZINI

12 ounces mushrooms,
  sliced
1 small green bell pepper,
  cut into strips
1/4 cup butter
3 tablespoons flour
2 teaspoons salt
1/4 teaspoon pepper
2 1/2 cups half and half
4 cups chopped cooked
  chicken
2 pimentos, chopped
2 tablespoons Sherry
2 egg yolks, slightly beaten
8 ounces thin spaghetti,
  cooked
Parmesan cheese

Sauté mushrooms and green pepper in butter in large skillet for 5 minutes. Blend in flour, salt and pepper. Add half and half. Cook over low heat until thickened, stirring constantly. Add chicken, pimentos and Sherry; mix well. Stir small amount of hot mixture into egg yolks; stir egg yolks into hot mixture. Place spaghetti in baking dish. Pour chicken mixture over spaghetti. Sprinkle with cheese. Bake at 300 degrees for 45 minutes. Yield: 6 servings.

Linda Chaney

CHICKEN TETRAZZINI WITH RIBBON MACARONI

1 3-pound chicken
2 cups water
1 cup dry white wine
2 carrots, chopped
1 medium onion, finely
  chopped
2 sprigs of parsley
1/2 teaspoon thyme
1 1/2 teaspoons salt
3 tablespoons butter
5 tablespoons flour
1/2 cup light cream
6 ounces Parmesan
  cheese
1 cup sliced mushrooms
1 tablespoon butter
2 quarts water
3 teaspoons salt
8 ounces ribbon macaroni

Combine chicken, 2 cups water, wine, carrots, onion, parsley, thyme and 1 1/2 teaspoons salt in saucepan. Bring to a boil; skim and reduce heat. Simmer, covered, for 40 minutes. Remove chicken; cool. Skin and bone chicken; cut into slices. Strain 3 cups broth. Combine 3 tablespoons butter and flour in medium saucepan. Stir in broth 1 cup at a time. Cook until

thickened, stirring constantly. Stir in cream. Cook for 5 minutes longer. Reserve a small amount of Parmesan cheese for topping. Stir in remaining cheese. Sauté mushrooms in 1 tablespoon butter in skillet until tender. Bring mixture of 2 quarts water and 3 teaspoons salt to a boil. Add macaroni. Cook just until tender. Drain. Rinse under running water; drain. Combine mushrooms and macaroni in large baking dish. Place chicken over macaroni mixture. Pour sauce over top. Sprinkle with reserved Parmesan cheese. Bake at 350 degrees for 15 minutes.
Yield: 6 to 8 servings.

Wilma Allen

CHICKEN SPAGHETTI WITH OLIVES

2 chicken bouillon cubes
2 cups water
2 onions
4 stalks celery
1 green bell pepper
Oil
1   15-ounce can stewed
   tomatoes
2   5-ounce cans chunk
   chicken
1   8-ounce package
   spaghetti, cooked
Salt and pepper to taste
1   4-ounce jar sliced
   mushrooms
1/2 cup green olives
1 cup shredded American
   cheese

Combine bouillon cubes and water in saucepan. Bring to a boil; reduce heat. Simmer until bouillon cubes dissolve, stirring occasionally. Chop onions, celery and green pepper. Sauté in a small amount of oil in large skillet until tender. Add broth and tomatoes; mix well. Simmer for 30 minutes, stirring occasionally. Stir in chicken, spaghetti and salt and pepper. Simmer until heated through. Add mushrooms, olives and cheese just before serving. Yield: 6 servings.

Aggie Burks

CHICKEN SPAGHETTI

1 chicken, cut up
2 20-ounce packages
　vermicelli
1/2 cup chopped onion
1/2 cup chopped celery
Oil
1 can cream of chicken
　soup

1 can cream of mushroom
　soup
1 can Ro-Tel tomatoes
1 1/2 pounds Velveeta
　cheese, cubed

Cook chicken in water to cover in large saucepan. Remove chicken. Cool slightly. Skin and bone chicken; chop into pieces. Cook vermicelli in chicken broth until tender; drain. Sauté onion and celery in a small amount of oil in skillet. Add chopped chicken, sautéed vegetables, soups, tomatoes and cheese to hot vermicelli; mix well. Pour into large casserole. Bake at 350 degrees until bubbly. Yield: 20 servings.

Norma Gray

CHICKEN PIE

1 5-pound chicken
4 to 5 hard-boiled eggs,
　sliced
1 8-ounce can
　mushrooms, drained
3 tablespoons chopped
　pimento

3 tablespoons chopped
　parsley
2 1/4 cups flour
2 teaspoons baking powder
1 teaspoon salt
1/3 cup shortening
3/4 cup milk

Cook chicken in water to cover in stockpot until tender. Remove chicken. Cool slightly. Cut into serving-sized pieces. Arrange chicken in 9x13-inch baking dish. Layer eggs, mushrooms and pimento over chicken. Sprinkle with parsley. Stir 1/4 cup flour into chicken broth in stockpot. Cook until thickened, stirring constantly. Pour over layers. Sift remaining 2 cups flour, baking powder and salt into bowl. Cut in shortening until crumbly. Add milk; mix well. Roll dough into thin rectangle on lightly floured surface. Cut with biscuit cutter. Place over layers in dish. Bake at 400 degrees for 15 minutes or until biscuits are brown. Yield: 8 servings.

Yocianne Everett

STUFFED CORNISH HENS

2 tablespoons minced
  onion
1/3 cup rice
2 tablespoons butter
1 tablespoon lemon juice
1/2 cup cream of celery
  soup, undiluted
1 teaspoon chopped
  chives

1 teaspoon parsley flakes
3/4 cup water
1 chicken bouillon cube
2　1 to 11/4-pound Cornish
  hens
Salt and pepper to taste
Melted butter

Sauté onion and rice in 2 tablespoons butter in saucepan until onions are tender and rice is golden. Add lemon juice, soup, chives, parsley flakes, water and bouillon cube. Bring to a boil; reduce heat to low. Simmer, covered, for 25 minutes. Remove giblets from hens. Wash hens and pat dry. Sprinkle cavities with salt and pepper. Stuff hens with rice mixture. Secure with wooden picks; truss. Place breast side up in roasting pan. Brush with melted butter. Roast, covered, at 375 degrees for 30 minutes. Roast, uncovered, for 1 hour, basting with melted butter and pan drippings. Yield: 2 servings.

Mary Mosier

TURKEY

TURKEY ARCADIA

1 package dry stuffing mix
1 cup melted butter
3 to 4 cups ground turkey
1 can cream of mushroom
  soup

1 can cream of celery soup
1　8-ounce can sliced
  water chestnuts
3 tablespoons minced
  onion

Combine stuffing mix and butter in bowl. Press half the mixture into bottom of 9x13-inch baking dish. Brown turkey in skillet, stirring until crumbly. Combine with soups, water chestnuts and onion in bowl. Spoon into prepared dish. Top with remaining stuffing mixture. Bake, covered, at 300 degrees for 45 minutes. Yield: 6 to 8 servings.

Ton Ali

TURKEY ASPARAGUS CASSEROLE

2 cups noodles
2 cups sliced cooked
  turkey
1/4 cup finely chopped
  green bell pepper

2 cans asparagus, drained
2 cans cream of chicken
  soup
1/2 cup milk
1 cup shredded cheese

Cook noodles using package directions; drain. Place in greased 9x13-inch baking dish. Layer turkey, green pepper and asparagus over noodles. Pour mixture of soup and milk over top. Sprinkle with cheese. Bake at 375 degrees until cheese is bubbly and beginning to brown. Yield: 6 servings.

Lois Barger

TURKEY CASSEROLE

1 tablespoon sugar
1 teaspoon salt
4 cups chopped cooked
  turkey
3/4 cup chopped celery
3/4 cup chopped green bell
  pepper
1/4 cup chopped pimento

1/4 cup chopped onion
1/4 cup lemon juice
1 cup mayonnaise
8 ounces Swiss cheese,
  shredded
1 can cream of mushroom
  soup
2 cups cracker crumbs

Combine sugar, salt, turkey, celery, green pepper, pimento, onion, lemon juice, mayonnaise, cheese, soup and 1 cup cracker crumbs in baking dish. Sprinkle with remaining 1 cup cracker crumbs. Bake at 350 degrees for 45 minutes.
Yield: 6 to 8 servings.

Nancy Winstead

TURKEY HASH

3 cups chopped onions
2 tablespoons butter
3 cups chopped cooked
  turkey

3 cups giblet gravy
Salt and pepper to taste
Turkey dressing

Sauté onions in butter in skillet until tender. Add turkey, gravy, salt and pepper. Simmer to desired consistency. Shape leftover dressing into walnut-sized balls. Drop dressing balls into hash. Heat to serving temperature. Spoon dressing balls onto serving plates. Spoon hash over top. Yield: 6 servings.

Mary Cook

HOT TURKEY SALAD

4 cups chopped cooked
  turkey
2 cups chopped celery
4 hard-boiled eggs,
  chopped
3/4 cup mayonnaise
3/4 cup cream of chicken
  soup

1 teaspoon minced onion
2 teaspoons lemon juice
1 teaspoon salt
1 small jar pimentos
1 cup crushed potato chips
1 cup shredded cheese
2/3 cup slivered almonds

Combine turkey, celery, eggs, mayonnaise, chicken soup, onion, lemon juice, salt and pimentos in baking dish. Chill in refrigerator overnight. Top with mixture of crushed potato chips, cheese and almonds. Bake at 400 degrees for 20 minutes. Yield: 6 to 8 servings.

Joseph B. Snodgrass

HOT TURKEY CASSEROLE

1 to 1 1/2 cups chopped
  cooked turkey
1/2 cup mayonnaise
1/2 can cream of chicken
  soup
1/2 can cream of
  mushroom soup
1/2 teaspoon minced onion

2 hard-boiled eggs,
  chopped
1   8-ounce can water
  chestnuts, drained
1/2 cup toasted sliced
  almonds
1/3 cup bread crumbs

Combine turkey, mayonnaise, soups, onion, eggs, water chestnuts and almonds in bowl; mix well. Pour into greased 1 1/2-quart baking dish. Sprinkle with bread crumbs. Bake at 350 degrees for 20 minutes. Yield: 6 servings.

Sandi Tipton Clark

TURKEY AND STUFFING BAKE

1/2 cup butter
1 1/4 cups boiling water
3 1/2 cups dry stuffing mix
1   3-ounce can French-
   fried onions
1 can cream of celery soup

3/4 cup milk
1 1/2 cups chopped cooked
   turkey
1   10-ounce package
   frozen peas

Melt butter in water. Pour over stuffing mix in bowl; mix well. Stir in half the French-fried onions; mix well. Press over bottom and side of 1 1/2-quart baking dish. Combine soup, milk, turkey and peas in bowl; mix well. Pour into prepared baking dish. Bake, covered, at 350 degrees for 30 minutes. Top with remaining onions. Bake, uncovered, for 5 minutes longer. May substitute leftover dressing for mixture of stuffing mix, butter and water. Yield: 4 to 6 servings.

Patricia J. Tudor

TURKEY ZUCCHINI LASAGNA

9 ounces ground turkey
2 cloves of garlic, crushed
2 teaspoons corn oil
2 cups canned tomatoes
1/2 cup tomato paste
1/4 cup water
1 package low-calorie beef
   broth and seasoning mix
1 tablespoon onion flakes
1/2 teaspoon basil
1/2 teaspoon oregano

1/2 teaspoon salt
1/4 teaspoon allspice
1/4 teaspoon pepper
1 package artificial
   sweetener
6 medium zucchini
1 1/3 cups ricotta cheese
6 ounces shredded
   mozzarella cheese
2 ounces Parmesan
   cheese

Brown turkey with garlic in oil in skillet, stirring until turkey is crumbly. Stir in next 10 ingredients. Bring to a boil; reduce heat. Simmer for 45 minutes, stirring occasionally. Remove from heat. Stir in sweetener; mix well. Steam zucchini until tender-crisp. Cool. Cut into 1/4-inch slices. Spray 9x13-inch baking dish with nonstick cooking spray. Alternate layers of sauce, zucchini and cheeses in baking dish until ingredients are used, beginning and ending with sauce. Bake at 350 degrees for 1 hour. Yield: 8 servings.

Jean Geary

SEAFOOD

FISH CHOWDER À LA PETE FOUNTAIN

1   6-ounce can minced
  clams
1 can cream of mushroom
  soup
1 can cream of celery soup
4 cups half and half

4 medium potatoes,
  chopped
1 small onion, chopped
1½ to 2 pounds fish fillets,
  cubed
½ cup butter

Combine clams, mushroom soup, celery soup, half and half, potatoes and onion in 5-quart stockpot; mix well. Bring to a slow boil, stirring constantly. Add fish. Return to a slow boil, stirring constantly. Cook for 20 minutes, stirring constantly. Add butter. Cook until butter melts, stirring constantly. To prevent clams from burning and sticking, continual stirring is necessary. May vary recipe by adding mushrooms, shrimp and crab meat. This recipe was given to me by Al Jorfe, an Illinois Bell telephone man, whose uncanny resemblance to the musician earned him the nickname Pete Fountain. Yield: 6 servings.

Gerald Turley

DEVILED BLUEGILL

1 cup milk
4 thick slices white bread,
  trimmed
½ cup butter
3 tablespoons chopped
  parsley
4½ teaspoons finely
  chopped onion
¾ teaspoon salt
Dash of pepper

Dash of Tabasco sauce
3 tablespoons
  Worcestershire sauce
1 teaspoon dry mustard
1 green bell pepper,
  chopped
1 pimento, finely chopped
4 cups flaked cooked
  Bluegill
Crushed cornflakes

Combine first 12 ingredients in large saucepan; mix well. Cook for 10 minutes, stirring constantly. Add fish. Cook for 5 minutes longer, stirring constantly. Spoon into shallow casserole; sprinkle with crushed cornflakes. Bake at 350 degrees for 10 to 15 minutes or until brown. Yield: 6 servings.

Henry Bennett

MICROWAVE HERB-BAKED FISH

2/3 cup saltine cracker
  crumbs
1/4 cup Parmesan cheese
1/2 teaspoon basil

1/2 teaspoon oregano
1/4 teaspoon garlic powder
1 pound whitefish
1/2 cup melted butter

Combine cracker crumbs, Parmesan cheese, basil, oregano and garlic powder in shallow dish; mix well. Dip fish into butter; coat with crumbs. Place in 9x13-inch glass baking dish. Microwave on High for 7 to 8 minutes or until fish flakes easily. Yield: 4 servings.

Ida L. Omer

BAKED FISH ROSENSTROM

4 whitefish fillets
2 eggs
3/4 cup shredded Monterey
  Jack cheese
1/2 teaspoon salt

1 clove of garlic, minced
1 tablespoon butter,
  softened
1 tablespoon chopped
  parsley

Arrange fish fillets in greased baking dish. Beat eggs in mixer bowl until light. Add cheese, salt, garlic, butter and parsley; mix well. Pour over filets. Bake, covered, at 400 degrees for 20 minutes or until fish flakes easily. Yield: 4 servings.

Beverly Both

MOTHER'S RED SNAPPER

1/2 cup flour
1 teaspoon salt
1/2 teaspoon pepper
1   4-pound red snapper
5 teaspoons (heaping)
  butter
1/2 cup chopped onion
1/4 cup chopped green bell
  pepper

1 1/2 cups chopped celery
3   14-ounce cans stewed
  tomatoes
2 bay leaves
1/8 teaspoon garlic powder
1/8 teaspoon red pepper
2 tablespoons
  Worcestershire sauce
Lemon wedges

Combine flour, salt and pepper in bowl; mix well. Rub red snapper inside and out with flour mixture. Place in greased baking dish. Melt butter in skillet. Add onion, green peppers and celery. Sauté until onion is transparent and vegetables are tender-crisp. Mix tomatoes, bay leaves, garlic powder, red pepper and Worcestershire sauce in bowl. Press through colander. Add to sautéed vegetables; mix well. Pour over red snapper. Bake at 350 degrees for 45 minutes. Garnish with lemon wedges. Yield: 6 servings.

Joyce Branham

BAKED ORANGE ROUGHY FILLETS

Melted butter
Orange Roughy fillets
Dillweed
Chopped chives
Red bell peppers, chopped

Green bell peppers,
  chopped
Dash of garlic powder
Lemon juice

Pour melted butter in shallow bowl. Dip fillets in butter. Arrange in baking dish. Sprinkle with dillweed, chives, red and green peppers and garlic powder. Drizzle with lemon juice. Bake at 350 degrees for 15 to 18 minutes or until fish flakes easily.

Aggie Burks

JANE'S SALMON

1   15-ounce can salmon
1 egg
1/2 cup flour

1 teaspoon (heaping)
  baking powder
Oil for deep frying

Drain salmon, reserving 1/4 cup liquid. Place salmon in bowl. Add egg; mix well. Stir in flour. Add baking powder to reserved salmon liquid in small bowl. Beat with fork until foaming has stopped. Pour into salmon mixture; mix well. Drop by teaspoonfuls into hot oil. Deep-fry until light brown. Remove from oil; drain. Yield: 2 servings.

Helen Lovan

SALMON CROQUETTES

1 15-ounce can salmon
1 small onion, finely
 chopped
1 tablespoon parsley
1/2 cup flour
1/2 cup buttermilk

2 eggs
1/4 teaspoon soda
2 tablespoons (heaping)
 shortening
3 dashes of
 Worcestershire sauce

Bone and finely mince salmon in bowl. Add onion, parsley, flour, buttermilk, eggs and soda 1 at a time, mixing well after each addition. Chill for several hours. Melt shortening in skillet. Drop salmon mixture by rounded tablespoonfuls into hot shortening. Fry until brown on both sides. Drain on paper towels. Serve hot. May eliminate chilling of salmon mixture before frying.
Yield: 4 servings.

Alice Ward

SALMON LOAF

1 15-ounce can salmon,
 drained, flaked
1/2 cup mayonnaise-type
 salad dressing
1 can cream of celery soup
1 cup dry bread crumbs
1 egg, beaten
1/2 cup chopped onion

1 tablespoon lemon juice
1 teaspoon salt
1/2 cup sour cream
1/2 cup mayonnaise-type
 salad dressing
1/2 cup finely chopped
 cucumber

Combine salmon, 1/2 cup salad dressing, soup, bread crumbs, egg, onion, lemon juice and salt in bowl; mix well. Spoon into greased 4x8-inch loaf pan. Bake at 350 degrees for 1 hour. Spoon sour cream into small bowl. Fold in remaining 1/2 cup salad dressing and cucumber. Serve with salmon loaf.
Yield: 8 servings.

Christy Michelle Lewis

SALMON STEAKS TERIYAKI

4 ½-inch thick salmon
  steaks
½ teaspoon sesame oil
4 teaspoons soy sauce

2 teaspoons lemon juice
1 clove of garlic, minced
1 tablespoon melted butter

Place salmon steaks in shallow baking dish. Combine oil, soy sauce, lemon juice and garlic in small bowl; mix well. Pour over steaks. Marinate for 20 minutes, turning occasionally. Remove steaks from marinade. Brush both sides with melted butter. Place on rack in broiler pan. Broil for 5 to 7 minutes on each side or until brown and flakes easily. Yield: 4 servings.

Ann Zimmerman

TUNA CAKES

2 6-ounce cans water-
  pack tuna
1 medium onion, chopped
3 egg whites

Black pepper to taste
1 stack saltine crackers,
  crushed
Oil

Drain and flake tuna in bowl. Add onion, egg whites, pepper and crushed crackers; mix well. Shape into patties. Cook in a small amount of oil in skillet over medium heat until light brown. May crush crackers in the package before opening. Yield: 4 servings.

Mary Beeler

TUNA CASSEROLE

1 can cream of mushroom
  soup
½ cup milk
2 hard-boiled eggs, sliced

1 6-ounce can tuna,
  drained
1 cup cooked peas
1 cup crushed potato chips

Combine soup and milk in 1-quart casserole; mix well. Stir in eggs, tuna and peas. Sprinkle with potato chips. Bake at 350 degrees for 30 minutes. Yield: 2 to 3 servings.

Dana Fendley

TUNA AND NOODLE CASSEROLE

1 medium onion, chopped
1/2 cup sliced celery
2 tablespoons butter
1 can cream of celery soup
1 soup can milk
1   6-ounce can tuna,
  drained, flaked

2 tablespoons chopped
  pimento
1   8-ounce package
  medium egg noodles
1/2 cup shredded Cheddar
  cheese

Sauté onion and celery in butter in saucepan over medium heat until tender. Stir in soup and milk; mix well. Remove from heat. Stir in tuna and pimento. Prepare noodles using package directions; drain. Fold into tuna mixture. Spoon into 2-quart casserole. Bake at 350 degrees for 25 minutes. Sprinkle with cheese. Bake for 5 minutes longer or until bubbly.
Yield: 6 servings.

Wilma Allen

ORIENTAL TUNA

2 onion bouillon cubes
3/4 cup boiling water
1 can cream of mushroom
  soup
1/2 cup chow mein noodles
1   6-ounce can tuna,
  drained

1 1/2 cups sliced celery
1/8 teaspoon pepper
2 tablespoons chopped
  pimento
Hot cooked rice
1/2 cup chow mein noodles

Dissolve bouillon cubes in water in skillet. Add soup, 1/2 cup chow mein noodles, tuna, celery and pepper; mix well. Bring to a boil, stirring constantly. Reduce heat. Simmer, covered, for 20 minutes. Stir in pimento. Spoon over hot rice. Sprinkle with remaining 1/2 cup chow mein noodles. Yield: 3 servings.

Terry White

SEAFOOD MOUSSE

2 tablespoons unflavored
  gelatin
1/2 cup cold water
16 ounces cream cheese,
  softened
1 can tomato soup
3 onions, minced
1/2 cup minced celery
1/2 cup sweet pickle relish
1 6-ounce can tuna,
  drained
1 15-ounce can salmon,
  drained, flaked
1 teaspoon Tabasco sauce
1/2 cup mayonnaise
Pinch of red pepper

Dissolve gelatin in cold water in bowl. Combine cream cheese and tomato soup in saucepan. Cook over medium heat until cheese melts, stirring constantly. Pour into gelatin; mix well. Let stand until cool. Combine onion, celery, relish, tuna, salmon, Tabasco sauce, mayonnaise and pepper in bowl; mix well. Add cooled gelatin mixture; mix well. Spoon into lightly greased fish-shaped mold. Chill until firm. Unmold onto serving plate. Garnish with olive for eye and green pepper for fins.
Yield: 8 servings.

Shirley Smith

CRAB SUPPER PIE

1 cup shredded Swiss
  cheese
1 unbaked 9-inch pie shell
1 7-ounce can crab meat,
  drained
2 green onions, sliced
3 eggs, beaten
1 cup light cream
1/2 teaspoon salt
1/2 teaspoon grated lemon
  rind
1/2 teaspoon dry mustard
1/4 cup sliced almonds

Sprinkle cheese over bottom of pie shell. Arrange crab meat over cheese layer. Sprinkle with onions. Combine eggs, cream, salt, lemon rind and mustard in bowl; mix well. Pour over layers. Sprinkle with almonds. Bake at 350 degrees for 45 minutes or until set. Yield: 6 servings.

Pete Manning

QUICK CRAB QUICHE

1 unbaked 9-inch pie shell
3 eggs, beaten
1 6-ounce can crab meat,
   drained, flaked
1 cup sour cream

1 3-ounce can French-
   fried onions, crushed
1/2 cup shredded sharp
   Cheddar cheese

Prick bottom and sides of pie shell with fork. Bake at 400 degrees for 6 minutes. Combine eggs, crab meat, sour cream and onions in bowl; mix well. Spoon into baked pie shell. Reduce oven temperature to 350 degrees. Bake for 35 minutes or until set. Let stand for 10 minutes before serving. Yield: 4 to 6 servings.

Janice Boud

DEVILED OYSTERS

2 quarts oysters
Oyster liquid
Oyster shells
1 cup bread crumbs
1 cup butter
1 onion, chopped
1 red bell pepper, chopped
1 green bell pepper,
   chopped

4 sweet pickles, chopped
1 egg
1 to 2 tablespoons
   Worcestershire sauce
Salt and pepper to taste
Paprika to taste
2 to 3 tablespoons minced
   parsley

Shell and drain oysters, reserving liquid and shells. Chop oysters. Cook bread crumbs in 2 tablespoons butter in skillet until crisp and brown, stirring constantly. Remove from skillet. Add remaining butter, oysters, onion, red pepper, green pepper, pickles, egg, Worcestershire sauce, salt, pepper, paprika and parsley to skillet; mix well. Cook for 10 minutes, stirring frequently. Add enough oyster liquid to make of desired consistency. Spoon into reserved oyster shells; place in baking dish. Chill for several hours. Sprinkle with reserved bread crumbs. Bake at 300 degrees for 40 minutes. Yield: 4 servings.

Gwen Mills

SCALLOPS NEWBURG

4½ teaspoons butter
1 pint scallops, finely
  chopped
½ cup sliced mushrooms
½ teaspoon salt
Dash of paprika

⅛ teaspoon nutmeg
2 tablespoons Sherry
2 egg yolks, beaten
½ cup half and half
6 slices bread, toasted

Melt butter in double boiler. Add scallops and mushrooms. Cook for 3 to 5 minutes, stirring constantly. Mix in salt, paprika, nutmeg and Sherry. Cook for 1 minute, stirring constantly. Remove from heat. Mix egg yolks and half and half in bowl. Add to scallop mixture; mix well. Return to heat. Cook for 1 minute or just until thickened, stirring constantly. Spoon over toast. Yield: 6 servings.

Lucy Davis

SHRIMP CREOLE

½ cup chopped onion
½ cup chopped celery
1 clove of garlic, minced
3 tablespoons oil
1 16-ounce can tomatoes
1 8-ounce can seasoned
  tomato sauce
1½ teaspoons salt
½ to 1 teaspoon chili
  powder

1 teaspoon sugar
1 tablespoon
  Worcestershire sauce
Dash of Tabasco sauce
1 teaspoon cornstarch
2 teaspoons water
12 ounces shrimp, shelled
½ cup chopped green bell
  pepper

Sauté onion, celery and garlic in hot oil in skillet just until vegetables are tender. Add tomatoes, tomato sauce, salt, chili powder, sugar, Worcestershire sauce and Tabasco sauce; mix well. Simmer, uncovered, for 45 minutes, stirring frequently. Dissolve cornstarch in water. Stir into sauce mixture. Cook until thickened, stirring constantly. Add shrimp and green pepper. Simmer, covered, for 5 minutes or until shrimp is cooked through. Serve with hot cooked rice. Yield: 5 to 6 servings.

Joan Echsner

SHRIMP KABOBS

1/2 cup soy sauce	Mushrooms
1/4 cup oil	Small onions
1/4 cup Sake	Cherry tomatoes
1 teaspoon ginger	Rice pilaf
1 1/2 pounds large shrimp, shelled	

Combine soy sauce, oil, Sake and ginger in bowl; mix well. Add shrimp. Marinate for 2 hours. Thread shrimp onto skewers alternately with mushrooms, onions and tomatoes. Place on rack in broiler pan. Broil for 10 to 12 minutes, turning frequently. Serve with hot rice pilaf. Yield: 6 servings.

Ed Jamison

MICROWAVE SHRIMP SCAMPI

1 pound shrimp, cleaned	1 1/2 cups water
1 onion, chopped	1 red pepper, chopped
4 to 6 cloves of garlic, minced	1 tablespoon lemon juice
	1/2 teaspoon salt
2 tablespoons butter	1 1/2 cups uncooked
1 envelope chicken gravy mix	minute rice
	1/4 cup chopped parsley

Combine shrimp, onion, garlic and butter in 7x12-inch glass baking dish. Microwave, covered, on High for 2 minutes. Combine gravy mix and water in bowl; mix well. Pour over shrimp mixture. Add pepper, lemon juice, salt and rice; mix well. Microwave, covered, on High for 7 to 8 minutes, stirring once. Let stand for 5 minutes. Stir in parsley. Yield: 4 servings.

Betty Krueger

SANDWICHES

ITALIAN BEEF

1 beef roast
1/2 teaspoon onion salt
1/2 teaspoon oregano
1/2 teaspoon Italian
 seasoning
1/2 teaspoon garlic salt

1/2 teaspoon basil
1/2 teaspoon seasoned salt
1 teaspoon MSG
1 teaspoon seasoned
 pepper

Cook roast in water to cover in Crock•Pot overnight. Shred into roasting pan, reserving 1 1/2 cups broth. Add seasonings to reserved broth in saucepan. Bring to a boil. Pour over shredded roast. Bake at 350 degrees for 30 minutes. Serve on French bread or steak rolls. Garnish with hot green peppers.

Judy Seitz

PIMENTO CHEESE

8 ounces shredded sharp
 Cheddar cheese
1 4-ounce jar pimentos
8 ounces small-curd
 cottage cheese

1/4 to 1/2 cup mayonnaise
2 or 3 drops of Tabasco
 sauce
1/2 teaspoon salt
1/2 teaspoon pepper

Combine Cheddar cheese, pimentos, cottage cheese, mayonnaise, Tabasco sauce, salt and pepper in bowl; mix well. Chill in airtight container in refrigerator. Yield: 4 cups.

Brenda Rates

★ Keep a variety of breads available for sandwiches. Wrap sliced bread in moisture-proof wrapping to freeze. Don't forget that English muffins, bagels, pita rounds and tortillas are suitable for sandwiches.

PIMENTO CHEESE SPREAD

1 12-ounce can
 evaporated milk
16 ounces American
 cheese, shredded
2 tablespoons vinegar
1/2 teaspoon dry mustard
1 7-ounce can pimentos,
 drained, chopped
1/2 teaspoon salt
Cayenne to taste (optional)

Heat evaporated milk in double boiler. Add cheese; stir until cheese is melted and mixture is smooth. Remove from heat. Cool, stirring frequently. Add vinegar, dry mustard, pimentos, salt and cayenne; mix until well blended. Store in covered container in refrigerator. Will keep for several weeks.

Judy Seitz

SWEET SANDWICH SPREAD

4 red bell peppers
4 green bell peppers
1 quart green tomatoes
1 cup water
1 1/2 cups sugar
1/4 cup (rounded) flour
2 tablespoons salt
1 cup vinegar
6 eggs, well beaten
1/4 cup mustard
1 cup sour cream
12 medium sweet pickles,
 chopped

Grind red peppers, green peppers and tomatoes. Combine with water in saucepan. Bring to a boil. Remove from heat; drain. Add sugar, flour and salt. Cook until sugar dissolves. Stir in vinegar gradually. Add eggs; mix well. Cook for 5 minutes. Stir in mustard and sour cream; mix well. Cook for 10 minutes longer. Add pickles. Simmer until heated through. Spoon into hot sterilized jars; seal with 2-piece lids.

Louisa Rosser

SANDWICH SPREAD

14 green bell peppers
6 red bell peppers
8 red onions
8 green tomatoes
Boiling water
1 1/2 cups vinegar
2 cups packed brown
 sugar
3 tablespoons mustard
6 tablespoons flour
4 cups mayonnaise-type
 salad dressing

Grind peppers, onions and tomatoes in food grinder. Cover with boiling water. Let stand for 10 minutes. Drain well. Combine with vinegar and brown sugar in saucepan; mix well. Bring to a boil; reduce heat. Simmer for 8 minutes. Stir in mixture of mustard and flour. Cook for 3 minutes longer. Add salad dressing. Cook for 4 minutes or to desired consistency. Spoon into hot sterilized 1-pint jars; seal with 2-piece lids.

Gwen Mills

BARBECUE SANDWICHES

2 pounds ground beef
1 large onion, chopped
2 tablespoons
   Worcestershire sauce
1/4 cup catsup
2 cans chicken gumbo
   soup
1 tablespoon mustard
Hamburger buns

Brown ground beef with onion in skillet, stirring until ground beef is crumbly; drain. Add Worcestershire sauce, catsup, soup and mustard; mix well. Simmer until heated through. Serve on buns. Yield: 24 sandwiches.

Pat Wilhelm

BARBECUE SAUCE AND MEAT

3 tablespoons margarine
1/3 cup minced onion
1 8-ounce bottle of catsup
1/3 cup vinegar
3 tablespoons brown sugar
1/2 cup water
1/8 teaspoon salt
1/2 teaspoon garlic powder
2 teaspoons prepared
   mustard
2 tablespoons
   Worcestershire sauce
1 2 to 3 pound roast,
   cooked, shredded
Hamburger buns

Melt margarine in large saucepan. Add onion, catsup, vinegar, brown sugar, water, salt, garlic powder, mustard and Worcestershire sauce; mix well. Bring to a boil; reduce heat. Simmer until onion is tender. Add shredded roast. Simmer until heated through. Serve on buns. Pork or beef roast can be used. Yield: 10 servings.

Maxine Beavin

COWBOY BEANS

2 pounds ground beef
1 cup finely chopped
  onion
1 cup finely chopped green
  bell pepper
1 cup finely chopped
  celery
1 cup water

1 clove of garlic, minced
1 cup catsup
2 tablespoons mustard
1½ teaspoons salt
1   46-ounce can pork and
    beans
Hamburger Buns

Brown ground beef in Crock•Pot, stirring until crumbly. Add onion, green pepper, celery and water; mix well. Cook on Low until water has evaporated and vegetables are tender. Stir in garlic, catsup, mustard, salt and pork and beans. Cook on High until bubbly. Simmer on Low until serving time. Serve on buns. Yield: 16 sandwiches.

Maxine Beavin

DAD'S HAMBURGERS

1 pound hamburger
¾ to 1 stack crackers,
  crushed

1 medium onion, chopped
3 egg whites
Salt and pepper to taste

Combine hamburger, cracker crumbs, onion, egg whites, salt and pepper in bowl; mix well. Shape into patties. Brown on both sides in skillet. Yield: 4 to 6 servings.

Mary Beeler

LASAGNA IN A BUN

¾ pound ground beef
1   8-ounce can tomato
    sauce
½ envelope dry onion
  soup mix
¼ teaspoon oregano

¼ teaspoon basil
1 egg, well beaten
¾ cup ricotta cheese
½ cup shredded
  mozzarella cheese
8   6-inch hard rolls

Brown ground beef in skillet, stirring until crumbly; drain. Add tomato sauce, dry soup mix, oregano and basil; mix well.

Cook, covered, over low heat for 5 minutes. Cook, uncovered, for 10 to 15 minutes longer, stirring frequently. Combine egg, ricotta cheese and mozzarella cheese in bowl; mix well. Cut thin slice from top of rolls. Hollow out centers leaving 1/2-inch shells. Spoon half the meat mixture into the rolls. Spread cheese mixture over meat layer. Top with remaining meat mixture. Cover with roll tops. Wrap each sandwich in foil. Bake at 400 degrees for 20 to 25 minutes or until heated through. Yield: 8 servings.

Patricia J. Tudor

SLOPPY JOES

1 pound ground beef
1 medium onion, finely
  chopped
1 teaspoon salt
1/8 teaspoon pepper
2 tablespoons flour

1 1/4 cups water
1/2 teaspoon
  Worcestershire sauce
3/4 cup catsup
8 sandwich rolls, split,
  heated

Brown ground beef with onion in skillet, stirring until ground beef is crumbly; drain. Season with salt and pepper. Stir in flour. Add water, Worcestershire sauce and catsup; mix well. Simmer for 15 to 20 minutes or until heated through, stirring frequently. Serve on rolls. Yield: 8 servings.

Antoinette Monroe

OLD-FASHIONED CONEY ISLAND SAUCE

1 pound ground beef
1 medium onion, chopped
3 tablespoons chili powder
1 teaspoon salt
3/4 teaspoon oregano

3/4 teaspoon cumin
1/4 teaspoon red pepper
  flakes
2 cups water
Tomato sauce to taste

Brown ground beef with onions in skillet, stirring until ground beef is crumbly; drain. Add chili powder, salt, oregano, cumin, red pepper flakes and water. Simmer for 1 hour. Add tomato sauce just before serving. Serve over grilled frankfurters. Garnish with shredded cheese. Yield: 6 to 8 servings.

Antoinette Monroe

CORN DOGS

2/3 cup cornmeal
1 cup flour
1 1/2 teaspoons baking
  powder
1 tablespoon sugar

1 teaspoon salt
3/4 cup milk
1 egg
1 pound frankfurters
Oil for deep frying

Combine cornmeal, flour, baking powder, sugar, salt, milk and egg in bowl; mix well. Cook frankfurters in water until done; drain on paper towels. Dip in batter to coat. Deep-fry until golden brown. Insert sticks after frying if desired. Yield: 8 to 10 servings.

Sam Young

PIGS IN A BLANKET

1 pound frankfurters
10 strips cheese

1 10-count package
  refrigerator biscuits

Split frankfurters lengthwise. Place cheese strip in each frankfurter. Roll biscuits to frankfurter length. Wrap around frankfurters; seal edges. Place on baking sheet. Bake at 350 degrees for 10 minutes. Yield: 5 servings.

Dana Fendley

MONTE CRISTO SANDWICH

2 slices white bread
Butter, softened
1 thin slice cooked ham
1 thin slice Swiss cheese
1 thin slice cooked chicken
1 thin slice American
  cheese

1 egg
Salt and pepper to taste
1 tablespoon cold water
1 tablespoon oil
Butter and oil for frying

Spread bread with softened butter. Layer ham, Swiss cheese, chicken and American cheese on 1 slice bread. Top with remaining slice bread. Press sandwich firmly together. Wrap in damp towel. Chill in refrigerator. Combine egg, salt, pepper, cold water and 1 tablespoon oil in small bowl; beat well with wire whisk. Dip sandwich in egg mixture, coating both sides. Brown sandwich in 1/8-inch mixture of butter and oil in skillet. Place in shallow baking dish. Bake at 350 degrees for 8 to 10 minutes. Drain on paper towels. Yield: 1 serving.

Buddy Cunningham

HAM AND SWISS CHEESE SANDWICHES

1/2 **cup margarine, softened**	2 **tablespoons poppy seed**
2 **tablespoons grated**	**Sandwich rolls**
onion	**Cooked ham**
2 **tablespoons horseradish**	**Swiss cheese**

Combine margarine, onion, horseradish and poppy seed in small bowl; mix well. Spread mixture on rolls. Top with ham and Swiss cheese. Wrap each sandwich in foil. Bake at 350 degrees until heated through and cheese is melted.

Virginia Emmitt

HOT CHICKEN AND CHEESE HEROES

2 **cups cooked chopped**	1 **teaspoon salt**
chicken	1/8 **teaspoon pepper**
1 1/2 **cups chopped celery**	1/2 **cup mayonnaise**
1/4 **cup slivered almonds,**	4 **large French rolls**
toasted	1/4 **pound Cheddar cheese,**
1 **tablespoon grated onion**	**shredded**
1 **tablespoon lemon juice**	

Combine chicken, celery, almonds, onion, lemon juice, salt, pepper and mayonnaise in bowl; mix well. Cut thin slice from top of rolls. Hollow out centers. Fill with chicken mixture. Arrange in baking dish. Chill, covered, in refrigerator until cooking time. Sprinkle rolls with cheese. Bake at 375 degrees for 25 minutes or until cheese begins to bubble. Yield: 4 servings.

Joseph Snodgrass

SALMON FRENCH TOAST SANDWICHES

1 16-ounce can salmon
6 tablespoons mayonnaise
2 teaspoons grated onion
¼ teaspoon Mrs. Dash
  seasoning

12 slices bread
2 eggs
2 tablespoons milk
Oil for browning

Drain salmon, reserving liquid. Bone and flake salmon in bowl. Add mayonnaise, onion and seasoning; mix well. Spread mixture on 6 slices bread. Top with remaining slices bread. Beat eggs, milk and reserved salmon liquid in shallow dish. Dip sandwiches in mixture. Brown on both sides in a small amount of oil in skillet. Serve immediately. Yield: 6 servings.

Peggy Posante

MICROWAVE TURKEY DIVAN SANDWICH

1½ cups chopped cooked
  turkey
1 8-ounce jar American
  process cheese spread

1 10-ounce package
  frozen broccoli spears
4 English muffins, split

Combine turkey and cheese in 1-quart glass bowl. Microwave on Medium for 3 to 5 minutes or until heated through, stirring once or twice. Microwave broccoli using package directions; drain well. Toast and butter English muffins; place on serving plate. Place broccoli spears on muffins. Spoon turkey and cheese sauce over top. Microwave on High for 30 seconds to reheat. Yield: 4 servings.

Pamela Simms

★ You do not need to cook a turkey for just a few slices. Buy sliced turkey breast in the deli or turkey that is packaged like lunch meat in the meat case.

This horse picture best describes Kentucky, with its many horse farms near Lexington, Kentucky.

Vegetables
and Side Dishes

MEIER '89

HORSE FARM

VEGETABLES

ASPARAGUS CASSEROLE

4 pats of butter
1 16-ounce can
   asparagus
2 to 3 slices cheese
3 or 4 hard-boiled eggs,
   chopped

Ritz cracker crumbs
2 to 3 slices cheese
1 can cream of mushroom
   soup
Paprika

Place butter in bottom of baking dish. Drain asparagus, reserving liquid. Arrange asparagus over butter. Place 2 to 3 slices cheese over asparagus. Add layers of eggs, cracker crumbs and remaining cheese. Top with soup and additional cracker crumbs. Pour reserved liquid over all. Sprinkle with paprika. Bake at 400 degrees for 30 to 45 minutes or until bubbly. Yield: 4 servings.

Helen Lovan

BAKED ASPARAGUS

5 slices bread
1 16-ounce can
   asparagus, drained
3 eggs, beaten

2 cups milk
1 teaspoon salt
1 cup shredded Cheddar
   cheese

Trim bread and cut into cubes. Sprinkle in buttered baking dish. Layer asparagus over bread. Beat eggs with milk and salt. Pour over asparagus. Top with cheese. Bake at 325 degrees for 1 hour. Yield: 4 servings.

Jenny Corp

ASPARAGUS AND CARROT CASSEROLE

2 tablespoons butter
2 tablespoons flour
1½ cups milk
1 cup shredded cheese
½ teaspoon salt
⅛ teaspoon paprika

1 16-ounce can carrots,
   drained
1 16-ounce can
   asparagus, drained
¼ cup buttered crumbs

Melt butter in saucepan. Stir in flour. Add milk gradually. Cook until thickened and smooth, stirring constantly. Reduce heat. Stir in cheese until melted. Season with salt and paprika. Alternate layers of carrots, asparagus and sauce in baking dish until all ingredients are used. Bake at 350 degrees until bubbly. Top with crumbs. Bake until crumbs are brown. Yield: 4 servings.

Nancy Heil

ASPARAGUS CASSEROLE WITH CHEESE SAUCE

2 chicken bouillon cubes
1 cup water
6 tablespoons butter
6 tablespoons flour
2 cups milk
5 cups shredded Cheddar
  cheese
1/2 teaspoon salt
1/2 teaspoon pepper
4 slices bread, toasted
1 16-ounce can
  asparagus, drained

Dissolve bouillon cubes in water. Melt butter in saucepan over very low heat. Stir in flour. Stir in milk, then bouillon and cheese. Cook until thickened and creamy, stirring constantly. Add salt and pepper. Trim toasted bread and cut into quarters. Arrange in baking dish. Top with asparagus and cheese sauce. Bake at 350 degrees for 20 minutes or until bubbly. Yield: 6 servings.

Debbie Renn

EASY BAKED BEANS

1 20-ounce can pork and
  beans
1/4 cup catsup
2 tablespoons brown sugar
2 tablespoons corn syrup
1 tablespoon bacon
  drippings
1/2 cup (or more) chopped
  onion
Bacon slices

Combine pork and beans, catsup, brown sugar, corn syrup, bacon drippings and onion in bowl; mix well. Spoon into baking dish. Top with bacon. Bake at 375 degrees for 45 minutes to 1 hour or until brown. Yield: 4 servings.

Betty Jo Daniel

BOSTON BAKED BEANS

4 cups dried pea beans
8 ounces salt pork
1/3 cup sugar
1/3 cup molasses

1/2 teaspoon dry mustard
1 teaspoon soda
1 teaspoon salt
Boiling water

Soak beans in cold water to cover in bowl overnight; drain. Combine with fresh water to cover in saucepan. Simmer until bean skins burst; drain. Place beans in bean pot, filling 3/4 full. Score pork; press on top of beans. Add sugar, molasses, dry mustard, soda and salt. Cover with boiling water. Bake, covered, at 250 degrees for 7 1/2 hours; do not stir. Add additional water if necessary for beans to remain covered. Remove cover. Bake for 30 minutes longer. Yield: 10 servings.

Mary Cook

GRANNY'S BAKED BEANS

1 pound ground beef
2 cups chopped onions

1 cup catsup
1 large can pork and beans

Brown ground beef in skillet, stirring until crumbly; drain. Add onions, catsup and pork and beans; mix well. Simmer for 15 to 20 minutes or to desired consistency. Yield: 6 servings.

Mrs. Vernon (Sandy) Ortenzi

QUICK BEANS

1 can pork and beans
1/3 cup packed brown
   sugar
1 medium onion, chopped

2 tablespoons catsup
1 tablespoon molasses
1/2 teaspoon pepper

Combine pork and beans, brown sugar, onion, catsup, molasses and pepper in 2-quart saucepan. Cook over medium heat for 10 minutes or until onion is tender. Serve with barbecued ribs or chicken. Yield: 4 servings.

Peggy Posante

CUBAN BEANS

2 cups dried pinto beans
Salt to taste
1 pound hot sausage
1 large onion, chopped
3 large potatoes, chopped
1 green bell pepper,
  chopped
1 clove of garlic, chopped
1 small can tomatoes,
  chopped
1 small can tomato sauce
1/4 teaspoon oregano
1 bay leaf

Combine pinto beans with water to cover in 4 to 6-quart saucepan. Cook for 30 minutes. Remove from heat; let stand for 1 hour. Add salt if desired. Cook until tender, adding additional water if necessary. Brown sausage in skillet, stirring until crumbly. Remove sausage to paper towel to drain. Drain all but 2 tablespoons drippings from skillet. Sauté onion, potatoes, green pepper and garlic in drippings in skillet. Combine with tomatoes, tomato sauce, sausage, oregano and bay leaf in bean pot; mix well. Cook until vegetables are tender or to desired consistency. Remove bay leaf. Yield: 6 servings.

Ida L. Omer

BLUE-RIBBON GREEN BEANS

8 cups cooked green
  beans, drained
1 package frozen onion
  rings
10 ounces mozzarella
  cheese, shredded
2 tomatoes, sliced
Almonds, chopped
1 can cream of chicken
  soup
1 can cream of celery
  or cream of mushroom
  soup
Buttered cracker crumbs

Layer half the green beans, onion rings, cheese, tomatoes and almonds in baking dish. Top with cream of chicken soup. Add layers of remaining beans, onion rings, cheese, tomatoes and almonds. Top with cream of celery soup and buttered crumbs. Bake at 350 degrees for 30 minutes. I cook the green beans without salt. Yield: 12 servings.

Norma Gray

COUNTRY GREEN BEANS

3 slices bacon
1 can green beans

1/2 onion, chopped
Cooked ham pieces

Fry bacon in saucepan until transparent. Add beans, onion and ham. Season to taste. Simmer for 20 minutes. Drain beans and discard seasoning meat before serving. Yield: 2 servings.

Dana Fendley

GREEN BEAN CASSEROLE

1 can French-style green
  beans, drained
1 can Shoe Peg corn,
  drained
1/4 to 1/2 cup chopped onion
1/4 to 1/2 cup chopped
  green bell pepper
1/4 cup chopped celery

1 can cream of celery or
  cream of mushroom soup
1/2 cup sour cream
1/3 to 1 cup shredded
  Cheddar cheese
1/2 cup slivered almonds
Ritz cracker crumbs
1/2 cup butter

Combine green beans, corn, onion, green pepper, celery, soup, sour cream, cheese and almonds in bowl; mix well. Spoon into 1 1/2-quart baking dish. Top with cracker crumbs. Drizzle or dot with butter. Bake at 350 degrees for 45 minutes. May omit cheese from casserole and add to top during last 15 minutes of baking time if preferred. Yield: 6 servings.

Linda Broyles, Juyne Bushart

GREEN BEAN CASSEROLE DELUXE

1 8-ounce can sliced
  mushrooms
1/2 cup chopped onion
1 8-ounce can sliced
  water chestnuts, drained
1/4 cup butter
1/2 cup flour
1 teaspoon salt
1/2 teaspoon pepper
1/2 cup melted butter

1 cup milk
2 teaspoons Tabasco
  sauce
2 cups shredded sharp
  cheese
3 10-ounce packages
  frozen French-style green
  beans, thawed, drained
1 3-ounce can French-
  fried onions

Drain mushrooms, reserving ½ cup liquid. Sauté onion, mushrooms and water chestnuts in ¼ cup butter in skillet until onion is tender; set aside. Blend flour, salt and pepper into ½ cup melted butter in saucepan. Add milk and reserved mushroom liquid gradually. Cook until thickened, stirring constantly. Stir in Tabasco sauce and cheese. Layer sautéed vegetables, green beans and cheese sauce ½ at a time in buttered 9x13-inch baking dish. Bake at 350 degrees for 15 minutes. Sprinkle with fried onions. Bake for 10 minutes longer. Yield: 8 to 10 servings.

Sandy Adams

SWISS GREEN BEANS

1 medium onion, chopped
1 green bell pepper, chopped
Butter
1 can sliced mushrooms, drained
1 cup sour cream
3   16-ounce cans green beans, drained
2 cups shredded Swiss cheese
Sugar to taste
Salt and pepper to taste

Sauté onion and green pepper in a small amount of butter in saucepan. Add mushrooms, sour cream, beans and cheese; mix well. Season to taste. Spoon into baking dish. Bake at 350 degrees for 30 minutes. Yield: 10 servings.

Roberta Walker

LIMA BEAN CASSEROLE

1   10-ounce package frozen lima beans
1 can Cheddar cheese soup
½ cup milk
¾ cup chopped celery
¼ cup pimento
1   3-ounce can French-fried onions

Cook beans according to package directions for 4 to 5 minutes; drain. Combine soup, milk, celery, pimento, beans and half the onions in bowl; mix well. Spoon into baking dish. Bake at 350 degrees for 30 minutes. Top with remaining onions. Bake for 10 minutes longer. Yield: 4 servings.

Dot Berry

SPANISH CHEESE LIMAS

2½ cups fresh lima beans
1 cup thinly sliced celery
½ cup finely chopped
  onion
2 tablespoons oil
3 tomatoes, peeled,
  chopped

2 teaspoons
  Worcestershire sauce
½ teaspoon salt
⅛ teaspoon pepper
Dash of red pepper
1½ cups shredded
  American cheese

Cook beans in boiling water in saucepan until tender; drain. Sauté celery and onion in oil in large skillet. Add tomatoes; reduce heat. Simmer, covered, for 10 minutes, stirring frequently. Stir in beans, Worcestershire sauce, salt, pepper and red pepper. Simmer for 10 minutes. Layer half the bean mixture, half the cheese and remaining bean mixture in lightly greased 2-quart baking dish. Bake at 350 degrees for 20 minutes. Sprinkle with remaining cheese. Bake for 5 minutes longer or until cheese melts. Yield: 6 servings.

Norma Gray

JEAN'S LIMA BEAN CASSEROLE

2 10-ounce packages
  frozen lima beans
1 can cream of mushroom
  soup
½ soup can milk

1 small jar sliced pimento
8 ounces Cheddar cheese,
  shredded
Ritz cracker crumbs
Butter

Cook beans according to package directions; drain. Combine soup, milk, undrained pimento and cheese in saucepan. Cook over low heat until cheese melts. Layer beans and soup mixture ½ at a time in buttered baking dish. Top with cracker crumbs. Dot with butter. Bake at 300 degrees until bubbly. Yield: 6 servings.

Jean Real

GLAZED ORANGE BEETS

2 tablespoons butter
2 tablespoons flour
Juice and grated rind of
  1 large orange

1/2 cup sugar
Salt to taste
1 29-ounce can tiny
  beets, drained

Melt butter in saucepan. Stir in flour. Add orange juice, orange rind, sugar and salt. Cook until thickened, stirring constantly. Add beets. Heat to serving temperature over low heat. May add additional juice if needed for desired consistency. Yield: 6 servings.

Aggie Burks

HARVARD BEETS

3/4 cup vinegar
1/2 cup water
2 teaspoons dry mustard
1 teaspoon caraway seed
1/3 cup sugar

1 teaspoon salt
1/2 teaspoon pepper
1 can beets, drained
1 medium onion, chopped

Bring vinegar, water, dry mustard, caraway seed, sugar, salt and pepper to a boil in saucepan; mix well. Combine with beets and onion in bowl. Marinate in refrigerator overnight. Yield: 4 servings.

Debbie Renn

BROCCOLI CASSEROLE

2 10-ounce packages
  frozen chopped broccoli
1 can cream of chicken
  soup

4 ounces sliced Velveeta
  cheese
Ritz cracker crumbs
1/2 cup melted margarine

Cook broccoli according to package directions; drain. Add soup; mix well. Spoon into greased 9x13-inch baking dish. Top with cheese and mixture of cracker crumbs and margarine. Bake at 350 degrees for 30 minutes. Yield: 8 servings.

Jean Geary, Laverne Hollingsworth
Carmen Stilger

PAULA'S BROCCOLI CASSEROLE

2 10-ounce packages
   frozen broccoli
1 can cream of mushroom
   soup
3/4 cup sour cream
1 2-ounce jar pimento,
   drained

1 cup finely chopped
   celery
1 teaspoon salt
1/2 teaspoon pepper
1 cup shredded Cheddar
   cheese

Cook broccoli according to package directions; drain. Add soup, sour cream, pimento, celery, salt and pepper; mix well. Spoon into greased baking dish. Top with cheese. Bake at 350 degrees for 25 minutes. Yield: 6 servings.

Paula Goodlett

BROCCOLI KRISP

2 10-ounce packages
   frozen broccoli
1 can cream of mushroom
   soup
1/2 envelope onion soup
   mix

1 cup sour cream
1 can sliced water
   chestnuts
3 cups crisp rice cereal
1/2 cup melted butter

Cook broccoli according to package directions; drain well. Layer broccoli, mushroom soup, dry soup mix, sour cream and water chestnuts in 9x13-inch baking dish. Top with mixture of cereal and butter. Bake at 350 degrees for 30 minutes. Yield: 6 to 8 servings.

June Brewer

BROCCOLI AND RICE CASSEROLE

2 10-ounce packages
   frozen chopped broccoli
1/2 cup chopped onion
1/2 cup chopped celery
1/2 cup butter

1 to 2 cans cream of
   chicken or cream of
   mushroom soup
2 cups cooked rice
1 8-ounce jar Cheez Whiz

Cook broccoli according to package directions; drain. Sauté onion and celery in butter in skillet. Add to broccoli. Add soup, rice and Cheez Whiz; mix well. Spoon into buttered 9x13-

inch baking dish. Bake at 350 degrees for 30 minutes or until bubbly. May add chopped red bell pepper if desired. Yield: 8 servings.

Aggie Burks, Mrs. Richard Hargrove
Patti Reece, Roberta Walker
Jane Wallace, Pat Wilhelm

SESAME BROCCOLI

1 tablespoon sesame seed
1 pound fresh broccoli
1 tablespoon olive or
  safflower oil
1 tablespoon vinegar
1 tablespoon lite soy sauce
1 teaspoon sugar
  (optional)

Sprinkle sesame seed on baking sheet. Toast in slow oven until light brown. Trim broccoli and cut into spears. Steam in saucepan until tender-crisp. Bring oil, vinegar, soy sauce, sugar and sesame seed to a boil in saucepan. Pour over broccoli in serving dish, turning to coat evenly. Yield: 6 servings.

Betty Jo Daniel

WOW-WEE BROCCOLI

2 10-ounce packages
   frozen chopped broccoli
1 cup mayonnaise
1 can cream of mushroom
  or cream of celery soup
2 teaspoons minced onion
2 cups shredded sharp
  Cheddar cheese
2 eggs, well beaten
1 cup cheese cracker
  crumbs

Cook broccoli according to package directions; drain. Add mayonnaise, soup, onion, cheese and eggs; mix well. Spoon into buttered baking dish. Bake at 400 degrees for 20 to 30 minutes. Top with cracker crumbs. Bake until crackers are light brown. Yield: 6 servings.

Christine D. Rankin, L. Wilburn

BROCCOLI AND CAULIFLOWER CASSEROLE

1 10-ounce package
   frozen chopped broccoli
1 10-ounce package
   frozen chopped
   cauliflower
1 medium onion, chopped
1/2 cup butter
1 cup cooked minute rice

1 small can mushrooms,
   drained
4 ounces Cheez Whiz or
   Velveeta cheese
1 can cream of mushroom
   or golden mushroom
   soup
1/2 cup milk

Cook broccoli and cauliflower using package directions; drain. Sauté onion in butter in saucepan. Add rice, broccoli, cauliflower, mushrooms, cheese, soup and milk; mix well. Spoon into buttered 2-quart baking dish. Bake at 350 degrees for 30 minutes. Yield: 6 servings.

Bernidea Fort

BRUSSELS SPROUTS IN CASSEROLE

2 10-ounce packages
   frozen Brussels sprouts
1 can cream of celery soup
1/2 teaspoon salt

1/4 teaspoon pepper
1/2 cup dry bread crumbs
2 tablespoons butter

Cook Brussels sprouts using package directions until tender; drain. Add soup, salt and pepper; mix well. Spoon into greased baking dish. Top with bread crumbs; dot with butter. Bake at 400 degrees for 20 minutes. Yield: 5 to 6 servings.

Debbie Renn

CABBAGE AU GRATIN

4 cups shredded cabbage
1 1/2 tablespoons flour
1 tablespoon sugar
1/2 teaspoon salt
1/2 teaspoon pepper
2 tablespoons melted
   margarine

1 cup milk
1 cup shredded Cheddar
   cheese
2 cups Ritz cracker crumbs
4 tablespoons melted
   butter

Cook cabbage in water to cover in saucepan for 5 minutes; drain well. Stir mixture of flour, sugar, salt and pepper into margarine in saucepan. Add milk. Cook until thickened, stirring constantly. Stir in cheese. Alternate layers of cabbage and cheese sauce in greased 1½-quart casserole until all ingredients are used. Top with mixture of cracker crumbs and butter. Bake at 350 degrees for 25 minutes. Yield: 6 servings.

Jean Real

BAKED CABBAGE

1 head cabbage, cut into
  12 wedges
1 teaspoon salt
1 cup water
2 tablespoons flour
2 tablespoons sugar

1 teaspoon salt
⅛ teaspoon pepper
3 tablespoons margarine
1 cup hot milk
1 cup shredded cheese

Cook cabbage, covered, in salted water in saucepan for 10 minutes; drain well. Place in 8x12-inch baking dish. Sprinkle with mixture of flour, sugar, 1 teaspoon salt and pepper; dot with margarine. Pour heated milk over top. Top with cheese. Bake at 350 degrees for 35 minutes. Yield: 8 servings.

Ruth Shearer

CABBAGE CASSEROLE

1 onion, chopped
Butter
1 head cabbage, chopped,
  cooked
1 can cream of mushroom
  soup

1 can cream of celery soup
1 can Cheddar cheese
  soup
Shredded Cheddar cheese
Buttered bread crumbs

Sauté onion in a small amount of butter in saucepan. Add cabbage and soups; mix well. Spoon into buttered baking dish. Top with cheese and bread crumbs. Bake at 350 degrees for 30 minutes. Yield: 8 servings.

Bernidea Fort

CHEESY CABBAGE CASSEROLE

1 medium head cabbage
1 can cream of celery soup
1 cup shredded American
  or Cheddar cheese
Pepper to taste
1 cup soft bread crumbs
1/4 cup melted butter

Separate cabbage into leaves. Soak in cold water to cover in bowl for 10 minutes; drain. Cut into 1/2-inch strips. Cook in boiling salted water to cover in saucepan for 5 to 8 minutes. Let stand for 2 minutes; drain well. Layer cabbage, soup, cheese and pepper 1/2 at a time in greased 11/2-quart baking dish. Top with mixture of bread crumbs and butter. Bake at 350 degrees for 25 to 30 minutes or until golden brown. May top with crushed cheese crackers if preferred. May substitute cream of chicken or cream of mushroom soup. May substitute cream cheese and 1/4 cup milk for cheese, heat with soup and pour over cabbage.
Yield: 8 servings.

Bea Gritton, Molly Hisel
Anna Lee Pruitt

BACON FRIED CARROTS

3 or 4 slices bacon
1 pound carrots, sliced
1 medium onion, chopped
Dash of sugar
1/2 teaspoon salt
1/4 teaspoon pepper

Cook bacon in skillet until crisp. Remove bacon to drain. Add carrots and onion to bacon drippings in skillet; sprinkle with sugar, salt and pepper. Cook, covered, over low heat for 15 minutes or until tender-crisp. Cook, uncovered, until carrots are light brown, turning occasionally. Add crumbled bacon. May use frozen carrots and cook for a shorter time. Yield: 4 servings.

Dorothy Lee Henn

BUTTERED CARROTS

11/2 pounds carrots
3/4 cup water
1 teaspoon sugar
3 tablespoons butter
1/2 teaspoon salt
1/8 teaspoon pepper
1 tablespoon chopped
  parsley

Peel carrots and cut into julienne strips. Combine with water, sugar, butter, salt and pepper in saucepan. Bring to a boil; reduce heat. Simmer, covered, for 10 to 15 minutes or until carrots are tender and liquid is absorbed, removing cover toward end of cooking time if necessary. Spoon into serving bowl. Sprinkle with parsley. Yield: 6 servings.

Wilma Allen

CARROT CASSEROLE

8 carrots, scraped, sliced
1 can cream of celery soup
3 tablespoons margarine

1/3 cup slivered almonds
1/3 cup Parmesan cheese
1/2 cup cornflake crumbs

Cook carrots in boiling salted water in saucepan until tender-crisp; drain. Place in 1 1/2-quart baking dish. Mix soup, margarine and almonds in bowl. Spoon over carrots. Sprinkle with cheese and cornflake crumbs. Bake at 350 degrees for 30 minutes. Yield: 6 servings.

Christy Michelle Lewis

DILL CARROTS

6 to 8 carrots
1 cup sliced onion
1 clove of garlic, finely
   minced
1/4 cup oil
1 tablespoon flour

1 can cream of celery soup
1 cup milk
1/2 teaspoon dillseed
1 teaspoon sugar
Garlic powder, salt and
   pepper to taste

Peel carrots and cut into julienne strips. Sauté carrots, onion and garlic in oil in saucepan for 5 minutes. Sprinkle with flour. Stir in soup and milk. Add dillseed and sugar. Simmer until carrots are tender. Season with garlic powder, salt and pepper. Yield: 6 servings.

Betty Sanders

CHEESE SCALLOPED CARROTS

12 medium carrots, sliced, cooked
2 cups shredded American or sharp Cheddar cheese
1/4 cup chopped onion
1/4 cup butter
1/4 cup flour
1/4 teaspoon dry mustard
1 teaspoon salt
1/8 teaspoon pepper
2 cups milk
1 cup buttered bread crumbs

Alternate layers of carrots and cheese in 9x13-inch baking dish. Sauté onion in butter in saucepan until tender. Stir in flour, mustard, salt and pepper. Cook for 1 minute, stirring constantly. Add milk gradually. Bring to a boil over low heat, stirring constantly. Cook for 1 minute, stirring constantly. Pour over carrots. Sprinkle with bread crumbs. Bake at 350 degrees for 35 to 45 minutes or until bubbly. Yield: 6 to 8 servings.

Trudie Gadjen

★ For glazed carrots, cook 2 cups carrot slices in 3 cups club soda until tender-crisp and drain. Add 1/4 cup butter and brown sugar to taste and heat until glazed. It is easier to slice or shred carrots if you leave an inch or so of green top on to use as a handle.

★ Onions should be selected for their intended use. Large Spanish or Bermuda onions and small white onions are usually mild in flavor. Globe types such as red and brown and small yellow onions are stronger in flavor.

CAULIFLOWER AU GRATIN

Flowerets of 1 head
  cauliflower
2¹/₂ tablespoons butter
3 tablespoons flour
2 cups milk

Salt and pepper to taste
¹/₂ cup bread crumbs
1 tablespoon melted butter
1 cup shredded Cheddar
  cheese

Cook cauliflower in boiling water in saucepan for 5 to 10 minutes or until tender-crisp; drain well. Melt 2¹/₂ tablespoons butter in medium saucepan. Stir in flour with wire whisk. Cook for 2 minutes. Stir in milk gradually, beating constantly. Add salt and pepper. Bring to a boil. Cook for 2 minutes, stirring constantly. Spoon ¹/₂ cup sauce into 2-quart baking dish. Add cauliflower. Spoon remaining sauce over cauliflower. Top with mixture of bread crumbs and melted butter. Sprinkle with cheese. Bake at 375 degrees for 20 to 30 minutes or until bubbly.
Yield: 6 to 8 servings.

Patricia J. Tudor

BAKED CELERY CASSEROLE

4 cups chopped celery
1 5-ounce can water
  chestnuts, drained
1 large jar chopped
  pimento, drained

1 can cream of chicken
  soup
1 cup buttered bread
  crumbs
¹/₄ cup almonds

Cook celery in boiling water in saucepan for 8 minutes; drain. Add water chestnuts, pimento and soup; mix well. Spoon into buttered 2-quart baking dish. Sprinkle with bread crumbs and almonds. Bake at 350 degrees for 25 minutes. Yield: 8 servings.

Grace Murphy

★ Peel celery stalks with a potato peeler for quick and easy removal of strings.

CELERY VICTORIA

1 bunch celery
1 10-ounce can beef broth
1/2 cup oil
3 tablespoons cider
  vinegar
1 tablespoon water
1 tablespoon minced fresh
  parsley
1 medium clove of garlic,
  minced

1 teaspoon Italian
  seasoning
1/4 teaspoon curry powder
1/2 teaspoons salt
1/8 teaspoon freshly
  ground pepper
1 whole pimento, cut into
  strips

Trim root end of celery, leaving stalks together. Discard coarse outer stalks; reserve some leaves for garnish. Cut six 1-inch thick slices from bottom of bunch. Reserve top portion for another use. Tie each slice around outside with string. Place in 12-inch skillet. Add broth. Bring to a boil over medium heat. Cook for 15 minutes or until tender-crisp. Remove celery with slotted spoon; place in shallow dish. Combine oil, vinegar, water, parsley, garlic, Italian seasoning, curry powder, salt and pepper in blender container. Process until smooth. Pour over celery. Chill, covered, for 3 hours, turning celery several times. Drain celery. Place on serving plates; remove string. Garnish with pimento strips and reserved leaves. Yield: 6 servings.

Juyne Bushart

SCALLOPED CELERY

3 tablespoons butter
3 tablespoons flour
1 cup chicken broth
3/4 cup half and half
3 1/4 cups chopped celery
1/2 cup sliced water
  chestnuts
1/4 cup toasted slivered
  almonds

3/4 cup sliced fresh
  mushrooms
1 package shrimp
  (optional)
Salt and pepper to taste
1 cup Parmesan cheese
2 tablespoons butter
1/2 cup bread crumbs

Melt 3 tablespoons butter in saucepan. Stir in flour. Cook until light brown. Stir in broth and half and half gradually. Cook over low heat until thickened, stirring constantly. Combine celery, water chestnuts, almonds, mushrooms and shrimp in bowl. Add sauce. Stir in salt, pepper and half the cheese. Spoon into 2-quart baking dish. Top with remaining cheese. Dot with 2 tablespoons butter; sprinkle with bread crumbs. Bake at 350 degrees for 30 minutes or until bubbly. Yield: 6 servings.

Wanda Wiegand

CORN CASSEROLE

1 or 2 cans Shoe Peg
  corn, drained
1 large can French-style
  green beans, drained
1 cup sour cream
1 can cream of celery soup
1/2 cup shredded Cheddar
  cheese (optional)
1/2 cup chopped onion

1/2 cup chopped celery
1/4 cup chopped green bell
  pepper
1/2 cup water chestnuts
  (optional)
Salt and pepper to taste
11/2 packages Ritz
  crackers, crushed
1/2 cup melted margarine

Combine corn, green beans, sour cream, soup, cheese, onion, celery, green pepper, water chestnuts and salt and pepper in bowl; mix well. Spoon into 9x13-inch baking dish. Top with mixture of crackers and margarine. Bake at 350 degrees for 45 minutes. Yield: 6 to 8 servings.

Dot Berry, Carolyn Hamon
Betty Wedding

GOLDEN CORN CASSEROLE

8 ounces Velveeta cheese,
  cubed
1/2 cup milk
1 12-ounce can whole
  kernel corn, drained

2 eggs, slightly beaten
1/4 cup chopped green bell
  pepper
1/2 teaspoon basil
1/8 teaspoon pepper

Combine cheese and milk in saucepan. Cook over low heat until cheese is melted and smooth. Add corn, eggs, green pepper, basil and pepper; mix well. Spoon into 6x10-inch baking dish. Bake at 350 degrees for 30 minutes. Yield: 8 servings.

Debbie Windhorst

CORN PUDDING

1/4 cup margarine
1 20-ounce can cream-
   style corn
3 eggs

1 tablespoon to 2/3 cup
   sugar
3 tablespoons flour

Melt margarine in baking dish. Combine corn, eggs, sugar and flour in bowl; mix well. Spoon into prepared dish. Bake at 400 degrees for 45 minutes. Yield: 6 servings.

Bernidea Fort, Molly Hisel
Celesta Wilson

BERNADETTE'S CORN PUDDING

1 16-ounce can corn,
   drained
3 eggs, slightly beaten
3 tablespoons melted
   shortening

1 cup plus 2 tablespoons
   milk, scalded
3 tablespoons sugar
1 teaspoon salt
1/2 teaspoon pepper

Combine corn, eggs, shortening, milk, sugar, salt and pepper in bowl; mix well. Spoon into baking dish. Bake at 325 degrees for 30 to 40 minutes or until set. Yield: 6 servings.

Bernadette Mills

NEW ORLEANS CORN PUDDING

1 tablespoon sugar
2 1/2 teaspoons flour
3/4 teaspoon baking
   powder
2 eggs, beaten
1/4 cup half and half

3 tablespoons melted
   butter
1 can cream-style corn
1 tablespoon brown sugar
1 tablespoon melted butter
1/8 teaspoon cinnamon

Mix sugar, flour and baking powder in bowl. Add eggs, half and half, 3 tablespoons butter and corn; mix well. Spoon into buttered 1 1/2-quart baking dish. Bake at 325 degrees for 45 minutes or until set. Combine brown sugar, 1 tablespoon butter and cinnamon in small bowl; mix well. Drizzle over casserole. Bake for 5 minutes longer. Yield: 6 servings.

Roberta Walker

HOT CORN CASSEROLE

2 16-ounce cans cream-
  style corn
2 eggs
3/4 cup cornmeal
2 tablespoons corn oil

1 onion, chopped
4 or 5 hot peppers, minced
2 teaspoons garlic salt
2 cups shredded Cheddar
  cheese

Combine corn, eggs, cornmeal, oil, onion, peppers and garlic salt in bowl; mix well. Alternate layers of corn mixture and cheese in greased 9x13-inch baking dish. Bake at 350 degrees for 35 to 45 minutes or until set. Yield: 8 servings.

Opal Miracle

MOM'S STEWED CORN

6 ears fresh white corn
6 slices bacon
1 small green bell pepper,
  chopped

3 medium tomatoes,
  peeled, chopped

Cut corn kernels from cobs. Fry bacon in skillet until crisp. Remove bacon to drain. Sauté green pepper in bacon drippings in skillet. Add tomatoes. Cook for 5 to 7 minutes or until tender. Add corn. Cook until corn is tender, adding water if needed. Stir crumbled bacon into corn just before serving.
Yield: 5 to 6 servings.

Violet Mullaney

MICROWAVE CORN ON THE COB

4 ears fresh corn

1/4 cup water

Husk corn; remove all silk. Place corn in glass baking dish, leaving space between ears. Add water. Microwave, tightly covered with plastic wrap, for 14 minutes. Let stand for 5 minutes. Serve with butter if desired. This is the most delicious way of preparing corn on the cob. Yield: 4 servings.

Peggy Posante

CORN OYSTERS

1 cup fresh corn kernels
2 egg yolks
1/4 cup sifted flour
1/2 teaspoon baking
  powder

1 teaspoon grated onion
1 teaspoon salt
1/8 teaspoon pepper
2 egg whites, stiffly beaten

Combine corn and egg yolks in bowl; mix well. Mix flour, baking powder, onion, salt and pepper in small bowl. Stir into corn mixture. Fold in stiffly beaten egg whites. Drop by teaspoonfuls onto hot greased griddle. Cook until golden brown on both sides. Yield: 4 servings.

Gary Lee Figg

EGGPLANT CASSEROLE

1 medium eggplant
1 egg, beaten
1/2 cup milk
2 to 3 tablespoons melted
  butter

1 small onion, chopped
1 green bell pepper, finely
  chopped
1 cup bread crumbs

Peel eggplant and cut into cubes. Cook in boiling salted water in saucepan for 8 minutes; drain. Add egg, milk, butter, onion, green pepper and bread crumbs; mix well. Spoon into baking dish. Bake at 350 degrees for 30 minutes. Yield: 6 servings.

Pearl Robinson

EASY BAKED EGGPLANT

1/4 cup wine
1 envelope Italian herb
  salad dressing mix
1   15-ounce can tomato
  sauce
4 cloves of garlic, minced
2 tablespoons oil

2 small eggplant, cut into
  1/2-inch slices
2 cloves of garlic, minced
10 ounces mozzarella
  cheese, sliced
Minced parsley

Combine wine, salad dressing mix, tomato sauce and 4 cloves of garlic in bowl; mix well. Marinate for 8 hours. Coat

medium baking dish with oil. Place eggplant in prepared dish. Sprinkle with 2 cloves of garlic. Layer 3/4 of the tomato mixture, cheese and remaining tomato mixture over eggplant. Sprinkle with parsley. Bake at 350 degrees for 45 minutes.
Yield: 4 servings.

Juyne Bushart

MUSHROOM-STUFFED EGGPLANT

1 medium eggplant
1/2 cup chopped onion
1/4 cup butter
1 4-ounce can sliced
   mushrooms, drained

3/4 cup soft bread crumbs
1/4 teaspoon pepper
1 cup shredded Cheddar
   cheese

Cut eggplant into halves lengthwise. Scoop out and chop pulp, leaving 1/4-inch shells. Sauté chopped eggplant and onion in butter in skillet until tender. Add mushrooms. Sauté for 5 minutes. Stir in bread crumbs and pepper. Spoon into eggplant shells. Place in 9x9-inch baking dish. Bake at 350 degrees for 15 minutes. Sprinkle with cheese. Bake for 5 minutes longer.
Yield: 2 servings.

Sandi Tipton Clark

SCALLOPED EGGPLANT

1 1¼-pound eggplant
1 large tomato, sliced
1 large onion, sliced
1/4 cup melted butter
1/2 teaspoon salt
1/2 teaspoon basil

1 cup shredded
   mozzarella cheese
1/2 cup bread crumbs
1/2 cup melted butter
1/4 cup freshly grated
   Parmesan cheese

Peel eggplant; cut into 1/2-inch slices. Soak for 10 minutes in salted water to cover in bowl; drain. Layer eggplant, tomato and onion in 2-quart baking dish. Drizzle with 1/4 cup butter. Sprinkle with salt and basil. Bake, covered, at 450 degrees for 20 minutes. Top with mozzarella cheese and mixture of bread crumbs and 1/2 cup butter. Sprinkle with Parmesan cheese. Bake, uncovered, for 10 minutes longer Yield: 6 servings.

Wanda Wiegand

STUFFED MUSHROOMS

1/2 cup chopped onion
1 tablespoon butter
2 teaspoons cornstarch
1/2 teaspoon salt
1/4 teaspoon thyme
1/2 cup water

1 cup frozen peas and
  carrots, cooked
1 pound fresh large
  mushroom caps
1/4 teaspoon salt

Sauté onion in butter in skillet for 4 minutes. Sprinkle mixture of cornstarch, 1/2 teaspoon salt and thyme over onion; mix well. Add water. Bring to a boil, stirring constantly. Add peas and carrots. Spoon into mushroom caps. Sprinkle 1/4 teaspoon salt into shallow baking dish. Arrange mushrooms in dish. Add enough hot water to cover bottom of dish to a depth of 1/2 inch. Bake at 350 degrees for 20 minutes. Yield: 6 servings.

Alma Brite

FRIED OKRA

4 cups sliced okra
1/2 cup milk
1/4 teaspoon salt

1/4 teaspoon pepper
3/4 cup cornmeal
Oil for deep frying

Combine okra with milk, salt and pepper in shallow dish; mix well. Let stand for 1 hour or until most of milk is absorbed. Coat okra with cornmeal. Deep-fry in 375-degree oil until golden brown. Drain on paper towel. Yield: 4 servings.

Jenny Corp

OKRA AND CORN WITH TOMATO

Water
Salt to taste
Bacon drippings to taste
2 10-ounce packages
  frozen cut okra
1 large green bell pepper,
  chopped

1 large onion, chopped
1 large tomato, chopped
1 small can tomato sauce
Kernels cut from 3 ears of
  fresh corn
1 teaspoon vinegar
Garlic powder to taste

Combine amount of water called for in okra cooking directions with salt and bacon drippings to taste in saucepan. Bring to a boil. Add okra, green pepper and onion. Simmer for several minutes. Add tomato, tomato sauce, corn, vinegar and garlic powder. Simmer until vegetables are tender. Yield: 8 servings.

Pauline Sweatt

OKRA PANCAKES

1 cup steamed okra
1 egg, beaten
1 teaspoon minced onion

1 cup (or more) sifted
cornmeal
Oil for deep frying

Combine okra, egg and onion in bowl. Add enough cornmeal to make a stiff batter. Drop into deep hot oil. Deep-fry until brown. Serve with tomato sauce, catsup or cheese. Yield: 6 servings.

Dorothy O'Neal

CREAMED ONIONS

3 tablespoons butter
12 small onions, thickly
  sliced
1/4 teaspoon salt

2 tablespoons flour
1 cup milk
1/4 cup Sherry
1/4 cup chopped pecans

Melt butter in saucepan. Add onion slices; sprinkle with salt. Simmer, covered, for 15 to 20 minutes or until tender, adding s small amount of water if needed. Sprinkle with flour; mix gently. Stir in milk. Cook for 3 minutes or until thickened, stirring constantly. Stir in Sherry and pecans. Yield: 4 servings.

Mary J. Thompson

ONION RINGS

Bermuda onions
Milk

Pancake batter
Oil for deep frying

Cut onions into 1/4-inch slices. Separate into rings. Soak in milk to cover in bowl for several minutes; drain. Dip into pancake batter, coating well. Deep-fry in hot oil until golden brown.

Dana Fendley

VIDALIA ONION CASSEROLE

6 or 7 large Vidalia onions
½ cup margarine

Parmesan cheese
Ritz crackers, crushed

Cut onions into thin slices. Sauté in margarine in skillet until tender. Layer with remaining ingredients ½ at a time in baking dish. Bake at 325 degrees for 30 minutes Yield: 8 servings.

Margaret Taylor

CHINESE-STYLE BAKED PEAS

1 6-ounce can sliced
   mushrooms
½ cup chopped onion
¼ cup margarine
1 10-ounce package
   frozen peas, thawed
1 8-ounce can water
   chestnuts

1 can cream of mushroom
   soup
⅓ cup milk
1 16-ounce can bean
   sprouts, drained
1 teaspoon salt
Dash of pepper
Chinese noodles

Sauté mushrooms and onion in margarine in skillet. Add peas and chestnuts. Combine soup, milk, bean sprouts, salt and pepper in bowl. Stir in pea mixture. Spoon into greased 1½-quart baking dish. Bake at 350 degrees for 45 minutes. Garnish with Chinese noodles. Yield: 8 servings.

Gwen Mills

ONION KUCHEN

1 package hot roll mix
3 to 3¾ pounds onions,
   sliced
¾ cup butter
3 eggs

1½ cups milk, scalded
1½ teaspoons salt
1½ teaspoons sugar
1½ teaspoons caraway
   seed

Prepare roll mix according to package directions through 1 rising. Punch dough down. Knead and spread thinly in three 9-inch pie plates. Sauté onions in butter in skillet until tender but not brown. Cool. Place in prepared pie plates. Beat eggs in large bowl. Add milk gradually, stirring constantly. Stir in salt and sugar. Pour over onions. Sprinkle with caraway seed. Bake at 350 degrees for 25 to 30 minutes or until knife inserted in center comes out clean. Yield: 18 to 24 servings.

Margaret Kurz

PEAS ORIENTAL

3 10-ounce packages
   frozen peas
2 8-ounce cans sliced
   water chestnuts, drained
1 15-ounce can bean
   sprouts, drained

1 4-ounce can sliced
   mushrooms, drained
2 cans cream of
   mushroom soup
2 3-ounce cans French-
   fried onion rings

Cook peas according to package directions just for several minutes; drain. Add water chestnuts, bean sprouts, mushrooms and soup; mix well. Spoon into 2-quart baking dish. Bake at 350 degrees for 30 minutes. Crumble onion rings over top. Bake for 5 to 10 minutes longer or until brown. Yield: 10 servings.

Gail Gardner

ENGLISH PEA CASSEROLE

1/3 cup chopped celery
1/3 cup chopped onion
1/3 cup chopped green bell
   pepper
1/4 cup butter
2 cups frozen peas
1 can water chestnuts,
   drained, chopped

1 can cream of mushroom
   soup
1/4 cup milk
1 small can chopped
   pimento, drained
Salt and pepper to taste
Cracker crumbs
Butter

Sauté celery, onion and green pepper in 1/4 cup butter in skillet until tender. Add peas, water chestnuts, soup, milk and pimento; mix well. Add salt and pepper. Spoon into baking dish. Top with cracker crumbs. Dot with butter. Bake at 350 degrees for 25 minutes. May top with cheese if desired. Yield: 6 servings.

Mrs. Vernon (Sandy) Ortenzi

PEAS AND DUMPLINGS

1 pound fresh peas
1/4 cup butter
2 cups buttermilk baking
  mix

2/3 cup milk

Cook peas with water to cover and butter in saucepan until tender. Add water if necessary to cover peas well. Combine baking mix and milk in bowl; mix well. Drop by spoonfuls into boiling peas; reduce heat. Simmer, covered, for 12 to 15 minutes or until dumplings are cooked through. Yield: 6 servings.

Helen Yaeger

PEA CASSEROLE

1 can cream of mushroom
  soup
1 cup sour cream
1/4 teaspoon garlic salt
1 teaspoon salt
2 large cans peas, drained

1 cup shredded Cheddar
  cheese
1 cup cracker crumbs
1   3-ounce can French-
  fried onion rings
1/4 cup melted margarine

Combine soup, sour cream, garlic salt and salt in bowl; mix well. Stir in peas. Spoon into shallow baking dish. Sprinkle with cheese and cracker crumbs. Top with onion rings and melted margarine. Bake at 350 degrees for 20 to 30 minutes or until bubbly. Yield: 8 servings.

Marylene Otte, Shirley Smith

BELL PEPPER CASSEROLE

Green bell peppers,
  chopped
Cracker crumbs

Shredded cheese
Butter
Milk

Cook peppers in boiling water to cover just until tender-crisp; drain. Alternate layers of peppers, cracker crumbs and cheese in baking dish until all ingredients are used. Dot with butter. Pour milk over layers. Bake at 350 degrees until bubbly.

Pearl Robinson

EASY POTATO CASSEROLE

1 32-ounce package
frozen hashed brown
potatoes, thawed
1/2 cup chopped onion
1/2 cup chopped green bell
pepper

1 can cream of potato soup
1 can cream of celery soup
1 cup sour cream
Salt and pepper to taste
1 cup shredded Cheddar
cheese

Combine potatoes, onion, green pepper, soups, sour cream, salt and pepper in bowl; mix well. Spoon into shallow greased 2-quart baking dish. Bake at 350 degrees for 1 hour. Sprinkle with cheese. Bake until cheese is melted. May sauté onion and green pepper or omit them entirely if preferred. May use cream of chicken soup. Yield: 8 servings.

Phyllis L. Allen, Sue Downing
Shirley Smith

POTATO CASSEROLE

1 32-ounce package
frozen hashed brown
potatoes
1/2 cup chopped onion
2 cups sour cream
1/2 cup melted butter
(optional)

2 cans cream of chicken
soup
2 cups shredded cheese
Salt and pepper to taste
2 cups cracker crumbs or
cornflake crumbs
Melted butter

Combine potatoes, onion, sour cream, 1/2 cup butter, soup, cheese, salt and pepper in bowl; mix well. Spoon into 9x13-inch baking dish. Top with cracker crumbs; drizzle with additional butter. Bake at 350 degrees for 1 hour. May omit 1 can of soup or substitute 1 can cream of mushroom soup for 1 can cream of chicken soup if preferred. Yield: 8 to 10 servings.

Brenda Collins, Betty Donovan
Sandra Free, Nancy Lockard
Judy Roberts, Patricia J. Tudor
Roberta Walker

HASHED BROWN QUICHE

3 cups frozen hashed
  brown potatoes, thawed
1/3 cup melted butter
1 cup chopped cooked
  ham
1 cup shredded hot
  pepper cheese

1 cup shredded Gouda or
  Swiss cheese
1/2 cup light cream
2 eggs
1/4 teaspoon seasoned salt

Press potatoes between paper towels to remove excess moisture. Press over bottom and side of 9-inch pie plate. Drizzle with melted butter. Bake at 425 degrees for 25 minutes. Reduce temperature to 350 degrees. Combine ham and cheeses in bowl. Spread in potato crust. Beat cream, eggs and seasoned salt in bowl until smooth. Bake at 350 degrees for 25 to 30 minutes or until knife inserted near center comes out clean. Let stand for 10 minutes before serving. Yield: 6 servings.

Pati Funk

MICROWAVE SCALLOPED POTATOES

3 tablespoons butter
3 tablespoons flour
1 1/2 teaspoons salt
1/4 teaspoon pepper

3 cups milk
9 medium potatoes
2 tablespoons minced
  onion

Microwave butter in 1-quart glass bowl on High for several seconds or until melted. Add flour, salt and pepper; blend well. Stir in milk gradually. Microwave on High for 9 minutes, stirring every 3 minutes. Peel and slice potatoes. Layer potatoes, onion and sauce 1/2 at a time in 2-quart glass casserole. Microwave on High for 25 minutes. I brown the finished casserole under the broiler. Yield: 6 to 8 servings.

Terry Neihoff

CRISP OVEN-ROASTED POTATOES

1 envelope onion or
  mushroom-onion
  soup mix
1/2 cup olive oil
1/4 cup melted butter

1 teaspoon thyme
1 teaspoon marjoram
1/4 teaspoon pepper
2 pounds potatoes, cut
  into quarters

Combine first 6 ingredients in baking pan; mix well. Add potatoes, turning to coat well. Bake at 450 degrees for 1 hour or until tender and golden brown. Yield: 8 servings.

Juyne Bushart

OVEN-FRIED PARMESAN POTATOES

3 medium potatoes
3 tablespoons melted
  margarine
1 1/2 teaspoons marjoram
1/2 teaspoon paprika

1/2 teaspoon garlic powder
1/4 teaspoon salt
1/4 teaspoon pepper
1/4 cup grated Parmesan
  cheese

Cut unpeeled potatoes into thin slices. Arrange in single layer on baking sheet. Combine margarine, marjoram, paprika, garlic powder, salt and pepper in bowl. Brush on both sides of potatoes. Bake at 350 degrees for 20 minutes or until potatoes begin to brown. Turn potatoes with spatula. Sprinkle with cheese. Bake for 10 minutes longer. Yield: 4 servings.

Dena Sue Montgomery

NANA'S CURRY POTATO PATTIES

3 potatoes, grated
1 carrot, grated
2 onions, grated
1 egg
1/2 cup milk
1 cup flour

1 tablespoon baking
  powder
1 1/2 teaspoons curry
  powder
2 teaspoons salt
Oil for deep frying

Combine first 9 ingredients in bowl; mix well. Drop by heaping tablespoonfuls into hot oil. Deep-fry until golden brown on both sides. This recipe is from New Zealand. Yield: 6 servings.

Melanie Bond

POTATO AND ONION PANCAKES

4 cups drained shredded
   potatoes
1 egg

1 envelope onion soup mix
3 tablespoons flour
1/4 cup butter

Combine potatoes, egg, dry soup mix and flour in bowl; mix well. Heat butter in 10-inch skillet until foamy but not brown. Drop potato mixture by 1/4 cupfuls into butter. Cook on each side for 3 minutes or until golden brown. Drain on paper towels. Serve with sour cream and applesauce. Do not use instant soup mix. Yield: 4 servings.

Juyne Bushart

FRIED POTATO CAKES

2 cups mashed potatoes
6 tablespoons flour
1 egg

1/4 cup milk
1 medium onion, chopped
1/4 cup oil

Combine potatoes, flour, egg, milk and onion in bowl; mix well. Drop by spoonfuls into hot oil in skillet. Brown on both sides, pressing with spatula to flatten. Yield: 12 cakes.

Peggy Posante

MUSHROOM POTATOES

8 medium potatoes
Salt and freshly ground
   pepper to taste
Fresh mushrooms,
   chopped

2 cans cream of
   mushroom soup
3/4 soup can milk
Butter

Cook potatoes in jackets in water to cover in saucepan until tender; drain and cool. Peel and chop potatoes. Place in buttered baking dish. Season with salt and pepper. Sprinkle with mushrooms. Combine soup and milk in bowl; mix well. Stir in additional pepper to taste. Pour over potatoes. Dot with butter. Bake at 350 degrees for 25 to 30 minutes or until bubbly. Yield: 6 to 8 servings.

Wilma Sullivan

POTATOES AU GRATIN

2 tablespoons butter
1 teaspoon salt
1/4 cup flour
2 cups milk

1 cup shredded cheese
4 cups chopped cooked
potatoes
2/3 cup buttered crumbs

Blend butter, salt and flour in small saucepan. Stir in milk. Cook until thickened, stirring constantly. Stir in cheese until melted. Add potatoes; mix gently. Spoon into 9x12-inch baking dish. Top with buttered crumbs. Bake at 400 to 450 degrees until golden brown. Cook potatoes in jackets to preserve nutrients. Yield: 8 servings.

Joyce Nally

SOUTHERN BELL POTATOES

1 16-ounce package
frozen golden crinkle
potatoes
1/4 cup melted butter
1 cup shredded Cheddar
cheese

1 1/3 cups milk
3 eggs
1 1/4 teaspoons seasoned
salt
1/4 teaspoon onion powder

Toss potatoes with melted butter in 6x10-inch baking dish. Bake at 400 degrees for 15 minutes. Reduce temperature to 350 degrees. Toss cheese with potatoes. Combine milk, eggs, seasoned salt and onion powder in bowl. Pour over potatoes. Bake at 350 degrees for 20 to 25 minutes or until set. Cool for 5 minutes before cutting. Yield: 4 to 5 servings.

Linda Fenwick

POTATO WEDGES

4 to 6 large potatoes
1/2 cup melted margarine

1 tablespoon seasoned salt
1/2 cup Parmesan cheese

Cut unpeeled potatoes into 1-inch wedges. Place skin side down in 9x13-inch baking dish. Drizzle with melted margarine. Sprinkle with seasoned salt and cheese. Bake at 375 degrees for 20 to 25 minutes or until golden brown. Yield: 4 to 6 servings.

Cindy Rayhill

STUFFED BAKED POTATOES

6 large baking potatoes
2 tablespoons margarine
1¼ cups finely chopped
  onion
1¼ cups finely chopped
  green bell pepper
3 tablespoons oil
½ cup hot milk
1 teaspoon paprika
1¼ teaspoons salt
½ teaspoon pepper
1½ cups shredded
  Cheddar cheese

Rub potatoes with margarine; pierce skins with fork. Bake at 425 degrees for 50 minutes to 1 hour or until tender. Cut shallow slice from 1 side of each potato; squeeze potatoes gently. Scoop out pulp, reserving shells. Mash potato with fork in bowl. Sauté onion and green pepper in oil in skillet until tender. Add to mashed potatoes. Add milk, paprika, salt, pepper and 1 cup cheese; mix well. Spoon lightly into potato shells. Sprinkle with remaining 1 cup cheese. Place on baking sheet. Bake for 15 minutes or until heated through. Yield: 6 servings.

Walter Mathis

BACON TATER TOTS

½ cup mustard
¼ cup packed brown
  sugar
½ teaspoon ginger
Bacon slices, cut into
  halves
Frozen Tater Tots
American cheese slices,
  cut into strips

Combine mustard, brown sugar and ginger in bowl; mix well and set aside. Cook bacon in skillet until light brown but not crisp; drain. Cook Tater Tots according to package directions. Wrap 1 strip cheese around each Tater Tot. Wrap bacon around cheese; secure with toothpicks. Place on rack in broiler pan. Broil until bacon is crisp. Serve with mustard sauce.

Linda Mathis

SPINACH CASSEROLE

2 10-ounce packages
  frozen chopped spinach
8 ounces cream cheese,
  softened

1 small onion, chopped
1/2 cup milk
1/2 cup shredded Cheddar
  cheese

Cook spinach according to package directions; press with spoon to drain well. Place in 1-quart baking dish. Combine cream cheese and onion in bowl; mix well. Add milk gradually; mixing well. Pour over spinach. Sprinkle with cheese. Bake at 350 degrees for 20 minutes. Yield: 8 servings.

Clara Nance

SQUASH CASSEROLE

2 pounds yellow squash,
  chopped
1 medium onion, chopped
1 tablespoon sugar
  (optional)
3 tablespoons melted
  butter

2 eggs, beaten
1 teaspoon sage (optional)
Salt and pepper to taste
Paprika to taste
2 cups shredded Cheddar
  cheese

Cook squash in small amount of water in saucepan until tender; drain. Combine with onion, sugar, butter, eggs, sage, salt and pepper in bowl; mix well. Add paprika and half the cheese. Spoon into buttered baking dish. Sprinkle with remaining cheese and additional paprika. Bake at 350 degrees for 30 minutes or until bubbly. May add 1 cup evaporated milk and 2 cups cracker crumbs if desired. Yield: 6 servings.

Juyne Bushart, Sandi Tipton Clark

★ Yellow summer squash and zucchini can be used interchangeably or in combination in most summer squash recipes.

CHEESY SQUASH CASSEROLE

12 medium yellow squash
6 slices bacon
3/4 cup chopped onion
1 1/2 cups shredded
  Cheddar cheese
3 eggs, beaten
1 1/2 tablespoons
  Worcestershire sauce
Pepper to taste

Cook squash in small amount of water in saucepan until tender; drain. Mash squash in bowl. Cook bacon in skillet until crisp; drain on paper towel. Sauté onion in bacon drippings until tender. Add onion, cheese, eggs, Worcestershire sauce, pepper and crumbled bacon to squash; mix well. Spoon into 1 1/2-quart baking dish. Bake at 350 degrees for 30 minutes.
Yield: 10 servings.

Grace Murphy

SPECIAL SQUASH CASSEROLE

4 cups chopped squash
1 large onion, chopped
1 egg
1/2 cup butter
Corn bread crumbs
Sugar, sage, salt and
  pepper to taste

Cook squash with onion in water in saucepan until tender; drain. Add remaining ingredients; mix well. Spoon into baking dish. Bake at 450 degrees until brown. Yield: 8 servings.

Helen Lovan

CELESTA'S SQUASH CASSEROLE

4 cups cooked yellow
  squash, drained
1 can cream of mushroom
  or cream of celery soup
1/4 cup chopped onion
1/2 cup margarine
3 eggs, beaten
1 cup dry bread crumbs
1 cup shredded cheese
Paprika to taste

Combine squash, soup, onion, margarine, eggs, bread crumbs and cheese in bowl; mix well. Spoon into buttered baking dish. Sprinkle with paprika. Bake at 325 degrees for 45 minutes or until brown. Yield: 12 servings.

Celesta Wilson

SQUASH SUPREME

2 to 3 cups chopped
  squash
1 medium onion, chopped
1 cup sour cream
1 can cream of chicken
  soup

Salt and pepper to taste
1/2 cup melted margarine
1/2 package herb-seasoned
  stuffing mix
1/2 package corn bread
  stuffing mix

Cook squash with onion in water in saucepan for 5 minutes or until tender; drain. Stir in sour cream and soup. Season to taste. Mix margarine with stuffing mixes. Sprinkle half the stuffing in 2-quart baking dish. Top with squash mixture and remaining stuffing. Bake at 350 degrees for 30 minutes. Yield: 6 servings.

Antoinette Monroe, Della Mundy
Clara Nance

SQUASH FRITTERS

2 cups grated squash
1 teaspoon minced onion
6 tablespoons flour
2 eggs
2 teaspoons melted butter

2 teaspoons sugar
1 teaspoon salt
Pepper to taste
Oil for deep frying

Combine squash, onion, flour, eggs, butter, sugar, salt and pepper in bowl; mix well. Drop by tablespoonfuls into hot oil. Deep-fry until brown. Yield: 4 servings.

Patsy Ford

ORANGE SQUASH

2 cups mashed cooked
  Hubbard squash
1/2 cup orange juice
2 to 3 tablespoons butter

1/2 teaspoon salt
Dash of pepper
1/4 cup chopped pecans

Combine squash, orange juice, butter, salt and pepper in bowl; mix until smooth. Spoon into greased baking dish. Top with pecans. Bake at 450 degrees until light brown. Yield: 4 servings.

Mary J. Thompson

STUFFED YELLOW SQUASH

2 medium onions, chopped
2 medium green bell
  peppers, chopped
1/2 cup margarine
2 pounds small yellow
  squash

2 or 3 eggs
1/4 cup flour
1/2 cup sugar
Salt and pepper to taste
Buttered bread crumbs

Sauté onions and green peppers in margarine in skillet until tender. Cut squash into halves lengthwise. Cook in water to cover in saucepan until just tender; drain. Scoop out pulp, reserving shells. Add pulp to onion mixture. Stir in next 4 ingredients. Spoon into squash shells. Place in baking dish. Sprinkle with crumbs. Bake at 325 degrees for 15 minutes. Yield: 8 servings.

Gwen Mills

WHITE PATTYCAKE SQUASH

Pattycake squash
Cream

Sugar to taste
Cinnamon to taste

Peel and chop squash. Cook in water in saucepan until tender; drain well. Mash squash in bowl. Add cream, sugar and cinnamon; mix until smooth.

Dolly Frick

MOM'S SWEET POTATO AND APPLE CASSEROLE

2 large sweet potatoes
1 21-ounce can apple pie
  filling
3 tablespoons butter

1/4 cup graham cracker
  crumbs
Cinnamon to taste
Sugar to taste

Cook sweet potatoes in water in saucepan until tender. Peel and chop sweet potatoes. Combine with pie filling in bowl; mix gently. Spoon into greased 1 1/2-quart baking dish. Dot with butter. Combine cracker crumbs with cinnamon and sugar in bowl. Sprinkle over casserole. Bake at 350 degrees for 25 minutes or until brown and bubbly. Yield: 6 to 8 servings.

Patti Reece

SWEET POTATO CASSEROLE

3 cups mashed sweet
 potatoes
2 eggs, beaten
1/3 to 1/2 cup milk
1 cup sugar
1/2 cup butter, softened

1 teaspoon vanilla extract
1 cup packed brown sugar
1/2 cup flour
1/3 cup butter
1 cup chopped nuts

Combine sweet potatoes, eggs, milk, sugar, 1/2 cup butter and vanilla in bowl; mix well. Spoon into baking dish. Mix remaining ingredients in bowl. Sprinkle over sweet potato mixure. Bake at 350 degrees for 25 minutes. Yield: 8 servings.

Virginia Emmitt, Clara Nance

BETTY'S SWEET POTATO CASSEROLE

4 sweet potatoes
1/4 cup margarine
1/2 cup chopped pecans

1/2 cup packed brown
 sugar
Miniature marshmallows

Cook potatoes in jackets in water in saucepan until tender; drain. Cool and peel potatoes. Combine with margarine in bowl; mash until smooth. Stir in pecans and brown sugar. Spoon into buttered baking dish. Top with marshmallows. Bake at 350 degrees until marshmallows are light brown. Yield: 4 servings.

Betty Krueger

SINFULLY RICH SWEET POTATOES

3 cups mashed cooked
 sweet potatoes
1/4 cup butter
2 eggs, beaten
3/4 cup sugar

1 teaspoon vanilla extract
1 cup coconut
1 cup packed brown sugar
1/3 cup butter
1 cup chopped pecans

Combine potatoes with 1/4 cup butter, eggs, sugar and vanilla in bowl; mix well. Spoon into greased baking dish. Mix coconut, brown sugar, 1/3 cup butter and pecans in small bowl. Sprinkle over potatoes. Bake at 375 degrees until brown. Yield: 6 servings.

Jo Ann Thompson

SWEET POTATO SOUFFLÉ

3 cups mashed cooked
  sweet potatoes
1/3 stick margarine
1/3 cup milk
1/3 cup sugar
1 teaspoon vanilla extract

1 teaspoon butter flavoring
Salt to taste
1 cup packed brown sugar
1/3 cup margarine
1/3 cup flour
1 cup chopped pecans

Combine sweet potatoes, 1/3 stick margarine, milk, sugar, flavorings and salt in mixer bowl; mix until smooth. Spoon into greased baking dish. Mix brown sugar, 1/3 cup margarine, flour and pecans in bowl. Sprinkle over sweet potato mixture. Bake at 350 degrees for 30 minutes. Yield: 10 servings.

Laverne Hollingsworth

MARY'S SWEET POTATO SOUFFLÉ

2 cups mashed cooked
  sweet potatoes
1 cup packed brown sugar
1/4 cup margarine
2 eggs
1 teaspoon cinnnamon
Dash of nutmeg

1 cup graham cracker
  crumbs
1/3 cup packed brown
  sugar
6 tablespoons melted
  margarine
1/2 cup chopped pecans

Combine sweet potatoes, 1 cup brown sugar, 1/4 cup margarine, eggs, cinnamon and nutmeg in bowl; mix well. Spoon into 8-inch baking dish. Bake at 350 degrees for 20 minutes. Mix cracker crumbs, 1/3 cup brown sugar, melted margarine and pecans in bowl. Sprinkle over sweet potato mixture. Bake for 20 minutes longer. Yield: 6 servings.

Mary Whitaker

★ Be sure to sample your sweet potatoes to know whether to adjust the amount of sugar. Sweet potatoes vary in sweetness as much as apples, pears and other fruit.

SWEET POTATO SURPRISE

1 16-ounce can sweet
potatoes, drained
1 16-ounce can apricot
halves
1¼ cups packed brown
sugar
1½ tablespoons
cornstarch

2 tablespoons margarine
1 teaspoon grated orange
rind
⅛ teaspoon cinnamon
¼ teaspoon salt
½ cup pecan halves

Place sweet potatoes in 6x10-inch baking dish. Drain apricots, reserving 1 cup syrup. Add apricots to sweet potatoes. Combine brown sugar, cornstarch, margarine, orange rind, cinnamon, salt and reserved apricot syrup in saucepan; mix well. Cook until thickened, stirring constantly. Pour over sweet potatoes and apricots. Top with pecans. Bake at 350 degrees for 30 minutes. Yield: 6 servings.

Roberta Walker

LOUISIANA WHIPPED YAMS

8 medium yams, peeled,
cut into quarters
½ cup sugar
¼ cup butter
Pinch of salt
1 cup cream

2 egg yolks
Rum extract to taste
2 egg whites
1 tablespoon sugar
1 teaspoon vanilla extract
Pinch of cream of tartar

Cook yams in water to cover in deep saucepan until tender; drain. Add ½ cup sugar, butter and salt; mash well. Add cream; beat until smooth. Add egg yolks lightly beaten with rum extract. Spoon into buttered baking dish. Bake at 350 degrees for 30 minutes or until set. Beat egg whites in bowl until stiff peaks form. Add 1 tablespoon sugar, vanilla and cream of tartar; mix well. Spread over casserole, sealing to edge of dish. Bake until meringue is light brown. Yield: 8 to 10 servings.

Helen Courtney

FRIED GREEN TOMATOES

4 large green tomatoes,
  sliced
1 cup self-rising flour

¼ cup sugar
¼ cup oil

Soak tomatoes in ice water to cover in bowl for 15 minutes; drain. Sift flour and sugar into shallow dish. Coat tomatoes well on both sides. Fry in oil in skillet over medium heat for 2½ minutes on each side or until golden brown. Serve at once. Yield: 4 servings.

Peggy Posante

TOMATO PROVENÇALE

1 firm tomato
Salt and pepper to taste

Butter
Cornflake crumbs

Cut tomato into halves crosswise. Place cut side up in small baking dish. Sprinkle with salt and pepper. Top with butter and cornflake crumbs. Bake at 350 degrees just until tomato is tender. Yield: 2 servings.

Rhonda Austin

PICKLED TURNIPS

4 small white turnips
3 tablespoons coarse salt
1 cup white vinegar

¾ cup sugar
½ teaspoon paprika

Peel turnips and cut crosswise into thin slices. Mix with salt in bowl. Let stand for 1 hour; drain. Bring vinegar, sugar and paprika to a boil in saucepan. Add turnips. Bring to a boil; reduce heat. Simmer for 3 minutes. Pour into dish; cool. Chill until serving time. Serve cold. Yield: 6 servings.

Gwen Mills

STUFFED TURNIPS

6 medium turnips
1 cup shredded sharp
  Cheddar cheese
1/4 cup butter
Pinch of sugar
1/4 teaspoon salt
1/4 teaspoon white pepper
Cornstarch

Peel turnips. Scoop out centers, leaving shells. Cook shells and scooped out portions in salted water in saucepan until tender. Invert shells to drain. Combine pulp with cheese, butter, sugar, salt and pepper in saucepan; mash until smooth. Mix in enough cornstarch to thicken to desired consistency. Cook until of desired consistency. Spoon into shells. Place in baking dish. Bake at 375 degrees for 30 minutes. Garnish with parsley. Yield: 6 servings.

Zora Logsdon

ZUCCHINI CASSEROLE

1 cup sliced onion
1 cup green bell pepper
  strips
3 tablespoons butter
3 medium zucchini, sliced
1 tablespoon cornstarch
3/4 teaspoon basil
Salt and pepper to taste
3 medium tomatoes,
  chopped
Parmesan cheese

Sauté onion and green pepper in butter in skillet. Add zucchini. Cook for 10 minutes. Stir in cornstarch, basil, salt and pepper. Alternate layers of zucchini mixture and tomatoes in baking dish until all ingredients are used. Sprinkle with cheese. Bake at 350 degrees for 45 minutes. May substitute 1 can of tomatoes for fresh tomatoes and mix with zucchini instead of layering. May add cracker crumbs and pats of butter to top if desired. Yield: 6 servings.

Gwen Mills, Shirley Smith

ZUCCHINI PATTIES

2 cups grated peeled
  zucchini
1 small onion, grated
1 egg
1/2 cup flour
2 tablespoons sugar
1 teaspoon salt
Oil for frying

Combine zucchini, onion, egg, flour, sugar and salt in bowl; mix well. Drop by tablespoonfuls into hot oil in skillet. Fry until golden brown on both sides. Yield: 6 to 8 servings.

Patti Reece

ZUCCHINI PARMESAN

1 to 2 eggs, beaten
1/4 cup milk
2 to 3 zucchini, sliced
  1/4 inch thick
1 to 2 cups Italian bread
  crumbs
Oil for frying
1 jar spaghetti sauce
1 pound mozzarella
  cheese, shredded
1/2 cup Parmesan cheese

Combine eggs and milk in bowl; mix well. Dip zucchini in egg mixture; roll in bread crumbs, coating well. Fry in oil in skillet until golden brown on both sides; drain on paper towel. Alternate layers of spaghetti sauce, zucchini, mozzarella cheese and Parmesan cheese in 8x8-inch baking dish, ending with mozzarella cheese. Bake at 350 degrees for 30 minutes. May substitute eggplant for zucchini. Yield: 6 to 8 servings.

Marylucy Caron

TOM'S ZUCCHINI SQUASH

1 or 2 large zucchini, sliced
1 large onion, sliced
3 to 4 medium tomatoes,
  chopped
2 ounces red wine
Butter
1 1/2 teaspoons oregano
1/8 teaspoon garlic powder
  (optional)
Seasoning salt to taste
1 cup shredded mozzarella
  or provolone cheese

Combine zucchini with onion and tomatoes in bowl; mix gently. Spoon into greased 10 or 12-inch baking dish. Add wine. Dot with butter. Sprinkle with oregano, garlic powder and seasoning salt. Bake at 350 degrees for 45 minutes to 1 hour. Top with cheese. Bake for 15 to 20 minutes longer or until cheese is melted. Yield: 4 to 6 servings.

Thomas Waldrop

ITALIAN STUFFED ZUCCHINI

6   5-inch zucchini
2 slices white bread
2 tablespoons milk
1/2 cup ricotta cheese

1/3 cup Parmesan cheese
1 egg
1/2 teaspoon garlic juice
1/4 teaspoon oregano

Parboil zucchini in water in saucepan for 5 minutes; drain. Cut into halves lengthwise. Scoop out and chop centers, reserving shells. Trim bread. Soak in milk in bowl for several minutes. Squeeze milk out of bread, reserving milk. Combine bread, chopped zucchini, ricotta cheese, Parmesan Cheese, egg, garlic juice and oregano in bowl; mix well. Add enough reserved milk to make of desired consistency. Spoon into zucchini shells. Place in oiled 9x13-inch baking dish. Bake at 375 degrees for 40 minutes or until tender and golden brown. Yield: 6 servings.

Peggy Posante

MICROWAVE ZUCCHINI BAKE

2 cups thinly sliced
   zucchini
1 large tomato, thinly
   sliced
1 large onion, thinly sliced

1 teaspoon thyme
2 tablespoons Parmesan
   cheese
1 tablespoon butter

Layer zucchini, tomato, onion, thyme and cheese 1/2 at a time in 11/2-quart glass casserole. Dot with butter. Microwave on High for 14 minutes or until vegetables are tender-crisp, turning dish once. Yield: 4 servings.

Glenda Rogers

ZUCCHINI AND POTATO CASSEROLE

Potatoes, thinly sliced
Zucchini, thinly sliced
Onion, thinly sliced
Tomatoes, thinly sliced

Parmesan cheese
Butter
Salt and pepper to taste

Layer potatoes, zucchini, onion, and tomatoes in buttered 2-quart baking dish, topping each layer with cheese, pats of butter and salt and pepper. Sprinkle additional cheese over all. Bake at 325 degrees until vegetables are tender.

Julia Hayden

ABC CASSEROLE

1 10-ounce package
   frozen asparagus
1 10-ounce package
   frozen broccoli
1 10-ounce package
   frozen cauliflower
1 can water chestnuts

8 ounces Velveeta cheese,
   cubed
1/2 cup melted margarine
1 can cream of mushroom
   soup
Butter
Crumbs

Cook asparagus, broccoli and cauliflower according to package directions; drain. Combine with water chestnuts, cheese, margarine and soup in bowl; mix well. Spoon into greased 6x9-inch baking dish. Dot with butter; sprinkle with crumbs. Bake at 350 degrees for 20 minutes. Yield: 6 servings.

Edith Hester

MEXICAN CASSEROLE

1/2 green bell pepper,
   chopped
1 onion, chopped
3 tablespoons bacon
   drippings
1 16-ounce can chili con
   carne without beans
1 16-ounce can kidney
   beans, drained

1 12-ounce can whole
   kernel corn, drained
1 3-ounce can
   mushrooms, drained
1 cup shredded sharp
   Cheddar cheese

Sauté green pepper and onion in bacon drippings in small skillet. Pour into 2-quart baking dish, spreading to grease bottom and sides. Layer remaining ingredients in prepared dish. Chill, covered, for 1½ hours. Bake, covered, at 325 degrees for 1 hour. Bake, uncovered, for 30 minutes longer. Yield: 8 servings.

Kim Clinton, Mary J. Thompson

MIXED VEGETABLE CASSEROLE

1 large package frozen
  mixed vegetables
1 cup chopped onion
1 cup chopped celery

1 cup shredded cheese
1 cup mayonnaise
½ cup melted margarine
1 tube crackers, crushed

Cook mixed vegetables according to package directions just until tender; drain. Place in greased baking dish. Combine onion, celery, cheese and mayonnaise in bowl. Spread over vegetables. Top with mixture of margarine and cracker crumbs. Bake at 350 degrees for 25 to 30 minutes or until heated through. Yield: 6 servings.

Dewey Clifton

VEG-ALL CASSEROLE

2 to 3 16-ounce cans
  mixed vegetables,
  drained
1 or 2 cans water
  chestnuts, drained
1 cup chopped onion
  (optional)
1 cup chopped celery
  (optional)

2 to 3 cups shredded
  cheese
1 to 2 tablespoons sugar
  (optional)
½ to 1 cup mayonnaise
1 tube Ritz crackers,
  crushed
¼ cup melted butter

Combine first 7 ingredients in bowl; mix well. Spoon into greased 3-quart baking dish. Top with mixture of cracker crumbs and butter. Bake at 350 degrees for 20 to 25 minutes or until golden brown. Yield: 8 to 10 servings.

Betty Donovan, Norma Hamilton
Barbara C. Hendrick, Gale Marcum
Delores Richardson

VEGETABLE LASAGNA

8 ounces lean ground beef
1/2 cup chopped onion
1/2 cup chopped green bell
   pepper
1 clove of garlic, crushed
1 8-ounce can tomatoes
1 8-ounce can tomato
   sauce
2 tablespoons chopped
   fresh parsley
1 teaspoon oregano

1 teaspoon basil
1/2 teaspoon salt
1 large or 3 medium
   zucchini
1 1/2 cups low-fat cottage
   cheese
1 egg
2 tablespoons chopped
   fresh parsley
1 cup shredded mozzarella
   cheese

Brown ground beef with onion, green pepper and garlic in large saucepan, stirring until ground beef is crumbly; drain. Add tomatoes, tomato sauce, 2 tablespoons parsley, oregano, basil and salt; mix well. Bring to a boil, stirring occasionally; reduce heat. Simmer for 1 hour. Parboil zucchini in saucepan. Cut into nine 1/4-inch thick slices. Combine cottage cheese, egg and 2 tablespoons parsley in bowl. Spoon a small amount of sauce into 8x8-inch baking dish. Layer zucchini, remaining sauce, mozzarella and cottage cheese mixture 1/3 at a time in prepared dish. Bake at 350 degrees for 45 minutes. Let stand for 15 minutes. Yield: 4 servings.

Jane Wallace

VEGETABLE CASSEROLE

1 package frozen
   California-style vegetables
1 cup sour cream
1 can cream of mushroom
   soup

1 can cream of celery soup
1 cup shredded Cheddar
   cheese
1 can French-fried onion
   rings

Thaw and drain vegetables. Combine with sour cream, soups, cheese and half the onion rings in bowl; mix well. Spoon into 1 1/2-quart baking dish. Bake at 350 degrees for 25 minutes. Sprinkle with remaining onion rings. Bake just until topping is brown. Yield: 6 servings.

Jayne Roberts

EASY GARDEN VEGETABLE PIE

1 cup water
1/2 teaspoon salt
2 cups chopped fresh
 broccoli
1/2 cup chopped green bell
 pepper
1 cup shredded Cheddar
 cheese
1/2 cup chopped onion
1 1/2 cups milk
3/4 cup buttermilk baking
 mix
3 eggs
1 teaspoon salt
1/4 teaspoon pepper

Bring water and 1/2 teaspoon salt to a boil in saucepan. Add broccoli. Cook, covered, for 5 minutes or until tender-crisp; drain. Combine with green pepper, cheese and onion in lightly greased 10-inch pie plate. Combine milk, baking mix, eggs, 1 teaspoon salt and pepper in blender. Process for 15 seconds or until smooth. Pour over broccoli in pie plate. Bake at 400 degrees for 35 to 40 minutes. Let stand for 5 minutes. Yield: 6 servings.

Shirley Smith

VEGETABLE PIZZA

1 12-ounce package
 refrigerator crescent
 rolls
8 ounces cream cheese,
 softened
1 cup mayonnaise
1/2 teaspoon onion powder
1/2 teaspoon garlic powder
1 teaspoon dillweed
1 head cauliflower,
 chopped
3 spears broccoli, chopped
1/2 green bell pepper,
 chopped
2 stalks celery, chopped
2 carrots, chopped
1 large package shredded
 Velveeta cheese

Unroll crescent roll dough on ungreased baking sheet, pressing to seal edges and perforations. Bake at 350 degrees for 5 minutes or until golden brown. Cool completely. Combine cream cheese, mayonnaise, onion powder, garlic powder and dillweed in bowl; mix until smooth. Spread over crust. Layer cauliflower, broccoli, green pepper, celery and carrots over cream cheese layer. Top with Velveeta cheese. Cover with plastic wrap; press vegetables gently into cream cheese. Chill for 4 hours or longer. Cut into squares. Yield: 15 squares.

Terri Arnold

VEGETABLE BATTER

2 teaspoons oil
1 egg
1/2 cup water
1 teaspoon sugar

1/2 cup flour
1/2 teaspoon baking
   powder
1/2 teaspoon salt

Combine oil, egg, water, sugar, flour, baking powder and salt in mixer bowl; mix until smooth. Use to coat vegetables for frying. Yield: 1 cup.

Carmen Stilger

VEGETABLE BATTER MIX

3 cups self-rising flour
2   1-serving envelopes
   tomato instant soup mix
1 tablespoon paprika

2 envelopes Italian salad
   dressing mix
1 teaspoon salt

Combine flour, soup mix, paprika, salad dressing mix and salt in airtight container; mix well. Store in refrigerator. Mix desired amount with enough water to make a smooth batter in bowl. Use to coat zucchini, onion rings, banana peppers, etc. for deep frying.

Pat Cole

★ Use bite-sized vegetables for frying so the batter will cook brown and crisp quickly and the vegetable inside will be tender-crisp. Serve with dipping sauces or a sprinkle of Parmesan cheese.

SIDE DISHES

BASIC MICROWAVE GRAVY

2 tablespoons flour
1/4 teaspoon salt

1/4 cup water
3/4 cup liquid*

Combine flour, salt and water in 2-cup glass measure; blend well. Stir in liquid gradually. Microwave on High for 2 1/2 minutes or until thickened, stirring every 30 seconds. *Liquid may be pan drippings plus enough water to measure 3/4 cup; 1 bouillon cube dissolved in 3/4 cup water; or reserved vegetable cooking liquid. May add gravy browning sauce.

Mary Cook

GRITS AU GRATIN

3 cups boiling water
1 teaspoon salt
3/4 cup quick-cooking grits
4 ounces sharp cheese

1/2 cup milk
1/2 cup buttered bread
   crumbs
Paprika to taste

Boil water and salt in saucepan. Add grits. Cook for 2 1/2 to 5 minutes. Alternate layers of grits and sliced cheese in greased 1 1/2-quart baking dish. Pour milk over top. Top with crumbs and paprika. Bake at 325 degrees until set. Yield: 6 servings.

Paula Goodlett

CHEESE GRITS

4 cups milk
1 cup quick-cooking grits
1 cup butter

1 pound Gruyère cheese
Salt and pepper to taste
1 cup Parmesan cheese

Bring milk to a boil in saucepan. Add grits and half the butter gradually. Cook over medium heat until of desired consistency, stirring constantly; remove from heat. Beat for 3 minutes. Add remaining butter, shredded Gruyère cheese, salt and pepper. Spoon into greased 9x13-inch baking dish. Sprinkle with Parmesan cheese. Bake at 350 degrees for 30 minutes or until brown. May add jalapeño peppers if desired. Yield: 8 to 10 servings.

Marge O'Daniel

DELUXE CHEESE GRITS SOUFFLÉ

Butter, softened
Parmesan cheese
1 cup grits
4 cups boiling salted water
3 tablespoons butter
3 tablespoons flour
1 cup milk
1 cup cream
1 cup shredded Cheddar
   cheese
1/2 cup Parmesan cheese
6 egg yolks
6 egg whites
Pinch of cream of tartar

Butter 3-quart soufflé dish. Fit with buttered foil collar. Dust dish and collar with Parmesan cheese. Stir grits into boiling salted water in saucepan. Bring to a boil; reduce heat. Cook over medium-high heat until grits are of the consistency of mashed potatoes. Melt 3 tablespoons butter in large saucepan. Stir in flour. Cook over medium-high heat for 2 minutes, whisking constantly. Heat milk and cream in saucepan. Stir into flour gradually. Cook until thickened, whisking constantly. Stir in grits, Cheddar cheese and 1/2 cup Parmesan cheese; remove from heat. Beat egg yolks in bowl until lemon-colored. Add to grits; mix well. Beat eggs at high speed in mixer bowl until foamy. Add cream of tartar. Beat until medium-soft peaks form. Fold gently into grits; do not overmix. Spoon into prepared dish. Place in 400-degree oven; reduce temperature to 375 degrees. Bake for 30 minutes or until brown on top. Serve immediately. May bake for 20 minutes in two 1 1/2-quart soufflé dishes or shallow baking dish.
Yield: 10 servings.

Shirley Smith

HOMINY CASSEROLE

1 large can hominy,
   drained
1 can cream of mushroom
   soup
1/2 cup cream
1 teaspoon celery seed
1 teaspoon
   Worcestershire sauce
1/2 teaspoon coarsely
   ground pepper
1/4 teaspoon cayenne
   pepper
8 ounces blanched
   slivered almonds, toasted
1 cup bread crumbs

Place hominy in baking dish. Combine soup, cream, celery seed, Worcestershire sauce, pepper and cayenne pepper in saucepan. Simmer until flavors are well mixed. Stir in almonds. Pour over hominy. Top with bread crumbs. Bake at 350 degrees for 30 to 40 minutes or until bubbly. Yield: 4 servings.

Zora Logsdon

CREAMY HOMINY CASSEROLE

2　29-ounce cans hominy, drained
2　4-ounce cans chopped green chilies, drained
8 ounces sour cream
1 cup whipping cream
Salt and pepper to taste
1/4 cup margarine
1 cup shredded Monterey Jack or Gruyère cheese

Combine hominy, chilies, sour cream, cream, salt and pepper in bowl; mix well. Spoon into deep baking dish. Dot with margarine; sprinkle with cheese. Bake, covered, at 350 degrees for 30 minutes. Yield: 8 servings.

Lillian Muller

FETTUCINI AND VEGETABLES

1 pound fettucini
1 cup sliced fresh mushrooms
1 cup coarsely chopped onion
1/2 cup sliced carrots
1 cup chopped broccoli
2 tablespoons oil
1/2 cup butter
1/3 cup Parmesan cheese

Cook fettucini using package directions; drain and set aside. Stir-fry mushrooms, onion, carrots and broccoli in hot oil in nonstick skillet for 6 minutes or until tender-crisp. Reduce heat. Add butter and fettucini. Toss until butter is melted. Spoon into serving dish. Top with cheese. Yield: 6 servings.

Cindy Rayhill

RICE WITH CASHEWS

¾ large can cashews
¼ cup butter
½ small can coconut

¼ cup margarine
2 servings minute rice

Sauté cashews in ¼ cup margarine in electric skillet at 200 to 250 degrees for 45 minutes, stirring occasionally. Add coconut and ¼ cup margarine. Cook for 15 minutes or until coconut is brown and crisp. Toss with rice in serving bowl. Yield: 2 servings.

Johnnie Harper

RICE CASSEROLE

2 cups rice
¾ cup margarine
2 cans beef consommé

1 large onion, chopped
1 large can chopped
   mushrooms

Sauté rice in margarine in skillet over low heat until light brown. Combine consommé with enough water to measure 4 cups liquid. Combine with rice and onion in baking dish; mix well. Bake, covered, at 325 to 350 degrees for 1 hour. Stir in undrained mushrooms. Bake for 30 to 40 minutes longer or until rice is tender and casserole is of desired consistency.
Yield: 12 servings.

Antoinette Monroe

DIRTY RICE

1 pound sausage
Bacon drippings or oil
½ cup flour
2 medium onions, finely
   chopped
1 green bell pepper, finely
   chopped
2 stalks celery, finely
   chopped
3 cloves of garlic, crushed

8 ounces chicken giblets,
   finely chopped
2 cups water
Tabasco sauce to taste
Salt and pepper to taste
6 green onion tops,
   chopped
6 sprigs of parsley,
   chopped
10 cups hot cooked rice

Brown sausage in large saucepan, stirring until crumbly; remove with slotted spoon. Add enough bacon drippings to pan drippings to measure 1/2 cup. Stir in flour. Cook until very brown, stirring constantly; do not burn. Add onions, green pepper, celery and garlic. Cook for several minutes. Add chicken giblets. Cook until no longer pink. Add water, sausage, Tabasco sauce, salt and pepper. Simmer for 1 1/2 hours or longer. Stir in onion tops and parsley. Cook for 30 minutes longer. Stir in rice just before serving. Yield: 16 to 20 servings.

Bob Garrison

FRIED RICE

3/4 **cup chopped onion**
2 **tablespoons oil**
2 **cups cooked rice, chilled**

2 **eggs, slightly beaten**
1 **tablespoon soy sauce**
1/2 **teaspoon salt**

Sauté onion in oil in skillet. Add rice. Sauté for several minutes. Stir in mixture of eggs, soy sauce and salt. Cook for 2 minutes or until eggs are set, stirring constantly. The secret to this recipe is to make sure the rice is cold. Yield: 4 servings.

Frank Fendley

GREEN RICE

2 **cups long grain rice**
2 **eggs, slightly beaten**
2 **cups milk**
1 1/2 **teaspoons lemon juice**
1 **teaspoon salt**
1/2 **teaspoon white pepper**
1/3 **cup oil**
1/3 **cup olive oil**

3 **medium onions, chopped**
2 **green bell peppers, chopped**
2 **cloves of garlic, chopped**
1 **bunch parsley, chopped**
2 **cups shredded mild Cheddar or American cheese**

Steam rice in saucepan until tender. Combine eggs, milk, lemon juice, salt and pepper in mixer bowl; mix well. Stir in oil and olive oil. Add rice, onions, green pepper, garlic, parsley and cheese. Spoon into buttered 2-quart baking dish. Bake at 350 degrees for 45 minutes. Yield: 12 to 14 servings.

Patricia J. Tudor

JAYNE'S GREEN RICE

3/4 cup chopped onion
3/4 cup chopped celery
3 tablespoons margarine
1 cup cooked rice
1 10-ounce package
  chopped broccoli, cooked

1 can cream of chicken
  soup
1/2 cup milk
1 small jar Cheez Whiz
Salt and pepper to taste

Sauté onion and celery in margarine in skillet. Add rice, broccoli, soup, milk, Cheez Whiz, salt and pepper; mix well. Spoon into baking dish. Bake at 350 degrees for 15 to 20 minutes or until bubbly. Yield: 6 servings.

Jayne Roberts

GREEN CHILI RICE

1 cup chopped onion
1/4 cup butter
3 cups cooked rice
2 cups sour cream
1 cup creamed cottage
  cheese
1 bay leaf, crumbled

1/2 teaspoon salt
1/4 teaspoon pepper
3 4-ounce cans whole
  green chilies, drained
1 cup shredded Cheddar
  cheese

Sauté onion in butter in saucepan until tender but not brown. Combine with rice, sour cream, cottage cheese, bay leaf, salt and pepper in bowl; mix well. Cut chilies into quarters lengthwise. Rinse and discard seed. Chop half the chilies. Stir into rice mixture. Spoon into 7x12-inch baking dish. Top with chili quarters and cheese. Bake at 375 degrees for 30 minutes. Yield: 8 to 10 servings.

Patricia J. Tudor

RICE PILAF

1/2 cup broken vermicelli
1/4 cup shortening
1 cup rice
31/2 cups cold water

1 large chicken or beef
  bouillon cube
1 teaspoon salt

Brown vermicelli in shortening in saucepan. Stir in rice, water and bouillon cube. Cook, covered, over medium heat until bouillon is dissolved. Add salt; reduce heat. Simmer, covered, until liquid is completely absorbed. Yield: 6 servings.

Betty Krueger

TAHITI PINEAPPLE RICE

1 large can crushed
  pineapple or pineapple
  chunks

4 cups cooked rice
Butter
1 cup packed brown sugar

Drain pineapple, reserving juice. Place 1 layer rice in baking dish; dot with butter. Top with 1 layer pineapple; sprinkle with brown sugar. Repeat layers until all ingredients are used. Pour reserved juice carefully over layers. Bake at 350 degrees for 10 to 15 minutes or until heated through. Yield: 8 servings.

Patsy Leffler

SPANISH RICE

2 slices bacon
1 medium onion, chopped
1 green bell pepper, sliced
1/2 cup minute rice
1/2 cup tomato sauce

1/4 cup water
1/4 teaspoon Mrs.Dash salt-
  free seasoning
1 bay leaf

Cook bacon in skillet until crisp. Drain, leaving 1 tablespoon drippings in skillet. Add onion and green pepper. Sauté for several minutes. Stir in rice, tomato sauce, water and seasoning; mix well. Top with bay leaf. Simmer, covered, for 10 minutes. Remove bay leaf. Crumble bacon over top.
Yield: 4 servings.

Peggy Posante

★ Do not rinse rice before cooking nor drain rice after cooking to avoid losing valuable nutrients.

WILD RICE CASSEROLE

2 6-ounce packages wild
   rice, cooked
2 to 3 stalks celery,
   chopped
2 to 3 green onions,
   chopped
1/2 green bell pepper,
   chopped
8 to 10 fresh mushrooms,
   sliced
1/2 cup whipping cream
1/2 cup Parmesan cheese

Combine first 6 ingredients in bowl; mix well. Spoon into 2-quart baking dish. Pour cream over top. Sprinkle with cheese. Bake at 350 degrees for 15 minutes or until heated through. Serve with fowl or game. Yield: 6 to 8 servings.

Ann Zimmerman

CORN BREAD DRESSING

3 cups crumbled corn
   bread
2 slices bread, crumbled
1 egg
3 stalks celery, chopped
1/2 small onion, chopped
2 tablespoons sage
1/4 teaspoon pepper
Chicken or beef broth

Combine first 7 ingredients in bowl; mix well. Add enough broth for desired consistency. Spoon into buttered baking dish. Bake at 350 degrees until golden brown. Yield: 6 servings.

Gwen Bond, Lila Sykes Stovall

STUFFING

1/4 cup chopped celery
1 medium onion, chopped
1 cup chicken broth
4 cups crumbled corn
   bread
2 cups crumbled biscuits
2 eggs
5 cups chicken broth
1 tablespoon sage
Salt and pepper to taste

Cook celery and onion in 1 cup broth in saucepan until tender. Combine with remaining ingredients in bowl; mix well. Spoon into greased 9x13-inch baking dish. Bake at 350 degrees for 1 hour. May make broth by dissolving 6 chicken bouillon cubes and 1/4 cup butter in 6 cups hot water. Yield: 8 servings.

Norma Hamilton

CHICKEN STUFFING

1 slice white bread
Milk
2 hard-boiled eggs,
  chopped
1 small onion, finely
  chopped

Parsley, salt and pepper to
  taste
1 egg
Bread crumbs

Soak bread in a small amount of milk in bowl for 30 minutes. Squeeze out excess milk. Combine bread with boiled eggs, onion, parsley, salt and pepper in bowl; mix well. Add egg and enough bread crumbs to hold stuffing together. Stuff into chicken and bake as desired.

Tibor Both

SLOW-COOKER BAKED APPLES

6 to 8 apples
Raisins
Chopped pecans
Brown sugar

1 teaspoon cinnamon
1/2 teaspoon nutmeg
2 tablespoons butter
1/2 cup water

Peel top 1/3 of apples; remove core. Fill cavities with mixture of raisins, pecans and brown sugar. Place in slow cooker. Sprinkle with cinnamon and nutmeg; dot with butter. Add water. Cook on Low for 8 hours to overnight. Yield: 6 to 8 servings.

Patricia J. Tudor

BAKED APPLESAUCE

Applesauce
Cinnamon

Sugar
Miniature marshmallows

Combine applesauce with cinnamon and sugar in saucepan. Heat to the simmering point. Spoon into shallow baking dish. Top with marshmallows. Bake at 350 degrees until marshmallows are golden brown. Serve immediately.

Sally Trent

ALMOND CURRIED FRUIT

1 29-ounce can sliced peaches
1 16-ounce can pineapple chunks
1 16-ounce can pear
1 6-ounce jar maraschino cherries

1/2 cup slivered almonds, toasted
1/3 cup melted butter
3/4 cup packed brown sugar
1 tablespoon curry powder (optional)

Drain peaches, pineapple, pears and cherries. Combine in 9x13-inch baking dish. Sprinkle with almonds. Combine butter, brown sugar and curry powder in bowl; mix well. Sprinkle over fruit. Bake at 325 degrees for 1 hour. Yield: 8 to 10 servings.

Terry Neihoff

FRIED APPLES

2 quarts small tart apples
1/3 package light brown sugar

1/2 teaspoon cinnamon
1/3 stick butter

Slice each unpeeled apple into 6 wedges, discarding seed. Place in skillet. Sprinkle with brown sugar and cinnamon; dot with butter. Cook, covered, until tender, stirring occasionally. Cook, uncovered, for 3 to 5 minutes longer. Yield: 16 servings.

Sally Trent

HOT PINEAPPLE

2 to 3 large cans pineapple chunks, drained
1 to 1 1/3 cups sugar
5 tablespoons flour
2 tablespoons margarine

1 cup shredded Cheddar cheese
1 tube Ritz crackers, crushed
1/2 cup melted margarine

Combine pineapple, sugar and flour in bowl; mix well. Melt 2 tablespoons margarine in baking dish. Add pineapple mixture. Top with cheese and cracker crumbs. Drizzle with melted margarine. Bake at 350 degrees for 20 to 45 minutes or until bubbly. Yield: 6 servings.

Ladonna Darnell, Debbie Morris

ACCOMPANIMENTS

HOMEMADE BUTTER WITHOUT THE COW

1 pound margarine,
    softened
4 ounces cream cheese,
    softened

1 small can evaporated
    milk

Combine margarine, cream cheese and evaporated milk in mixer bowl; beat until smooth. Store in refrigerator or freezer. Yield: 1 1/2 pounds.

Mitzie Black

CRANBERRY AND ORANGE BUTTER

1 cup butter, softened
1/3 cup whole cranberry
    sauce

2 tablespoons sweet
    orange marmalade

Cream butter in mixer bowl until fluffy. Add cranberry sauce and marmalade; beat until well mixed. Store in covered container in refrigerator for up to 3 weeks. Yield: 1 1/2 cups.

Juyne Bushart

STRAWBERRY BUTTER

1   10-ounce package
    frozen sliced strawberries
1 cup confectioners' sugar

1 cup 40% butter and 60%
    margarine spread,
    softened

Drain strawberries, reserving juice. Combine strawberries, confectioners' sugar and butter in mixer bowl. Beat until well mixed, adding a small amount of reserved juice if needed for desired consistency or color. Yield: 2 1/2 cups.

Bernidea Fort

MICROWAVE AROMATIC APPLE JELLY

2 cups apple juice
1   1¾-ounce package
  powdered fruit pectin
1 tablespoon aromatic
  bitters

2 tablespoons lemon juice
Red food coloring
3½ cups sugar

Pour apple juice into 2-quart glass bowl. Add pectin; mix well. Microwave on High for 5 to 7 minutes or until mixture comes to a boil. Add bitters, lemon juice and desired amount of food coloring; mix well. Add sugar. Microwave on Medium for 6 to 8 minutes or until mixture is slightly thickened, stirring once to dissolve sugar. Skim. Pour into hot sterilized 8-ounce jars; seal with 2-piece lids. Yield: four 8-ounce jars.

Mary Cook

APRICOT AND PINEAPPLE MARMALADE

1 pound dried apricots
9 cups water
1 cup pineapple juice

6 cups sugar
1 cup crushed pineapple

Combine apricots with water in bowl. Let stand for 2 days. Place undrained apricots in saucepan. Add pineapple juice. Bring to a boil; reduce heat. Simmer for 1 hour. Stir in sugar and pineapple. Cook to 220 degrees on candy thermometer, stirring frequently. Pour into hot sterilized jars, leaving ½-inch headspace; seal with 2-piece lids. Yield: 2 pints.

Gwen Mills

DRIED APRICOT AND PINEAPPLE JAM

2 cups dried apricots
2 cups drained crushed
  pineapple

Juice of ½ lemon
4 cups sugar

Combine apricots with water to cover in bowl. Let stand overnight. Place undrained apricots in saucepan. Cook, covered, until tender. Mash well. Add pineapple, lemon juice and sugar. Simmer until sugar is dissolved, stirring frequently. Cook over high heat for 30 minutes or until thickened to desired consistency, skimming foam. Pour into hot sterilized jars, leaving 1/2-inch headspace; seal with 2-piece lids. Yield: 2 pints.

Gwen Bond

BLACKBERRY PRESERVES

4 quarts blackberries   **8 cups sugar**

Place blackberries in colander. Pour boiling water over berries; drain well. Place in heavy saucepan. Cook over low heat until juicy. Bring to a boil. Cook for 15 minutes. Stir in sugar. Bring to a second boil. Cook for 15 minutes. Pour into hot sterilized jars, leaving 1/2-inch head space; seal with 2-piece lids. Yield: 8 pints.

Gwen Mills

PEACH JELLY

4 cups fresh peach juice   **51/2 cups sugar**
1 package Sure-Jel

Bring peach juice to a rolling boil in saucepan. Stir in Sure-Jel. Bring to a rolling boil. Stir in sugar with wooden spoon. Bring to a rolling boil. Boil for 2 minutes. Remove from heat; skim off foam. Pour into hot sterilized jars, leaving 1/4 inch headspace; seal with 2-piece lids. I make peach juice by boiling and straining fresh peach peelings. I also use juice left over from canning peaches and reduce the sugar. Yield: 21/2 pints.

Gwen Bond

PEAR HONEY

8 cups chopped peeled   **6 cups sugar**
   pears
1 20-ounce can crushed
   pineapple

Bring pears and pineapple to a boil in saucepan. Stir in sugar. Cook for 20 to 30 minutes or until thickened, stirring constantly. Pour into hot sterilized jars, leaving 1/2-inch headspace; seal with 2-piece lids. Yield: 21/2 quarts.

Jayne Roberts

JACK'S PEAR PRESERVES

3 cups sliced pears   **2 cups sugar**

Bring pears and sugar to a boil in covered saucepan; remove cover. Cook until pears are tender and rosy colored. Spoon into jars. Store in pantry. Yield: 1 pint.

Patsy Ford

HOT PEPPER JELLY

¼ cup chopped red or   **6½ cups sugar**
  green hot peppers   **1½ cups vinegar**
1½ cups chopped green   **1 bottle of liquid pectin**
  bell peppers

Bring peppers, sugar and vinegar to a boil in saucepan. Boil for 3 minutes. Stir in pectin. Boil for 1 minute longer; remove from heat. Let stand for 5 minutes. Spoon into hot sterilized jars, leaving ¼-inch headspace; seal with 2-piece lids. Yield: 1 pint.

Martha Hooper

STRAWBERRY JAM

4 cups fresh strawberry   **2 tablespoons vinegar**
  halves   **4 cups sugar**

Combine strawberries and vinegar in saucepan. Cook for 3 minutes. Add sugar. Cook over high heat for 10 minutes; reduce heat. Simmer for 8 minutes. Stir well and skim foam. Spoon into hot sterilized jars, leaving ½-inch headspace; seal with 2-piece lids. Yield: 2 pints.

Norma Hamilton

HAM BASTE

1/4 cup margarine
3 tablespoons white wine
1/4 cup water
3 tablespoons
  Worcestershire sauce

Garlic powder to taste
Onion salt to taste

Combine margarine, wine, water, Worcestershire sauce, garlic powder and onion salt in saucepan. Bring to a boil, stirring to mix well; remove from heat. Use to baste thick ham slice on grill. Yield: 1 cup.

Patsy Ford

MARVELOUS MEAT MARINADE

1 1/2 cups oil
1/2 cup red wine vinegar
3/4 cup soy sauce
1/4 cup Worcestershire
  sauce
1/4 cup packed brown
  sugar

1 1/2 teaspoons chopped
  parsley
2 cloves of garlic, crushed
2 tablespoons dry mustard
Grated fresh ginger to
  taste
Lemon juice to taste

Combine oil, vinegar, soy sauce, Worcestershire sauce, brown sugar, parsley, garlic, dry mustard, ginger and lemon juice in dish; mix well. Add meat to be marinated. Refrigerate overnight. Yield: 3 1/2 cups.

Gloria McClave

ORIENTAL MARINADE

1/2 cup soy sauce
1/4 cup water
2 tablespoons vinegar
1 tablespoon oil

1 teaspoon sugar
1/4 teaspoon pepper
Garlic powder to taste

Combine all ingredients in bowl. Add beef, chicken or fish. Marinate for 4 hours. Use drained marinade as basting sauce during grilling or broiling. Yield: 2 cups.

Carmen Stilger

KENTUCKY DILL PICKLES

3 gallons cucumbers
Fresh dill
Hot peppers
Garlic

1 gallon vinegar
1/2 gallon water
2 cups non-iodized salt

Pack cucumbers into sterilized quart jars. Add 1 sprig of dill, 1 hot pepper and 2 or 3 cloves of garlic to each jar. Bring vinegar, water and salt to a boil in saucepan. Pour vinegar mixture into jars, leaving 1/2-inch headspace; seal with 2-piece lids. I insert a silver knife into each jar before adding hot liquid. This recipe can be made using fresh okra or green cherry tomatoes instead of cucumbers. Yield: 12 quarts.

Gwen Mills

BREAD AND BUTTER PICKLES

1 gallon cucumbers, thinly sliced
2 green bell peppers, cut into strips
8 medium onions, thinly sliced
1/2 cup non-iodized salt
4 cups crushed ice

5 cups 5% white vinegar
5 cups sugar
1/2 teaspoon turmeric
2 teaspoons mustard seed
1 teaspoon celery seed
2 teaspoons powdered alum

Alternate layers of cucumbers, peppers, onions, salt and ice in deep bowl. Let stand for 3 hours. Drain and rinse with cold water. Bring vinegar, sugar, turmeric, dry mustard, celery seed and alum to a boil in large saucepan. Add cucumber mixture. Heat gradually to boiling point. Spoon into hot sterilized jars, leaving 1/2-inch headspace; seal with 2-piece lids. Process in boiling water bath for 10 minutes. Yield: 14 to 16 pints.

Janet Arnold

MARIE'S PICKLES

4 quarts thinly sliced
  medium cucumbers
6 medium onions, thinly
  sliced
6 to 8 medium green
  tomatoes, thinly sliced
1/3 cup non-iodized salt

3 cups white vinegar
4 cups sugar
1 1/2 teaspoons turmeric
1 1/2 teaspoons celery seed
2 tablespoons mustard
  seed

Combine cucumbers, onions, tomatoes and salt in large bowl. Add ice to cover; mix well. Let stand for 3 hours; drain well. Combine vinegar, sugar, turmeric, celery seed and mustard seed in large saucepan. Add cucumbers. Cook until mixture comes to a rolling boil. Spoon into hot sterilized jars, leaving 1/2-inch headspace; seal with 2-piece lids. Yield: 8 pints.

Joan Echsner

MOM'S FROZEN CUCUMBERS

1 cup vinegar
2 cups sugar
1 tablespoon canning salt
1 teaspoon celery seed

7 cups thinly sliced
  cucumbers
3 onions, thinly sliced

Combine vinegar, sugar, salt and celery seed in bowl. Pour over cucumbers and onions in glass bowl; mix well. Refrigerate for 24 hours. Spoon into freezer containers. Store in freezer. May combine cucumbers and onion with additional salt, let stand for 2 hours and drain before packing in vinegar mixture. Yield: 5 pints.

Patricia R. Henson, Rosaleen Robertson

★ Make your own easy pickled beets by adding well-drained canned beets to the juice remaining from sweet or dill pickles. Chill for a day or 2 and the beets are ready to serve.

JUG PICKLES

1 cup non-iodized salt
1 gallon sliced cucumbers
1 tablespoon alum
Distilled vinegar

1 tablespoon whole
　allspice
9 cups sugar

　　Sprinkle salt over cucumbers in 1-gallon jug; press down. Fill jug with water. Let stand for 14 days. Drain and measure liquid from cucumbers. Rinse cucumbers twice with fresh water, leaving in jug. Measure fresh water to equal liquid poured off of cucumbers. Bring to a boil in saucepan. Add alum; cool. Pour over cucumbers. Let stand for 24 hours. Drain cucumbers and rinse twice. Add vinegar to fill jug and allspice. Let stand for 24 hours. Drain all but 3 inches vinegar, reserving drained portion. Add 3 cups sugar; shake to mix. Let stand for 24 hours, shaking several times. Add 2 cups sugar. Let stand for 24 hours, shaking several times. Repeat addition of 2 cups sugar 2 more times. Add reserved vinegar if necessary to cover pickles completely for storage. Yield: 1 gallon.

Chrissy Robey

FAVORITE SWEET PICKLES

1 quart sliced dill pickles
1 tablespoon alum
1 cup vinegar

3 cups sugar
1 tablespoon pickling spice

　　Drain pickles. Sprinkle alum over pickles. Bring vinegar, sugar and pickling spice to a boil in saucepan. Pour over pickles; seal tightly. Store in refrigerator. Yield: 1 quart.

Elizabeth Vaught

MUSTARD PICKLES

Cucumbers
1 quart 5% cider vinegar
1 cup sugar
1 cup water

1 tablespoon prepared
　mustard
1/3 cup canning salt

　　Slice ends from small cucumbers or slice medium cucumbers lengthwise. Pack into hot sterilized jars. Bring vinegar, sugar, water, mustard and salt to a boil in saucepan. Pour over cucumbers, leaving 1/2-inch headspace; seal with 2-piece lids. Store for 3 to 4 weeks before opening.

Celesta Wilson

PICKLED OKRA

6 pints small okra
6 cloves of garlic
2 tablespoons dillseed
6 small hot peppers

1 quart cider vinegar
2 cups water
1/4 cup canning salt

Trim okra, leaving 3/8-inch stems. Pack into pint jars. Add 1 clove of garlic, 1 teaspoon dillseed and 1 hot pepper to each jar. Bring vinegar, water and salt to a boil in saucepan. Pour over okra, leaving 1/2-inch headspace; seal with 2-piece lids. Yield: 6 pints.

Celesta Wilson

PEACH PICKLES

2 cups sugar
2 cups water
3 cups vinegar
1 piece gingerroot
2 cinnamon sticks

1 tablespoon whole
  allspice
1 teaspoon whole cloves
24 firm ripe peaches
3 to 4 cups sugar

Bring 2 cups sugar, water, vinegar, gingerroot, cinnamon, allspice and cloves to a boil in saucepan. Add peaches a few at a time. Cook until heated through, removing with slotted spoon when hot. Return peaches to syrup. Let stand until cool. Drain, reserving syrup. Add 2 cups sugar to reserved syrup in saucepan. Cook until sugar is dissolved, stirring frequently. Cool slightly. Add peaches. Let stand overnight. Pack peaches into hot sterilized jars. Add remaining 1 to 2 cups sugar to syrup. Cook to desired consistency. Pour over peaches, leaving 1/2-inch headspace; seal with 2-piece lids. Process in boiling water bath for 10 minutes. I prefer clingstone peaches but freestone may be used. Yield: 4 quarts.

Helen Lenz

COLD PACK RELISH

2 large heads cabbage
12 large carrots
12 onions
12 red or green bell
 peppers
1/2 cup salt

6 cups vinegar
6 cups sugar
2 teaspoons celery seed
2 teaspoons mustard seed
1 teaspoon turmeric

Grind cabbage, carrots, onions and peppers in food grinder or processor container. Combine with salt in large bowl; mix well. Let stand for 2 hours. Drain, pressing to remove liquid. Combine vinegar, sugar, celery seed, mustard seed and turmeric in bowl. Add cabbage mixture; mix well. Pack into jars; seal. Yield: 10 to 12 pints.

Aggie Burks

GREEN PEPPER RELISH

12 large green bell peppers
2 hot red peppers
12 large onions

2 cups white vinegar
2 cups sugar

Grind peppers and onions. Combine in sieve. Pour hot water over pepper mixture. Drain for 10 minutes. Combine vinegar and sugar in saucepan. Add pepper mixture. Bring to a boil. Spoon into hot sterilized jars, leaving 1/2-inch headspace; seal with 2-piece lids. Process in boiling water bath for 10 minutes. Yield: 5 pints.

Janet Arnold

CUCUMBER RELISH

3 cups sugar
2 cups vinegar
2 teaspoons celery seed
1 teaspoon cinnamon
1 teaspoon turmeric

8 cups chopped
 cucumbers
3 green bell peppers,
 chopped
4 medium onions, chopped

Combine sugar, vinegar, celery seed, cinnamon and turmeric in saucepan, stirring to dissolve sugar. Add cucumbers, peppers and onions. Bring to a boil. Cook for 20 minutes. Spoon into hot sterilized jars, leaving 1/2-inch headspace; seal with 2-piece lids. May substitute 1 red bell pepper for 1 green bell pepper. Yield: 8 to 10 pints.

Betty Schweinhart

SWEET RELISH

12 tomatoes, peeled, chopped
4 onions, chopped
4 apples, peeled, chopped
3 green bell peppers, chopped
3 to 6 hot peppers, chopped
3 cups vinegar
3 cups sugar
2 teaspoons cinnamon
2 teaspoons allspice

Combine tomatoes, onions, apples, peppers, vinegar, sugar, cinnamon and allspice in saucepan. Cook until thickened to desired consistency. Spoon into hot sterilized jar, leaving 1/2-inch headspace; seal with 2-piece lids. Yield: 4 pints.

Pamela J. Turner

HOT GREEN TOMATO CATSUP

2 gallons green tomatoes
2 gallons green bell peppers
2 gallons red bell peppers
Hot peppers to taste
10 pounds onions
1 gallon vinegar
5 pounds sugar
1/4 cup salt

Grind tomatoes, peppers and onions together. Pour boiling water over vegetables in large bowl. Let stand for 15 minutes. Drain well. Combine with vinegar, sugar and salt in saucepan. Cook for 20 minutes or until mixture comes to a full boil. Spoon into hot sterilized jars, leaving 1/2-inch headspace; seal with 2-piece lids. Yield: 10 to 12 quarts.

Nancy Winstead

HOT CHILI SAUCE

1 gallon tomatoes
1/2 stalk celery, chopped
2 large onions, chopped
3 hot peppers, chopped
2 cups vinegar
2 cups sugar

1 teaspoon cinnamon
1 teaspoon allspice
1/2 teaspoon nutmeg
2 teaspoons salt
Pepper to taste

Scald and peel tomatoes. Cook in saucepan for 15 minutes. Add celery, onions, peppers, vinegar, sugar, cinnamon, allspice, nutmeg, salt and pepper; mix well. Cook for 2 hours or until thickened to desired consistency. Spoon into hot sterilized jars, leaving 1/2-inch headspace; seal with 2-piece lids. Yield: 5 to 6 pints.

Ida L. Omer

HOT BANANA PEPPER RELISH

16 hot banana peppers, chopped
1 gallon green tomatoes, chopped
1 gallon large cucumbers, chopped
8 medium onions, chopped

2 tablespoons salt
6 cups vinegar
1 cup (or more) sugar
1 cup packed brown sugar
1 tablespoon horseradish
1 tablespoon celery seed
2 tablespoons turmeric

Combine peppers, tomatoes, cucumbers and onions in bowl. Sprinkle with salt; mix well. Let stand for 3 to 4 hours. Drain well, squeezing out excess moisture. Combine with vinegar, sugar, brown sugar, horseradish, celery seed and turmeric in saucepan. Bring to a boil over medium heat. Cook for 20 to 25 minutes or to desired consistency. Spoon into hot sterilized jars, leaving 1/2-inch headspace; seal with 2-piece lids. Yield: 10 pints.

Chasteen Thompson

SQUASH RELISH

4 cups chopped yellow
  squash
4 cups chopped zucchini
2 cups chopped onion
1 tablespoon canning salt
3 cups sugar

2 cups 5% cider vinegar
2 cups chopped green bell
  peppers
2 teaspoons dry mustard
2 teaspoons celery seed

Combine yellow squash, zucchini, onion and salt in bowl. Let stand for 1 hour. Drain, pressing lightly to remove excess moisture. Combine sugar, vinegar, green pepper, dry mustard and celery seed in saucepan; mix well. Add squash mixture. Bring to a boil. Cook for 10 minutes. Spoon into hot sterilized jars, leaving 1/2-inch headspace; seal with 2-piece lids. Yield: 4 pints.

Celesta Wilson

ZUCCHINI RELISH

10 cups ground zucchini
4 cups ground onions
1 green bell pepper,
  ground
1 red bell pepper, ground
5 tablespoons salt
2 1/4 cups vinegar

4 cups sugar
1 tablespoon cornstarch
2 teaspoons celery seed
1 teaspoon nutmeg
1 teaspoon turmeric
1/2 teaspoon dry mustard

Combine zucchini, onions, peppers and salt in bowl; mix well. Let stand overnight. Drain and rinse with cold water; drain well. Combine with vinegar, sugar, cornstarch, celery seed, nutmeg, turmeric and dry mustard in saucepan. Cook for 30 minutes. Spoon into hot sterilized jars, leaving 1/2-inch headspace; seal with 2-piece lids. Process in boiling water bath for 10 minutes. Yield: 6 pints.

Gwen Mills

FOOLPROOF FRIED CHICKEN GRAVY

2 tablespoons flour
3 tablespoons pan
  drippings from frying
  chicken

1 cup milk
Salt and pepper to taste

Combine flour with drippings in skillet, stirring to deglaze. Cook until light brown; remove from heat. Stir in milk gradually. Cook until thickened, stirring constantly. Season with salt and pepper. Yield: 1½ cups.

Particia J. Tudor

SKILLET GRAVY

3 tablespoons flour
3 tablespoons meat
  drippings

2 cups liquid
Salt and pepper to taste

Sprinkle flour into drippings in skillet. Cook over low heat until brown, stirring constantly. Add liquid gradually. Cook until thickened, stirring constantly. Use milk as liquid for milk gravy. Decrease flour and drippings to 2 tablespoons for thinner gravy; increase to 4 tablespoons for thicker gravy. Yield: 2 cups.

Cindy Jones

BARBECUE MARINADE

¾ cup margarine
½ cup Maull's sauce
½ cup zesty Italian salad
  dressing

1 large dash of Wham
  sauce
Juice of 1 lemon
2 dashes of hot sauce

Melt margarine in saucepan. Add Maull's sauce, salad dressing, Wham sauce, lemon juice and hot sauce; mix well. Simmer until well blended. Use as marinade and basting sauce for beef or pork. Yield: 2 cups.

Juyne Bushart

BARBECUE SAUCE

2 cups sugar
1 tablespoon salt
1 1/2 teaspoons pepper
1 teaspoon red pepper
  (optional)
1 1/4 cups catsup

1/2 cup water
2 1/2 cups vinegar
1 cup mustard
1/2 cup margarine
1/4 cup cornstarch
1/2 cup sugar

Mix 2 cups sugar, salt, pepper and red pepper in saucepan. Add catsup, 1/2 cup water, vinegar, mustard and margarine. Simmer for 1 hour. Blend cornstarch and 1/2 cup sugar with enough water to make a paste in small bowl. Stir into sauce. Cook for 30 minutes longer. Store sauce indefinitely. Yield: 8 cups.

Patsy Ford

MITZIE'S BARBECUE SAUCE

1 32-ounce bottle of
   vinegar
4 cups water
1 3 1/2-ounce bottle of
   liquid smoke

1/2 cup butter
2 tablespoons garlic
  powder
1/4 to 1/2 cup salt
1 1/2 teaspoons red pepper

Combine vinegar, water, liquid smoke, butter, garlic powder, salt and pepper in saucepan. Cook until butter is melted and flavors are well blended. Store for up to 2 weeks. Use with beef, pork and chicken. Yield: 5 cups.

Mitzie Black

MARY LOU'S BARBECUE SAUCE

2 cups vinegar
1/2 bottle of catsup
4 teaspoons sugar
1/2 teaspoon chili powder

1 teaspoon (heaping) salt
1 teaspoon pepper
1 teaspoon red pepper

Combine vinegar, catsup, sugar, chili powder, salt, pepper and red pepper in saucepan. Simmer until flavors are well blended. Store indefinitely. Yield: 3 cups.

Mary Lou Harris

MANCILL ALLEN'S BARBECUE SAUCE

1   12-ounce bottle of catsup
1/2 cup cider vinegar
1/2 cup water
1 cup oil
1/2 cup melted butter
1/3 cup Worcestershire
  sauce
Juice of 1 large lemon
1/4 cup sugar

1 large onion, finely
  chopped
4 teaspoons liquid smoke
3 or 4 cloves of garlic,
  minced
2 bay leaves
1/2 teaspoon dry mustard
1/4 teaspoon red pepper
Tabasco sauce to taste

Combine catsup, vinegar, water, oil, butter, Worcestershire sauce, lemon juice, sugar, onion, liquid smoke, garlic, bay leaves, dry mustard, red pepper and Tabasco sauce in saucepan. Bring to a boil. Cook for 15 minutes. Remove bay leaves. Keep warm while basting beef, pork or chicken.
Yield: 5 cups.

Judy Seitz

LEA'S BARBECUE SAUCE

2 cups vinegar
1 small bottle of catsup
1/2 jar prepared
  horseradish
1 tablespoon cayenne
  pepper

1 tablespoon dry mustard
1 tablespoon sugar
1 tablespoon salt
1/2 teaspoon pepper

Combine vinegar, catsup, horseradish, cayenne pepper, dry mustard, sugar, salt and pepper in saucepan. Cook until flavors are well blended. Use to baste spareribs or pork roast.
Yield: 3 cups.

Billie Y. Weatherington

JUDY'S BARBECUE SAUCE

1 cup catsup
1/2 cup water
1/2 cup vinegar
1 large onion, chopped
3 tablespoons brown sugar

2 tablespoons
  Worcestershire sauce
1/2 cup butter
2 teaspoons salt

Combine catsup, water, vinegar, onion, brown sugar, Worcestershire sauce, butter, and salt in saucepan. Cook until butter is melted and flavors are well blended. Use as basting sauce for chicken or ribs. Yield: 3 cups.

Judy Seitz

ZESTY ORANGE BARBECUE SAUCE

1   6-ounce can frozen
   orange juice concentrate,
   thawed
1/2 cup Worcestershire
   sauce
1 tablespoon light brown
   sugar
1/4 teaspoon garlic powder
1/2 teaspoon salt

Combine orange juice concentrate, Worcestershire sauce, brown sugar, garlic powder and salt in bowl; mix well. Use to baste chicken during last 30 minutes of grilling time. Yield: 1 1/3 cups.

Cindy Jones

BEARNAISE SAUCE

2 egg yolks
3 tablespoons lemon juice
1/2 cup cold butter
1 tablespoon white wine
   vinegar
1 tablespoon finely
   chopped onion
1 teaspoon tarragon
1/2 teaspoon chervil

Beat egg yolks and lemon juice with wooden spoon in 1-quart saucepan. Add half the butter. Cook over very low heat until butter is melted, stirring constantly. Add remaining butter. Cook until butter is melted and sauce is thickened, stirring vigorously. Stir in vinegar, onion, tarragon and chervil. Serve with filet mignon, beef tenderloin or flank steak. Yield: 3/4 cup.

Frank Fendley

BUTTERMILK SAUCE

1/2 teaspoon soda
1/2 cup buttermilk
1/2 cup butter

1 cup sugar
1 teaspoon vanilla extract

Dissolve soda in buttermilk in saucepan. Add butter and sugar. Bring to a boil. Cook for 2 minutes; remove from heat. Add vanilla. Use over pancakes or ice cream or as icing for cake. Store in refrigerator. Yield: 2 cups.

Wanda Regan

COCKTAIL SAUCE

1/2 cup catsup
1/2 cup chili sauce
2 tablespoons prepared
    horseradish

2 teaspoons lemon juice
1 teaspoon
    Worcestershire sauce

Combine catsup, chili sauce, horseradish, lemon juice and Worcestershire sauce in bowl; mix well. Use as sauce for shrimp. Yield: 1 cup.

Mary Cook

HOLLANDAISE SAUCE

1 egg
2 tablespoons vinegar
1 teaspoon sugar
1 tablespoon butter

1 tablespoon flour
2 tablespoons (heaping)
    mayonnaise

Beat egg, vinegar and sugar in measuring cup. Add enough water to measure 1/2 cup. Melt butter in saucepan. Blend in flour. Add vinegar mixture gradually. Cook over low heat until thickened, stirring constantly. Remove from heat; cool. Blend in mayonnaise. Yield: 3/4 cup.

Olivia Ratterman

SWEET AND SOUR SAUCE

1/3 cup white vinegar
1/2 cup sugar
1/4 cup crushed pineapple

1/2 teaspoon soy sauce
2 tablespoons cornstarch
3/4 cup cold water

Combine vinegar, sugar, pineapple and soy sauce in saucepan. Cook until bubbly. Dissolve cornstarch in cold water in measuring cup. Add gradually to pineapple mixture. Cook until thickened to desired consistency, stirring constantly.
Yield: 1 1/4 cups.

Frank Fendley

TARTAR SAUCE

2 cups mayonnaise
2 tablespoons chopped
  onion

1 dill pickle, chopped
Salt and pepper to taste
1/8 teaspoon red pepper

Combine mayonnaise, onion, pickle, salt, pepper and red pepper in bowl; mix well. Serve with fish. Yield: 2 1/2 cups.

Sally Trent

QUICK WHITE SAUCE

2 tablespoons butter
1 1/2 to 2 tablespoons flour

1 cup milk

Melt butter in saucepan over low heat. Stir in flour. Cook for 3 minutes, stirring constantly. Add milk gradually. Simmer until thickened, stirring constantly with wire whisk. Yield: 1 cup.

Carmen Stilger

★ Add some shredded cheese and Worcestershire sauce to taste to hot white sauce; stir until cheese melts and you have a sauce for vegetables.

HOT WINE FOR VEGETABLES

1/4 cup dry white wine
1 tablespoon minced onion
2 tablespoons chopped
   fresh parsley
1 tablespoon lemon juice
3/4 cup mayonnaise

    Combine wine, onion, parsley, lemon juice and mayonnaise in double boiler. Cook over hot water until heated through. Serve over vegetables cooked until tender-crisp. Yield: 1 1/2 cups.

Mary Butler Wessel

WORCESTERSHIRE SAUCE

1/2 cup butter
1/2 cup cider vinegar
1/2 cup water
1 bottle of Worcestershire
   sauce
Juice of 1/2 lemon
2 tablespoons Tabasco
   sauce
2 tablespoons salt
1 1/2 teaspoons pepper
1/2 teaspoon cayenne
   pepper

    Combine butter, vinegar, water, Worcestershire sauce, lemon juice, Tabasco sauce, salt, pepper and cayenne pepper in saucepan. Cook for 3 minutes, stirring constantly. Yield: 4 cups.

Pat Berry

★ When an enameled saucepan burns, fill it with water and add salt. Let stand until the next day, then bring slowly to a boil. The burn will disappear.

Churchill Downs, home of the Kentucky Derby; one of the greatest two minutes in sports.

Breads

CHURCHILL DOWNS

BREADS

BISCUITS

4 cups flour
1 tablespoon baking
   powder
1 teaspoon salt

1 teaspoon sugar
3/4 cup shortening
13/4 cups milk

Sift flour, baking powder, salt and sugar into mixer bowl. Cut in shortening until crumbly. Stir in milk. Knead gently on lightly floured surface. Roll dough 1/2 inch thick. Cut with biscuit cutter. Place on baking sheet. Let rise for 15 minutes. Bake at 400 to 425 degrees for 10 to 12 minutes or until light brown.
Yield: 20 biscuits.

Shirley Smith

BEER BISCUITS

1 package dry yeast
2 tablespoons warm water
3 cups buttermilk baking
   mix

1/4 cup sugar
Beer

Dissolve yeast in lukewarm water. Combine baking mix and sugar in bowl. Add yeast and enough beer to make a soft dough. Roll on floured surface; cut with biscuit cutter. Place on baking sheet. Bake at 400 degrees until light brown. May store in refrigerator for several days. Yield: 1 1/2 dozen.

BUTTERMILK BISCUITS

2 cups soft wheat flour
2 teaspoons baking
   powder
1 teaspoon salt
1 teaspoon sugar

1/2 teaspoon soda
5 tablespoons corn oil
   margarine
2/3 to 3/4 cup low-fat
   buttermilk

Combine first 5 ingredients in bowl. Cut in margarine until crumbly. Make a well in center of mixture; pour in buttermilk. Mix lightly for 30 seconds. Knead on floured surface for 30 seconds. Pat dough to 1/4-inch thickness; cut with biscuit cutter. Place on ungreased baking sheet. Bake immediately at 450 degrees for 15 minutes. Soft wheat flour may be purchased at health food stores. Biscuits will be tender. Yield: 1 dozen.

Patricia Ann Lock

CREAM BISCUITS

2 cups sifted flour
1 teaspoon baking powder
1 teaspoon soda

1 teaspoon salt
1 cup cream
Melted butter

Sift flour, baking powder, soda and salt into bowl. Add cream; mix with fork. Knead lightly on floured surface. Roll dough to 1/2-inch thickness; cut with biscuit cutter or glass. Place on baking sheet. Bake at 425 degrees for 10 minutes. Brush tops with butter. Yield: 1 1/2 dozen .

Pat Cole

DROP BISCUITS

1 cup self-rising flour
Dash of salt

1/2 cup milk
2 tablespoons mayonnaise

Combine flour and salt in bowl. Stir in milk and mayonnaise. Drop by spoonfuls onto baking sheet or into muffin cups. Bake at 425 degrees until brown. May substitute oil for mayonnaise. Yield: 1/2 dozen.

Celesta Wilson

MAYONNAISE BISCUITS

2 cups self-rising flour
1 tablespoon baking
  powder

3/4 cup mayonnaise
Milk

Combine flour and baking powder in bowl; mix well. Add mayonnaise and enough milk to make batter slightly thicker than cake batter. Spoon into muffin cups. Bake at 500 degrees until golden brown. Yield: 1 dozen.

Mitzie Black

MAYONNAISE SPOON ROLLS

1 cup self-rising flour
1/2 cup milk

2 tablespoons mayonnaise

Combine flour, milk and mayonnaise in bowl; mix well. Fill greased muffin cups 2/3 full. Bake at 375 degrees for 14 minutes. Yield: 1/2 dozen.

Mary J. Abell, Peggy Posante

NUT BREAD CUPS

2 cups buttermilk baking
mix
1/2 cup sugar
1/4 cup flour

1 egg, beaten
3/4 cup milk
1 cup chopped nuts

Combine baking mix, sugar and flour in bowl. Stir in mixture of egg and milk. Add nuts; mix well. Fill greased and floured miniature muffin cups 2/3 full. Bake at 350 degrees until brown. Cool. Scoop out centers of muffins. Fill with chicken salad or other filling. Yield: 1 1/2 dozen.

Peggy Graviss

REFRIGERATOR BISCUITS

2 packages dry yeast
2 tablespoons warm water
5 cups flour
1/2 cup sugar
1 tablespoon baking
powder

1 teaspoon soda
1 1/2 teaspoons salt
1/2 cup shortening
2 cups buttermilk
Melted butter

Dissolve yeast in warm water. Let stand for 5 to 10 minutes. Sift flour, sugar, baking powder, soda and salt into bowl. Cut in shortening until crumbly. Add 1 cup buttermilk; mix well. Stir in yeast and remaining 1 cup buttermilk. Knead on floured surface. Roll dough to 1/4-inch thickness. Dip into melted butter. Place on baking sheet. Let rise for 1 hour or longer. Bake at 400 to 425 degrees for 5 to 10 minutes or until brown. May store dough in refrigerator in airtight container for up to 1 week. Yield: 4 dozen.

Susan Rice

BLACK WALNUT COFFEE CAKE

1   2-layer package yellow
cake mix
1   4-ounce package
vanilla instant pudding
mix
3/4 cup oil
3/4 cup water

4 eggs
1 teaspoon butter extract
1/4 cup sugar
2 teaspoons cinnamon
3/4 cup chopped black
walnuts
Confectioners' sugar glaze

Combine cake mix, pudding mix, oil, water, eggs and butter extract in mixer bowl. Beat for 5 minutes. Mix sugar, cinnamon and walnuts in small bowl. Alternate 4 layers of batter and 3 layers of cinnamon mixture in greased and floured tube pan. Bake at 350 degrees for 50 to 60 minutes. Cool in pan for 10 minutes. Invert onto cake plate. Drizzle with confectioners' sugar glaze. Yield: 16 servings.

Judy Seitz

CHEESE COFFEE CAKE

1/2 cup margarine, softened
1 1/4 cups sugar
2 eggs
8 ounces cream cheese,
softened
1 teaspoon vanilla extract
2 cups flour
1 teaspoon baking powder

1/2 teaspoon soda
1/4 teaspoon salt
1/3 cup milk
1/3 cup flour
2 tablespoons butter
1/3 cup packed brown
sugar
1 teaspoon cinnamon

Cream margarine and sugar in mixer bowl until light and fluffy. Blend in eggs and cream cheese. Add mixture of 2 cups flour, baking powder, soda and salt alternately with milk, mixing well after each addition. Pour into greased and floured tube pan. Sprinkle with mixture of 1/3 cup flour, butter, brown sugar and cinnamon. Bake at 350 degrees for 35 to 40 minutes or until coffee cake tests done. Yield: 16 servings.

Norma Hamilton

CINNAMON COFFEE CAKE

4 teaspoons sugar
1 tablespoon cinnamon
3/4 cup chopped pecans
1 cup butter, softened
2 cups sugar
2 eggs

1 cup sour cream
1/2 teaspoon vanilla extract
2 cups flour
1 teaspoon baking powder
Pinch of salt

Combine 4 teaspoons sugar, cinnamon and pecans in small bowl; mix well. Cream butter and sugar in bowl until light and fluffy. Add eggs, sour cream and vanilla; blend well. Sift flour, baking powder and salt into bowl. Add to creamed mixture; mix well. Pour half the batter into greased tube pan. Sprinkle with half the cinnamon mixture. Repeat layers. Bake at 350 degrees for 50 to 55 minutes or until cake tests done. Cool in pan for 10 minutes. Invert onto cake plate. Garnish with confectioners' sugar. Yield: 16 servings.

Martha S. Harper

EASY-BAKE COFFEE CAKE

1/2 cup margarine
1 cup buttermilk baking
  mix
1 cup sugar
1 cup milk

1 1/2 cups packed brown
  sugar
1/2 cup English walnuts
1/2 cup coconut
1 tablespoon cinnamon

Melt margarine in 9x13-inch baking dish. Blend baking mix, sugar and milk in bowl. Pour over margarine in baking dish. Mix remaining ingredients in bowl. Sprinkle over batter. Bake at 350 degrees for 30 minutes. Yield: 12 servings.

Janet Milburn

SOUR CREAM COFFEE CAKE

1/4 cup packed brown
  sugar
2 teaspoons cinnamon
3/4 cup chopped pecans
1 2-layer package white
  cake mix

1/2 cup sugar
1 cup sour cream
3/4 cup oil
4 eggs
1 cup confectioners' sugar
2 tablespoons milk

Combine brown sugar, cinnamon and pecans in small bowl; mix well. Combine cake mix, sugar, sour cream and oil in bowl; mix well. Add eggs 1 at a time, beating well after each addition. Pour half the batter into greased and floured tube pan. Sprinkle with half the cinnamon mixture. Repeat layers. Bake at 325 degrees for 1 hour or until cake tests done. Cool in pan for 10 minutes. Remove to wire rack to cool completely. Glaze with mixture of confectioners' sugar and milk. Yield: 16 servings.

Mrs. Leonard H. Frazier

AUNT MARY'S ALABAMA SOUR CREAM CORN BREAD

1 1/2 cups self-rising cornmeal
1 cup sour cream
1 onion, chopped

1 small can cream-style corn
2 eggs
3/4 cup oil

Combine cornmeal, sour cream, onion, corn, eggs and oil in bowl; mix well. Pour into preheated greased cast-iron skillet. Bake at 375 degrees for 20 to 30 minutes or until brown. Yield: 6 servings.

Grace Murphy

CORN BREAD

2 eggs
1 1/2 cups cornmeal
1 cup shredded cheese
1   8-ounce can cream-style corn

1 cup sour cream
1 tablespoon baking powder
Salt to taste
Jalapeño pepper to taste

Combine eggs, cornmeal, cheese, corn, sour cream and baking powder in bowl. Add salt and jalapeño pepper to taste. Sprinkle additional cornmeal in skillet; pour in batter. Place in cold oven. Set temperature to 450 degrees. Bake until brown. Yield: 8 servings.

Juyne Bushart

EGG CORN BREAD

1 cup cornmeal
1 cup flour
3 to 4 teaspoons baking
  powder
1 to 3 tablespoons sugar

1 teaspoon salt
1 to 1¹/₂ cups milk
1 to 2 eggs, beaten
2 to 3 tablespoons oil

Sift cornmeal, flour, baking powder, sugar and salt into bowl. Add milk, eggs and oil; beat well. Pour into greased heavy baking pan or cast-iron skillet. Bake at 400 degrees until brown. Yield: 6 servings.

Pat Wilhelm, Celesta Wilson

CORN BREAD SUPREME

1 cup self-rising cornmeal
1   8-ounce can cream-
  style corn

¹/₂ cup oil
2 eggs, beaten
1 cup sour cream

Combine cornmeal, corn, oil, eggs and sour cream in bowl; mix well. Pour into preheated greased cast-iron skillet. Bake at 400 degrees for 35 to 40 minutes or until brown. May double recipe, but using just 1 can of corn. Yield: 6 servings.

Hazel Cundiff, Helen Lovan

JALAPEÑO CORN BREAD

3 cups corn bread mix
2¹/₂ cups milk
¹/₂ cup oil
3 eggs, beaten
1 onion, grated
2 tablespoons sugar
1 cup cream-style corn
¹/₄ cup chopped pimento

¹/₂ cup finely chopped
  jalapeño peppers
1¹/₂ cups shredded sharp
  cheese
¹/₃ pound bacon, crisp-
  fried, crumbled
¹/₂ clove of garlic, chopped

Combine corn bread mix and milk in large bowl; mix well. Add oil, eggs, onion, sugar, corn, pimento, peppers, cheese, bacon and garlic; mix well. Pour into 3 greased 8x8-inch pans. Bake at 400 degrees for 35 minutes. Yield: 18 servings.

Martha Hooper

CHEDDAR-JALAPEÑO BREAD

5 slices bacon
2 eggs
1¼ cups milk
2 cups self-rising cornmeal
1 tablespoon sugar
¼ teaspoon garlic powder
¾ cup shredded mild
  Cheddar cheese

1 cup chopped onion
2 tablespoons chopped
  pimento
1 8-ounce can cream-
  style corn
2 tablespoons canned
  chopped jalapeño

Cook bacon in 9-inch cast-iron skillet until crisp. Drain and crumble bacon, reserving 5 tablespoons drippings. Coat bottom and side of skillet with 1 tablespoon drippings. Preheat skillet in 400-degree oven. Beat eggs in bowl. Stir in milk and remaining 4 tablespoons drippings. Add bacon, cornmeal, sugar, garlic powder, Cheddar cheese, onion, pimento, corn and jalapeño; mix well. Pour into hot skillet. Bake for 35 minutes or until golden brown. Yield: 8 to 10 servings.

Norma Gray

MEXICAN CORN BREAD

1½ cups self-rising
  cornmeal
1 cup cream-style corn
1 cup buttermilk
1 medium onion, chopped
1 large green bell pepper,
  chopped

3 jalapeño peppers,
  chopped
3 eggs, beaten
⅔ cup oil
1 cup shredded Cheddar
  cheese

Combine cornmeal, corn, buttermilk, onion, green pepper, jalapeño peppers, eggs and oil in bowl; mix well. Sprinkle greased 9x13-inch baking dish with additional cornmeal. Pour in half the batter. Top with Cheddar cheese. Add remaining batter. Bake at 375 degrees for 45 minutes. Yield: 12 servings.

Opal Miracle

HOT WATER CORN CAKES

1 cup cornmeal
1/2 teaspoon sugar
1/2 teaspoon baking powder
1/4 teaspoon salt
1 1/2 cups boiling water
Shortening for frying

Combine cornmeal, sugar, baking powder and salt in bowl; mix well. Pour boiling water into cornmeal mixture; mix well. Drop by spoonfuls into 1/8 inch hot shortening in skillet. Cook over medium heat until brown, turning once. Yield: 12 servings.

Phyllis L. Allen

CORN STICKS

2 cups white cornmeal
1/2 cup flour
1 teaspoon baking powder
1/2 teaspoon salt
1/2 teaspoon soda
2 cups buttermilk
1/4 cup melted lard
2 eggs, beaten

Sift cornmeal, flour, baking powder and salt into bowl. Mix soda with buttermilk. Add to dry ingredients; mix well. Add melted lard gradually, stirring well. Add eggs; beat well. Fill preheated greased corn stick pan to top. Place on lower rack of oven. Bake at 450 to 500 degrees for 8 minutes. Move to upper rack. Bake for 5 to 10 minutes longer or until brown. This recipe came from Boone's Tavern in Berea, Kentucky. Yield: 12 servings.

Elizabeth Vaught

B.C. CORN BREAD

2 cups flour
1/2 cup sugar
1 tablespoon baking powder
1 teaspoon salt
1 egg, slightly beaten
1 cup milk
1/2 cup shredded Cheddar cheese
1 8-ounce can corn, drained
1 cup oil

Combine all ingredients in bowl in order listed. Stir just until moistened; batter will be lumpy. Pour into greased 8x8-inch baking dish. Bake at 400 degrees for 35 minutes. Yield: 9 servings.

Bea Senn

CORN BREAD MUFFINS

1 cup self-rising cornmeal
2 eggs
1/2 cup oil

1 cup sour cream
1 cup cream-style corn

Combine cornmeal, eggs, oil, sour cream and corn in bowl; mix well. Pour into greased muffin cups. Bake at 450 degrees for 15 to 20 minutes or until brown. Yield: 18 muffins.

Debbie Windhorst

MOONLITE BAR-B-QUE'S CORN BREAD MUFFINS

2 eggs
1 1/2 cups milk
1 1/2 cups buttermilk
1/2 cup oil

1/2 cup melted butter
3 tablespoons sugar
1/2 cup self-rising flour
3 cups self-rising cornmeal

Beat eggs in large mixer bowl. Add milk, buttermilk, oil and melted butter; beat well. Add sugar, flour and cornmeal; mix well. Pour into greased muffin cups. Bake at 500 degrees for 10 minutes. May bake in greased 10-inch skillet for 20 minutes. Yield: 16 muffins.

Barbara Struck

ALMOND BREAD

2 1/4 cups flour
2 1/4 teaspoons baking
  powder
3/4 teaspoon cinnamon
3/4 teaspoon ginger
1 cup milk

1/2 cup sugar
1/4 cup oil
1 egg
1 egg white
1/4 teaspoon almond
  extract

Combine flour, baking powder, cinnamon and ginger in large bowl; mix well. Combine milk, sugar, oil, egg and egg white in medium bowl. Beat with wire whisk until smooth. Add to flour mixture; blend well. Pour into greased 5x9-inch loaf pan. Bake at 350 degrees for 35 minutes. Yield: 8 to 12 servings.

Jean Gray

APPLE BREAD

1 cup sugar
1/2 cup shortening
2 eggs
2 cups sifted flour
1 teaspoon baking powder
1 teaspoon soda
1/2 teaspoon salt
1 1/2 cups diced apples
1/2 cup chopped pecans
1 teaspoon vanilla extract
Cinnamon-sugar to taste

Cream sugar and shortening in bowl until light and fluffy. Add eggs; mix well. Sift flour, baking powder, soda and salt together. Add to creamed mixture; mix well. Stir in apples, pecans and vanilla. Pour into greased loaf pan. Sprinkle with cinnamon-sugar. Bake at 350 degrees until bread tests done. Place pan on side to cool. Yield: 12 servings.

Pearl Robinson

APPLE RAISIN LOAVES

3 cups self-rising flour
2 cups sugar
1 teaspoon cinnamon
4 eggs
2/3 cup oil
2 cups grated peeled
   apples
1 cup raisins

Combine flour, sugar and cinnamon in bowl. Beat eggs and oil in large bowl. Add flour mixture; mix well. Add apples and raisins; mix well. Spoon batter into 2 well-greased loaf pans. Bake at 350 degrees for 40 to 50 minutes or until loaves test done. May bake in 24 muffin cups for 30 to 40 minutes. Yield: 2 loaves.

Tammy Brasher

SPICY APPLESAUCE LOAVES

1   2-layer package yellow
   cake mix
1   4-ounce package
   vanilla instant pudding
   mix
1 cup applesauce
1/2 cup water
1/4 cup oil
4 eggs
1/2 teaspoon cinnamon
1/2 teaspoon nutmeg
1/2 teaspoon allspice
1/2 cup raisins, finely
   chopped

Combine cake mix, pudding mix, applesauce, water, oil, eggs, cinnamon, nutmeg, allspice and raisins in mixer bowl; mix well. Beat at medium speed for 4 minutes. Pour into 7 greased 4x8-inch loaf pans. Bake at 350 degrees for 45 minutes or until loaves test done. Yield: 7 loaves.

Martha Hooper

HAWAIIAN BANANA NUT BREAD

3 cups flour
2 cups sugar
1 teaspoon salt
1 teaspoon soda
1 teaspoon cinnamon
1 cup chopped nuts
2 teaspoons vanilla extract

3 eggs, beaten
1 1/2 cups oil
2 cups mashed ripe
  bananas
1   8-ounce can crushed
  pineapple, drained

Combine flour, sugar, salt, soda and cinnamon in bowl. Stir in nuts. Mix vanilla, eggs, oil, bananas and pineapple in bowl. Add to flour mixture; mix just until moistened. Spoon into greased and floured bundt pan. Bake at 350 degrees for 1 hour or until bread tests done. Cool in pan for 10 minutes. Remove to wire rack to cool completely. Pan may be prepared with nonstick baking spray. May substitute 2 loaf pans for bundt pan. Yield: 16 servings.

Dena Sue Montgomery, Patricia J. Tudor

BANANA NUT BREAD

1 3/4 cups flour
1/4 teaspoon soda
2 teaspoons baking
  powder
1/2 teaspoon salt

2/3 cup sugar
1/3 cup shortening
2 eggs
1 cup mashed bananas
1/2 cup chopped nuts

Sift flour, soda, baking powder, salt and sugar into bowl. Add shortening, eggs and bananas; mix well. Fold in nuts. Pour into greased 5x9-inch loaf pan. Bake at 350 degrees for 1 hour. Yield: 10 servings.

Terry Neihoff

BANANA RAISIN BREAD

2 cups flour
1/2 teaspoon baking
  powder
1/2 teaspoon soda
1/2 teaspoon salt
1/2 cup butter, softened

1 cup sugar
2 tablespoons oil
2 eggs
3 bananas, mashed
1/2 cup raisins or nuts

Sift flour, baking powder, soda and salt into bowl. Cream butter and sugar in bowl until light and fluffy. Add oil. Beat in eggs 1 at a time. Stir in bananas. Add flour mixture gradually, mixing well after each addition. Stir in raisins. Pour into well-greased loaf pan. Bake at 350 degrees for 40 to 60 minutes or until bread tests done. Cool in pan for 10 minutes. Remove to wire rack to cool completely. Yield: 10 servings.

Alice Arterburn

BANANA ZUCCHINI BREAD

3 eggs
2 cups sugar
1 cup oil
2 1/2 cups self-rising flour
1 cup shredded unpeeled
  zucchini
1 cup mashed bananas

1 tablespoon vanilla
  extract
1 teaspoon cinnamon
1 teaspoon nutmeg
1 cup chopped nuts
  (optional)

Beat eggs in bowl until fluffy. Add sugar, oil, flour, zucchini, bananas, vanilla, cinnamon, nutmeg and nuts; mix well. Pour into 2 greased 5x9-inch loaf pans. Bake at 350 degrees for 1 hour. May substitute 9x13-inch pan for loaf pans. Serve hot with cream cheese or sour cream. Yield: 16 servings.

Charlene P. Atkinson

★ Freeze bananas whole and unpeeled or mash and freeze in recipe-sized portions.

BLUEBERRY BREAD

2 cups flour
1 cup sugar
1¹/₂ teaspoons baking
  powder
¹/₂ teaspoon soda
¹/₄ teaspoon salt
2 tablespoons shortening

1 egg, beaten
¹/₄ cup orange juice
1 tablespoon grated
  orange rind
1 cup blueberries
¹/₄ cup chopped pecans

Combine flour, sugar, baking powder, soda and salt in bowl; mix well. Mix in shortening. Stir in egg. Add enough boiling water to orange juice and rind to measure 1 cup; stir into flour mixture. Add blueberries and pecans; mix gently. Pour into greased 5x9-inch loaf pan. Bake at 350 degrees for 1 hour. May substitute lemon rind for orange rind or walnuts for pecans. Yield: 1 loaf.

Trudie Gadjen

CARROT PINEAPPLE BREAD

2 eggs
2 cups sugar
1¹/₃ cups oil
2 cups shredded carrots
1 cup drained crushed
  pineapple
1 teaspoon vanilla extract

1 teaspoon lemon juice
¹/₂ teaspoon almond
  extract
3 cups flour
1 teaspoon soda
1 teaspoon cinnamon
¹/₂ teaspoon salt

Combine eggs, sugar, oil, carrots, pineapple, vanilla, lemon juice and almond extract in bowl; mix well. Sift flour, soda, cinnamon and salt into bowl. Stir into egg mixture. Pour into 7 greased 3x6-inch loaf pans. Bake at 350 degrees until bread tests done. Yield: 7 loaves.

Martha Hooper

CHERRY PECAN BREAD

2 cups flour
1/2 teaspoon soda
1 teaspoon salt
1/2 cup butter, softened
3/4 cup sugar
2 eggs

1/2 teaspoon vanilla extract
1 cup buttermilk
1 10-ounce jar
  maraschino cherries,
  drained, chopped
1 cup chopped pecans

Combine flour, soda and salt in bowl. Cream butter, sugar and eggs in bowl until light and fluffy. Add mixture of vanilla and buttermilk alternately with flour mixture, mixing well after each addition. Fold in cherries and pecans. Pour into greased loaf pans or small tube pan. Bake at 325 degrees for 30 minutes or until slightly brown. Remove to wire rack to cool. Yield: 8 servings.

Francele Black

CAPE COD CRANBERRY BREAD

13/4 cups flour
1 teaspoon soda
3/4 teaspoon baking
  powder
1/2 teaspoon salt
1/2 teaspoon cinnamon
1/4 teaspoon nutmeg
1/2 cup butter, softened

3/4 cup sugar
1 egg
1/4 cup light corn syrup
1 cup hot water
11/2 cups cranberries,
  coarsely chopped
2 cups 40% bran flakes

Combine flour, soda, baking powder, salt, cinnamon and nutmeg in medium bowl. Cream butter and sugar in large bowl until light and fluffy. Add egg; mix well. Beat in corn syrup and water gradually. Add flour mixture; beat until smooth. Stir in cranberries and bran flakes. Pour into greased and floured 5x9-inch loaf pan. Bake at 350 degrees for 1 hour and 15 minutes or until loaf tests done. Yield: 8 to 10 servings.

Nancy Winstead

COLONIAL BROWN BREAD

4 cups whole wheat flour
1¹/₃ cups flour
2 cups packed brown sugar

4 teaspoons soda
1 teaspoon salt
4 cups buttermilk

Combine flours, brown sugar, soda and salt in large bowl. Add buttermilk gradually, blending well after each addition. Pour into 2 greased 5x9-inch loaf pans. Bake at 350 degrees for 1 hour. Serve warm. Wrap in foil to reheat. Yield: 2 loaves.

Trudie Gadjen

GINGERBREAD

2¹/₂ cups flour
1¹/₂ teaspoons soda
¹/₂ teaspoon salt
1 teaspoon cinnamon
¹/₂ cup butter, softened

¹/₂ cup sugar
1 egg, beaten
1 cup molasses
1 cup hot water

Combine flour, soda, salt and cinnamon in bowl. Cream butter and sugar in bowl until light and fluffy. Beat in egg and molasses. Add flour mixture; mix well. Add hot water; beat until smooth. Pour into greased shallow baking pan. Bake at 325 degrees for 35 minutes. Serve warm with whipped cream. Yield: 6 to 8 servings.

Phyllis Davis

PEANUT BUTTER BREAD

1¹/₂ cups packed brown
  sugar
¹/₂ cup melted butter
1³/₄ cups milk
3 eggs
4¹/₂ cups sifted flour

2 tablespoons baking
  powder
1 teaspoon salt
2 cups crunchy peanut
  butter

Combine first 4 ingredients in bowl; blend well. Add dry ingredients; stir just until moistened. Add peanut butter; mix well. Pour into 2 well-greased loaf pans. Bake at 350 degrees until loaves test done. Cool in pan for 20 minutes. Yield: 2 loaves.

Martha Hooper

PINEAPPLE NUT BREAD

2¼ cups sifted flour
¾ cup sugar
1 tablespoon baking
powder
½ teaspoon soda
1½ teaspoons salt
1 cup prepared bran cereal

¾ cup chopped walnuts
1½ cups undrained
crushed pineapple
1 egg, beaten
3 tablespoons shortening,
melted

Sift flour, sugar, baking powder, soda and salt into large bowl. Combine bran cereal, walnuts, pineapple, egg and shortening in bowl; mix well. Stir into flour mixture. Pour into greased 4x9-inch loaf pan. Bake at 350 degrees for 1 hour and 15 minutes. Bread will stay moist for 7 to 10 days; it slices best after 1 day. Yield: 10 servings.

Clara Nance

RAISIN BREAD

1½ cups seedless raisins
1½ cups orange juice
1 egg, slightly beaten
1 cup packed brown sugar
3 tablespoons oil
Grated rind of 1 orange

2½ cups flour
1 teaspoon salt
2 teaspoons baking
powder
½ teaspoon soda

Combine raisins and orange juice in saucepan. Bring to a boil. Cool to room temperature. Combine egg, brown sugar, oil and orange rind in bowl; mix well. Stir in raisin mixture. Add flour, salt, baking powder and soda; beat well. Pour into greased and floured 5x9-inch loaf pan. Bake at 325 degrees for 1 hour. May bake in 2 small loaf pans. Yield: 10 servings.

Mildred Cunningham

PUMPKIN BREAD

3 cups sugar
1 cup oil
1   16-ounce can pumpkin
4 eggs, beaten
3^1/$_2$ cups flour
2 teaspoons soda
2 teaspoons salt

1 teaspoon baking powder
1 teaspoon cinnamon
1 teaspoon nutmeg
1 teaspoon allspice
^{1}/$_2$ teaspoon cloves
^{2}/$_3$ cup water

Combine sugar, oil, pumpkin and eggs in bowl; beat until light and fluffy. Sift flour, soda, salt, baking powder, cinnamon, nutmeg, allspice and cloves together. Add to pumpkin mixture alternately with water, mixing well after each addition. Pour into 2 greased and floured 5x9-inch loaf pans. Bake at 350 degrees for 45 minutes or until loaves test done. Cool in pans for 10 minutes. Remove to wire rack to cool completely. Yield: 2 loaves.

Nona Marie Besendorf

PUMPKIN RAISIN BREAD

1^1/$_2$ cups sugar
2 eggs
^{1}/$_2$ cup oil
1^1/$_2$ cups mashed pumpkin
1^2/$_3$ cups flour
1 teaspoon soda
1^1/$_2$ teaspoons baking
  powder

^{3}/$_4$ teaspoon salt
1 teaspoon cinnamon
1 teaspoon cloves
1 teaspoon nutmeg
^{1}/$_2$ cup chopped walnuts
^{1}/$_2$ cup raisins

Combine sugar, eggs and oil in bowl; mix well. Sift in flour, soda, baking powder, salt, cinnamon, cloves and nutmeg; mix well. Stir in walnuts and raisins. Pour into greased and floured 5x9-inch loaf pan. Bake at 325 degrees for 50 minutes or until bread tests done. May substitute 1 tablespoon pumpkin pie spice for spices. Yield: 10 servings.

Nancy A. Thiry

STRAWBERRY BREAD

3 cups flour
1 teaspoon soda
1 teaspoon salt
1 tablespoon cinnamon
2 cups sugar
4 eggs, beaten

2 10-ounce packages
frozen strawberries,
thawed
1 1/2 cups oil
1 1/2 cups chopped nuts

Sift flour, soda, salt, cinnamon and sugar into bowl. Stir in eggs, strawberries and oil. Add nuts. Pour into 2 greased loaf pans. Bake at 350 degrees for 1 hour. Yield: 2 loaves.

Janice Davis

STRAWBERRIES AND CREAM BREAD

1 cup butter, softened
1/2 cup sugar
1 teaspoon vanilla extract
1 teaspoon lemon extract
4 eggs
3 cups flour
1 teaspoon salt

1 teaspoon cream of tartar
1/2 teaspoon soda
1 cup strawberry jam
1 cup sour cream
1 cup chopped nuts
Confectioners' sugar

Cream butter, sugar, vanilla and lemon extract until light and fluffy. Add eggs 1 at a time, beating well after each addition. Sift flour, salt and cream of tartar into bowl. Combine jam and sour cream in bowl; mix well. Add to creamed mixture alternately with flour mixture, mixing well after each addition. Stir in chopped nuts. Pour into greased loaf pan. Bake at 350 degrees for 50 to 55 minutes or until bread tests done. Cool in pan for 10 minutes. Remove to wire rack to cool completely. Sprinkle with confectioners' sugar. Yield: 10 servings.

Norma Gray

ZUCCHINI BREAD

1 cup oil
2 cups sugar
3 eggs
1 tablespoon vanilla
 extract
3 cups flour

1 tablespoon cinnamon
1 teaspoon baking powder
1 teaspoon soda
1 teaspoon salt
2 cups finely shredded
 zucchini

Combine oil, sugar, eggs and vanilla in large bowl. Sift flour, cinnamon, baking powder, soda and salt in bowl. Add to oil mixture; mix well. Stir in zucchini. Pour into 2 greased loaf pans. Bake at 350 degrees for 1 hour. Yield: 2 loaves.

Janice Yost

SCOTCH APPLE MUFFINS

2 cups flour
2 teaspoons cinnamon
1 teaspoon soda
1/2 teaspoon salt
2 eggs
1 cup oil
1/2 cup sugar

1/2 cup packed brown
 sugar
1 teaspoon vanilla extract
4 cups chopped tart apples
3/4 cup butterscotch chips
1 cup walnuts

Combine flour, cinnamon, soda and salt in bowl. Beat eggs in large bowl. Add oil, sugar, brown sugar, vanilla and apples; mix well. Add flour mixture; stir just until moistened. Add butterscotch chips and walnuts; mix well. Spoon into greased muffin cups. Bake at 350 degrees for 15 to 20 minutes or until muffins test done. Yield: 12 muffins.

Danny F. Compton

★ Most recipes for 12 muffins can also be baked in a greased 5x9-inch loaf pan. Bake at 350 degrees, remove to wire rack, cool and slice.

BANANA OAT MUFFINS

1/2 cup quick-cooking oats
1/2 cup flour
1/2 cup whole wheat flour
2 teaspoons baking
  powder
1/4 teaspoon salt

1/2 teaspoon cinnamon
1/4 cup oil
2/3 cup mashed banana
1 egg, slightly beaten
2 tablespoons honey
1/3 cup milk

Place oats in blender container; process to fine texture. Combine oats, flour, whole wheat flour, baking powder, salt and cinnamon in bowl; mix well. Combine oil, bananas, egg, honey and milk in small bowl; mix well. Add to flour mixture; stir just until moistened. Fill greased muffin cups 1/2 to 2/3 full. Bake at 400 degrees for 12 minutes or until golden brown.
Yield: 10 to 12 muffins.

Patricia J. Tudor

ALMOND BLUEBERRY MUFFINS

5 tablespoons slivered
  almonds
1 1/2 cups cake flour
2 tablespoons sugar
2 teaspoons baking
  powder
1/4 teaspoon salt
1/2 teaspoon cinnamon
2 eggs

1/2 cup low-fat buttermilk
1/4 cup honey
1/4 cup water
1/4 cup melted unsalted
  margarine
1/2 teaspoon almond
  extract
1 cup fresh blueberries
1/4 cup sliced almonds

Process 5 tablespoons almonds in blender container until finely ground. Combine ground almonds, flour, sugar, baking powder, salt and cinnamon in bowl; mix well. Combine eggs, buttermilk, honey, water, margarine and almond extract in blender container; process until smooth. Make a well in center of dry ingredients. Pour in egg mixture; stir just until moistened. Fold in blueberries. Fill miniature muffin cups sprayed with nonstick cooking spray 2/3 full. Sprinkle with sliced almonds. Bake at 400 degrees for 15 to 20 minutes or until golden brown. Remove from pans immediately. Yield: 12 muffins.

Patricia J. Tudor

BLUEBERRY CORN MUFFINS

1 8-ounce package corn
  muffin mix
1 tablespoon brown sugar

1 egg
1/3 cup milk
1/2 cup drained blueberries

Combine muffin mix, brown sugar, egg and milk; mix well. Stir in blueberries. Fill greased muffin cups 1/2 full. Bake at 400 degrees for 15 to 20 minutes or until golden brown. Yield: 8 to 12 muffins.

Clara Nance

BLUEBERRY STREUSEL MUFFINS

1/4 cup margarine, softened
1/3 cup sugar
1 egg
2 1/3 cups flour
4 teaspoons baking
  powder
1/2 teaspoon salt

1 cup milk
1 teaspoon vanilla extract
1 1/2 cups blueberries
1/2 cup sugar
1/3 cup flour
1/2 teaspoon cinnamon
1/4 cup margarine

Cream 1/4 cup margarine in mixer bowl. Add 1/3 cup sugar gradually, beating until light and fluffy. Add egg; mix well. Combine 2 1/3 cups flour, baking powder and salt in bowl. Add to creamed mixture alternately with milk, mixing well after each addition. Stir in vanilla. Fold in blueberries. Fill greased muffin cups 2/3 full. Combine 1/2 cup sugar, 1/3 cup flour and cinnamon in bowl. Cut in 1/4 cup margarine until crumbly. Sprinkle over batter in muffin cups. Bake at 375 degrees for 25 to 30 minutes or until golden brown. Remove from pan immediately. If using frozen blueberries, rinse and drain thawed berries and pat dry with paper towels. Yield: 18 muffins.

Patricia J. Tudor

★ Frozen, canned and fresh blueberries can be used interchangeably in loaves and muffins. Be sure frozen and canned berries are well drained unless the recipe has other instructions.

REFRIGERATOR BRAN MUFFINS

2 cups boiling water
2 cups All-Bran cereal
1¼ cups shortening
2½ cups sugar
4 eggs

4 cups buttermilk
4 cups Bran Buds cereal
6 cups flour
5 teaspoons soda

Pour boiling water over All-Bran in bowl. Let stand for several minutes. Cream shortening and sugar in bowl. Add eggs; mix well. Add buttermilk, All-Bran mixture and Bran Buds; mix well. Beat in flour and soda. Spoon into greased muffin cups. Bake at 400 degrees for 15 to 20 minutes or until brown. May store in refrigerator for up to 4 weeks. Yield: 5 dozen.

Barbara C. Hendrick

APPLESAUCE OAT BRAN MUFFINS

2 egg whites
1¼ cups applesauce
½ cup raisins

1 cup oat bran
1 cup self-rising flour
1 tablespoon cinnamon

Beat egg whites in small bowl until frothy. Add applesauce and raisins; mix well. Combine oat bran, flour and cinnamon in medium bowl. Add applesauce mixture; mix just until moistened. Fill greased muffin cups ⅔ full. Bake at 400 degrees for 15 minutes or until golden brown. Yield: 10 muffins.

Delores Richardson

BANANA OAT BRAN MUFFINS

¼ cup honey
3 egg whites
½ cup oil
½ cup oat bran

½ cup oat flour
3 bananas, mashed
½ cup chopped pecans

Combine honey, egg whites and oil in bowl; mix well. Add mixture of oat bran and oat flour alternately with bananas, mixing lightly after each addition. Stir in pecans. Spoon into muffin cups sprayed with nonstick cooking spray. Bake at 350 degrees for 35 minutes. Yield: 12 muffins.

Irene McKinney

HONEY OAT BRAN MUFFINS

1³/₄ cups flour
1 tablespoon baking
  powder
¹/₄ teaspoon salt
1¹/₂ cups skim milk

¹/₂ cup honey
2 egg whites
3 tablespoons oil
3 cups oat bran cereal

Combine flour, baking powder and salt in bowl; mix well. Combine milk, honey, egg whites and oil in large bowl; beat until well mixed. Add flour mixture and cereal; mix until just moistened. Spoon into greased 2¹/₂-inch muffins cups. Bake at 400 degrees for 25 minutes. Yield: 12 muffins.

Wellness Committee

RAISIN OAT BRAN MUFFINS

¹/₂ cup apple juice
¹/₂ cup oat bran
1¹/₄ cups whole wheat flour
³/₄ cup oat bran
¹/₄ teaspoon salt
1 egg, slightly beaten
¹/₂ cup packed brown
  sugar

¹/₄ cup oil
1¹/₂ teaspoons vanilla
  extract
1 teaspoon cinnamon
1 cup buttermilk
1¹/₄ teaspoons soda
³/₄ cup raisins
¹/₃ cup chopped pecans

Bring apple juice to a boil in saucepan. Combine with ¹/₂ cup oat bran in bowl. Combine whole wheat flour, ³/₄ cup oat bran and salt in large bowl. Blend egg, brown sugar, oil, vanilla and cinnamon in medium bowl. Add mixture of buttermilk and soda. Stir in raisins and pecans. Add to dry ingredients. Add bran and apple juice mixture; mix just until moistened. Spoon into greased large muffin cups. Bake at 400 degrees for 20 minutes. Muffins freeze well, are breakfast treats and are low in cholesterol. Yield: 1 dozen.

Mary C. Masterson

SPICE OAT BRAN MUFFINS

1¼ cups whole wheat flour
1¼ cups oat bran
2 tablespoons wheat germ
1 teaspoon soda
1 teaspoon cinnamon
½ teaspoon ginger
¼ teaspoon allspice

1 egg
⅔ cup buttermilk
⅓ cup honey
⅓ cup safflower oil
½ cup raisins
½ cup chopped pecans

Combine whole wheat flour, oat bran, wheat germ, soda, cinnamon, ginger and allspice in large bowl. Combine egg, buttermilk, honey and oil in bowl; mix well. Add to flour mixture; mix just until moistened. Fold in raisins and pecans. Spoon into muffin cups sprayed with nonstick cooking spray. Bake at 375 degrees for 16 to 20 minutes or until muffins test done.
Yield: 12 to 16 muffins.

Alma Brite

MAYONNAISE MUFFINS

2 cups self-rising flour
¼ cup mayonnaise

1 cup milk
1 tablespoon sugar

Combine flour, mayonnaise, milk and sugar in bowl; mix well. Spoon into greased muffin cups. Bake at 400 degrees for 15 to 20 minutes or until golden brown. Yield: 12 muffins.

Donna Browning

FRENCH BREAKFAST PUFFS

½ cup sugar
⅓ cup shortening
1 egg
1½ cups sifted flour
1½ teaspoons baking
  powder
½ teaspoon salt

¼ teaspoon nutmeg
½ cup milk
6 tablespoons melted
  butter
½ cup sugar
1 teaspoon cinnamon

Cream 1/2 cup sugar, shortening and egg in bowl until light and fluffy. Sift flour, baking powder, salt and nutmeg together. Add to creamed mixture alternately with milk, beating well after each addition. Fill greased muffin cups 2/3 full. Bake at 350 degrees for 20 to 25 minutes or until brown. Dip muffins into melted butter. Roll in mixture of 1/2 cup sugar and cinnamon. Yield: 12 muffins.

Erma S. Messer

JUSTINE'S MUFFINS

2 cups flour
1 tablespoon baking
  powder
Pinch of salt

1 egg
1 cup milk
2 tablespoons melted
  butter

Sift flour, baking powder and salt into medium bowl. Beat egg in bowl. Add milk and butter; mix well. Make a well in flour mixture. Pour in egg mixture; mix well. Spoon into greased muffin cups. Bake at 425 degrees for 10 minutes or until brown. Yield: 12 muffins.

Justine Both

COUNTRY PECAN MUFFINS

1 1/2 cups flour
1 cup chopped pecans
1/2 cup packed brown
  sugar
2 teaspoons baking
  powder

Pinch of salt
1/2 cup milk
1/4 cup melted butter
2 eggs, beaten
1/2 teaspoon vanilla extract

Combine flour, pecans, brown sugar, baking powder and salt in large bowl. Make a well in center. Combine milk, butter, eggs and vanilla in bowl. Add to dry ingredients; mix just until moistened. Fill greased and floured muffin cups 1/2 full. Bake at 350 degrees for 20 to 25 minutes or until brown. Yield: 15 muffins.

Wilma Allen

YOGURT WHOLE WHEAT MUFFINS

1 cup whole wheat flour
1/2 cup all-purpose flour
1 teaspoon baking powder
1 teaspoon soda
1/3 cup sugar
1/3 cup chopped pecans

1 egg, slightly beaten
8 ounces plain low-fat
  yogurt
5 tablespoons melted
  reduced-calorie
  margarine

Combine whole wheat flour, all-purpose flour, baking powder, soda, sugar and pecans in large bowl. Make a well in center of mixture. Mix egg with yogurt and margarine in bowl. Add to dry ingredients; stir just until moistened. Fill greased muffin cups 3/4 full. Bake at 350 degrees for 18 to 20 minutes or until lightly browned. Yield: 12 muffins.

Robbie Lowery

ORANGE DOUGHNUT BALLS

2 cups flour
1/4 cup sugar
1 tablespoon baking
  powder
1 teaspoon salt
1 tablespoon grated
  orange rind

1 teaspoon nutmeg
1/4 cup oil
1/2 cup milk
1/2 cup orange juice
1 egg
Oil for frying
Cinnamon-sugar

Combine first 6 ingredients in bowl. Add oil, milk, orange juice and egg; stir with fork until well mixed. Drop by teaspoonfuls into hot oil. Fry for 2 to 3 minutes or until golden brown on all sides. Drain on paper towels. Roll warm doughnut balls in cinnamon-sugar mixture. Serve warm. Yield: 2 1/2 dozen.

Trudie Gadjen

ORANGE FRENCH TOAST

1/4 cup margarine
1/3 cup sugar
1/4 teaspoon cinnamon
1 teaspoon grated orange
  rind

2/3 cup orange juice
4 eggs, slightly beaten
8 slices bread
Chopped pecans (optional)

Melt margarine with sugar and cinnamon in saucepan. Pour into 9x13-inch baking dish. Mix orange rind, orange juice and eggs in bowl. Dip bread into egg mixture; arrange in baking dish. Pour remaining egg mixture over bread. Sprinkle with pecans. Bake at 350 degrees until golden brown.
Yield: 4 to 8 servings.

Robbie Lowery

HOMEMADE CRACKERS

1 cup flour
2 teaspoons butter
1/2 teaspoon salt

1 egg, beaten
1/4 cup milk
Salt to taste

Combine flour, butter, salt, egg and milk in bowl; mix well. Roll to 1/8-inch thickness on lightly floured surface. Sprinkle with salt. Cut into squares. Pierce surface of each cracker with fork. Place on baking sheet. Bake at 350 degrees until golden brown and crispy. Great for snacks. Yield: 1 dozen.

Sandi Tipton Clark

GERMAN PANCAKES

4 eggs
1 tablespoon sugar
1/2 teaspoon salt
2/3 cup sifted flour

2/3 cup milk
2 tablespoons butter,
softened

Beat eggs in bowl until light. Add sugar, salt, flour, milk and butter; mix until smooth. Pour into 2 buttered 9-inch cake pans. Bake at 400 degrees for 20 minutes. Reduce temperature to 350 degrees. Bake for 10 minutes longer. Slide onto hot plates. Serve with lemon slices, confectioners' sugar and butter.
Yield: two 9-inch pancakes.

Mrs. Homer Quiggins

WHOLE WHEAT PANCAKES

1 egg
1 cup buttermilk
2 tablespoons oil
3/4 cup whole wheat flour

1 tablespoon brown sugar
1 teaspoon baking powder
1/2 teaspoon soda
1/2 teaspoon salt

Beat egg in medium bowl. Add buttermilk, oil, whole wheat flour, brown sugar, baking powder, soda and salt; beat well. Bake on hot greased griddle or skillet. May add small amount of sugar to pancake or waffle batter for faster browning. Serve with Maple Syrup. Yield: ten 4-inch pancakes.

Maple Syrup

4 cups sugar
1/2 cup packed light brown sugar

2 cups water
1 teaspoon vanilla extract
1 teaspoon maple flavoring

Combine sugar, brown sugar and water in saucepan; stir until dissolved. Bring to a boil; reduce heat. Simmer, covered, for 10 minutes. Remove from heat; add flavorings. Yield: 4 cups.

Donna Hearn

FRENCH BREAD

1 package dry yeast
1/2 cup warm water
1 tablespoon sugar
1 1/2 teaspoons salt

1 cup warm water
1 tablespoon shortening
4 cups flour
Melted butter

Dissolve yeast in 1/2 cup warm water. Dissolve sugar and salt in 1 cup warm water in large bowl. Add shortening and yeast; mix well. Add flour; mix well. Let dough rest for 10 minutes. Knead with spoon. Repeat resting and kneading four times. Divide into 2 portions on lightly floured surface. Let rest for 10 minutes. Roll each portion into 9x12-inch rectangle. Roll as for jelly roll from long sides, sealing edges and ends. Place on greased baking sheet. Score tops diagonally 6 times with sharp knife. Let rise, covered, for 1 1/2 hours. Bake at 400 degrees for 30 to 35 minutes or until golden brown. Brush tops with butter. Yield: 2 loaves.

May E. Merklein

ONION-POPPY SEED BREAD

1 package dry yeast	1/4 cup sugar
1/2 cup warm water	1 3/4 teaspoons salt
4 1/2 to 5 cups flour	1 egg
1/2 cup melted butter	Poppy Seed Filling
1 cup warm milk	1 egg, beaten

Dissolve yeast in warm water in large mixer bowl. Add 2 cups flour, melted butter, milk, sugar, salt and 1 egg. Beat at medium speed for 2 minutes, scraping sides of bowl occasionally with wooden spoon. Add 2 cups flour or enough to make stiff dough. Knead on lightly floured surface for 8 to 10 minutes or until smooth and elastic. Place in greased bowl, turning to grease surface. Cover and let rise in warm place for 1 hour or until doubled in bulk. Roll into 8x20-inch rectangle on floured surface. Cut into two 4x20-inch rectangles. Spread Poppy Seed Filling to within 1/2 inch of edges. Fold 20-inch sides together; pinch seams to seal, forming rope. Twist ropes together. Shape into ring on greased baking sheet; seal ends together. Let rise, covered, for 1 hour or until doubled in bulk. Brush with beaten egg. Sprinkle with additional poppy seed and chopped onion if desired. Bake for 40 minutes. Cool slightly on wire rack. Yield: 28 servings.

Poppy Seed Filling

1 cup chopped onion	3 tablespoons poppy seed
1/4 cup melted butter	1/4 teaspoon salt

Combine onion, melted butter, poppy seed and salt in bowl; mix well.

Linda Wieland

★ Try substituting unbleached or whole wheat flour for all-purpose flour in bread recipes for a different flavor and texture.

NO-KNEAD CINNAMON RAISIN LOAVES

6 cups sifted flour
2 teaspoons salt
1/4 cup sugar
1 teaspoon cinnamon
1 package dry yeast

1 cup milk
1/2 cup water
1/2 cup butter
3 eggs
1 cup raisins

Combine 1 1/2 cups flour, salt, sugar, cinnamon and dry yeast in bowl. Heat milk, water and butter to 120 to 130 degrees in saucepan. Pour into mixer bowl. Beat in flour mixture gradually. Beat for 2 minutes. Add eggs and 1/2 cup flour. Beat at high speed for 2 minutes. Stir in raisins and enough remaining 4 1/2 cups flour to make soft dough. Let rise, covered, for 50 minutes or until doubled in bulk. Punch dough down. Spoon into 2 well-greased 1 1/2-quart casseroles. Let rise, covered, for 40 minutes. Bake at 375 degrees for 35 minutes or until loaves test done. Yield: 2 loaves.

Clara Nance

SWEDISH RYE BREAD

2 packages dry yeast
1/2 cup lukewarm water
4 cups milk, scalded
1/4 cup shortening
1 cup packed brown sugar
2 tablespoons molasses

4 teaspoons salt
3 cups medium rye flour
3 cups Bohemian rye flour
6 to 7 cups all-purpose
  flour
1 teaspoon (scant) fennel

Dissolve yeast in lukewarm water. Pour scalded milk into large bowl. Add shortening, brown sugar, molasses and salt; stir until shortening melts. Cool to lukewarm. Add yeast. Beat in rye flour, 6 cups all-purpose flour and fennel. Knead on floured surface for 10 minutes, kneading in remaining 1 cup all-purpose flour. Place in greased bowl, turning to grease surface. Let rise for 1 1/2 hours or until doubled in bulk. Punch dough down. Let rise for 45 minutes or until almost doubled in bulk. Shape into 4 loaves. Place in greased 5x9-inch loaf pans. Let rise to top of pans. Bake at 350 degrees for 20 minutes. Reduce oven temperature to 300 degrees. Bake for 25 minutes longer. This bread freezes well. Yield: 4 loaves.

Marie Matsen

BUTTERHORN ROLLS

1 package dry yeast
1 tablespoon sugar
1/4 cup warm water
1/2 cup butter, softened
1/2 cup sugar

1 cup lukewarm milk
3 eggs
1/2 teaspoon salt
4 cups flour

Dissolve yeast and 1 tablespoon sugar in warm water. Let stand until bubbly. Combine butter, 1/2 cup sugar, milk, eggs and salt in large bowl; mix well. Add flour; mix well. Let rise for several hours to overnight. Knead on floured surface; dough will be very soft. Divide into 2 portions. Roll each portion into circle. Cut into wedges; roll up from wide end. Shape into crescents on greased baking sheet. Let rise until doubled in bulk. Bake at 375 degrees for 10 minutes. Yield: 2 dozen.

Ladonna Darnell

BUTTERMILK ROLLS

1 cake yeast
2 cups fresh buttermilk
1/4 teaspoon baking
   powder
1/4 teaspoon soda

3 tablespoons sugar
1 tablespoon shortening
1 teaspoon salt
3 cups flour
Melted butter

Dissolve yeast in a small amount of buttermilk. Cream baking powder, soda, sugar and shortening in bowl until light and fluffy. Add yeast, salt and remaining buttermilk; mix well. Add enough flour to make soft dough. Knead on floured surface until smooth and elastic. Roll to 3/4-inch thickness; cut as desired. Place on greased baking sheet. Brush with melted butter. Let rise for 1 hour or until light. Bake at 400 degrees for 15 to 20 minutes or until golden brown. Yield: 1 1/2 dozen.

Pearl Hodges

DINNER ROLLS

1 package dry yeast
1/4 cup warm water
1 teaspoon sugar
1 egg, at room temperature
1/4 cup butter, softened

1 cup warm water
1/4 cup sugar
1 1/2 teaspoon salt
3 cups flour
Melted butter

Combine yeast, 1/4 cup warm water and 1 teaspoon sugar in large bowl. Let stand for 15 minutes. Add egg; beat lightly. Add butter, 1 cup warm water, 1/2 cup sugar and salt; mix well. Add flour 1 cup at a time, beating well after each addition; dough will be soft. Let rise, covered, in refrigerator until doubled in bulk. Divide into 4 portions. Roll each portion into circle on floured surface. Cut each into 8 wedges; roll up from wide end. Shape into crescents on greased baking sheet. Let rise until doubled in bulk. Bake at 350 degrees for 10 to 12 minutes or until golden. Drizzle with melted butter. Yield: 2 3/4 dozen.

Jean LeMaster

EASY ONE-BOWL ROLLS

1 package dry yeast
1 cup warm water
1/4 cup sugar
1 teaspoon salt

3 cups sifted flour
1/4 cup melted margarine
1 egg, beaten
Melted butter

Dissolve yeast in warm water in large bowl; mix well. Add sugar, salt and 1 cup flour; mix well. Beat in melted margarine and egg. Add 1 cup flour; mix well. Add remaining 1 cup flour 1/3 at a time, mixing well after each addition. Let rise, covered, until doubled in bulk. Pat out on floured surface; cut as desired. Dip into melted butter and fold over to make Parker House rolls. Place on baking sheet. Let rise until doubled in bulk. Bake at 375 degrees for 12 to 15 minutes or until brown. Rolls may be frozen before second rising or after baking. Yield: 3 dozen.

Betty Schweinhart

NEVER-FAIL ROLLS

2 packages dry yeast
1 cup warm water
3/4 cup sugar
3/4 cup shortening

1 teaspoon salt
1 cup boiling water
2 eggs
6 cups flour

Dissolve yeast in warm water. Combine sugar, shortening, salt and boiling water in bowl; mix well. Cool to lukewarm. Add yeast and eggs; beat well. Add flour; mix well. Chill, covered with greased waxed paper, for up to 10 days. Roll to desired thickness on floured surface; cut as desired. Place on greased baking sheet. Let rise until doubled in bulk. Bake at 400 degrees until brown. Yield: 6 dozen.

Carolyn Burgess

PAN ROLLS

3 1/4 cups flour
3 tablespoons sugar
1/2 teaspoon salt
1 package dry yeast

1 cup warm (120 to 130 degree) water
3 tablespoons butter, softened

Combine 1 cup flour, sugar, salt and yeast in bowl. Add water gradually, beating until smooth. Stir in butter and 1 1/4 cups flour; beat until smooth. Place remaining 1 cup flour on work surface; make a well in center. Pour batter into well. Knead for 8 minutes or until smooth, kneading in additional flour as necessary. Place in greased bowl, turning to grease surface. Let rise, covered, in warm place for 1 hour or until doubled in bulk. Punch dough down. Knead lightly on floured surface until smooth. Shape into 24 balls. Arrange in 2 well-greased 9-inch round pans. Let rise, covered, for 1 hour or until doubled in bulk. Bake at 400 degrees for 12 to 15 minutes or until golden. Yield: 2 dozen.

Joyce Alexander

REFRIGERATOR YEAST ROLLS

1 teaspoon sugar
1 teaspoon salt
1 package dry yeast
1/2 cup water
2 eggs

7 cups flour
1/2 cup sugar
1 cup shortening
2 cups water

Combine 1 teaspoon sugar, salt, yeast, water and eggs in mixer bowl. Beat at low speed for 2 minutes. Combine flour with 1/2 cup sugar, shortening and 2 cups water in large bowl. Beat at medium speed for 3 minutes. Add yeast mixture. Beat at medium speed for 3 minutes. Let rise, covered, for 3 hours or until doubled in bulk. Punch dough down. Chill, covered, overnight. Shape dough into 1 1/2-inch balls. Place in 3 greased 9-inch round pans. Let rise for 2 hours or until doubled in bulk. Bake at 400 degrees for 10 to 12 minutes or until golden brown. Dough may be stored in refrigerator for up to 4 days. Yield: 2 1/2 dozen.

Emma Lee Hester

BEGINNER'S REFRIGERATOR YEAST ROLLS

1 cup butter
2/3 cup sugar
1 teaspoon salt
1 3/4 cups cold water

2 eggs, beaten
2 packages dry yeast
1/4 cup lukewarm water
6 cups (about) flour

Heat butter, sugar and salt in saucepan until sugar is dissolved. Add cold water. Pour into large bowl. Cool to lukewarm. Stir in eggs. Dissolve yeast in 1/4 cup lukewarm water. Add to egg mixture; mix well. Stir in flour gradually to make soft dough. Let rise, covered, for 1 hour or until doubled in bulk. Punch dough down. Chill, covered, overnight. Shape rolls as desired. Arrange in greased baking pan. Bake at 350 degrees until brown. Dough may be used to make cinnamon rolls. This recipe is from an elementary school that makes its own rolls. Yield: 3 dozen.

Ann Schmitt

CECILE'S FAMOUS ROLLS

2 packages dry yeast
1 cup lukewarm water
1 cup hot water
1/4 to 1/2 cup honey
3/4 cup oil

2 teaspoons salt
2 eggs, beaten
6 1/2 cups flour
Melted butter

Dissolve yeast in lukewarm water for 5 minutes or until bubbly. Combine hot water, honey, oil and salt in large bowl; stir until honey is dissolved. Add eggs; mix well. Stir in yeast. Add flour; mix well. Shape rolls as desired. Place in greased baking pan. Let rise until doubled in bulk. Bake at 425 degrees for 10 minutes. Brush with melted butter. May store dough in refrigerator for several days. Omit 1/2 cup flour if dough is not used immediately. May freeze rolls after shaping. This recipe is excellent for hamburger buns, English muffins and sweet rolls. Yield: 3 to 4 dozen.

CINNAMON ROLLS

1 cup milk, scalded
1/2 cup shortening
1/2 cup sugar
1 teaspoon salt
2 eggs, beaten
1 package dry yeast
1/2 cup warm water

4 cups flour
1/2 cup melted butter
3/4 cup sugar
2 tablespoons cinnamon
2 cups confectioners' sugar
1/4 cup milk

Combine scalded milk, shortening, sugar and salt in large mixer bowl. Cool to lukewarm. Add eggs; mix well. Dissolve yeast in warm water. Add to milk mixture; mix well. Add flour gradually, mixing to make a soft dough. Let rise, covered, until doubled in bulk. Punch dough down. Roll into rectangle on floured surface. Brush with melted butter. Sprinkle with mixture of sugar and cinnamon. Roll as for jelly roll, sealing edge and ends. Place seam side up in buttered baking pan. Brush lightly with melted butter. Let rise until doubled in bulk. Bake at 400 degrees for 15 minutes or until brown. Frost with mixture of confectioners' sugar and milk. This recipe is from Mayfield City School cafeteria. It freezes well. Yield: 2 dozen.

Louise Chambers

HOT CROSS BUNS

1 cup milk, scalded
1/3 cup butter
1/4 cup sugar
1 teaspoon salt
1 cake yeast, crumbled
1 egg, beaten

3/4 teaspoon cinnamon
4 to 5 cups flour
3/4 cup raisins
1 egg, beaten
Confectioners' sugar
   frosting

Combine milk, butter, sugar and salt in large bowl. Cool to lukewarm. Add yeast. Let stand for 3 minutes. Add 1 egg, cinnamon and enough flour to make soft dough. Mix in raisins. Let rise, covered, until doubled in bulk. Shape into large biscuits. Place 1 inch apart in buttered baking pan. Let rise, covered, until doubled in bulk. Brush with egg. Bake at 400 degrees for 20 minutes. Cool. Drizzle frosting cross on each. Yield: 1 1/2 dozen.

Cindy Jones

NUT ROLLS

1 cup lukewarm milk
1/3 cup butter
1/3 cup sugar
1 teaspoon salt
3 packages dry yeast
1 teaspoon sugar

2 tablespoons warm water
1 egg, beaten
4 cups flour
Ground nuts
Sugar to taste
1 egg, beaten

Combine first 4 ingredients in bowl. Dissolve yeast and 1 teaspoon sugar in 2 tablespoons warm water. Combine 1 egg, milk mixture, yeast and flour in large bowl; mix well. Roll by handful-sized portions into rectangles on floured surface. Combine nuts with sugar and enough boiling water to make of spreading consistency. Spread on rectangles. Roll as for jelly roll, sealing edges and ends. Place seam sides down in greased pans. Brush with beaten egg. Bake at 350 degrees for 35 to 45 minutes. Brush with melted butter. Cool in pans for 10 to 15 minutes. Remove to wire racks to cool completely. May substitute poppy seed filling for nut filling. Yield: 8 servings.

Marilyn Zippay

The Belle of Louisville cruises the Ohio River through Louisville, Kentucky. The Delta Queen from Cincinnati, Ohio, comes to town during Derby Festival week for a real riverboat race.

Desserts

BELLE OF LOUISVILLE

MISCELLANEOUS DESSERTS

APPLE BROWN BETTY

1/4 cup flour
1/8 teaspoon soda
1/8 teaspoon baking
powder
1/8 teaspoon salt
1/2 cup oats
1/2 cup packed brown
sugar

1/4 cup margarine
2 cups sliced apples
1 tablespoon flour
1/4 teaspoon cinnamon
1/4 cup packed brown
sugar
1/4 teaspoon nutmeg

Sift 1/4 cup flour, soda, baking powder and salt into bowl. Add oats and 1/2 cup brown sugar; mix well. Cut in margarine until crumbly. Combine apples, 1 tablespoon flour, cinnamon, 1/4 cup brown sugar and nutmeg in small bowl; mix well. Spoon into greased casserole. Sprinkle with oats mixture. Bake at 325 degrees for 50 to 60 minutes or until apples are tender. Yield: 2 servings.

Gwen Mills

APPLE AND CHEDDAR GRATIN

2 pounds Granny Smith
apples, peeled, sliced
1/2 cup raisins
1/2 teaspoon cinnamon
1/4 cup fresh lemon juice
3/4 cup packed brown
sugar

1/2 cup flour
1/8 teaspoon salt
1/4 cup unsalted butter, cut
into squares
1 cup shredded extra-
sharp Cheddar cheese

Arrange apple slices in buttered 1-quart shallow baking dish. Sprinkle with raisins, cinnamon and lemon juice. Combine brown sugar, flour and salt in small bowl; mix well. Cut in butter until crumbly. Add cheese; toss well. Sprinkle over apples. Bake at 350 degrees in upper 1/3 of the oven for 30 minutes or until apples are tender. Serve as dessert or accompaniment to roast pork or ham. Yield: 4 to 6 servings.

Ladonna Darnell

APPLE CRISP

4 to 6 apples, peeled,
  sliced
1/2 cup flour
3/4 cup packed brown sugar
1/2 teaspoon cinnamon

1/2 teaspoon nutmeg
Salt to taste
1/2 cup quick-cooking oats
Chopped pecans
3/4 cup melted butter

Place apples in casserole. Combine flour, brown sugar, cinnamon, nutmeg, salt, oats and pecans in bowl; mix well. Pour in melted butter; mix well. Sprinkle evenly over apples. Bake at 375 degrees for 35 minutes. Serve with ice cream or whipped topping. Yield: 6 servings.

Molly Hisel

APPLE AND CRANBERRY BAKE

3 cups apples, peeled,
  chopped
2 cups cranberries
1 1/2 teaspoons lemon juice
1 1/2 cups sugar
1 cup chopped pecans

1 1/3 cups quick-cooking
  oats
1/3 cup packed brown
  sugar
1/2 cup melted butter

Combine apples, cranberries, lemon juice and sugar in bowl; mix well. Spoon into baking dish. Mix pecans, oats, brown sugar and butter in bowl. Sprinkle over apple mixture. Bake at 325 degrees for 1 hour and 15 minutes. Yield: 4 servings.

Joanne Berry

FRIED APPLES

5 medium apples
1/2 cup water
1/2 cup sugar

2 tablespoons oil
1/2 cup butter

Peel and thinly slice apples. Place in skillet. Add water. Simmer until apples are tender; drain. Add sugar and oil; mix well. Cook over low heat until thickened; stirring constantly. Remove from heat; dot with butter. Let stand until butter melts. Stir in melted butter. Serve immediately. Yield: 4 servings.

Peggy Posante

APPLE CRUMB DELIGHT

1 can sliced apples
1/3 cup sugar
1/2 teaspoon cinnamon
3 tablespoons water
2 tablespoons butter

1/2 cup butter
1/2 cup packed brown
   sugar
1/2 cup flour

Arrange apples in buttered 9-inch baking dish. Sprinkle with sugar, cinnamon and water. Dot with 2 tablespoons butter. Combine 1/2 cup butter, brown sugar and flour in bowl; mix until crumbly. Sprinkle over apple mixture. Bake at 350 degrees for 1 hour. May use fresh apples or peaches if preferred.
Yield: 6 servings.

Mae Pate

APPLE DUMPLINGS

1 10-count package
   refrigerator Butter-Me-Not
   biscuits
2 cans fried apples
10 tablespoons butter

10 tablespoons sugar
1/4 cup butter
1/2 cup sugar
1 teaspoon cinnamon
Flour

Roll biscuits into thin rounds. Drain apples, reserving liquid. Place 1 heaping tablespoonful apples on each biscuit. Dot with 1 tablespoon butter; sprinkle with 1 tablespoon sugar. Bring edges together to enclose filling. Pinch edges to seal. Place in 10x13-inch baking dish. Bake at 375 degrees for 30 to 45 minutes or until well browned. Add enough water to reserved apple liquid to make 2 cups. Pour into saucepan. Add 1/4 cup butter, 1/2 cup sugar and cinnamon. Cook until butter melts, stirring constantly. Add enough flour to thicken. Cook until thickened, stirring constantly. Pour over baked dumplings before serving.
Yield: 10 servings.

Peggy Noel

APPLE PUDDING CAKE

1/2 cup margarine, softened
1 cup sugar
1 teaspoon vanilla extract
1 egg
1 cup self-rising flour
1/4 teaspoon salt
1 teaspoon soda

1/4 cup golden raisins
1 cup chopped black
  walnuts
1/4 cup coconut
2 cups chopped peeled
  apples
Whipped topping

Cream margarine and sugar in mixer bowl. Add vanilla and egg; mix well. Add flour, salt, soda, raisins, walnuts and coconut. Stir in apples. Spoon into 9x13-inch cake pan. Bake at 350 degrees for 40 minutes. Serve warm with whipped topping. Yield: 9 servings.

Gwen Mills

FROZEN APRICOT DESSERT

2 envelopes whipped
  topping mix
8 ounces cream cheese,
  softened
1 6-ounce package
  apricot gelatin

2/3 cup sugar
2/3 cup water
1 6-ounce jar baby food
  apricots
2 small cans crushed
  pineapple

Prepare whipped topping mix in mixer bowl using package directions. Beat in cream cheese. Chill in refrigerator. Combine gelatin, sugar, water, apricots and pineapple in saucepan. Bring to a boil, stirring constantly. Chill in freezer until partially set. Fold in cream cheese mixture. Spoon into 9x13-inch dish. Freeze, covered, overnight. Cut into squares. Can be prepared and frozen several days ahead. Yield: 24 servings.

Judy Henry

APRICOT STACK CAKE

1 cup shortening	6 tablespoons milk
2 cups sugar	5¹/₂ cups self-rising flour
2 teaspoons vanilla extract	16 ounces dried apricots
3 eggs	1 cup sugar

Cream shortening, 2 cups sugar and vanilla in mixer bowl until light and fluffy. Add eggs; beat well. Add milk and flour; mix well. Chill for several hours. Divide dough into 6 portions. Roll each portion to ¹/₈-inch thickness on floured surface. Cut into 9¹/₂-inch cookies, using plate as pattern. Place on cookie sheet. Bake at 375 degrees for 6 to 8 minutes or until lightly browned. Remove to wire rack to cool completely. Combine apricots with water to cover in saucepan. Simmer until tender, stirring occasionally. Add 1 cup sugar; mix well. Cook until thickened, stirring constantly. Cool. Alternate layers of cookies and filling on serving plate, beginning and ending with cookies. Flavor improves if allowed to stand for 2 or 3 days. Yield: 16 to 20 servings.

Philip and Sarah Chaudoin

APRICOT STRUDEL

1 cup butter	Frozen coconut, thawed
2 cups flour	Chopped pecans
1 cup sour cream	Raisins
Apricot preserves	Confectioners' sugar
Sugar	

Cut butter into flour in bowl until crumbly. Add sour cream; mix well. Divide dough into 8 portions. Wrap in waxed paper. Chill for several hours. Roll each portion into 8-inch square. Spoon small amount apricot preserves on ¹/₃ of square. Sprinkle sugar, coconut, pecans and raisins on remaining ²/₃ of square. Roll to enclose filling. Place seam side down on baking sheet. Bake at 400 degrees for 5 minutes. Reduce temperature to 350 degrees. Bake for 45 minutes longer. Cut each strudel into 7 slices. Remove to wire rack to cool. Sprinkle with confectioners' sugar. Yield: 56 servings.

Kim Clinton

BANANA FRITTERS

1½ cups self-rising flour
6 tablespoons sugar
3 eggs
1 cup milk

4 to 5 ripe bananas,
  mashed
Oil for deep frying
Confectioners' sugar

Mix flour and sugar in large mixer bowl. Add eggs 1 at a time, beating well after each addition. Add milk gradually. Beat for 2 minutes or until smooth. Add bananas; mix well. Ladle by ¼ cupfuls into hot oil in deep fryer. Deep-fry 2 to 3 fritters at a time for 3 minutes or until golden brown, turning to brown evenly. Drain on paper towels. Sprinkle with confectioners' sugar. Yield: 20 fritters.

Patsy Ford

BANANA SPLIT CAKE

2 cups graham cracker
  crumbs
½ cup melted margarine
2 eggs
2 cups confectioners'
  sugar
½ cup margarine, softened
1 teaspoon vanilla extract

4 bananas
1 large can crushed
  pineapple
16 ounces whipped
  topping
Chopped nuts
12 maraschino cherries

Mix graham cracker crumbs and ½ cup melted margarine in bowl until crumbly. Press into 9x13-inch dish. Combine eggs, confectioners' sugar, ½ cup margarine and vanilla in mixer bowl. Beat for 15 minutes. Spread over graham cracker layer. Slice bananas lengthwise. Layer bananas, pineapple and whipped topping over top. Sprinkle with nuts. Top each serving with cherry. Yield: 12 servings.

Nancy Heil

BANANA SPLIT LEMON CAKE

1½ packages graham
  crackers, crushed
½ cup melted margarine
4 to 5 bananas, sliced
1 14-ounce can
  sweetened condensed
  milk

Juice of 2 lemons
1 large can crushed
  pineapple, drained
Whipped topping
Maraschino cherries
Crushed peanuts

    Mix graham cracker crumbs and melted margarine in bowl until crumbly. Press into greased 9x13-inch cake pan. Arrange bananas over graham cracker layer. Combine condensed milk and lemon juice in mixer bowl. Beat for 2 minutes. Spread over bananas. Top with pineapple, whipped topping, cherries and peanuts. Chill, loosely covered with foil, until serving time. Yield: 12 servings.

Bernadette Mills

BANANA SPLIT PUDDING

1 15-ounce can crushed
  pineapple
1 14-ounce can
  sweetened condensed
  milk
1 4-ounce package
  banana cream instant
  pudding mix

2 cups whipping cream,
  whipped
1 15-ounce package
  chocolate wafers
4 medium bananas, sliced
Lemon juice

    Drain pineapple, reserving liquid. Add enough cold water to reserved pineapple liquid to make 1½ cups. Combine with condensed milk and pudding mix in mixer bowl; mix well. Add pineapple; mix well. Chill for 10 minutes. Fold in whipped cream. Spoon 1½ cups mixture into 4-quart serving bowl. Layer chocolate wafers, bananas and remaining pudding mixture ⅓ at a time in serving bowl. Chill for several hours. Yield: 8 to 10 servings.

Cindy Jones

BLUEBERRY DELIGHT

2 cups vanilla wafer
  crumbs
1 6-ounce package
  lemon gelatin
1 cup sour cream

9 ounces whipped topping
4 cups blueberries
2 cups vanilla wafer
  crumbs

Press 2 cups vanilla wafer crumbs in 10x14-inch pan. Prepare gelatin using package directions. Chill until partially set. Fold in sour cream, whipped topping and blueberries. Pour over crumb layer. Sprinkle with remaining 2 cups crumbs. Chill overnight. Yield: 24 servings.

Mildred Kretschman

BUTTERFINGER DESSERT

12 graham crackers,
  crushed
12 saltine crackers,
  crushed
1/2 cup melted margarine
1/4 cup sugar
2 packages vanilla instant
  pudding mix

2 cups cold milk
1 quart vanilla ice cream,
  softened
12 ounces whipped
  topping
2 large Butterfinger candy
  bars, crushed

Mix cracker crumbs, margarine and sugar in bowl. Press into 9x13-inch pan. Mix pudding mix and milk in bowl until slightly thickened. Stir in ice cream. Pour over cracker crust. Spread whipped topping over ice cream layer. Sprinkle with crushed candy bars. Chill or freeze until serving time. Yield: 12 servings.

Jayne Roberts

★ Keep brown sugar soft by storing it in the refrigerator. To soften brown sugar that is hard, place it in an airtight container with a slice of bread for several hours to overnight.

BUTTER PECAN LAYER DESSERT

2 cups flour
1 cup melted butter
1 cup chopped pecans
1 cup sugar
8 ounces cream cheese,
  softened
16 ounces whipped
  topping

2 packages butter pecan
  instant pudding mix
3 cups milk
16 ounces whipped
  topping
Toasted coconut

Combine flour, butter and pecans in bowl; mix well. Press into 9x13-inch baking dish. Bake at 350 degrees for 25 minutes. Cool completely. Cream sugar and cream cheese in mixer bowl until light and fluffy. Fold in 16 ounces whipped topping. Spread over cooled baked layer. Combine pudding mix and milk in mixer bowl. Beat until thickened. Spread over cream cheese layer. Spread remaining 16 ounces whipped topping over top. Sprinkle with coconut. Chill for several hours before serving.
Yield: 12 servings.

Molly Hisel

CHARLOTTE RUSSE

2 eggs, separated
1 cup sugar
1 package unflavored
  gelatin
1/4 cup cold water

1 teaspoon (scant) vanilla
  extract
2 cups whipping cream
Egg white, unbeaten
24 ladyfingers, split

Beat 2 egg whites in mixer bowl until stiff peaks form. Add 1/2 cup sugar gradually. Beat egg yolks in large mixer bowl until light and fluffy. Add remaining 1/2 cup sugar; beat well. Soften gelatin in cold water in double boiler. Cook over hot water, stirring until gelatin is dissolved. Beat into egg yolk mixture rapidly. Fold in beaten egg whites and vanilla. Whip cream in bowl until soft peaks form. Fold 1 cup whipped cream into egg mixture. Brush bottom and sides of large bowl with unbeaten egg white. Arrange ladyfingers across bottom and around side of bowl. Pour in filling. Spread remaining 1 cup whipped cream over top. Garnish with cherries. Chill for 6 hours or longer. Yield: 12 servings.

Trudie Gadjen

BLACK FOREST DUMP CAKE

1 20-ounce can crushed
   pineapple
1 21-ounce can cherry
   pie filling

1 2-layer package devil's
   food cake mix
1 cup chopped pecans
1/2 cup melted butter

Drain pineapple, reserving juice. Spread pineapple in lightly greased 9x13-inch cake pan. Spoon pie filling over top. Sprinkle cake mix over pie filling. Sprinkle with pecans. Combine melted butter and reserved juice in bowl; mix well. Pour over top. Bake at 350 degrees for 35 to 40 minutes or until brown.
Yield: 12 servings.

Clara White

LEMONADE CHEESECAKE

1 2-layer package white
   cake mix
1 cup sour cream
1 6-ounce can frozen
   lemonade concentrate,
   thawed

3 ounces cream cheese,
   softened
3 eggs
1/4 cup sugar
1 cup sour cream

Combine cake mix, 1 cup sour cream, lemonade concentrate, cream cheese and eggs in mixer bowl; beat at low speed until moistened. Beat at high speed for 4 minutes. Pour into greased and floured bundt pan. Bake at 350 degrees for 50 to 65 minutes or until toothpick inserted in center comes out clean. Cool upright in pan for 10 minutes. Remove from pan. Cool completely. Combine sugar and 1 cup sour cream in bowl; mix well. Spread over cooled cheesecake. Yield: 16 servings.

Diane Murphy

★ Reduce the fat and calories in recipes by substituting yogurt for sour cream and Neufchâtel cheese or cottage cheese for cream cheese.

WORLD'S BEST CHEESECAKE

1 1/2 cups graham cracker
   crumbs
1/4 cup butter, softened
1/4 cup sugar
1 cup sugar
24 ounces cream cheese,
   softened

1 teaspoon vanilla extract
5 eggs
2 cups sour cream
1/2 cup sugar
1 teaspoon vanilla extract

Mix graham cracker crumbs, butter and 1/4 cup sugar in bowl until crumbly. Press into bottom of 10-inch springform pan. Bake at 375 degrees for 5 minutes. Cream 1 cup sugar and cream cheese in mixer bowl until smooth. Add 1 teaspoon vanilla and eggs; beat until creamy. Spoon into prepared pan. Bake for 40 minutes. Combine sour cream, 1/2 cup sugar and 1 teaspoon vanilla in bowl; mix well. Spoon over cheesecake layer. Increase oven temperature to 475 degrees. Bake for 5 minutes longer. Yield: 8 servings.

Joseph B. Snodgrass

CHEESE GEMS

3/4 cup graham cracker
   crumbs
3/4 cup sugar
16 ounces cream cheese,
   softened
3 egg yolks

3 egg whites, stiffly beaten
1/2 to 3/4 cup sour cream
7 1/2 teaspoons
   confectioners' sugar
1 teaspoon vanilla extract

Press graham cracker crumbs into buttered miniature muffin cups. Cream sugar and cream cheese in mixer bowl until smooth. Add egg yolks; beat well. Fold in egg whites. Spoon into muffin cups. Bake at 350 degrees for 15 to 20 minutes or until set. Cool in pans. Remove from pans. Combine sour cream, confectioners' sugar and vanilla in bowl; mix well. Spread on cooled cheese gems. Yield: 3 to 5 dozen.

Darlene L. Dutko

CHOCOLATE ÉCLAIR CAKE

1 package graham
  crackers
2 packages French vanilla
  instant pudding mix
3 cups milk

12 ounces whipped
  topping
1 16-ounce can
  chocolate frosting

Line bottom of 9x13-inch cake pan with graham crackers. Beat pudding mixes and milk in bowl until thickened. Fold in whipped topping. Spoon half the pudding mixture over graham crackers. Layer graham crackers, remaining pudding mixture and graham crackers over pudding layer. Spread frosting over top. May add small amount of milk to frosting to make of spreading consistency. Chill until serving time. May substitute 1 package vanilla instant pudding mix for French vanilla if preferred. Yield: 15 servings.

Cathy Beckham, Paula Goodlett
Nancy Heil, Patricia J. Tudor

WHITE CHOCOLATE MOUSSE

5 ounces white chocolate,
  chopped

1½ cups whipping cream
1 teaspoon vanilla extract

Melt chocolate in top of double boiler over simmering water, stirring occasionally. Remove from heat; stir in chilled whipping cream. Beat at medium speed for 5 minutes or until soft peaks form, adding vanilla while beating. Do not overbeat. Spoon into stemmed glasses. Chill for several hours to overnight. Yield: 6 servings.

Patricia J. Tudor

★ Whipping cream will whip higher and quicker if the cream is whipped with chilled beaters in a chilled mixer bowl.

CHOCOLATE PUDDING YUM-YUM

1 cup sugar
2 tablespoons (heaping)
  baking cocoa
3 tablespoons (heaping)
  flour
2¹/₂ cups milk
3 egg yolks

1 teaspoon vanilla extract
1 package graham
  crackers
3 egg whites
6 tablespoons sugar
Pinch of cream of tartar

Combine sugar, cocoa and flour in saucepan; mix well. Stir in milk gradually until of smooth consistency. Add egg yolks; mix well. Cook over medium to low heat until thickened, stirring constantly. Add vanilla; mix well. Arrange 1 layer of graham crackers in deep baking dish. Alternate layers of pudding and crackers, ending with pudding. Beat egg whites in mixer bowl until foamy. Add sugar 1 tablespoon at a time, beating until stiff. Fold in cream of tartar. Spread over layers, sealing to edges. Bake at 350 degrees until lightly browned. Yield: 5 servings.

Wilma Sullivan

CHOCOLATE CHIP MUFFINS

1¹/₂ cups flour
³/₄ cup sugar
2 teaspoons baking
  powder
¹/₂ teaspoon salt
1 cup sour cream
¹/₂ cup oil
2 eggs

¹/₂ cup semisweet
  chocolate chips
¹/₄ cup sugar
1 teaspoon cinnamon
¹/₂ cup chopped nuts
¹/₄ cup semisweet
  chocolate chips

Combine flour, ³/₄ cup sugar, baking powder and salt in bowl; mix well. Make a well in center. Combine sour cream, oil and eggs in small bowl; mix well. Pour into dry ingredients, mixing just until moistened. Fold in ¹/₂ cup chocolate chips. Fill greased muffin cups ²/₃ full. Combine ¹/₄ cup sugar, cinnamon, nuts and ¹/₄ cup chocolate chips in bowl. Sprinkle over muffins. Bake at 350 degrees for 25 to 30 minutes or until golden brown.
Yield: 12 to 14 muffins.

Grace Dabney

DIRT CAKE

2 6-ounce packages
  vanilla instant
  pudding mix
4 cups milk
8 to 16 ounces cream
  cheese, softened

2 cups confectioners'
  sugar or sugar
16 ounces whipped
  topping
1 20-ounce package
  Oreo cookies, crushed

Beat pudding mix and milk in bowl. Beat cream cheese, sugar and whipped topping in mixer bowl until creamy. Add to pudding; mix well. Alternate layers of cookies and pudding in 8-inch terra-cotta flowerpot. Place artificial flower in center of pot. May use French vanilla pudding. Yield: 20 servings.

Rebecca Scheer, Shirley Wood

EASY COBBLER

1/2 cup butter
2 cups fruit, drained
2 cups sugar
2 cups water

1/2 cup shortening
1 1/2 cups sifted self-rising
  flour
1/3 cup milk

Melt butter in 9x13-inch baking dish. Arrange fruit evenly in butter. Heat sugar and water in saucepan until sugar dissolves, stirring constantly. Cut shortening into flour in bowl until crumbly. Stir in milk with fork. Knead on lightly floured surface just until smooth. Roll to 1/8-inch thickness. Cut into strips; arrange over fruit. Pour sugar syrup over pastry. Bake at 350 degrees for 55 to 60 minutes or until fruit is tender and liquid is absorbed. Add 1 teaspoon cinnamon if using apples. Yield: 8 servings.

Janis Arnett

MICROWAVE COBBLER

1 1-layer package yellow
  cake mix

1 stick butter, sliced
1 can fruit pie filling

Layer cake mix, pie filling and butter 1/2 at a time in 2-quart glass baking dish. Microwave on High for 15 minutes. Cool slightly. Serve plain or with ice cream. Yield: 4 to 6 servings.

Melinda Miller

LAZY DAY COBBLER

1/2 cup butter	1/4 teaspoon salt
1 cup sugar	3/4 cup milk
1 cup flour	2 cups fruit
1 1/2 teaspoons baking powder	1/2 cup sugar

Melt butter in deep baking dish. Combine 1 cup sugar, flour, baking powder, salt and milk in bowl; mix until smooth. Pour into melted butter; do not stir. Arrange fruit over batter. Sprinkle with 1/2 cup sugar. Bake at 350 degrees for 30 minutes. Batter will rise to top. Omit salt and baking powder if using self-rising flour. Yield: 12 servings.

Donna Browning, Betty Hunter
Peggy Posante, Judy Roberts

PEACH COBBLER

3 cups cake flour	2 tablespoons flour
1 teaspoon salt	1/4 teaspoon nutmeg
1 cup shortening	3 tablespoons butter
1/3 to 1/2 cup ice water	Melted butter
7 cups thinly sliced peeled peaches	1 teaspoon sugar
3/4 cup sugar	1 cup milk
	Dash of nutmeg

Mix cake flour and salt in bowl. Cut in shortening until crumbly. Stir in water gradually until soft dough forms. Reserve 1/3 of the dough. Roll remaining dough into 12x12-inch square on waxed paper. Press over bottom and sides of 8x8-inch baking dish; trim edges. Combine peaches, 3/4 cup sugar, 2 tablespoons flour and 1/4 teaspoon nutmeg in bowl; mix well. Spoon into pastry. Dot with 3 tablespoons butter. Roll reserved dough into 7x9-inch rectangle. Cut into 1-inch wide strips. Arrange over peaches. Trim edges. Brush with melted butter. Sprinkle with additional sugar and nutmeg. Bake at 375 degrees for 55 to 60 minutes or until crust is brown. Combine 1 teaspoon sugar, milk and dash of nutmeg in bowl; mix well. Drizzle over servings. May use raspberries or blackberries. Yield: 8 to 10 servings.

Pati Funk

ORANGE AND PINEAPPLE DELIGHT

60 butter crackers, crushed
1/4 cup sugar
1/2 cup melted butter
1 can sweetened
    condensed milk
1 small can frozen orange
    juice concentrate

2 11-ounce cans
    mandarin oranges,
    drained, chopped
1 20-ounce can crushed
    pineapple, drained
12 ounces whipped
    topping

Reserve 1 cup cracker crumbs. Mix remaining crumbs, sugar and butter in bowl. Press into 9x13-inch baking pan. Mix condensed milk and orange juice concentrate in bowl. Stir in fruit. Fold in whipped topping. Spread over crust. Sprinkle with reserved crumbs. Chill until serving time. Yield: 8 servings.

Agnes Potts

CURRIED FRUIT

1 20-ounce can peaches
1 20-ounce can pears
1 20-ounce can pineapple
1/2 cup butter

1 cup packed brown sugar
1 tablespoon curry powder
1/4 teaspoon salt

Drain fruit; place in baking dish. Heat remaining ingredients in saucepan until sugar dissolves. Pour over fruit. Bake at 350 degrees for 30 minutes. Yield: 8 to 10 servings.

Alma Lee Middleton

FRUIT CUPS

1 can chunky fruits
1 small can pineapple
    chunks
2 bananas, sliced
Strawberries, sliced

3 tablespoons orange
    breakfast drink mix
1 4-ounce package
    vanilla instant pudding
    mix

Drain canned fruit, reserving juice. Combine with bananas and strawberries in bowl. Blend reserved juice with drink mix and pudding mix. Pour over fruit. Chill until serving time. Yield: 8 servings.

Marylene Otte

ICE CREAM CRUNCH DESSERT

2 cups flour
1 cup chopped walnuts
1 cup butter, softened
1/2 cup packed brown
  sugar
1 18-ounce jar hot fudge
  ice cream topping
1/2 gallon vanilla ice
  cream, softened

Mix flour, walnuts, butter and brown sugar at low speed in mixer bowl until crumbly. Spoon into 11x17-inch baking pan. Bake at 375 degrees for 15 to 20 minutes or until light brown, stirring occasionally. Cool slightly. Sprinkle half the crumbs into 9x13-inch dish. Drizzle with half the hot fudge topping. Spoon ice cream over top. Drizzle remaining hot fudge topping over ice cream. Sprinkle with remaining crumbs. Freeze, covered, for 2 hours or until firm. Soften slightly in refrigerator before serving. May substitute butterscotch ice cream topping for hot fudge. Yield: 12 servings.

Patricia J. Tudor, Maxine Welch

HOMEMADE BANANA ICE CREAM

7 eggs
7 bananas
2 pints whipping cream
Sugar to taste
1 quart half and half
1 tablespoon vanilla
  extract
Milk

Combine eggs, bananas and whipping cream in blender container. Process until smooth. Pour into ice cream freezer container. Combine sugar, half and half and vanilla in blender container. Process until smooth. Add to banana mixture; mix well. Add milk to fill line. Freeze according to manufacturer's instructions. Let stand for 30 minutes before serving. Yield: 1 gallon.

Alice Ritchey

COCONUT ICE CREAM

1¹/₃ cups shredded
  coconut
1¹/₂ cups milk
1 tablespoon unflavored
  gelatin
2 tablespoons water

¹/₃ cup sugar
1 cup whipping cream,
  chilled
1 cup half and half
1 teaspoon vanilla extract
²/₃ cup shredded coconut

Combine 1¹/₃ cups coconut and milk in saucepan; mix well. Let stand for 30 minutes. Simmer for 10 minutes, stirring frequently. Cool. Strain through several thicknesses of cheesecloth, squeezing out as much liquid as possible, reserving liquid. Discard coconut. Soften gelatin in water in small bowl for 10 minutes. Stir in small amount of hot coconut liquid to gelatin mixture until gelatin is dissolved. Beat sugar and whipping cream in mixer bowl until soft peaks form. Add half and half, vanilla, gelatin mixture and coconut liquid; mix well. Stir in ²/₃ cup coconut. Spoon into freezer container. Freeze until partially set. Stir until well mixed. Freeze until firm. Yield: 6 servings.

Zora Logsdon

PAT'S PEACH ICE CREAM

2 quarts frozen nondairy
  creamer, thawed
1 14-ounce can
  sweetened condensed
  milk

12 ounces whipped
  topping
Sugar to taste
Peaches

Combine creamer, milk and whipped topping in bowl; mix well. Pour into ice cream freezer container. Add sweetened fruit to fill line. Freeze according to manufacturer's instructions. May use other fruit. Yield: 1 gallon.

Rhoda Bailey

VANILLA ICE CREAM

4 egg yolks
3/4 cup sugar
4 egg whites

6 cups half and half
3/4 cup sugar
2 teaspoons vanilla extract

Beat egg yolks in small mixer bowl until foamy. Add 3/4 cup sugar gradually, beating until yolks are lemon-colored and thick. Beat egg whites in mixer bowl until soft peaks form. Fold egg yolk mixture into egg whites. Stir in half and half and 3/4 cup sugar. Pour into 3-quart saucepan. Cook over medium heat until mixture coats spoon, stirring constantly. Do not boil. Cool to room temperature. Stir in vanilla. Chill thoroughly. Pour into ice cream freezer container. Freeze according to manufacturer's instructions. Yield: 3 quarts.

Shirley Smith

HOMEMADE BANANA ORANGE SHERBET

3 bananas, mashed
Juice of 3 oranges
Juice of 3 lemons

3 cups sugar
3 cups milk
3 cups cream

Combine bananas, orange juice, lemon juice, sugar, milk and cream in bowl; mix well. Pour into ice cream freezer container. Freeze according to manufacturer's instructions. May substitute half and half or milk for cream.

Chrissy Robey

LEMON DELIGHT

1 angel food cake
2 3-ounce packages
  lemon pudding and pie
  filling mix

1 3-ounce package lemon
  gelatin
12 ounces whipped topping

Crumble cake into 9x11-inch cake pan. Cook pudding using package directions. Prepare gelatin using package directions. Stir into cooked pudding. Pour over crumbled cake. Chill until firm. Spread whipped topping over top.
Yield: 8 to 10 servings.

Donna Browning, Betty Krueger

LIME BAVARIAN CREAM

1 3-ounce package lime
  gelatin
1/8 teaspoon salt
1 cup hot water
1 cup pineapple juice
1 cup whipping cream,
  whipped

1 cup crushed pineapple,
  drained
3 tablespoons sugar
1/2 cup chopped pecans
Cherries

Dissolve gelatin and salt in hot water in bowl. Stir in pineapple juice. Chill until partially set. Fold in whipped cream. Add pineapple, sugar and pecans; mix gently. Chill until set. Garnish with cherries. Yield: 8 servings.

Gwen Mills

ORANGE GELATIN DELIGHT

1 3-ounce package
  orange gelatin
16 ounces cottage cheese

1 can pineapple tidbits
1 can mandarin oranges
9 ounces whipped topping

Mix gelatin and cottage cheese in bowl. Drain pineapple and oranges. Add to gelatin; mix well. Fold in whipped topping. Chill until serving time. Yield: 4 servings.

Grace Murphy

SANGRIA ORANGE CUPS

3 large oranges
1 3/4 cups Sangria

1 3-ounce package
  orange gelatin

Mark a horizontal guideline around middle of each orange. Make even scallop cuts into orange above and below line. Pull halves apart gently. Remove orange sections with grapefruit knife; reserve. Scrape shells clean with large spoon. Heat Sangria just to the boiling point in small saucepan. Add gelatin, stirring until dissolved. Pour into bowl. Chill for 30 minutes or until mixture is partially set. Fold in reserved orange sections. Chill for 2 hours. Place orange shells in sherbet glasses. Spoon gelatin mixture into shells. Chill until serving time. Yield: 6 servings.

Billie Snelling

BAKED PEACHES

2 29-ounce cans peach
   halves
8 ounces cream cheese,
   softened
1/4 cup honey
Pecan halves

1/2 cup packed light brown
   sugar
1 teaspoon flour
1/4 cup margarine
1 teaspoon vanilla extract

Drain peaches, reserving 1 cup juice. Arrange peaches cut side up in baking dish. Blend cream cheese and honey in bowl. Spoon into center of peaches. Place pecan half on top of cream cheese mixture. Combine reserved peach juice, brown sugar, flour and margarine in saucepan. Cook until thickened, stirring constantly. Stir in vanilla. Pour over peaches. Bake at 350 degrees for 10 minutes. Yield: 12 to 14 servings.

Kathleen S. McDougal

PEACHES AND CREAM

2 cups flour
1 cup butter
1 cup chopped nuts
   (optional)
1 cup whipped topping
1 cup confectioners' sugar

8 ounces cream cheese,
   softened
1 jar peach filling
6 to 8 peaches, sliced
Whipped topping

Mix flour, butter and nuts in bowl until crumbly. Press into 9x13-inch baking dish. Bake at 350 degrees for 15 to 20 minutes. Cool completely. Mix 1 cup whipped topping, confectioners' sugar and cream cheese in bowl until smooth. Spread over baked layer. Mix peach filling and peaches in bowl. Spoon over cream cheese layer. Spread additional whipped topping over top. Yield: 12 servings.

Judy Seitz

LAZY PEACH PIE

1/2 cup butter
1 cup self-rising flour
1/2 cup sugar
1 egg

3/4 cup milk
1 quart peaches, sliced
1/2 cup sugar
1 teaspoon vanilla extract

Melt butter in 9x13-inch baking dish. Mix flour, ½ cup sugar, egg and milk in bowl. Pour into melted butter. Sprinkle peaches with ½ cup sugar in large bowl; stir until sugar is dissolved. Add vanilla; mix well. Spoon over flour mixture. Bake at 350 degrees for 45 minutes. Yield: 12 servings.

Phyllis L. Allen

PEACH AND ALMOND ROLL

3 eggs
1 cup sugar
1 cup self-rising flour
¾ cup puréed peaches
1 teaspoon almond extract
Confectioners' sugar
1 cup confectioners' sugar

8 ounces cream cheese, softened
½ teaspoon almond extract
2 tablespoons margarine, softened

Beat eggs in mixer bowl for 5 minutes or until very thick and lemon-colored. Beat in sugar gradually. Stir in flour and peaches. Add 1 teaspoon almond extract; mix well. Pour into greased and floured 10x15-inch baking pan, spreading evenly. Bake at 350 degrees for 15 minutes. Loosen cake from edges; invert onto towel sprinkled with confectioners' sugar. Roll hot cake from narrow end as for jelly roll. Cool for 30 minutes. Beat 1 cup confectioners' sugar, cream cheese, ½ teaspoon almond extract and margarine in mixer bowl until smooth and creamy. Unroll cake. Spread with cream cheese mixture. Roll as for jelly roll. Place on serving plate. Cut into pieces. Yield: 9 servings.

Dena Sue Montgomery

★ Cake rolls are versatile and festive. Use your favorite jam, frosting or ice cream as filling. Decorate for the occasion and enjoy the compliments.

SPICED PEACH HALVES

1 29-ounce can peach
   halves
1/4 cup packed brown
   sugar
1/2 teaspoon cinnamon
1/4 teaspoon nutmeg
1/4 cup melted margarine
1/4 cup crushed cornflakes
1/4 cup chopped nuts
1 cup whipped topping
1 tablespoon molasses

Drain peaches, reserving 1/4 cup juice. Arrange peaches cut side up in shallow 1 1/2-quart casserole. Combine reserved peach juice, brown sugar, cinnamon, nutmeg and 2 tablespoons melted margarine in bowl; mix well. Spoon over peaches. Bake at 350 degrees for 10 minutes. Combine remaining 2 tablespoons margarine, cornflakes and nuts in bowl; mix well. Sprinkle over peaches. Increase oven temperature to 400 degrees. Bake for 10 minutes. Mix whipped topping and molasses in bowl. Spoon over peaches. Serve warm. Yield: 6 to 8 servings.

Dot Berry

PEANUT BUTTER TREAT

30 Oreo cookies, crushed
1/3 cup melted margarine
1 small package vanilla
   instant pudding mix
1 3/4 cups milk
1 cup peanut butter
4 ounces German's sweet
   chocolate, chopped
12 ounces whipped
   topping

Mix cookies and margarine in bowl; reserve 1/4 cup. Press remaining cookie mixture into 9x13-inch baking pan. Bake at 375 degrees for 5 minutes. Cool completely. Prepare pudding mix according to package directions using 1 3/4 cups milk. Stir in peanut butter and chocolate. Fold in whipped topping. Spread evenly over cooled crust. Sprinkle with reserved crumbs. Chill, covered, for several hours to overnight. Yield: 15 servings.

Patricia J. Tudor

PEPPERMINT ICEBOX DESSERT

10 ounces vanilla wafers,
crushed
3 tablespoons melted
butter
3 cups whipping cream,
whipped

8 ounces marshmallows
3/4 cup chopped pecans
8 peppermint sticks,
crushed

Mix vanilla wafers and melted butter in bowl. Press half the crumbs into shallow baking dish. Combine whipped cream, marshmallows, pecans and peppermint candy in bowl; mix well. Spoon over crumb layer. Sprinkle with remaining crumbs. Chill for several hours. Yield: 8 to 10 servings.

Marie Matsen

HAWAIIAN PINEAPPLE WHIP

4 egg yolks
1 cup pineapple juice
2 envelopes unflavored
gelatin
1/2 cup sugar
Dash of salt
1 1/2 cups pineapple juice

3 tablespoons lemon juice
1   13-ounce can
pineapple tidbits, drained
10 maraschino cherries,
chopped
2 cups whipping cream,
whipped

Beat egg yolks in saucepan with wire whisk. Add 1 cup pineapple juice; mix well. Stir in gelatin, sugar and salt. Cook over medium heat just to the boiling point, stirring constantly; remove from heat. Add remaining 1 1/2 cups pineapple juice and lemon juice; mix well. Chill until partially set. Fold in pineapple, cherries and whipped cream. Spoon into mold. Chill until set. Unmold onto serving plate. Garnish with additional maraschino cherries. Yield: 8 servings.

Gwen Mills

PINEAPPLE DESSERT

1/2 package vanilla wafers,
  crushed
2 eggs
1 1/2 cups confectioners'
  sugar
1/2 cup butter, softened

1   16-ounce can crushed
  pineapple, drained
1 cup whipping cream,
  whipped
Crushed nuts

Press half the vanilla wafer crumbs into buttered 8x8-inch baking dish. Beat eggs, confectioners' sugar and butter in mixer bowl until light and fluffy. Spoon over crumb layer. Layer pineapple and whipped cream over top. Sprinkle with nuts and remaining crumbs. Yield: 9 servings.

Bea Senn

FRUIT PIZZA

1   2-layer package yellow
  cake mix
1/4 cup water
2 eggs
1/4 cup butter, softened
1/4 cup packed brown
  sugar
1/2 cup chopped nuts

16 ounces whipped
  topping
Strawberries
Pineapple
Grapes
Bananas
1/2 cup apricot preserves
2 tablespoons water

Combine cake mix, 1/4 cup water, eggs, butter, brown sugar and nuts in bowl; mix well. Mixture will be stiff. Spread in 2 greased and floured waxed paper-lined pizza pans. Bake at 350 degrees for 15 to 20 minutes or until light brown. Cool. Spread with whipped topping. Arrange fruits over whipped topping. Heat apricot preserves and 2 tablespoons water in saucepan, stirring constantly. Strain. Pour over pizza. Chill until serving time. Yield: 2 pizzas.

Peggy Graviss

STRAWBERRY PIZZA

1/2 cup margarine
1 cup self-rising flour
1/4 cup confectioners'
  sugar
8 ounces cream cheese,
  softened
1/4 cup lemon juice

1 14-ounce can
  sweetened condensed
  milk
1 teaspoon vanilla extract
1 quart strawberries
Strawberry glaze

Melt margarine in saucepan. Add flour and confectioners' sugar; mix well. Press into pizza pan. Bake at 350 degrees for 10 to 15 minutes or until edges are lightly browned. Cool. Combine cream cheese, lemon juice, condensed milk and vanilla in bowl; mix well. Spread over cooled crust. Combine strawberries and glaze in bowl; mix well. Spread over cream cheese mixture. Chill until serving time. Yield: 8 servings.

Judy Wallis

PRALINE PARFAIT

1 1/2 cups light corn syrup
1 1/2 cups dark corn syrup
1 1/2 cups chopped roasted
  pecans
1 teaspoon vanilla extract
Dash of nutmeg

Dash of cinnamon
12 scoops French vanilla
  ice cream
1 cup whipping cream,
  whipped
6 maraschino cherries

Mix corn syrups, pecans, vanilla, nutmeg and cinnamon in bowl. Spoon 2 tablespoonfuls sauce into each of 6 parfait dishes. Add two scoops ice cream to each dish. Drizzle additional sauce over ice cream. Top with whipped cream and cherries. Serve immediately. Yield: 6 servings.

Patricia J. Tudor

ALMOND AND COCONUT CUSTARD

3 tablespoons unflavored
   gelatin
1 cup water
1 cup milk

1/2 cup sugar
1 cup coconut cream
1 1/2 teaspoons almond
   extract

Soften gelatin in 1/2 cup water for 10 minutes. Combine remaining 1/2 cup water and milk in saucepan. Bring to a boil, stirring constantly. Add gelatin and sugar, stirring until dissolved. Stir in coconut cream and almond extract. Remove from heat. Cool. Pour into shallow dish. Chill until set. Yield: 4 servings.

Crystal Duke

APPLE NUT PUDDING

2 eggs
1 cup sugar
3/4 cup sifted flour
3/4 teaspoon salt
1 teaspoon baking powder

1/2 teaspoon cinnamon
1/4 teaspoon nutmeg
1 teaspoon almond extract
3/4 cup chopped walnuts
1 1/2 cups chopped apples

Beat eggs in large mixer bowl. Add sugar gradually; beat well. Sift in flour, salt, baking powder, cinnamon and nutmeg. Add almond extract, walnuts and apples; mix well. Pour into well-greased 8x8-inch cake pan. Bake at 325 degrees for 50 minutes. Cut into squares. Serve warm with whipped cream.
Yield: 8 servings.

Margaret Kurz

★ Serve warm puddings with ice cream, whipped cream, whipped topping or an appropriate sauce. Most puddings can be rewarmed in the microwave.

BANANA PUDDING

1 cup sugar
1 tablespoon flour
3 egg yolks, beaten
1 to 1½ cups milk
1 teaspoon butter,
    softened

1 teaspoon vanilla extract
Vanilla wafers
Bananas, sliced
3 egg whites
3 tablespoons sugar

Combine 1 cup sugar and flour in saucepan. Add egg yolks, milk and butter; mix well. Cook over medium heat until thickened, stirring constantly. Stir in vanilla. Alternate layers of vanilla wafers, bananas and hot pudding in baking dish. Beat egg whites and 3 tablespoons sugar in mixer bowl until stiff peaks form. Spread over pudding, sealing to edges. Bake at 350 degrees for 15 minutes or until brown. Yield: 6 servings.

Patsy Ford

LAYERED BANANA PUDDING

3 4-ounce packages
    vanilla instant pudding
    mix
1 14-ounce can
    sweetened condensed
    milk

3 cups milk
12 ounces whipped
    topping
Graham crackers
5 medium bananas, sliced

Combine pudding, condensed milk, milk and whipped topping in bowl; mix well. Layer graham crackers, bananas and pudding ½ at a time in 9x13-inch dish. Chill until serving time. May substitute vanilla wafers for graham crackers.
Yield: 20 servings.

Martha Duncan Wilson

★ Brush sliced bananas with lemon juice to keep them white or peel and slice just before serving.

EASY BANANA PUDDING

2 packages vanilla instant
  pudding mix
3 cups milk
8 ounces whipped topping

1 cup sour cream
2 packages vanilla wafers
6 large bananas, sliced

Combine pudding mix, milk, whipped topping and sour cream in bowl; mix gently. Crush a small amount of vanilla wafers; reserve. Alternate layers of remaining wafers, pudding and bananas in 9x13-inch dish, ending with pudding. Sprinkle with reserved crushed wafers. Chill until serving time.
Yield: 20 servings.

Donna Browning

BANANA AND CHOCOLATE PUDDING

3 packages vanilla wafers
1 6-ounce package
  chocolate instant
  pudding mix

1 6-ounce package
  vanilla instant pudding
  mix
6 bananas, sliced

Line bottom and side of large bowl with vanilla wafers. Prepare pudding mixes using package directions. Alternate layers of bananas, chocolate pudding, vanilla wafers, bananas and vanilla pudding. Chill until serving time.
Yield: 10 to 20 servings.

Donna M. Barnes

PEGGY BENTON'S
BANANA AND CHOCOLATE PUDDING

2 packages chocolate
  fudge instant pudding
  mix
6 to 8 bananas, sliced

32 ounces whipped topping
1 package ground nut
  topping
Maraschino cherries

Prepare pudding using package directions. Alternate layers of pudding, bananas, whipped topping and nuts in stemmed glasses. Place cherry on top. Chill until serving time.
Yield: 12 servings.

Shari Vaughn

BREAD PUDDING WITH AMARETTO SAUCE

4 eggs
1 cup packed brown sugar
1¼ teaspoons cinnamon
2 teaspoons vanilla extract
½ teaspoon salt
4½ cups milk

4 to 5 cups 1-inch cubed
  dry French bread
1 cup golden raisins
Amaretto Sauce (page 408)
Whipped cream
Maraschino cherries

Beat eggs and brown sugar in large mixer bowl until thick. Add cinnamon, vanilla and salt; mix well. Stir in milk. Fold in bread. Spoon into 2-quart casserole. Add raisins; mix well. Place casserole in baking pan containing 1-inch water. Bake at 350 degrees for 1½ hours. Spoon hot bread pudding into tall goblets. Pour warm Amaretto Sauce over pudding. Garnish with whipped cream and maraschino cherries. Yield: 8 servings.

Sandi Tipton Clark

CHOCOLATE BREAD PUDDING

1½ cups milk
1½ ounces baking
  chocolate
1 cup bread crumbs
½ cup sugar
3 egg yolks

½ cup milk
3 tablespoons margarine
¼ teaspoon salt
1 teaspoon vanilla extract
Whipped cream

Heat 1½ cups milk and chocolate in saucepan until chocolate is melted, stirring constantly. Add bread crumbs and sugar; mix well. Cook until sugar is dissolved. Beat egg yolks in mixer bowl until light. Fold into chocolate mixture. Add ½ cup milk, margarine and salt; mix well. Cook until thickened, stirring constantly. Stir in vanilla. Spoon into baking dish. Bake at 350 degrees for 30 minutes or until pudding tests done. Serve with whipped cream. Yield: 4 servings.

Gwen Mills

FRENCH BREAD PUDDING

6 cups cubed French bread
4 cups milk
3 eggs, slightly beaten
2 cups sugar
1 cup raisins

2 tablespoons vanilla
  extract
3 tablespoons margarine
Whiskey Sauce (page 410)

Place bread in large bowl. Add milk; mix well. Let stand for 10 minutes; mix well. Add eggs, sugar, raisins and vanilla; mix well. Melt margarine in 9x13-inch baking pan. Spoon pudding mixture into prepared pan. Bake at 325 degrees for 30 to 45 minutes or until very firm. Cool. Cut into small squares. Place in dessert dishes. Drizzle with Whiskey Sauce.
Yield: 6 to 8 servings.

Henry Bennett

VINCENT PRICE'S OLD-FASHIONED BREAD PUDDING

1 cup packed dark brown
  sugar
2 tablespoons butter,
  softened
3 slices bread

1 cup raisins
3 eggs
2 cups milk
1/8 teaspoon salt
1 teaspoon vanilla extract

Place brown sugar in top of double boiler. Butter 1 side of bread slices; chop. Sprinkle over brown sugar. Add raisins. Beat eggs, milk, salt and vanilla in mixer bowl. Pour over bread. Do not stir. Cook over simmering water for 1 hour. Spoon into serving bowl. Serve warm or cold. Yield: 4 servings.

Barbara Struck

RICE PUDDING

2 egg yolks
1/2 cup sugar
1 tablespoon melted
  shortening
1 teaspoon vanilla extract

1/4 teaspoon salt
1/2 cup raisins
1 1/2 cups milk
1 cup cooked rice
2 egg whites, stiffly beaten

Combine egg yolks, sugar, shortening, vanilla, salt, raisins, milk and rice in bowl; mix well. Fold in egg whites. Spoon into baking dish. Bake at 325 degrees for 40 to 60 minutes or until set. Serve with whipped topping. Yield: 4 servings.

Sandi Tipton Clark

PUMPKIN DESSERT

1 2-layer package yellow
   cake mix
1/2 cup melted margarine
1 egg
1 16-ounce can pumpkin
   pie filling

2 cups milk
2 eggs
1/4 cup margarine, softened
1/2 cup chopped pecans
1/4 cup sugar
1 teaspoon cinnamon

Reserve 1 cup cake mix. Combine remaining cake mix, melted margarine and 1 egg in bowl; mix well. Press into 9x13-inch baking pan. Combine pumpkin, milk and 2 eggs in bowl; mix well. Pour over crumb layer. Mix 1/4 cup margarine, reserved 1 cup cake mix, pecans, sugar and cinnamon in bowl until crumbly. Sprinkle over pumpkin mixture. Bake at 325 degrees for 1 hour or until set. Serve warm with whipped topping. Yield: 12 servings.

Donna Browning

★ Your Halloween pumpkin can be peeled, cooked and mashed. Store in freezer in recipe-sized portions.

PUMPKIN ICE CREAM SQUARES

1/4 cup melted margarine
1/4 cup sugar
1 cup gingersnap crumbs
1 teaspoon unflavored
  gelatin
1/4 cup cold water
1/2 cup cooked pumpkin

1/2 teaspoon salt
1 teaspoon cinnamon
1/4 teaspoon nutmeg
1 teaspoon vanilla extract
1 quart vanilla ice cream,
  softened

Mix margarine, sugar and gingersnap crumbs in bowl; reserve 1/3 cup. Press remaining crumb mixture into 8x8-inch dish. Soften gelatin in cold water in saucepan. Add pumpkin, salt, cinnamon, nutmeg and vanilla; mix well. Cook over low heat until gelatin dissolves, stirring constantly. Spoon into chilled bowl. Cool. Fold in ice cream. Spoon over crust. Sprinkle with reserved crumbs. Freeze until firm. Cut into 2-inch squares.
Yield: 16 servings.

Gwen Mills

PUNCH BOWL CAKE

1 2-layer package yellow
  cake mix
1 6-ounce package
  vanilla instant pudding
  mix
4 cups strawberries

1 large can crushed
  pineapple, drained
16 ounces whipped
  topping
1 cup chopped nuts
1 small package coconut

Prepare and bake cake mix using package directions for 9x13-inch cake pan. Crumble cake. Prepare pudding mix using package directions. Layer cake crumbs, strawberries, pineapple, pudding, whipped topping, nuts and coconut 1/2 at a time in large bowl. Yield: 12 servings.

Juyne Bushart

FRUITY PUNCH BOWL CAKE

1 2-layer package yellow
cake mix
2 6-ounce packages
vanilla instant pudding
mix
2 large cans crushed
pineapple, drained

2 20-ounce cans cherry
pie filling
6 bananas, sliced
32 ounces whipped
topping
1 cup chopped nuts

Prepare and bake cake mix using package directions for 9x13-inch cake pan. Prepare pudding mixes using package directions. Crumble half the cake into punch bowl. Layer half the pineapple, cherry pie filling, bananas and whipped topping over cake. Repeat layers. Sprinkle with nuts. Yield: 24 servings.

Karen Murphy

LARGE PUNCH BOWL CAKE

1 6-ounce package
vanilla instant pudding
mix
1 large angel food cake
5 bananas, sliced

1 small carton blueberries
1 quart fresh strawberries
Whipped topping
Crushed pecans

Prepare pudding mix using package directions. Crumble half the angel food cake into bottom of punch bowl. Layer half the bananas, blueberries and strawberries over cake layer. Repeat layers. Spread with whipped topping. Sprinkle with pecans. Yield: 12 servings.

Irene McKinney

★ For a quick but company elegant dessert, place a slice of pound cake spread with a favorite jam on a dessert plate, then spoon canned pudding on top and garnish with whipped cream and a cherry.

SNOWBALL CAKE

2 envelopes unflavored
gelatin
1/4 cup cold water
1 cup boiling water
1 large can crushed
pineapple

1 cup sugar
3 tablespoons lemon juice
Pinch of salt
4 envelopes whipped
topping mix
Angel food cake, crumbled

Soften gelatin in cold water in small bowl. Stir in boiling water until gelatin is dissolved. Cool. Combine pineapple, sugar, lemon juice and salt in bowl; mix well. Prepare whipped topping mix using package directions. Fold whipped topping and gelatin into pineapple mixture. Alternate layers of cake and pineapple mixture in large bowl until all ingredients are used. Chill for 2 to 3 hours. Yield: 12 servings.

Grace Murphy

STRAWBERRY BROWNIE TORTE

1 23-ounce package
brownie mix
1 14-ounce can
sweetened condensed
milk
1/2 cup cold water

1 4-ounce package
vanilla instant pudding
mix
4 ounces whipped topping
1 quart fresh strawberries

Line bottoms and sides of two greased 9-inch round cake pans with greased waxed paper. Prepare brownie mix using package directions for cake-like brownies. Pour into prepared pans. Bake at 350 degrees for 20 minutes or until brownies test done. Remove to wire rack to cool. Combine condensed milk and water in large mixer bowl; mix well. Add pudding mix; beat well. Chill in refrigerator for 5 minutes. Fold in whipped topping. Place 1 brownie layer on serving plate. Spread with half the pudding mixture. Arrange half the strawberries over pudding mixture. Repeat layers. Chill until serving time. Yield: 8 to 10 servings.

Rebecca Smith

FROZEN STRAWBERRY DELIGHT

1 cup flour
1/2 cup chopped nuts
1/2 cup melted butter
1/4 cup packed brown
  sugar
1 cup sugar

1 1/2 cups sliced
  strawberries
2 teaspoons lemon juice
2 egg whites
2 cups whipped topping

Combine flour, nuts, butter and brown sugar in 8x8-inch baking dish; mix well. Bake at 350 degrees for 20 minutes, stirring occasionally. Cool. Reserve 1/3 of crumb mixture. Press remaining crumbs into bottom of 9x13-inch dish. Combine sugar, strawberries, lemon juice and egg whites in large mixer bowl. Beat at high speed for 10 to 12 minutes. Fold in whipped topping; spread over crust. Sprinkle with reserved crumb mixture. Freeze until serving time. Yield: 12 servings.

Bernice J. Mills

STRAWBERRY DELIGHT DESSERT

8 ounces cream cheese,
  softened
16 ounces whipped
  topping
1 large angel food cake,
  crumbled

1 quart strawberries,
  sliced, drained
1/4 to 1/2 cup sugar
1 package strawberry glaze

Beat cream cheese and whipped topping in mixer bowl until smooth. Add cake; mix well. Press into 9x13-inch cake pan. Combine strawberries, sugar and glaze in bowl; mix well. Spoon over cake mixture. Chill for 2 hours or longer. Yield: 12 servings.

Danny Cook, Joy Keller

★ Do not wash strawberries or remove stems until ready to use in order to keep them as fresh and firm as possible.

HEAVENLY STRAWBERRY DELIGHT

1 10-ounce angel food
cake
1 14-ounce can
sweetened condensed
milk

1/2 cup lemon juice
16 ounces whipped
topping
2 1/2 cups sliced
strawberries

Break cake into bite-sized pieces. Mix condensed milk and lemon juice in large bowl. Fold in whipped topping and strawberries and cake. Chill for 6 hours to overnight. Yield: 12 servings.

Barbara C. Hendrick

STRAWBERRY ICEBOX DESSERT

16 ounces vanilla wafers,
finely crushed
1/4 cup melted margarine
1/2 cup margarine, softened
1 1/2 cups sugar
2 eggs

1 quart strawberries,
halved
2 cups whipping cream,
whipped
4 to 5 vanilla wafers

Mix wafer crumbs and melted margarine in bowl. Press into 9x13-inch dish. Cream softened margarine and sugar in mixer bowl until light and fluffy. Beat in eggs 1 at a time. Spread over crumb layer. Add layers of strawberries and whipped cream. Crush remaining wafers; sprinkle over top. Chill for several hours to overnight. Cut into squares. Yield: 12 servings.

Nona Marie Besendorf

HOMEMADE STRAWBERRY SHORTCAKE

2 cups sugar
2 cups self-rising flour
2 cups milk

2 teaspoons vanilla extract
2 eggs
Strawberries

Combine sugar, flour, milk, vanilla and eggs in mixer bowl; mix well. Pour into greased 9x13-inch cake pan. Bake at 350 degrees for 30 to 45 minutes. Cool. Top with strawberries. Garnish with whipped cream. Yield: 8 to 10 servings.

Janis Arnett

SHORTCAKE FOR STRAWBERRIES

3 egg yolks
1/2 cup sugar
1/2 cup boiling water
1 1/2 cups sifted flour
1 cup sugar

1 teaspoon baking powder
1/4 teaspoon salt
1/2 teaspoon vanilla extract
3 egg whites, stiffly beaten

Beat egg yolks in mixer bowl until light and lemon-colored. Add 1/2 cup sugar gradually, beating well. Stir in boiling water. Sift flour, 1 cup sugar, baking powder and salt into bowl. Add to egg yolk mixture; mix well. Stir in vanilla. Fold in egg whites gently. Spoon into 5x9-inch loaf pan. Bake at 350 degrees for 45 minutes or until shortcake tests done. Remove to wire rack to cool. Yield: 8 servings.

Mary E. Quinker

STRAWBERRY AND BANANA TWINKIE CAKE

1 package Twinkies
1 6-ounce package
   vanilla instant pudding
   mix
3 cups milk
4 to 5 bananas, sliced

1 16-ounce package
   frozen sweetened
   strawberries, thawed
1 cup chopped nuts
12 ounces whipped topping

Split Twinkies lengthwise. Arrange cream side up in 9x13-inch dish. Beat pudding and milk in mixer bowl until thickened. Spoon over Twinkies. Layer bananas and strawberries over pudding; sprinkle with nuts. Spread whipped topping over nuts. Chill for several hours to overnight. Yield: 12 servings.

Brenda Collins

★ Try substituting raspberries or other berries for strawberries in many recipes — you may be able to reduce the amount of berries if the flavors are more intense.

PINEAPPLE AND BANANA TWINKIE CAKE

1 package Twinkies
1 6-ounce package
   French vanilla instant
   pudding mix
3 to 4 bananas, sliced

1 can crushed pineapple,
   drained
8 ounces whipped topping
Strawberries
Chopped pecans

Cut Twinkies into small pieces. Place in 9x13-inch glass dish. Prepare pudding using package directions. Layer bananas, pineapple and pudding over Twinkies. Spread whipped topping over top. Garnish with strawberries and pecans. Chill until serving time. May use vanilla instant pudding. Yield: 12 servings.

Judy Seitz, Shirley Smith

AMARETTO SAUCE

2 cups sugar
1 cup unsalted butter
1/2 teaspoon cinnamon

1/4 teaspoon nutmeg
1/2 cup Amaretto

Combine sugar and butter in heavy saucepan. Cook over medium heat to 234 degrees on candy thermometer, soft-ball stage, stirring constantly. Stir in spices and Amaretto. Serve warm over warm Bread Pudding (page 399). Yield: 1 1/2 cups.

Sandi Tipton Clark

AMBROSIA SAUCE

1 16-ounce can fruit
   cocktail
2 tablespoons sugar
2 teaspoons cornstarch
Dash of salt
2 tablespoon water

2 tablespoons thawed
   frozen orange juice
   concentrate
1 orange, peeled, chopped
1/2 cup flaked coconut

Drain fruit cocktail, reserving 1 cup juice. Combine sugar, cornstarch and salt in saucepan. Stir in water, reserved juice and orange juice. Cook until thickened, stirring constantly. Add fruit cocktail, orange and coconut; mix well. Spoon into bowl. Chill until serving time. Yield: 2 1/2 cups.

Dot Berry

CHOCOLATE SYRUP

2¹/₂ cups sugar
1 cup baking cocoa
¹/₈ teaspoon salt

2 cups water
1 teaspoon vanilla extract

Combine sugar, cocoa, salt and water in saucepan; mix well. Bring to a boil, stirring constantly. Stir in vanilla. Boil for 2 minutes, stirring constantly. Cool. Yield: 2 cups.

Marilyn Heffernan

HOT FUDGE SAUCE

2 cups sugar
²/₃ cup baking cocoa
¹/₄ cup flour
¹/₄ teaspoon salt

2 cups water
2 tablespoons butter
1 teaspoon vanilla extract

Mix sugar, cocoa, flour and salt in heavy saucepan. Add water and butter; mix well. Bring to a boil, stirring constantly. Reduce heat. Cook for 8 minutes, stirring constantly. Cool. Stir in vanilla. Yield: 2¹/₂ cups.

Mary Cook

DESSERT SAUCE

2 cups milk
3 tablespoons flour
3 tablespoons sugar

1¹/₂ teaspoons margarine, softened
1 teaspoon vanilla extract

Combine milk, flour and sugar in saucepan. Cook until thickened, stirring constantly. Add margarine and vanilla; mix well. Pour over favorite dessert. Yield: 2 cups.

Catherine Watkins

★ Top a brownie with ice cream and hot or cold fudge sauce, whipped cream and a cherry.

DIP AND WOBBLE

2 cups milk
2 tablespoons butter
1 cup sugar

1 tablespoon flour
Dash of salt
1 teaspoon nutmeg

Heat milk and butter in saucepan until butter melts. Blend sugar, flour, salt and a small amount of cold water in bowl. Add to milk mixture. Cook until thickened, stirring constantly. Stir in nutmeg. Serve hot over gingerbread or cobblers. May substitute allspice or cinnamon for nutmeg. Yield: 2 cups.

George Alexander

FRUIT SAUCE

1 small jar marshmallow
  creme

1 small package cream
  cheese, softened

Process marshmallow cream and cream cheese in blender container until smooth. Serve as dip or sauce for fruit or lemon cake. Recipe may be doubled.

Ivory S. Henry

WHISKEY SAUCE

1/2 cup butter
1 cup sugar

1 egg, beaten
Whiskey to taste

Combine butter and sugar in top of double boiler. Cook until very hot and sugar is dissolved, stirring constantly. Stir a small amount of mixture into egg; stir egg into hot mixture. Cool. Stir in whiskey. Serve over French Bread Pudding (page 400). Yield: 1/2 cup.

Henry Bennett

★ Keep jars of ice cream topping in the refrigerator to use as an extra flavor touch on plain cake, pudding or large cookies.

CAKES

APPLE CAKE

2 cups flour
1 teaspoon salt
1 teaspoon soda
2 cups sugar
1 cup oil
3 eggs, well beaten
3 cups chopped peeled
  apples

1 cup chopped pecans
1 cup raisins
2 teaspoons vanilla extract
$1/2$ cup margarine, softened
1 cup packed light brown
  sugar
$1/4$ cup canned cream

Sift flour, salt and soda into bowl. Add sugar and oil; mix well. Pour eggs over mixture. Do not stir; let stand while preparing apples. Stir in apples, pecans, raisins and vanilla. Pour into greased 9x13-inch cake pan. Place in cold oven. Bake at 350 degrees for 1 hour or until cake tests done. Combine margarine, brown sugar and canned cream in saucepan; mix well. Boil for 2 to 3 minutes, stirring constantly. Pour over cake.
Yield: 12 servings.

Kathleen S. McDougal

SPICY APPLE CAKE

2 cups sugar
3 eggs, beaten
1 cup oil
1 teaspoon vanilla extract
$2^1/2$ cups self-rising flour

1 teaspoon cinnamon
1 teaspoon nutmeg
1 cup pecans
$1/2$ cup raisins
$2^1/2$ cups chopped apples

Beat sugar and eggs in bowl. Add oil, vanilla, flour, cinnamon and nutmeg; mix well. Stir in pecans, raisins and apples. Pour into greased and floured 9x13-inch cake pan. Bake at 350 degrees for 40 to 45 minutes or until cake tests done.
Yield: 12 servings.

Grace Murphy

GERMAN APPLE CAKE

3 eggs
1/2 cup oil
2 cups sugar
2 cups sifted flour
1/4 teaspoon salt
2 teaspoons cinnamon

1 teaspoon soda
2 teaspoons vanilla extract
4 cups finely chopped
  apples
1 cup chopped pecans

Beat eggs and oil in bowl until foamy. Add sugar; mix well. Sift flour, salt, cinnamon and soda into bowl; mix well. Stir in vanilla and mixture of apples and pecans. Pour into greased 9x13-inch cake pan. Bake at 350 degrees for 40 minutes or until cake tests done. Frost with Cream Cheese Frosting. Yield: 12 servings.

Cream Cheese Frosting

7 ounces cream cheese,
  softened
3 tablespoons margarine,
  softened

2 tablespoons vanilla
  extract
2 cups confectioners' sugar
Milk

Combine cream cheese, margarine, vanilla and confectioners' sugar in mixer bowl. Beat until smooth. Add enough milk to make of desired spreading consistency.

Margie Brodt

APPLE SPICE CAKE

3/4 cup butter, softened
2 1/2 cups sugar
3 eggs
3 1/4 cups sifted flour
2 teaspoons soda
1 1/2 teaspoons salt

1/2 teaspoon nutmeg
1/2 teaspoon cinnamon
5 cups chopped peeled
  apples
1 cup nuts

Cream butter and sugar in mixer bowl until light and fluffy. Add eggs; beat well. Add mixture of flour, soda, salt, nutmeg and cinnamon; mix well at low speed. Stir in apples and nuts. Pour into well-greased bundt pan. Bake at 350 degrees for 1 hour and 15 minutes or until cake tests done. Yield: 16 servings.

Cleo Hardin

FRESH APPLE CAKE

2¹/₂ cups flour
2 cups sugar
1 teaspoon salt
1 teaspoon soda
1 teaspoon baking powder
1 teaspoon cinnamon
1 cup oil

2 eggs
3 cups chopped peeled
    apples
1 cup chopped nuts
1   12-ounce package
    butterscotch chips

Sift flour, sugar, salt, soda, baking powder and cinnamon into bowl. Add oil and eggs; mix well. Stir in apples and nuts. Pour into greased 9x13-inch cake pan. Sprinkle butterscotch chips over top. Bake at 350 degrees for 45 to 50 minutes or until cake tests done. Yield: 12 servings.

Judy Long

LYNDA'S FRESH APPLE CAKE

1 cup packed brown sugar
1 cup sugar
1¹/₄ cups oil
2 eggs
3 cups flour
1 teaspoon cinnamon

1 teaspoon salt
2 teaspoons soda
3 cups chopped peeled
    apples
1 cup chopped walnuts
1 cup coconut

Beat brown sugar, sugar and oil in bowl until well mixed. Add eggs; mix well. Add flour, cinnamon, salt and soda; mix well. Stir in apples, walnuts and coconut. Pour into oiled and floured tube pan. Bake at 325 degrees for 1 hour and 30 minutes or until cake tests done. May add raisins and dates if desired. Yield: 16 servings.

Barbara Struck

★ When choosing apples for cooking, remember some are tart, some are sweet and some will stay firm while others become soft and mushy as they cook.

APRICOT NECTAR CAKE

1 package yellow cake mix
1 cup apricot nectar
5 eggs
1 cup oil
1 teaspoon lemon juice

1 4-ounce package lemon
   instant pudding mix
Apricot nectar
Confectioners' sugar

Combine cake mix, 1 cup nectar, eggs and oil in bowl; mix well. Add lemon juice and pudding mix; beat until well mixed. Pour into tube pan. Bake at 250 degrees for 1 hour. Increase temperature to 350 degrees. Bake for 20 to 30 minutes longer or until cake tests done. Add enough apricot nectar to confectioners' sugar to make of spreading consistency. Drizzle over cake. Invert cake onto serving plate. Spread remaining icing over top and side. Yield: 16 servings.

Dollie D. Billiter

BANANA-NUT CAKE

1 cup margarine, softened
2 cups sugar
2 eggs
3 bananas, mashed
2 cups flour

3 tablespoons sour cream
1 teaspoon soda
1 cup chopped black
   walnuts

Line 2 greased 9-inch cake pans with greased waxed paper. Cream margarine and sugar in bowl until light and fluffy. Add eggs and bananas; mix well. Add flour and mixture of sour cream and soda; mix well. Stir in walnuts. Pour into prepared pans. Bake at 350 degrees for 35 to 40 minutes or until cake tests done. Remove to wire rack to cool. Spread Caramel Icing between layers and over top and side of cake. Yield: 12 servings.

Caramel Icing

1/2 cup margarine
1 cup packed brown sugar
1/4 cup milk

1 3/4 to 2 cups
   confectioners' sugar

Bring margarine and brown sugar to a boil in saucepan. Add milk. Bring to a boil; remove from heat. Beat in enough confectioners' sugar to make of spreading consistency. Add additional milk if icing becomes too thick.

Ada P. Wheeler

BEER CAKE

1 package lemon deluxe
  cake mix
1 4-ounce package
  lemon instant pudding
  mix

4 eggs
1/4 cup oil
1 cup beer

Combine cake mix and pudding mix in bowl; mix well. Add eggs, oil and beer; mix well. Pour into greased and floured bundt pan. Bake at 350 degrees for 1 hour or until cake tests done. Remove to wire rack to cool. May add confectioners' sugar glaze. Yield: 15 servings.

BEST EVER CAKE

1 cup chopped nuts
2 eggs
2 cups sugar
2 cups flour
2 teaspoons soda
1 teaspoon vanilla extract
Dash of salt
1 20-ounce can crushed
  pineapple

1/2 cup margarine, softened
8 ounces cream cheese,
  softened
1 1/2 cups confectioners'
  sugar
1 teaspoon vanilla extract
Nuts

Combine 1 cup nuts, eggs, sugar, flour and soda in bowl; mix well. Add 1 teaspoon vanilla, salt and crushed pineapple; mix well. Pour into greased and floured 9x13-inch cake pan. Bake at 350 degrees for 40 to 45 minutes or until cake tests done. Combine margarine and cream cheese in bowl; mix well. Add confectioners' sugar; beat until smooth. Add 1 teaspoon vanilla; mix well. Spread over cake. Sprinkle with nuts.
Yield: 12 servings.

Betty Schweinhart

BETTER THAN SEX CAKE

1 package white cake mix
  with pudding
1 large can crushed
  pineapple
1 cup sugar

1 4-ounce package
  vanilla instant pudding
  mix
16 ounces whipped
  topping

Prepare and bake cake using package directions in 9x13-inch cake pan. Combine pineapple and sugar in saucepan. Boil for 5 minutes, stirring constantly. Pierce holes in hot cake with ice pick. Pour hot pineapple over cake; cool. Prepare pudding mix according to package directions. Spread over cooled cake. Spread with whipped topping. Store in refrigerator for up to 1 week. May substitute whipped cream for whipped topping. Yield: 18 servings.

Linda Thompson

BUTTERNUT CAKE

1 cup butter-flavor
  shortening or oil
2 cups sugar
4 eggs

2 cups self-rising flour
1 cup milk
1 to 2 tablespoons
  butternut flavoring

Cream shortening and sugar in bowl until light and fluffy. Beat in eggs. Add flour alternately with milk, mixing well. Add butternut flavoring; mix well. Pour into 3 greased and floured 9-inch cake pans. Bake at 350 degrees for 30 minutes or until cake tests done. Remove to wire rack to cool. Frost with Butternut Frosting. Yield: 16 servings.

Butternut Frosting

1/2 cup margarine, softened
8 ounces cream cheese
1 pound confectioners'
  sugar

1 tablespoon butternut
  flavoring
1 cup chopped pecans

Combine margarine and softened cream cheese in bowl; mix well. Beat in confectioners' sugar and butternut flavoring until smooth. Stir in pecans. May double recipe if desired.

Dorothea Jennings, Terry Neihoff

CARAMEL CAKES

1 package yellow cake mix
1/2 cup butter
1 pound light brown sugar
2 tablespoons flour

2 eggs, beaten
1 teaspoon vanilla extract
1 1/2 cups chopped pecans

Prepare cake mix using package directions. Pour into 2 greased 9x13-inch cake pans dusted with confectioners' sugar. Bake at 350 degrees for 20 minutes. Cool in pans. Melt butter in 2-quart saucepan. Combine brown sugar, flour and eggs in bowl; mix well. Add to butter. Simmer for 3 minutes, stirring constantly. Stir in vanilla and pecans. Pour over cooled cakes. Bake at 400 degrees for 8 minutes longer. Cut into squares.
Yield: 30 to 40 servings.

Norma Gray

CARROT CAKE

2 cups sugar
1 cup oil
4 eggs
2 cups flour
1 teaspoon soda
1 teaspoon salt
2 teaspoons cinnamon
2 teaspoons baking
powder

3 cups shredded carrots
1 cup chopped nuts
4 ounces cream cheese,
softened
2 cups confectioners'
sugar, sifted
1/4 cup butter, softened
1 teaspoon vanilla extract

Beat sugar and oil in bowl until thick. Add eggs; beat well. Sift flour, soda, salt, cinnamon and baking powder into mixture; mix well. Fold in carrots and nuts. Pour into greased and floured tube pan. Bake at 300 degrees for 1 hour or until cake tests done. Cool on wire rack. Combine cream cheese, confectioners' sugar, butter and vanilla in bowl; mix well. Spread over top and sides of cooled cake. Yield: 16 servings.

Shirley Smith

EASY CARROT CAKE

1 2-layer package yellow
   cake mix
1¼ cups mayonnaise-type
   salad dressing
4 eggs
¼ cup cold water

2 teaspoons cinnamon
2 cups finely shredded
   carrots
½ cup chopped walnuts
1 16-ounce can vanilla
   frosting

Combine cake mix, salad dressing, eggs, water and cinnamon in mixer bowl; beat until well blended. Stir in carrots and walnuts. Pour into greased 9x13-inch cake pan. Bake at 350 degrees for 35 minutes or until cake tests done. Cool and spread with favorite frosting. Yield: 12 servings.

Mary J. Abell

ALMOND JOY CAKES

1 package chocolate cake
   mix
1 13-ounce can
   evaporated milk
1 cup sugar
24 large marshmallows
1 14-ounce package
   coconut

1½ cups sugar
½ cup butter
12 ounces semisweet
   chocolate chips
1 3-ounce package sliced
   almonds

Prepare cake mix using package directions. Pour into 2 greased and floure 9x13-inch cake pans. Bake at package temperature for 15 to 20 minutes. Combine 1 cup evaporated milk and 1 cup sugar in saucepan. Bring to a boil, stirring constantly. Stir in marshmallows until melted. Add coconut. Pour over hot cakes. Combine remaining evaporated milk and 1½ cups sugar in saucepan. Bring to a boil, stirring constantly. Stir in butter and chocolate chips until melted. Add almonds; mix well. Pour over cakes. Chill in refrigerator for 2 hours.
Yield: 24 servings.

Shirley Smith

CHOCOLATE CARAMEL NUT CAKE

1 package German
  chocolate cake mix with
  pudding
1 14-ounce package
  caramels
1/2 cup butter
1/3 cup milk
1 cup chopped dry-
  roasted peanuts
3/4 cup milk chocolate
  chips

Prepare cake mix using package directions. Spoon half the batter into greased and floured 9x13-inch cake pan. Bake at 350 degrees for 10 minutes. Cool for 10 minutes. Heat caramels, butter and milk in saucepan until caramels melt, stirring constantly. Spread over baked cake. Sprinkle with peanuts and chocolate chips. Spread remaining batter over top. Bake at 350 degrees for 20 to 25 minutes or until cake tests done. Yield: 12 servings.

Patricia J. Tudor

CHOCOLATE COCONUT CAKE

1 package devil's food
  cake mix
1 cup sugar
1 cup evaporated milk
15 large marshmallows
2 cups flaked coconut
1 teaspoon vanilla extract
1 pound confectioners'
  sugar
1/2 cup butter, softened
1/2 cup baking cocoa
1/2 cup evaporated milk

Prepare cake mix using package directions. Pour batter into 3 greased and floured 9-inch round cake pans. Bake at 350 degrees for 20 to 25 minutes or until cake tests done. Cool in pans for 10 minutes; remove to wire rack to cool completely. Bring sugar, 1 cup evaporated milk and marshmallows to a boil in heavy saucepan for 5 minutes, stirring constantly. Remove from heat. Stir in coconut and vanilla. Cool for 10 to 15 minutes or until of spreading consistency. Spread between layers of cake. Sift confectioners' sugar into mixer bowl. Add butter, cocoa and 1/2 cup evaporated milk; beat until smooth and creamy. Spread over top and side of cake. Yield: 16 servings.

Patricia J. Tudor

CHOCOLATE MAYONNAISE CAKE AND SAUCE

1   2-layer package
   chocolate cake mix
1   4-ounce package
   chocolate instant pudding
   mix

4 eggs
1 cup mayonnaise
1 cup water
1 cup chopped pecans

Combine cake mix, pudding mix, eggs, mayonnaise and water in mixer bowl; beat well. Stir in pecans. Pour into greased and floured 9x13-inch cake pan. Bake at 350 degrees for 35 to 40 minutes or until cake begins to pull away from sides and tests done; do not underbake. Cool in pan for 15 minutes. Remove to wire rack to cool completely. Serve with vanilla ice cream and Hot Fudge Sauce. Yield: 12 servings.

Hot Fudge Sauce

1/2 cup melted margarine
1 cup sugar
Pinch of salt
2 tablespoons baking
  cocoa

3/4 cup sweetened
  condensed milk
1 teaspoon vanilla extract

Bring margarine, sugar, salt and cocoa to a boil in saucepan, stirring constantly. Cook until mixture looks grainy, stirring constantly. Add milk. Bring to a boil. Cook until mixture is smooth, stirring frequently. Stir in vanilla. Serve hot.

Opal Miracle

FROSTED CHOCOLATE SHEET CAKE

2 cups flour
2 cups sugar
1/2 cup margarine
1/4 cup baking cocoa
1 cup water
1/2 cup shortening
1/2 cup buttermilk
1 teaspoon soda
2 eggs
2 teaspoons vanilla extract

1 teaspoon cinnamon
1 pound confectioners'
  sugar
6 tablespoons cream or
  milk
3 to 4 tablespoons baking
  cocoa
1/2 cup melted margarine
1 teaspoon vanilla extract
1 cup chopped nuts

Combine flour and sugar in large bowl; mix well. Combine 1/2 cup margarine, 1/4 cup cocoa, water and shortening in saucepan. Bring to a boil, stirring frequently. Pour into flour mixture; mix well. Add mixture of buttermilk and soda; mix well. Add eggs, 2 teaspoons vanilla and cinnamon; mix well. Pour into greased 11x15-inch cake pan. Bake at 350 degrees for 15 to 20 minutes or until cake tests done. Combine confectioners' sugar, cream, 3 to 4 tablespoons cocoa, melted margarine and 1 teaspoon vanilla in bowl; mix well. Stir in nuts. Pour over hot cake. This cake is best if it is made 4 to 8 hours before serving. Yield: 30 small servings.

Loretta Ramey

FROSTED DARK CHOCOLATE CAKE

1³/₄ cups sugar
1/2 cup margarine, softened
2 eggs
1 cup sour cream
2 cups flour
1/2 teaspoon baking
   powder
Pinch of salt
1 tablespoon soda
1/2 cup hot coffee

³/₄ cup baking cocoa
1 teaspoon vanilla extract
2²/₃ cups confectioners'
   sugar
6 tablespoons melted
   margarine
5 to 6 tablespoons milk
³/₄ cup baking cocoa
1 teaspoon vanilla extract

Cream sugar and 1/2 cup margarine in bowl until light and fluffy. Add eggs and sour cream; mix well. Sift in flour, baking powder and salt; mix well. Add mixture of soda and hot coffee, ³/₄ cup cocoa and 1 teaspoon vanilla; beat well. Pour into 2 greased 9-inch cake pans coated with cocoa. Bake at 350 degrees for 30 minutes or until cake tests done. Cool in pans for 10 minutes. Remove to wire rack to cool completely. Combine confectioners' sugar with melted margarine, milk, ³/₄ cup cocoa and 1 teaspoon vanilla; mix well. Spread between layers and over top and side of cake. Yield: 16 servings.

Shirley Smith

CHRIS EVERT'S INSIDE-OUT CHOCOLATE CAKE

1 4-ounce package
   chocolate instant
   pudding mix
1 package devil's food or
   chocolate cake mix
1¾ cups milk

2 eggs
1 12-ounce package
   semisweet chocolate
   chips
1 cup chopped pecans

Combine pudding mix, cake mix, milk and eggs in large bowl; mix well. Stir in chocolate chips and pecans. Pour into greased 12-cup bundt pan. Bake at 350 degrees for 50 to 55 minutes or until cake tests done. Cool in pan for 30 minutes. Remove to wire rack to cool completely. Yield: 16 servings.

Nellie Leitne

COCA-COLA CAKE

2 cups sugar
2 cups flour
½ cup butter
½ cup oil
3 tablespoons baking
   cocoa
1 cup Coca-Cola

½ cup buttermilk
1 teaspoon soda
2 eggs
1 teaspoon vanilla extract
1½ cups miniature
   marshmallows

Sift sugar and flour into large bowl. Combine butter, oil, cocoa and Coca-Cola beverage in saucepan. Bring to a boil, stirring frequently. Pour into sugar mixture; mix well. Add buttermilk, soda, eggs and vanilla; mix well. Stir in marshmallows. Pour into well-greased 9x13-inch cake pan. Bake at 350 degrees for 45 minutes or until cake tests done. Spread Coca-Cola Frosting over hot cake. Yield: 16 servings.

Coca-Cola Frosting

½ cup butter
3 tablespoons baking
   cocoa
6 tablespoons Coca-Cola

1 pound confectioners'
   sugar
1 teaspoon vanilla extract
1 cup chopped nuts

Combine butter, cocoa and Coca-Cola in large saucepan. Bring to a boil, stirring frequently. Remove from heat. Add confectioners' sugar and vanilla; mix well. Stir in nuts.

Roberta Walker

DEVIL'S FOOD CAKE

1/2 cup butter, softened
1/4 cup shortening
2 cups sugar
1 teaspoon vanilla extract
2 eggs
3/4 cup baking cocoa

1 3/4 cups flour
3/4 teaspoon baking powder
3/4 teaspoon soda
1/8 teaspoon salt
1 3/4 cups milk

Cream butter, shortening and sugar in bowl until light and fluffy. Add vanilla and eggs; mix well. Combine cocoa, flour, baking powder, soda and salt in medium bowl; mix well. Add to creamed mixture alternately with milk, mixing well after each addition. Pour into 2 greased and floured 9-inch cake pans. Bake at 350 degrees for 35 minutes or until cake tests done. Cool in pans for 10 minutes. Remove to wire rack to cool completely. Spread Minute Fudge Frosting between layers and over top and side of cake. Yield: 16 servings.

Minute Fudge Frosting

2 ounces unsweetened chocolate, chopped
2 cups sugar
2/3 cup milk

1/2 cup shortening
1/2 teaspoon salt
2 teaspoons vanilla extract

Combine chocolate, sugar, milk, shortening and salt in saucepan. Bring to a boil. Boil for 1 minute, stirring constantly. Add vanilla. Beat until of spreading consistency. May add a small amount of milk if needed for desired consistency.

Norma Gray

FUDGE CAKE

1/2 cup baking cocoa
2 cups sugar
1 cup melted butter
4 eggs

1 1/4 cups flour
1 teaspoon baking powder
1 teaspoon vanilla extract
1 cup chopped pecans

Combine cocoa, sugar and butter in bowl; mix well. Add eggs 1 at a time, beating well after each addition. Sift in flour and baking powder; mix well. Stir in vanilla and pecans. Pour into greased 9x13-inch cake. Bake at 350 degrees for 10 minutes. Remove; shake baking dish until cake falls. Repeat baking and shaking 2 times. Top with favorite chocolate icing. Yield: 18 servings.

Nancy Winstead

FUDGE RIBBON CAKE

2 tablespoons butter,
  softened
1/4 cup sugar
1 tablespoon cornstarch
8 ounces cream cheese,
  softened
1 egg
2 tablespoons milk
1/2 teaspoon vanilla
  extract
2 cups sifted flour

2 cups sugar
1 teaspoon salt
1 teaspoon baking powder
1/2 teaspoon soda
1/2 cup shortening
1 1/2 cups milk
2 eggs
1 teaspoon vanilla extract
4 ounces unsweetened
  chocolate, melted

Cream butter, 1/4 cup sugar and cornstarch in mixer bowl until well blended. Add cream cheese; beat until light and fluffy. Add 1 egg, 2 tablespoons milk and 1/2 teaspoon vanilla; beat until smooth and creamy. Combine flour, 2 cups sugar, salt, baking powder and soda in large bowl; mix well. Add shortening and 1 1/2 cups milk; blend well. Add 2 eggs, vanilla and chocolate; beat well. Spread 3 cups batter in greased and floured 9x13-inch cake pan. Spoon cream cheese mixture over batter, spreading to cover. Top with remaining batter. Bake at 350 degrees for 50 minutes or until cake tests done. Cool. Frost with favorite icing. Yield: 12 servings.

Patricia J. Tudor

HEALTHY HEART CHOCOLATE CAKE

2 cups flour
1³/4 cups sugar
¹/2 cup baking cocoa
1 tablespoon soda

²/3 cup oil
1 cup buttermilk
1 cup strong decaffeinated
coffee

Mix flour, sugar, cocoa and soda in large bowl. Add oil and buttermilk; mix well. Bring coffee to a boil in saucepan. Stir into batter. Batter will be thin. Pour into greased and floured tube pan. Bake at 350 degrees for 40 minutes or until cake tests done. Invert onto wire rack to cool. Spread Skim Milk Frosting over top and sides of cake. Yield: 16 servings.

Skim Milk Frosting

3 tablespoons baking
cocoa
1 cup sugar
¹/4 cup margarine

¹/3 cup evaporated skim
milk
1 teaspoon vanilla extract

Bring cocoa, sugar, margarine and skim milk to a boil in saucepan. Simmer for 1 minutes. Remove from heat. Add vanilla; beat until of spreading consistency.

Mary Butler Wessel

MOUND'S CAKE

1 package sour cream
chocolate cake mix
1 cup milk
1 cup sugar
24 large marshmallows
4 ounces coconut

2 cups sugar
¹/2 cup milk
3 tablespoons baking
cocoa
¹/2 cup margarine

Bake cake mix using package directions for 9x13-inch cake pan. Combine 1 cup milk, 1 cup sugar and marshmallows in saucepan. Cook until marshmallows are melted, stirring constantly. Stir in coconut. Pour over hot cake. Combine 2 cups sugar, ¹/2 cup milk, cocoa and margarine in saucepan. Bring to a boil. Boil for 3 minutes, stirring constantly. Beat until mixture begins to thicken. Pour over cake. Yield: 12 servings.

Marty Hill

HERSHEY SYRUP CAKE

1/2 cup margarine
1 cup sugar
4 eggs
1 cup flour

1 teaspoon baking powder
1 16-ounce can Hershey
   syrup
1 teaspoon vanilla extract

Cream margarine and sugar in bowl until light and fluffy. Add eggs l at a time, beating well after each addition. Add flour, baking powder, chocolate syrup and vanilla; mix well. Pour into greased and floured 9x13-inch cake pan. Bake at 350 degrees for 30 minutes or until cake tests done. Cool. Spread Dark Chocolate Icing over cake. Yield: 12 servings.

Dark Chocolate Icing

3 ounces unsweetened
   chocolate
1/4 cup butter
1 pound confectioners'
   sugar

1 egg white, stiffly beaten
1 teaspoon vanilla extract
2 tablespoons milk, cream
   or coffee
1 cup chopped nuts

Melt chocolate and butter in saucepan. Fold in egg white. Add confectioners' sugar and vanilla; beat at medium speed. Add milk; beat until of spreading consistency. Stir in nuts.

Kris Russell

RAE'S CHOCOLATE CAKE

1 cup hot water
2 to 3 tablespoons
   (heaping) baking cocoa
2 teaspoons vanilla extract
2 cups packed light brown
   sugar

1/2 cup shortening
2 eggs
1 teaspoon soda
3/4 cup milk
2 cups flour

Combine hot water, cocoa and vanilla in bowl; mix well. Set aside. Cream brown sugar and shortening in mixer bowl until well blended. Add eggs; beat until light and fluffy. Add mixture of soda and milk; mix well. Sift in flour, beating until blended. Add cocoa mixture; mix well. Pour into greased 9x13-inch cake pan. Bake at 325 degrees for 30 minutes or until cake tests done. Spread Fudge Icing over cake. Yield: 12 servings.

Fudge Icing

2 cups sugar
1/4 cup light corn syrup
1/2 cup milk
1/2 cup shortening

2 ounces unsweetened
  chocolate, chopped
1/4 teaspoon salt
1 teaspoon vanilla extract

Combine sugar, corn syrup, milk, shortening, chocolate and salt in saucepan. Cook over low heat until shortening and chocolate are melted; mix well. Bring to a boil. Boil for 1 minute, stirring constantly. Remove from heat. Beat until lukewarm. Stir in vanilla.

Billie Y. Weatherington

TURTLE CAKE

1 package German
  chocolate cake mix
1 14-ounce package
  caramels
1/2 cup evaporated milk

1/2 cup butter
1 cup chopped pecans
1 cup semisweet
  chocolate chips

Prepare cake mix according to package directions, using 3/4 cup margarine and 1/2 cup evaporated milk. Pour half the mixture into greased 9x13-inch cake pan. Bake at 350 degrees for 10 minutes. Melt caramels, in 1/2 cup evaporated milk in saucepan, stirring constantly. Pour over cake. Sprinkle with pecans and chocolate chips. Top with remaining cake batter. Bake for 30 minutes longer or until cake tests done.
Yield: 12 servings.

Juyne Bushart, Bernidea Fort
Shirley Smith

TUDOR TURTLE CAKE

1 package German
  chocolate cake mix
1 14-ounce can
  sweetened condensed
  milk
3/4 cup melted butter

1 14-ounce package
  caramels
6 ounces semisweet
  chocolate chips
3/4 cup chopped nuts

Prepare cake mix according to package directions, using 1/3 cup sweetened condensed milk and half the melted butter; mix well. Pour half the mixture into greased and floured 9x13-inch cake pan. Bake at 350 degrees for 10 minutes. Heat caramels, remaining sweetened condensed milk and butter in saucepan until caramels are melted, stirring constantly. Pour over baked batter. Sprinkle with chocolate chips and nuts. Top with remaining batter. Bake for 20 minutes longer or until cake tests done. Frost with milk chocolate icing of your choice. Yield: 12 servings.

Patricia J. Tudor

WHITE CHOCOLATE CAKE

4 ounces white chocolate
1 cup margarine
2 cups sugar
4 eggs yolks
1 cup buttermilk
1 teaspoon vanilla extract

1 teaspoon baking powder
2 1/2 cups sifted cake flour
1 cup chopped pecans
1 cup flaked coconut
4 egg whites, stiffly beaten

Melt white chocolate in top of double boiler over hot water. Cream margarine and sugar in bowl until well blended. Add egg yolks; beat well. Add buttermilk, vanilla and mixture of baking powder and cake flour; mix well. Stir in melted chocolate, pecans and coconut. Fold in egg whites. Pour into tube cake pan. Bake at 350 degrees for 1 hour and 15 minutes or until cake tests done. Cool on wire rack. Frost with Snowy Icing. Yield: 16 servings.

Snowy Icing

2 cups sugar
1 cup butter
1 teaspoon vanilla extract

1 5-ounce can
  evaporated milk

Combine sugar, butter, vanilla and evaporated milk is saucepan. Boil for 20 minutes, stirring constantly. Remove from heat. Beat until of spreading consistency.

Betty H. Barton

COCONUT CAKE

1 package white or yellow cake mix
1 14-ounce can sweetened condensed milk
1 15-ounce can cream of coconut
8 ounces whipped topping
1 7-ounce can coconut

Bake cake mix according to package directions using greased 9x13-inch cake pan. Punch holes in hot cake with fork; pour mixture of condensed milk and cream of coconut over cake. Cover; cool completely. Spread whipped topping over cooled cake. Sprinkle with coconut. Store in refrigerator. Flavor improves overnight. Yield: 12 servings.

Dollie D. Billiter, Betty Hunter
Shirley Smith, Jeannie Wynn

COCONUT YELLOW CAKE

1 package yellow cake mix
4 eggs
1 cup water
1/4 cup oil
1 14-ounce can sweetened condensed milk
1 3-ounce package coconut cream instant pudding
8 ounces whipped topping
Coconut

Prepare cake mix according to package directions using eggs, water and oil. Pour into greased 9x13-inch cake pan. Bake using package directions. Pierce holes in hot cake with fork. Pour sweetened condensed milk over cake. Prepare instant pudding using package directions. Pour over cake. Frost with whipped topping; sprinkle with coconut. Store in refrigerator.
Yield: 12 servings.

Phyllis L. Allen

EXTRA MOIST AND CREAMY COCONUT CAKE

1 2-layer package yellow
cake mix
1½ cups milk
½ cup sugar

2 cups flaked coconut
or 6 ounces frozen
coconut
8 ounces whipped topping

Bake cake mix according to package directions for 9x13-inch cake pan. Cool for 15 minutes. Combine milk, sugar and ¼ cup coconut in saucepan. Bring to a boil. Simmer for 1 minute, stirring constantly. Punch holes in cake with fork. Pour milk mixture over cake. Cool completely. Fold ½ cup coconut into whipped topping in bowl. Spread over cake. Sprinkle remaining coconut over cake. Chill overnight. Store in refrigerator. Yield: 12 servings.

Madrid Shaw

PRIZE WINNING COCONUT CAKE

1 2-layer package yellow
cake mix
3 12-ounce packages
frozen coconut, thawed

8 ounces sour cream
1 pound confectioners'
sugar or 2 cups sugar

Bake cake mix using to package directions for 2 layer cake pans. Cool on wire rack. Slice layers horizontally with thread. Reserve enough coconut for topping. Combine remaining coconut, sour cream and sugar in bowl; mix well. Spread on plate between layers and on top of cake. Sprinkle reserved coconut over top. Chill in refrigerator for 24 hours to 3 days. May reserve 1 cup filling to mix with 1½ cups whipped cream as topping and ice top and side of cake if preferred. Yield: 16 servings.

Patsy Ford, Donald W. Noel

SOUR CREAM COCONUT CAKE

1 cup margarine, softened
2 cups sugar
4 eggs, at room
temperature
3 cups flour

1 tablespoon baking powder
1 teaspoon salt
1 cup milk, at room
temperature
2 teaspoons vanilla extract

Cream margarine and sugar in bowl until light and fluffy. Add eggs I at a time, beating well after each addition. Sift flour, baking powder and salt 3 times. Add to sugar mixture alternately with milk, beating just until blended. Add vanilla; mix well. Pour into 2 greased and floured 10-inch cake pans. Bake at 350 degrees for 30 minutes or until cake tests done. Cool on wire rack. Split each layer horizontally. Spread Sour Cream Filling between layers and on top and side of cake. Chill in airtight container for 3 days before serving. Yield: 16 servings.

Sour Cream Filling

16 ounces sour cream
1   16-ounce package
    frozen coconut, thawed

2 cups sugar
1/4 teaspoon salt

Combine sour cream, coconut, sugar and salt in bowl; mix well. Let stand for 1 hour.

Gwen Mills

GLAZED COFFEE CAKE

1 package yellow cake mix
1 package vanilla instant
   pudding mix
3/4 cup oil
3/4 cup water
1 teaspoon vanilla extract
1 teaspoon butter
4 eggs

1/4 cup packed brown
   sugar
1 cup nuts (optional)
1 cup confectioners' sugar
1 tablespoon milk
1 teaspoon vanilla extract
1 teaspoon butter

Combine cake mix, pudding mix, oil, water, 1 teaspoon vanilla, 1 teaspoon butter and eggs in bowl; mix well. Pour into greased and floured tube pan. Mix brown sugar and nuts in bowl. Swirl into cake batter. Bake at 350 degrees for 25 to 30 minutes or until cake tests done. Invert onto wire rack to cool. Combine confectioners' sugar, milk, 1 teaspoon vanilla and 1 teaspoon butter in bowl; beat until of spreading consistency. Drizzle over cake. Yield: 16 servings.

Jewell D. Sivels

GLAZED COMFORT CAKE

1 package yellow cake mix
1 3-ounce package
   vanilla instant pudding
   mix
4 eggs
1/2 cup cold water
1/2 cup oil
1/2 cup Southern Comfort

1 cup chopped nuts
1/4 cup butter
1/2 cup sugar
2 tablespoons water
1/4 cup Southern Comfort
1 tablespoon
   confectioners' sugar

Combine cake mix, pudding mix, eggs, 1/2 cup cold water, oil and 1/2 cup Southern Comfort in mixer bowl; beat for 2 minutes. Stir in nuts. Pour into greased and floured 10-inch tube pan. Bake at 325 degrees for 1 hour or until cake tests done. Cool. Combine butter, sugar and 2 tablespoons water in saucepan. Bring to a boil. Boil for 3 minutes, stirring constantly. Remove from heat. Stir in 1/4 cup Southern Comfort. Invert cake on serving plate. Pierce holes in cake with fork. Spread half the glaze over top and side of cake. Reheat glaze; spread over cake. Sift confectioners' sugar over top. Yield: 16 servings.

Nellie Leitner

DOODLE CAKE

2 cups self-rising flour
2 cups sugar
2 eggs
1 20-ounce can crushed
   pineapple
1 1/2 cups sugar

1/2 cup margarine
1 5-ounce can
   evaporated milk
1 cup coconut
1 cup chopped pecans

Combine flour, 2 cups sugar, eggs and pineapple in bowl; mix well. Pour into greased and floured 9x13-inch cake pan. Bake at 350 degrees for 25 minutes or until cake tests done. Combine 1 1/2 cups sugar, margarine and evaporated milk in saucepan. Bring to a boil. Boil for 3 minutes, stirring constantly. Remove from heat. Stir in coconut and pecans. Pour over warm cake. Yield: 12 servings.

Judy Seeders

FRUIT COCKTAIL CAKE

1½ cups sugar
2 eggs
½ cup oil
2 cups flour
½ teaspoon salt
2 teaspoons soda
1 medium can fruit
  cocktail

Flaked coconut
½ cup butter
1 cup sugar
1 5-ounce can
  evaporated milk
1 teaspoon vanilla extract
1 cup chopped nuts

Combine 1½ cups sugar, eggs and oil in bowl; mix well. Sift in flour, salt and soda; mix well. Add undrained fruit cocktail; mix well. Pour into greased 9x13-inch cake pan. Sprinkle with coconut. Bake at 350 degrees for 45 minutes or until cake tests done. Combine butter, 1 cup sugar and evaporated milk in saucepan. Boil for 5 minutes, stirring constantly. Remove from heat. Stir in vanilla and nuts. Pour over hot cake. Yield: 12 servings.

Molly Hisel

FIESTA FRUIT CAKE

1 cup shortening
2 cups sugar
5 eggs
⅔ cup milk
2½ cups flour
1 tablespoon baking
  powder
6 drops of yellow food
  coloring

1 8-ounce can crushed
  pineapple
2 cups chopped nuts
1½ cups coconut
1 9-ounce jar maraschino
  cherries

Cream shortening and sugar in bowl until light and fluffy. Add eggs and milk; beat well. Sift in flour and baking powder; mix well. Add food coloring; mix well. Stir in undrained pineapple, nuts, coconut and maraschino cherries. Pour into greased and floured tube pan. Bake at 350 degrees for 1 hour and 30 minutes or until cake tests done. Cool on wire rack. Yield: 16 servings.

Marty Hill

MY FAVORITE FRUITCAKES

1 pound raisins
1 pound dates, chopped
1 pound candied
　pineapple, chopped
1/2 pound candied red
　cherries, chopped
1/2 pound candied green
　cherries, chopped

1 to 2 pounds pecans,
　chopped
1 cup flour
2 cups sugar
8 eggs
1 cup flour
2 teaspoons baking
　powder

Grease four 2x7-inch loaf pans; line with greased brown paper. Combine fruit and nuts in large bowl; mix well. Add 1 cup flour. Toss to coat. Combine sugar and eggs in medium bowl; mix well. Add mixture of 1 cup flour and baking powder; mix well. Pour batter into fruit mixture; mix well. Place shallow pan of hot water on bottom oven rack. Spoon into prepared pans; press down well. Place loaf pans on center rack. Bake at 300 degrees for 1 1/2 hour to 2 hours or until cake tests done. Cool in pans. Store, tightly wrapped, in cool dark place. Yield: 4 small cakes.

George Alexander

FUZZY NAVEL CAKE

1 can peaches, chopped
1/2 cup peach schnapps
1 cup sugar
1/4 cup orange juice
1 package yellow cake mix
1 package vanilla instant
　pudding mix

4 eggs
2/3 cup oil
1 cup chopped nuts
1 1/2 cups confectioners'
　sugar

Combine first 4 ingredients in glass container. Chill, covered, in refrigerator for 24 hours. Combine cake mix, pudding mix, eggs and oil in mixer bowl; mix well. Stir in 1 cup chopped peaches and 1/2 cup liquid from schnapps mixture. Add nuts; mix well. Pour into greased and floured bundt pan. Bake at 350 degrees for 40 minutes or until cake tests done. Mix 1/4 cup liquid from schnapps mixture with confectioners' sugar in bowl. Invert cake onto serving plate. Spread glaze over cake.
Yield: 16 servings.

Carolyn Burgess

HICKORY NUT CAKE

2 cups packed brown
  sugar
1 cup sugar
2 cups self-rising flour

4 eggs
1 cup melted margarine
1 cup chopped nuts
1 teaspoon vanilla extract

Combine brown sugar, sugar and flour in bowl; mix well. Add eggs and margarine; mix well. Stir in nuts and vanilla . Pour into greased 9x13-inch cake pan. Bake at 350 degrees for 50 minutes or until cake tests done. Yield: 12 servings.

Patsy Ford

HUMMINGBIRD CAKE

3 cups flour, sifted
1 teaspoon soda
2 cups sugar
1 teaspoon salt
1 teaspoon cinnamon
1 1/4 to 1 1/2 cups oil
3 eggs, beaten
1 1/2 teaspoons vanilla
  extract
1 8-ounce can crushed
  pineapple
3/4 to 1 cup chopped
walnuts or pecans

2 cups chopped bananas
8 to 11 ounces cream
  cheese, softened
1/2 to 3/4 cup margarine,
  softened
1 to 2 teaspoons vanilla
  extract
1 to 2 pounds
  confectioners' sugar
1 cup chopped walnuts or
  pecans (optional)

Combine flour, soda, sugar, salt and cinnamon in bowl; mix well. Add oil and eggs, stirring just until flour mixture is moistened. Stir in 1 1/2 teaspoons vanilla, undrained pineapple, walnuts and bananas. Spoon into 3 greased and floured 9-inch layer pans. Bake at 350 degrees for 25 to 30 minutes or until cake tests done. Cool in pans for 1 minute. Remove to wire racks to cool completely. Combine cream cheese, margarine, 1 to teaspoons vanilla and confectioners' sugar in bowl. Beat until well blended and of spreading consistency. Spread between layers and over top and side of cake. Sprinkle with 1 cup walnuts. Yield: 16 servings.

Marty Hill, Shirley Smith

ITALIAN CREAM CAKE

1/2 cup margarine, softened
2 cups sugar
1 cup oil
5 egg yolks, beaten
2 cups flour
1 teaspoon soda
1 cup buttermilk
1 teaspoon vanilla extract
5 egg whites, stiffly beaten

1 small can coconut
1 cup chopped pecans
1/4 cup margarine, softened
8 ounces cream cheese,
  softened
1 pound confectioners'
  sugar
1 teaspoon vanilla extract
1 cup chopped pecans

Cream 1/2 cup margarine, sugar and oil in mixer bowl until light and fluffy. Add egg yolks; beat well. Sift in flour and soda; mix well. Add buttermilk and 1 teaspoon vanilla; mix well. Fold in egg whites, coconut and 1 cup pecans. Pour into 3 greased and floured 8-inch round cake pans. Bake at 350 degrees for 15 to 20 minutes or until cake tests done. Remove to wire rack to cool. Combine 1/4 cup margarine, cream cheese and confectioners' sugar in bowl; beat well. Stir in 1 teaspoon vanilla and 1 cup pecans. Spread between layers and over top and side of cake. Yield: 15 servings.

Paula Parks

BLACKBERRY JAM CAKE

1 cup butter, softened
1 cup sugar
3 eggs
13/4 cups flour
1 teaspoon soda
1 teaspoon cinnamon
1 teaspoon cloves

1 teaspoon nutmeg
1 teaspoon allspice
2/3 cup buttermilk
1 cup blackberry jam
Brown Sugar Icing
  (next page)

Cream butter and sugar in bowl until light and fluffy. Add eggs; beat well. Sift flour, soda and spices into medium bowl. Add to creamed mixture alternately with buttermilk, mixing well. Stir in jam. Pour into 2 greased and floured 9-inch cake pans. Bake at 350 degrees for 15 to 20 minutes or until cake tests done. Remove to wire rack to cool. Spread Brown Sugar Icing between layers and over top and side of cake. Yield: 16 servings.

Brown Sugar Icing

1 pound brown sugar
1 5-ounce can
   evaporated milk

3 tablespoons flour
1 teaspoon vanilla extract
3 tablespoons butter

Combine brown sugar, evaporated milk and flour in saucepan; mix well. Cook until mixture forms a soft ball when dropped in cold water. Stir in vanilla and butter. Beat until of spreading consistency.

Clara Nance

CHRISTMAS JAM CAKE

2 cups sugar
1½ cups margarine
1 cup blackberry jam
1 cup strawberry jam
1⅓ cups buttermilk
4 cups flour

2 teaspoons soda
1 tablespoon allspice
1 tablespoon cinnamon
6 egg whites
1 cup raisins

Cream sugar and margarine in bowl until light and fluffy. Add jams and buttermilk; mix well. Add mixture of flour, soda, allspice and cinnamon; mix well. Fold in unbeaten egg whites and raisins. Pour into 3 greased and floured 9-inch cake pans. Frost with Fruit Frosting. Yield: 16 servings.

Fruit Frosting

1 cup whipping cream
2⅔ cups sugar
10 egg yolks
2 cups butter

2 cups raisins
2 cups nuts
2 cups frozen coconut,
   thawed

Combine cream, sugar, egg yolks and butter in saucepan. Simmer until thickened, stirring constantly. Add remaining ingredients. Beat with spoon until of spreading consistency.

Marty Hill

KENTUCKY JAM CAKE

1³/₄ cups flour
1¹/₂ cups sugar
1 teaspoon soda
1 teaspoon baking powder
¹/₂ teaspoon salt
1 teaspoon cinnamon
1 teaspoon nutmeg
1 teaspoon allspice
¹/₂ teaspoon cloves
3 eggs
1 cup oil
1 cup blackberry jam
1 cup buttermilk
1 teaspoon vanilla extract
1 cup finely chopped
    pecans

Combine flour, sugar, soda, baking powder, salt and spices in large mixer bowl; mix well. Add eggs and oil, beating well. Add jam, buttermilk and vanilla; beat for 8 minutes. Stir in pecans. Pour into 3 greased and floured 9-inch cake pans. Bake at 350 degrees for 40 minutes or until cake tests done. Cool in pans. Remove to serving plate. Spread Vanilla Frosting between layers and on top and side of cake. Yield: 16 servings.

Vanilla Frosting

¹/₄ cup margarine, softened
¹/₂ teaspoon salt
2 teaspoons vanilla extract
¹/₄ cup milk
3 cups confectioners'
    sugar

Combine margarine, salt, vanilla, milk and 1 cup confectioners' sugar in bowl; mix well. Add remaining confectioners' sugar; beat until smooth and creamy.

Georgia B. Flora

JAM CAKE

2¹/₂ cups sugar
1 cup butter, softened
6 egg yolks, beaten
1 teaspoon soda
1 cup buttermilk
3³/₄ cups sifted cake flour
1 teaspoon cloves
1 teaspoon allspice
1 teaspoon cinnamon
1 cup jam or jelly
1 cup raisins
1 cup strawberry preserves
1 cup pear preserves,
    finely chopped
1 cup chopped nuts
6 egg whites, stiffly beaten
¹/₂ cup milk
1¹/₂ cups sugar
2 tablespoons butter

Cream sugar and 1 cup butter in large mixer bowl until light and fluffy. Add egg yolks; mix well. Add mixture of soda and buttermilk alternately with mixture of flour and spices; mix well. Add jam, raisins, strawberry preserves, pear preserves and nuts; mix well. Fold in egg whites. Reserve 1$\frac{1}{2}$ cups batter for filling. Pour remaining batter into 3 greased and floured cake pans. Bake at 350 degrees for 40 to 45 minutes or until cake tests done. Cool on wire racks. Spread Jam Cake Filling between layers of cake. Frost with Speedy Caramel Frosting. Yield: 16 servings.

Jam Cake Filling

**1$\frac{1}{2}$ cups reserved Jam
  Cake batter
$\frac{1}{2}$ cup milk**

**1$\frac{1}{2}$ cups sugar
2 tablespoons butter**

Combine reserved batter, milk, remaining sugar and butter in saucepan. Simmer until thickened, stirring constantly. Cool.

Speedy Caramel Frosting

**$\frac{1}{2}$ cup butter
1 cup packed brown sugar
$\frac{1}{4}$ teaspoon salt
$\frac{1}{4}$ cup milk**

**2$\frac{1}{2}$ cups sifted
  confectioners' sugar
$\frac{1}{2}$ teaspoon vanilla extract**

Melt butter in large saucepan. Blend in brown sugar and salt. Simmer for 2 minutes, stirring constantly. Add milk. Bring to a boil, stirring constantly. Remove from heat. Add confectioners' sugar; mix well. Stir in vanilla. Add additional cream if needed to make of spreading consistency.

Helen Courtney

★ Remember that even teflon cake pans should be greased and floured to be sure your cake will slip from the pans easily.

FROSTED STRAWBERRY JAM CAKE

1¹/₂ cups sugar
3 eggs
1 cup oil
2 cups flour
1 teaspoon salt
1 teaspoon cinnamon
1 teaspoon nutmeg
1 cup buttermilk
1 cup strawberry preserves

1 teaspoon vanilla extract
1 cup chopped pecans
¹/₂ cup butter
1 cup packed brown sugar
¹/₄ cup milk
1 pound confectioners'
  sugar
1 teaspoon vanilla extract

Beat sugar and eggs in mixer bowl until well blended. Add oil; mix well. Sift flour, salt, cinnamon and nutmeg into bowl. Add to sugar mixture alternately with buttermilk mixing well after each addition. Add preserves and 1 teaspoon vanilla; mix well. Stir in pecans. Pour into greased and floured tube pan. Bake at 350 degrees for 1 hour or until cake tests done. Invert onto wire rack to cool. Combine butter, brown sugar and milk in saucepan. Bring to a boil, stirring constantly. Simmer for 2 minutes or until sugar is dissolved, stirring constantly. Cool. Add confectioners' sugar; beat until of spreading consistency. Add remaining vanilla; mix well. Add additional milk if needed for desired consistency. Spread over top and side of cake. Yield: 16 servings.

Molly Hisel

LEMONY LEMON CAKE

1 package lemon cake mix
1 package lemon instant
  pudding mix
4 eggs
¹/₄ cup oil

1 cup water
1 6-ounce can frozen
  lemonade, thawed
1 cup confectioners' sugar

Combine cake mix, pudding mix and eggs in bowl; mix well. Add oil and water; beat until well blended. Pour into greased 9x13-inch cake pan. Bake at 350 degrees for 45 to 50 minutes or until cake tests done. Cool for 5 minutes. Combine lemonade and confectioners' sugar in bowl; beat until smooth. Pierce holes in cake with fork. Pour glaze over cake. Yield: 12 servings.

Donna Browning

COLONIAL MAPLE NUT CAKE

1 2-layer package white cake mix
1 cup water
1/3 cup oil
3 eggs
2 teaspoons maple extract
1/2 cup chopped nuts
1 cup confectioners' sugar
2 tablespoons margarine, softened
2 tablespoons (about) milk
1/4 teaspoon maple extract

Beat first 5 ingredients in mixer bowl. Stir in nuts. Pour into greased and floured 10-inch tube pan. Bake at 350 degrees for 35 minutes or until cake tests done. Cool in pan for 25 minutes. Invert onto serving plate. Cool completely. Blend confectioners' sugar, margarine, milk and 1/4 teaspoon flavoring in bowl. Spoon over cake. Garnish with additional nuts. Yield: 16 servings.

Jo Ann Thompson

OATMEAL CAKE

1 1/2 cups boiling water
1 cup oats
1/2 cup shortening or butter
1 cup sugar
1 cup packed brown sugar
2 eggs, beaten
1 1/2 cups flour
1/2 teaspoon salt
1 teaspoon soda
1/2 teaspoon cloves
1 teaspoon cinnamon
1/2 teaspoon nutmeg
5 to 8 tablespoons butter
1/4 to 1/2 cup evaporated milk or cream
1/2 to 2/3 cup packed brown sugar
3/4 cup coconut
3/4 to 1 cup chopped nuts
1 teaspoon vanilla extract

Pour boiling water over oats in bowl. Let stand for 20 minutes. Cream shortening, sugar and 1 cup brown sugar in bowl. Add eggs and oats; mix well. Sift in flour, salt, soda and spices; mix well. Pour into greased 9x13-inch cake pan. Bake at 350 degrees for 45 minutes. Bring butter, evaporated milk and 1/2 to 2/3 cup brown sugar to a boil in saucepan. Add coconut, nuts and vanilla. Spread over hot cake. Yield: 12 servings.

Judy B. Damron, Yocianne Everett
Johnnie Harper

ORANGE JUICE CAKE

1 package yellow butter-
flavored cake mix
4 eggs
1/2 cup oil

1 cup orange juice
1/2 cup margarine
1 cup sugar
1/2 cup orange juice

Combine cake mix, eggs, oil and 1 cup orange juice in bowl; mix well. Pour into greased and floured bundt pan. Bake at 350 degrees for 35 minutes or until cake tests done. Bring margarine, sugar and remaining orange juice to boil in saucepan, stirring constantly. Pour over hot cake in pan. Let cool for 30 minutes. Invert onto serving plate. Yield: 16 servings.

Patsy Ford

ORANGE CAKE

1 3-ounce package
orange gelatin
3/4 cup boiling water
1 package yellow cake mix
3/4 cup oil

3 eggs
Dash of salt
1 teaspoon lemon juice
1/2 cup orange juice

Combine gelatin and boiling water in large mixer bowl, mix well. Cool. Add cake mix, oil, eggs, salt and lemon juice. Beat for 8 minutes. Pour into greased and floured tube pan. Bake at 350 degrees for 50 to 60 minutes or until cake tests done. Pour orange juice over hot cake in pan. Let cool for 15 minutes. Invert onto serving plate. Yield: 16 servings.

Mrs. Vernon (Sandy) Ortenzi

ORANGE SLICE CAKE

1 cup margarine, softened
1 3/4 cups sugar
4 eggs
1/2 teaspoon salt
1 teaspoon soda
3 1/2 cups self-rising flour
1/2 cup buttermilk
1 1/2 cups raisins

1 pound orange slices,
finely chopped
1 to 1 1/2 cups coconut
1 1/2 cups chopped pecans
1 cup orange juice
2 cups confectioners'
sugar

Cream margarine and sugar in bowl until light and fluffy. Add eggs I at a time, beating well after each addition. Add mixture of salt, soda and flour alternately with buttermilk; mix well. Stir in raisins, orange slices, coconut and pecans. Pour into greased and floured tube pan. Bake at 275 degrees for 2½ hours or until cake tests done. Combine orange juice and confectioners' sugar in bowl; mix well. Pour over hot cake in pan. Cool for 30 minutes or until mixture is absorbed. Invert onto serving plate. Yield: 15 servings.

Johnnie Harper

MANDARIN ORANGE CAKE

1 package yellow cake mix
1 11-ounce can mandarin
  oranges
½ cup chopped pecans
4 eggs
½ cup oil

1 15-ounce can crushed
  pineapple
9 ounces whipped topping
1 3-ounce package
  vanilla instant pudding
  mix

Combine cake mix, undrained mandarin oranges, pecans, eggs and oil in mixer bowl. Beat at high speed for 2 minutes. Beat at low speed for 1 minute. Pour into 3 greased and floured 9-inch round cake pans. Bake at 350 degrees for 20 to 25 minutes or until cake tests done. Cool in pans for 10 minutes. Remove to wire rack to cool completely. Combine undrained pineapple, whipped topping and pudding mix in mixer bowl. Beat for 2 minutes at medium speed. Let stand for 5 minutes or until mixture is of spreading consistency. Spread between layers and on top and side of cake. Chill for 2 hours before serving. Store in refrigerator. Yield: 8 servings.

Evelyn McClure, Judy Roberts
Patricia J. Tudor

OUT OF THE WORLD CAKE

4 cups graham cracker
  crumbs
2 cups sugar
4 eggs, beaten
1 cup melted margarine
1 teaspoon baking powder
1 cup milk

1 teaspoon vanilla extract
1 cup coconut
1 cup chopped pecans
1   20-ounce can crushed
  pineapple
1/4 cup flour
1 cup sugar

Combine graham cracker crumbs, 2 cups sugar, eggs, margarine, baking powder, milk and vanilla in bowl; mix well. Stir in coconut and pecans. Pour into greased and floured 9x13-inch cake pan. Bake at 350 degrees for 35 to 40 minutes or until cake tests done. Combine undrained pineapple, flour and 1 cup sugar in saucepan. Simmer until thick, stirring constantly. Pour over warm cake. Let stand in refrigerator for several days before serving. Yield: 12 servings.

Grace Murphy

FRESH PEAR CAKE

2 cups sugar
3 eggs, beaten
1 1/2 cups oil
3 cups flour
1 teaspoon soda
1 teaspoon salt

1 teaspoon vanilla extract
3 cups thinly sliced pears
2 teaspoons cinnamon
1 1/4 cups confectioners'
  sugar
2 to 4 tablespoons milk

Combine sugar, eggs and oil in bowl; beat well. Add mixture of flour, soda and salt I cup at a time, mixing well after each addition. Stir in vanilla, pears and cinnamon. Spoon into well greased bundt pan. Bake at 350 degrees for 1 hour or until cake tests done. Remove to wire rack to cool. Glaze with mixture of confectioners' sugar and milk. Yield: 16 servings.

Nancy Winstead

PIÑA COLADA CAKE

1 package yellow cake mix
1   14-ounce can
    sweetened condensed
    milk

1 cup piña colada mix
8 ounces whipped topping
Coconut

Bake cake mix according to package directions for 9x13-inch cake pan. Pierce holes in cake with handle of wooden spoon. Mix condensed milk and piña colada mix in bowl. Pour over hot cake. Cool. Spread with whipped topping; sprinkle with coconut. Yield: 12 servings.

Elizabeth Vaught

PINEAPPLE PIÑA COLADA CAKE

1 package yellow cake mix
    with pudding
1   8-ounce can crushed
    pineapple

1/2 cup shredded coconut
2 teaspoons rum flavoring
8 ounces whipped topping
Toasted coconut

Prepare cake mix according to package directions, using undrained pineapple for liquid. Stir in coconut and flavoring. Pour into 2 greased and floured round cake pans or 9x13-inch cake pan. Bake at 350 degrees 30 to 45 minutes or until cake tests done. Cool in pans for 10 minutes. Remove to wire rack to cool completely. Spread whipped topping between layers and on top and side of cake. Sprinkle with toasted coconut. Chill until serving time. Store in refrigerator. Yield: 10 to 12 servings.

Patti Reece

★ Frozen coconut may be used in the same manner as canned or packaged coconut. It is slightly less sweet than canned.

PINEAPPLE UPSIDE-DOWN CAKE

2 tablespoons butter
1/2 cup packed brown
  sugar
1   20-ounce can
  pineapple, drained
3 egg yolks
1/2 cup sugar

1/2 cup boiling water
1 cup sugar
1 1/2 cups sifted cake flour
1 teaspoon baking powder
1/4 teaspoon salt
3 egg whites, stiffly beaten

Melt butter in iron skillet over low heat. Sprinkle evenly with brown sugar. Heat until sugar is melted. Remove from heat. Arrange pineapple in sugar. Beat egg yolks in bowl until light and lemon colored. Add 1/2 cup sugar and boiling water gradually, beating well. Sift 1 cup sugar, cake flour, baking powder and salt into bowl. Fold into batter. Fold in egg whites. Pour over pineapple in skillet. Bake at 350 degrees for 45 minutes or until cake tests done. Invert immediately onto wire rack to cool.
Yield: 12 servings.

Mary E. Quinker

GRANDMOTHER'S PINEAPPLE UPSIDE-DOWN CAKE

1/4 cup margarine
1 cup packed brown sugar
1   8-ounce can sliced
  pineapple
3 eggs
1 1/2 cups sugar

1/2 cup cold water
1 teaspoon vanilla extract
Pinch of salt
1 1/2 cups flour
1 1/2 teaspoons baking
  powder

Melt margarine in 9-inch round cake pan. Add brown sugar. Simmer until melted. Arrange pineapple in sugar. Combine eggs, sugar, cold water and vanilla in bowl; beat well. Add salt, flour and baking powder; mix well. Pour over pineapple. Bake at 350 degrees for 20 to 30 minutes or until cake tests done. Invert immediately onto serving plate. Yield: 12 servings.

Jean Geary

SWEDISH PINEAPPLE CAKE

2 eggs, beaten
2 cups sugar
2 cups flour
1/2 teaspoon salt
2 teaspoons soda
1 teaspoon vanilla extract
1 20-ounce can crushed
    pineapple in heavy syrup

1/2 cup chopped nuts
1 pound confectioners'
    sugar
1/2 cup margarine, softened
8 ounces cream cheese,
    softened
Milk

Beat eggs and sugar in bowl until well blended. Add flour, salt, soda, vanilla and undrained pineapple; mix well. Stir in nuts. Pour into greased 9x13-inch cake pan. Bake at 350 degrees for 40 to 45 minutes or until cake tests done. Combine confectioners sugar, margarine and cream cheese in bowl; mix well. Add milk if needed for spreading consistency. Spread over cake.
Yield: 12 servings.

Joan Butler

PINEAPPLE DELIGHT CAKE

1 package white cake mix
2 cups water
3 eggs
1/4 cup oil
1 6-ounce package
    vanilla instant pudding
    mix

1 large can crushed
    pineapple
Whipped topping
1 cup chopped pecans

Combine cake mix, water, eggs and oil in bowl; mix well. Pour into greased 9x13-inch cake pan. Bake at 350 degrees for 35 minutes or until cake tests done. Cool. Prepare pudding mix according to package directions. Chill until thickened. Pour un-drained pineapple over cooled cake. Spread pudding over pineapple. Top with whipped topping; sprinkle with pecans.
Yield: 12 servings.

Irene McKinney

MOTHER BLACK'S PINEAPPLE DELIGHT CAKE

1 package lemon supreme   4 eggs
  cake mix   3/4 cup oil
1 4-ounce package   10 ounces 7-Up
  pineapple or lemon
  instant pudding mix

     Combine cake mix, pudding mix, eggs, oil and 7-Up in mixer bowl; beat for 2 minutes. Pour into greased 9x13-inch cake pan. Bake at 325 degrees for 30 to 35 minutes or until cake tests done. Spread warm Pineapple Icing over cake. Yield: 12 servings.

Pineapple Icing

1 1/2 cups sugar   2 eggs, beaten
1/2 teaspoon flour   1/2 cup butter
1 20-ounce can crushed 1 can coconut
  pineapple

     Combine sugar, flour, undrained pineapple, eggs and butter in saucepan. Simmer until thickened, stirring constantly. Remove from heat. Stir in coconut.

Mary Black

DAY-AHEAD PINEAPPLE CAKE

1 package yellow cake mix   1/2 cup evaporated milk
1 20-ounce can crushed   1/2 cup water
  pineapple   1 cup sugar
2 tablespoons cornstarch   3/4 cup shortening
1/4 cup sugar   1/2 cup margarine
1 package vanilla instant   1 can coconut
  pudding mix

     Prepare cake mix using package directions using 2 greased and floured 9-inch cake pans. Combine undrained pineapple, cornstarch and 1/4 cup sugar in saucepan. Cook until thickened, stirring constantly. Cool. Combine pudding mix, evaporated milk and water in bowl; mix well. Add 1 cup sugar, shortening and margarine; beat until peaks form. Split cake layers into halves horizontally. Spread the remaining pudding mixture and pineapple mixture alternately between cake layers. Spread pudding mixture on side of cake. Spread remaining pineapple mixture over top; sprinkle with coconut. Chill until serving time. This cake is better if made day before serving. Yield: 15 servings.

L. J. McGuire

PINEAPPLE DREAM CAKE

2 eggs
2 cups sugar
2 cups flour
2 teaspoons soda
1 teaspoon vanilla extract
1 large can crushed
 pineapple

1/2 cup chopped nuts
8 ounces cream cheese,
 softened
1/2 cup butter, softened
1 teaspoon vanilla extract
1/2 to 3/4 cup confectioners'
 sugar

Beat eggs and sugar in bowl until well blended. Add mixture of flour and soda, 1 teaspoon vanilla and undrained pineapple; mix well. Stir in nuts. Pour into greased cake pan. Bake at 350 degrees for 1 hour or until cake tests done. Combine remaining ingredients in bowl; beat until smooth and of spreading consistency. Spread over cake. Yield: 12 servings.

Shirley Smith

PISTACHIO PUDDING CAKE

1 3-ounce package
 pistachio instant
 pudding mix
1 2-layer package yellow
 cake mix
4 eggs

1/2 teaspoon almond
 extract
1 1/4 cups water
1/4 cup oil
7 drops of green food
 coloring (optional)

Combine pudding mix, cake mix, eggs, almond extract, water, oil and food coloring in large mixer bowl; mix well. Beat for 2 minutes. Pour into greased and floured 10-inch tube pan. Bake at 350 degrees for 50 to 55 minutes or until cake tests done. Cool in pan for 15 minutes. Remove to rack to cool completely. Yield: 16 servings.

Martha S. Harper

DOUBLE PISTACHIO CAKE

1 3-ounce package
  pistachio instant
  pudding mix
1 package white or yellow
  cake mix
4 eggs
1 cup club soda or water

1/4 cup oil
1/2 cup chopped nuts
1 1/2 cups cold milk
1 envelope whipped
  topping mix
1 3-ounce package
  pistachio pudding mix

Combine 1 package pudding mix, cake mix, eggs, soda and oil in mixer bowl; mix well. Beat for 4 minutes. Stir in nuts. Pour into greased and floured 9x13-inch cake pan. Bake at 350 degrees for 40 to 45 minutes or until cake tests done. Cool in pan for 15 minutes. Remove to wire rack to cool completely. Combine milk, whipped topping mix and package pudding mix in mixer bowl; mix well. Beat for 4 to 6 minutes or until soft peaks form. Spread over cake. Yield: 12 servings.

Patricia J. Tudor

POUND CAKE

3 cups sugar
1 cup butter, softened
6 eggs
3 cups flour or cake flour

8 ounces whipping cream
1 teaspoon butternut
  flavoring

Cream sugar and butter in mixer bowl until light and creamy. Add eggs I at a time, beating well after each addition. Add flour alternately with cream, mixing well. Add flavoring; mix well. Pour into prepared bundt pan. Bake at 280 degrees for 2 hours or until top is brown and cake tests done. Cool in pan for 10 minutes. Remove to wire rack to cool completely. May substitute 2 teaspoons lemon flavoring and 1 teaspoon vanilla for butternut flavoring. May place in cold oven. Bake at 325 degrees for 1 1/4 hours. Yield: 16 servings.

Clare McFarland, Doris M. McNear

ELEVEN EGG POUND CAKE

1 cup plus 2 tablespoons
   butter, softened
1 cup cake flour
1½ teaspoons vanilla
   extract
1 cup cake flour
2 teaspoons baking
   powder
11 egg whites, at room
   temperature

¾ teaspoon salt
1½ cups sugar
2¼ cups confectioners'
   sugar
9 tablespoons butter,
   softened
3 tablespoons cream
2¼ teaspoons vanilla
   extract

Cream 1 cup plus 2 tablespoons butter and 1 cup sifted flour in mixer bowl until well blended. Beat in 1½ teaspoons vanilla. Sift 1 cup flour and baking powder into bowl. Beat egg whites and salt in large bowl until soft peaks form. Add sugar gradually, beating until stiff peaks form. Fold ¼ of the egg white mixture into creamed mixture. Add sifted flour. Fold in remaining egg white mixture. Pour into greased and waxed paper-lined tube cake pan. Cut mixture with table knife to eliminate air pockets. Bake at 350 degrees for 50 minutes or until cake tests done. Cool in pan for 10 minutes. Cream confectioners' sugar and 9 tablespoons butter in bowl until well blended. Add cream and 2¼ teaspoons vanilla; beat until fluffy and of spreading consistency. Invert cake onto serving plate. Spread with frosting.
Yield: 16 servings.

Betty Barton

★ If you are modifying your diet to reduce fat or cholesterol, use the following ingredient substitutions in your favorite recipes.

Milk — use 1 cup skim or nonfat dry milk plus 2 teaspoons polyunsaturated oil for 1 cup whole milk.
Eggs — use 1 egg white plus 2 teaspoons polyunsaturated oil or use commercially produced cholesterol-free egg substitutes according to package directions.
Shortening — use ¾ cup oil (safflower, sunflower or corn) in place of 1 cup solid shortening.

PRUNE CAKE

1½ cups sugar
1 cup oil
3 eggs
1 cup buttermilk
2 small jars baby food
  prunes
1½ teaspoons vanilla
  extract
2 cups flour
1½ teaspoons soda

1 teaspoon salt
1½ teaspoons nutmeg
1½ teaspoons cinnamon
1 cup chopped pecans
½ cup buttermilk
1 cup sugar
5 tablespoons light corn
  syrup
½ cup margarine

Cream 1½ cups sugar and oil in mixer bowl until well blended. Add eggs; beat well. Add buttermilk, prunes and vanilla; mix well. Add mixture of flour, soda, salt and spices; mix well. Stir in pecans. Pour into greased 9x11-inch cake pan. Bake at 350 degrees for 20 to 30 minutes or until cake tests done. Combine ½ cup buttermilk, 1 cup sugar, corn syrup and margarine in saucepan. Simmer for 2 minutes, stirring constantly. Pierce holes in cake with fork. Spoon icing over cake. Yield: 12 servings.

Patsy Akers

PEGGY'S PRUNE CAKE

2 cups sugar
1 cup oil
3 eggs, beaten
2 cups self-rising flour
1 teaspoon allspice
1 teaspoon cinnamon
1 teaspoon nutmeg

1 jar junior baby food
  prunes
¼ cup water
1 cup chopped pecans
Butter Rum Sauce
  (next page)

Cream sugar and oil in mixer bowl until well blended. Add eggs; beat well. Sift in flour and spices; mix well. Add prunes. Rinse jar with water; add to mixture. Stir in pecans. Pour into greased and floured bundt pan. Bake at 300 degrees for 1 hour or until cake tests done. Remove to wire rack to cool. Pour Butter Rum Sauce over cooled cake. Yield: 16 servings.

Butter Rum Sauce

1 cup sugar
1 tablespoon cornstarch
3/4 cup half and half

1/2 cup butter
2 tablespoons rum

Combine sugar, cornstarch, half and half and butter in glass bowl; mix well. Microwave on High for 3 minutes; stir. Microwave on High for 4 minutes. Stir in rum.

Peggy Posante

PUMPKIN CAKE

2 cups sugar
1 1/2 cups oil
4 eggs
2 cups self-rising flour
2 teaspoons soda
1 teaspoon salt
1 tablespoon cinnamon

1 1/2 cups canned pumpkin
8 ounces cream cheese,
   softened
1/2 cup margarine, softened
1 pound confectioners'
   sugar
Chopped walnuts

Cream sugar and oil in mixer bowl until well blended. Add eggs; beat well. Add mixture of flour, soda, salt and cinnamon; mix well. Add pumpkin; mix well. Pour into 3 greased and floured 9-inch cake pans. Bake at 350 degrees for 30 minutes or until cake tests done. Cool in pan for 5 minutes. Remove to wire rack to cool completely. Combine cream cheese, margarine and confectioners' sugar in bowl; mix well. Spread between layers and over top and side of cake. Sprinkle with walnuts. Let cake stand for 12 to 24 hours before serving. Yield: 16 servings.

H. Katherine Ray

★ Reduce calories by reducing the amount of frosting on a cake: a 9x13-inch cake left in the pan needs much less frosting than a layer cake; a layer cake need be frosted only between layers and on top or with just a ring around the top.

FROSTED RED CAKE

1½ to 2 cups oil
1½ cups sugar
2 eggs
2½ cups self-rising flour
1 teaspoon baking cocoa
1 teaspoon salt (optional)
1 teaspoon soda
1 cup buttermilk
¼ cup red food coloring
1 teaspoon white vinegar
1 to 2 teaspoons vanilla
   extract
½ cup butter
8 to 10 ounces cream
   cheese, softened
1 pound confectioners'
   sugar
2 cups chopped pecans
   (optional)

Cream oil and sugar in mixer bowl until well blended. Add eggs; mix well. Add mixture of flour, cocoa, salt and soda alternately with buttermilk. Add food coloring, vinegar and vanilla; mix well. Pour into three 9-inch cake pans sprayed with nonstick cooking spray. Bake at 350 degrees for 25 to 30 minutes or until cake tests done. Split layers horizontally. Cool in pan for 10 minutes. Remove to wire racks to cool completely. Combine butter, cream cheese and confectioners' sugar in mixer bowl; beat until smooth and creamy. Reserve ½ cup pecans. Stir in remaining pecans. Spread between layers and on top and side of cooled cake. Sprinkle reserved pecans over top of cake. Chill for 1 hour or longer before serving. Yield: 10 to 15 servings.

Johnnie Harper, Judy Long

RED VELVET CAKE

1 tablespoon vinegar
1 teaspoon soda
1 cup shortening
1½ cups sugar
2 eggs
2 ounces red food coloring
2 teaspoons baking cocoa
1 cup buttermilk
2½ cups flour
1 teaspoon salt
1 teaspoon vanilla extract
Red Velvet Frosting
   (next page)

Combine vinegar and soda in small bowl; mix well. Cream shortening and sugar in mixer bowl until well blended. Add eggs; beat well. Combine food coloring and cocoa in small bowl; mix well. Add to shortening mixture. Add buttermilk alternately with mixture of flour and salt; mix well. Add vanilla and vinegar mixture; mix well. Pour into 2 greased and floured 8-inch cake pans. Bake at 325 degrees for 30 minutes. Remove to wire rack to cool. Split layers into halves crosswise. Spread Velvet Frosting between layers and on top and side of cake. Yield: 16 servings.

Red Velvet Frosting

5 tablespoons flour
1 cup milk
1 cup butter, softened

1 cup sugar
1 teaspoon vanilla extract

Combine flour and milk in saucepan; mix well. Simmer until thickened, stirring constantly. Cool. Cream butter and sugar in bowl until light and fluffy. Add vanilla and flour mixture; beat until of spreading consistency.

Peggy Graviss

RUM CAKE

1 package lemon supreme
   cake mix
1   4-ounce package
   lemon instant pudding
   mix
4 eggs
3/4 cup oil
1 cup milk

1 teaspoon lemon extract
1/2 teaspoon rum extract
1 cup confectioners' sugar
1 tablespoon lemon juice
2 tablespoons rum or
   11/2 teaspoons rum
   extract

Combine cake mix, pudding mix and eggs in mixer bowl; beat well. Add oil, milk, 1 teaspoon lemon extract and 1/2 teaspoon rum extract. Beat for 10 minutes. Pour into greased and floured large bundt pan. Bake at 350 degrees for 45 minutes. Remove to wire rack to cool slightly. Combine confectioners' sugar, lemon juice and rum in mixer bowl. Beat until of spreading consistency. Drizzle over top and side of warm cake. Yield: 16 servings.

Marie Bundy

★ When cooking with alcohol, remember the contents evaporate leaving just the flavor.

SOCK IT TO ME CAKE

1 2-layer package yellow
  cake mix
1/2 cup sugar
4 eggs
3/4 cup oil
1 tablespoon vanilla
  extract

1 tablespoon melted butter
8 ounces sour cream
1 cup chopped nuts
2 tablespoons sugar
2 tablespoons cinnamon

Combine cake mix, 1/2 cup sugar and eggs in bowl; mix well. Add oil, vanilla, butter and sour cream; mix well. Stir in nuts. Pour half the batter into greased tube pan. Sprinkle with mixture of 2 tablespoons sugar and cinnamon. Top with remaining batter. Bake at 325 degrees for 1 hour or until cake tests done. Invert onto wire rack to cool. Yield: 16 servings.

Erma S. Messer

CINNAMON SOUR CREAM CAKE

1 cup butter, softened
1 1/4 cups sugar
2 eggs
8 ounces sour cream
2 cups sifted flour
1/2 teaspoon soda

1/2 teaspoon baking
  powder
1 teaspoon vanilla extract
3/4 cup finely chopped nuts
1 teaspoon cinnamon
2 tablespoons sugar

Cream butter and 1 1/4 cups sugar in mixer bowl until light and fluffy. Add eggs, beating well. Add sour cream; mix well. Sift in mixture of flour, soda and baking powder. Add vanilla; mix well. Mix nuts, cinnamon and 2 tablespoons sugar in bowl. Layer batter and nut mixture 1/2 at a time in greased tube pan. Bake at 350 degrees for 55 minutes or until cake tests done. Remove to wire rack to cool. Yield: 16 servings.

Betty Schweinhart

SOUR CREAM CAKE

2 cups sugar
1 cup margarine, softened
6 egg yolks
3 cups flour
1/4 teaspoon soda
8 ounces sour cream
6 eggs whites, stiffly
   beaten

1/3 cup packed brown
   sugar
1/4 cup sugar
1 teaspoon cinnamon
1 cup chopped nuts

Cream 2 cups sugar and margarine in mixer bowl until light and fluffy. Add egg yolks; beat well. Add mixture of flour and soda alternately with sour cream; mix well. Fold in egg whites. Combine brown sugar, 1/4 cup sugar, cinnamon and nuts in bowl; mix well. Layer cake batter and nut mixture 1/2 at a time in greased and floured tube pan. Bake at 300 degrees for 1 1/2 hours or until cake tests done. Cool on wire rack. Yield: 16 servings.

Grace Murphy

AUNT SARAH'S SOUR CREAM CAKE

1 cup whipped butter,
   softened
3 cups sugar
5 eggs
3 cups flour
1/4 teaspoon soda
8 ounces sour cream

1/2 teaspoon vanilla extract
1/2 teaspoon lemon
   flavoring
2/3 cup sugar
1/4 cup melted butter
1/3 cup orange juice

Cream 1 cup butter and 3 cups sugar in mixer bowl until light and fluffy. Add eggs, beating well. Add mixture of flour and soda alternately with sour cream, mixing well after each additon. Add flavorings; mix well. Pour into greased and floured 10-inch tube pan. Bake at 325 degrees for 1 1/2 hours or until cake tests done. Invert onto serving plate. Combine 2/3 cup sugar, 1/4 cup butter and orange juice in bowl; mix well. Pour over hot cake. Yield: 16 servings.

Barbara Struck

SPICE CAKE

1 package spice cake mix
1 3-ounce package vanilla
   instant pudding mix

4 eggs
1 cup water
1/2 cup oil

Combine cake mix, pudding mix, eggs, water and oil in mixer bowl; mix well. Beat for 3 minutes. Pour into greased and floured 10-inch tube pan. Bake at 350 degrees for 45 to 55 minutes or until cake tests done. Remove to wire rack to cool. Spread with favorite frosting or sprinkle with confectioners' sugar. Yield: 16 servings.

Betty Krueger

HOT MILK SPONGE CAKE

4 eggs
2 cups sugar
2 cups sifted flour
2 teaspoons baking
   powder

1 teaspoon salt
2 teaspoons vanilla extract
1 cup milk
2 tablespoons margarine

Beat eggs and sugar in mixer bowl until light and fluffy. Sift in flour, baking powder and salt. Add vanilla; beat well. Scald milk and margarine in saucepan. Add to batter; beat well. Pour into greased and floured tube pan. Bake at 350 degrees for 40 to 45 minutes or until cake tests done. Cool in pan inverted on wire rack. Yield: 16 servings.

Betty Schweinhart

OLD-FASHIONED STACK CAKE

2 eggs
1 cup sugar
1 cup molasses
14 tablespoons melted
   butter
2 teaspoons soda
1 teaspoon cinnamon

1/2 teaspoon nutmeg
2 teaspoons ginger
1/2 teaspoon allspice
3 cups flour
1 cup boiling water
Apple butter

Combine eggs, sugar and molasses in mixer bowl; beat well. Add butter and mixture of soda, spices and 1 cup flour; mix well. Add remaining flour and boiling water; mix well. Spoon 9 tablespoons into each of 7 greased 9-inch layer cake pans. Bake at 350 degrees for 8 to 10 minutes or until layers test done. Remove to wire rack to cool. Spread apple butter between layers. Yield: 16 servings.

Judy Damron

STRAWBERRY CAKE

2/3 **cup butter, softened**
1 cup sugar
1 3-ounce package
** strawberry gelatin**
4 eggs
2 1/2 **cups sifted cake flour**
1/2 **teaspoon salt**

2 teaspoons baking
** powder**
1 cup milk
1 cup flaked coconut
1 cup chopped pecans
1 cup chopped
** strawberries**

Cream butter, sugar and gelatin in bowl until light and fluffy. Add eggs, beating well. Sift flour, salt and baking powder in bowl. Add to creamed mixture alternately with milk, mixing well after each addition. Stir in coconut, pecans and strawberries. Pour into 3 greased and floured 8-inch cake pans. Bake at 350 degrees for 25 to 30 minutes or until cake tests done. Cool in pans for 3 or 4 minutes. Remove to wire racks to cool completely. Spread Strawberry Frosting between layers and on top and side of cake. Yield: 16 servings.

Strawberry Frosting

1/2 **cup butter, softened**
1 pound confectioners'
** sugar**
1 cup chopped pecans

1/4 **cup mashed**
** strawberries**
1 cup flaked coconut

Cream butter and 2 cups confectioners' sugar in bowl until well blended. Add remaining sugar, pecans, strawberries and coconut; mix well. Add additional mashed strawberries if needed for spreading consistency.

Brenda Collins

FROSTED SWEDISH NUT CAKE

2 eggs
2 cups sugar
1 20-ounce can crushed
   pineapple
2 cups sifted flour
2 teaspoons soda
1 teaspoon vanilla extract
1/2 cup chopped nuts

1 pound confectioners'
   sugar
8 ounces cream cheese,
   softened
1/2 cup butter, softened
1 teaspoon vanilla extract
1/2 cup chopped nuts

Beat eggs and sugar in bowl until well blended. Add undrained pineapple; mix well. Add mixture of flour and soda. Add 1 teaspoon vanilla; mix well. Stir in 1/2 cup nuts. Pour into greased 9x13-inch cake pan. Bake at 350 degrees for 35 to 40 minutes or until cake tests done. Cream confectioners' sugar, cream cheese and butter in mixer bowl until well blended. Add 1 teaspoon vanilla; mix well. Stir in 1/2 cup nuts. Spread over cake. Yield: 12 servings.

Joy Keller

BLACK WALNUT CAKE

1/2 cup butter, softened
1/2 cup shortening
2 cups sugar
5 egg yolks
2 cups flour
1 cup buttermilk
1 teaspoon soda
1 teaspoon vanilla extract

1 1/2 cups chopped black
   walnuts
1 3-ounce can flaked
   coconut
5 egg whites
1/2 teaspoon cream of tartar
Cream Cheese Frosting
   (next page)

Cream 1/2 cup butter, shortening and sugar in bowl until light and fluffy. Add egg yolks, beating well. Add flour alternately with mixture of buttermilk and soda. Stir in vanilla, black walnuts and coconut. Beat egg whites in bowl until soft peaks form. Add cream of tartar, beating until stiff. Fold into batter. Pour batter into 3 greased and floured 9-inch round cake pans. Bake at 350 degrees for 30 minutes or until cake tests done. Cool in pans for 10 minutes. Remove to wire rack to cool completely. Frost with Cream Cheese Frosting. Garnish with additional walnuts. Yield: 16 servings.

Cream Cheese Frosting

3/4 cup butter, softened
6 3/4 cups sifted
   confectioners' sugar
11 ounces cream cheese,
   softened

1 1/2 teaspoons vanilla
   extract

Combine butter, confectioners' sugar and cream cheese in bowl; beat until well blended. Add vanilla; mix well.

Ruth DeHaven

TREASURE TOFFEE CAKE

1/4 cup sugar
1 teaspoon cinnamon
1 cup sugar
1/2 cup butter, softened
2 eggs
2 cups flour
1/4 teaspoon nutmeg
1 1/2 teaspoons baking
   powder

1 teaspoon soda
1/4 teaspoon salt
1 teaspoon vanilla extract
8 ounces sour cream
1/4 cup chopped nuts
3   1-ounce bars chocolate
   toffee candy, crushed
1/4 cup melted butter
Confectioners' sugar

Combine 1/4 cup sugar and cinnamon in small bowl; mix well. Cream 1 cup sugar and 1/2 cup butter in mixer bowl until light and fluffy. Add eggs, beating well. Mix flour, nutmeg, baking powder, soda and salt in bowl. Add to creamed mixture. Add vanilla and sour cream; mix well. Spoon half the batter into buttered and floured 10-inch bundt pan. Sprinkle with 2 tablespoons cinnamon mixture. Spoon in remaining batter; sprinkle with remaining cinnamon mixture. Top with nuts. Sprinkle candy over mixture. Pour melted butter over top. Bake at 325 degrees for 45 to 50 minutes or until cake tests done. Cool in pan for 5 minutes. Remove to wire rack to cool completely. Sprinkle with confectioners' sugar. Yield: 10 to 12 servings.

Patricia J. Tudor

VANILLA WAFER CAKE

2 cups sugar
1 cup margarine or butter,
  softened
6 eggs
1/2 cup milk
12 ounces vanilla wafers,
  crushed

1 7-ounce package
  coconut
1 to 11/2 cups chopped
  pecans

Cream sugar and margarine in mixer bowl until light and fluffy. Add eggs l at a time, beating well after each addition. Add milk; mix well. Add vanilla wafers; beat well. Stir in coconut and pecans. Pour into greased bundt pan. Bake at 300 degrees for 1 hour and 45 minutes or until cake tests done. Cool in pan for 40 minutes. Remove to wire rack to cool completely. Garnish with whipped topping or whipped cream. Yield: 16 servings.

Mary Keen, Virginia Emmitt
Diane Murphy

WHITE LAYER CAKE

1 cup shortening
2 cups sugar
4 eggs
3 cups sifted cake flour
21/2 teaspoons baking
  powder
1/2 teaspoon salt
1 cup milk

1 teaspoon almond extract
1 teaspoon vanilla extract
1 12-ounce can flaked
  coconut
Lemon-Orange Filling
  (next page)
Luscious White Frosting
  (next page)

Cream shortening and sugar in bowl until light and fluffy. Add eggs, beating well. Mix flour, baking powder and salt in bowl. Add to shortening mixture alternately with milk. Add flavorings; mix well. Pour into 3 greased and floured 9-inch round cake pans. Bake at 375 degrees for 20 to 25 minutes or until cake tests done. Cool in pans for 10 minutes. Remove to wire rack to cool completely. Spread Lemon-Orange Filling between layers. Spread Luscious White Frosting over top and side of cake. Sprinkle coconut over top. Yield: 16 servings.

Lemon-Orange Filling

1/2 cup sifted cake flour
1 cup sugar
1/4 teaspoon salt
1/4 cup water
2 tablespoons grated
  orange rind

1 tablespoon grated lemon
  rind
11/4 cups orange juice
1/4 cup lemon juice
4 egg yolks, well beaten

Combine flour, sugar, salt and water in heavy saucepan; mix well. Stir in orange rind, lemon rind and juices. Simmer until thickened, stirring constantly. Stir about 1/4 of the hot mixture into egg yolks; stir egg yolks into hot mixture. Beat well. Cool completely. Yield: 21/2 cups.

Luscious White Frosting

11/2 cups sugar
1/2 teaspoon cream of
  tartar
1/8 teaspoon salt
1/2 cup hot water

4 egg whites
1/2 teaspoon almond
  extract
1/2 teaspoon coconut
  extract

Combine sugar, cream of tartar, salt and hot water in heavy saucepan; mix well. Simmer until mixture is clear, stirring constantly. Cook to 240 degrees on candy thermometer, soft-ball stage; do not stir. Beat egg whites in bowl until soft peaks form. Add flavoring and syrup gradually, beating constantly until frosting is stiff and of spreading consistency.

Ladonna Darnell

★ Add a quick and easy decorative look by heating a
  small amount of canned frosting in the microwave,
  then drizzle a pattern over plain or frosted cake.

YUM-YUM CAKE

2 eggs
2 cups sugar
2 cups undrained crushed
  pineapple
2 cups self-rising flour
1 cup sugar

1/2 cup margarine
1 5-ounce can
  evaporated milk
1/2 teaspoon vanilla extract
1 cup chopped pecans
1 cup flaked coconut

Beat eggs and 2 cups sugar in bowl until well blended. Add pineapple; mix well. Add flour; beat until well mixed. Spread in greased 9x13-inch cake pan. Bake at 350 degrees for 25 to 30 minutes or until cake tests done. Combine 1 cup sugar, margarine and evaporated milk in saucepan. Boil for 2 minutes, stirring constantly. Remove from heat. Stir in vanilla, pecans and coconut. Spread over hot cake. Yield: 12 servings.

Molly Hisel

ORANGE ZUCCHINI CAKE

1 cup butter, softened
1 tablespoon grated
  orange rind
1 teaspoon cinnamon
1/2 teaspoon nutmeg
1/4 teaspoon cloves
2 cups packed brown
  sugar
4 eggs
3 cups flour
1 tablespoon baking powder

1/2 teaspoon salt
1/3 cup orange juice
1 cup shredded unpeeled
  zucchini
11/2 cups sifted
  confectioners' sugar
1 tablespoon butter,
  softened
1/2 teaspoon vanilla extract
2 to 3 tablespoons orange
  juice

Cream 1 cup butter, orange rind, spices and brown sugar in bowl until light and fluffy. Beat in eggs. Add mixture of flour, baking powder and salt alternately with orange juice; mix well. Stir in zucchini. Pour into greased 10-inch tube pan. Bake at 350 degrees for 55 to 65 minutes or until cake tests done. Cool in pan for 10 minutes. Remove to wire rack to cool completely. Combine remaining ingredients in bowl; beat until smooth. Spread over cooled cake. Garnish with additional shredded orange rind and zucchini. Yield: 16 servings.

Betty Krueger

ZUCCHINI CAKE

3/4 cup melted butter
2 cups sugar
3 eggs, beaten
1/2 cup buttermilk
2 teaspoons vanilla extract
2 1/2 cups cake flour
1/4 cup baking cocoa

2 1/2 teaspoons baking
  powder
1/2 teaspoon soda
1 teaspoon cinnamon
2 cups grated peeled
  zucchini
Easy Penuche Icing

Cream butter and sugar in bowl until light and fluffy. Add eggs, beating well. Add buttermilk and vanilla; mix well. Mix cake flour, cocoa, baking powder, soda and cinnamon in bowl. Add to creamed mixture; mix well. Stir in zucchini. Pour into 3 greased and floured cake pans. Bake at 350 degrees for 25 minutes. Remove to wire rack to cool. Spread Easy Penuche Icing between layers and over top and side of cake. Yield: 16 servings.

Easy Penuche Icing

1/2 cup butter
1 cup packed light brown
  sugar

1/4 cup milk
1 3/4 to 2 cups
  confectioners' sugar

Combine butter and brown sugar in saucepan. Simmer for 2 minutes, stirring constantly. Add milk. Bring to a boil, stirring constantly. Cool to lukewarm or 120 degrees on candy thermometer. Add gradually to confectioners' sugar in bowl, beating until smooth and creamy.

Trudie Gadjen

★ Forget the frosting if you are watching calories. Place a paper doily on the cake and sift a little confectioners' sugar over chocolate cake or cocoa powder over yellow cake. Remove doily carefully.

CHEESECAKE MINIATURES

1 package devil's food
cake mix
1 egg, beaten
8 ounces cream cheese,
softened

1/2 cup sugar
1 cup semisweet
chocolate chips

Prepare cake mix according to package directions. Fill paper-lined miniature muffin cups 2/3 full. Combine egg, cream cheese and sugar in bowl; beat well. Stir in chocolate chips. Place 1 teaspoonful chocolate chip mixture in each prepared muffin cup. Bake according to package directions. Yield: 24 servings.

Ladonna Darnell

CREAM CHEESE CUPCAKES

9 ounces cream cheese,
softened
1 cup sugar
5 eggs
1 1/2 teaspoons vanilla
extract

1 1/2 cups sour cream
1/2 cup sugar
1/2 teaspoon vanilla extract

Combine cream cheese and 1 cup sugar in bowl; mix well. Add eggs, beating well. Add 1 1/2 teaspoons vanilla; mix well. Fill paper-lined muffin cups 2/3 full. Bake at 300 degrees for 30 minutes. Mix sour cream, 1/2 cup sugar and vanilla in bowl. Place 1 teaspoon in each prepared muffin cup. Bake for 5 to 10 minutes longer. Yield: 12 servings.

Myrtle Stogner

PINEAPPLE FROSTING

1 tablespoon flour
1 1/2 cups sugar
2 tablespoons milk

1   20-ounce can crushed
pineapple
2 tablespoons butter

Mix flour and sugar in saucepan. Add milk, pineapple and butter; mix well. Simmer until thickened, stirring constantly. Yield: Frosting for 3-layer cake.

Chrissy Robey

CANDY

NO-BAKE CHOCOLATE BOURBON BALLS

1 12-ounce package
vanilla wafers, crushed
1 cup confectioners' sugar
1 cup finely chopped
pecans

¼ cup light corn syrup
2 tablespoons baking
cocoa
½ cup Bourbon
½ cup sugar

Combine crushed vanilla wafers, confectioners' sugar, pecans, corn syrup, baking cocoa and Bourbon in large bowl; mix well. Shape into 1-inch balls. Roll in ½ cup sugar. Store in airtight container for 3 days or longer before serving. Will keep for 2 weeks. Do not freeze. Yield: 42 Bourbon balls.

Aggie Burks, Patricia J. Tudor

KENTUCKY BOURBON BALLS

1 cup margarine, softened
1 14-ounce can
sweetened condensed
milk
4½ to 5 pounds
confectioners' sugar

⅔ cup Kentucky Bourbon
Pecan halves
½ stick Para-Seal Wax
4 cups semisweet
chocolate
¼ cup butter

Cream margarine in mixer bowl until light and fluffy. Stir in condensed milk; mix well. Add sugar alternately with Bourbon, mixing well after each addition. Press 1 teaspoonful at a time around pecan half; shape into ball. Place on waxed paper-lined trays. Chill overnight. Melt paraffin in double boiler. Add chocolate and ¼ cup butter; stir until chocolate is melted and mixture is well blended. Dip Bourbon balls into chocolate mixture; place on waxed paper. Let stand until firm. Make coconut bonbons by omitting most of the Bourbon and the pecans and adding desired amount of coconut. Reduce confectioners' sugar as necessary. Yield: 16 dozen.

Wilma Sullivan

BUCKEYES

2 cups margarine, softened
4 cups peanut butter
2½ pounds confectioners' sugar

4 cups milk chocolate chips
1½ squares paraffin

Cream margarine, peanut butter and confectioners' sugar in bowl until light and fluffy. Shape into 1-inch balls. Chill in freezer until firm. Melt chocolate chips with paraffin in double boiler over hot water. Dip peanut butter balls in chocolate, leaving a small portion uncoated. Place on waxed paper. Yield: 12 dozen.

Pat Wilhelm

BUTTERSCOTCH AND PEANUT FUDGE

2 cups butterscotch chips
1½ cups miniature marshmallows
1   14-ounce can sweetened condensed milk

½ cup peanut butter
1 teaspoon vanilla extract
Salt to taste
1 cup chopped pecans

Melt butterscotch chips and marshmallows with condensed milk in saucepan, stirring constantly. Remove from heat. Beat in peanut butter, vanilla and salt until smooth. Fold in pecans. Pour into buttered 9x9-inch baking dish. Chill until firm. Cut into squares. Yield: 4 dozen.

Antoinette Monroe

MITZIE'S CANDY HASH

2 cups Cap'n Crunch's Crunch Berries cereal
2 cups Rice Krispies
2 cups slivered almonds

2 cups miniature marshmallows
2 cups dry-roasted peanuts
1 pound almond bark

Combine first 5 ingredients in large bowl; mix well. Melt almond bark in saucepan, stirring constantly. Pour over cereal mixture. Spread on baking sheet. Let stand until firm. Break into small pieces. Store in airtight container. Yield: 16 to 20 pieces.

Mitzie Black

CHOCOLATE CARAMELS

2¹/₂ cups sugar
³/₄ cup light corn syrup
¹/₂ cup butter
¹/₈ teaspoon cream of tartar

2¹/₂ cups milk
1 teaspoon vanilla extract
2¹/₂ ounces unsweetened chocolate

Combine sugar, corn syrup, butter, cream of tartar and 1 cup milk in saucepan. Bring to a boil, stirring constantly. Boil for 5 minutes. Add remaining 1¹/₂ cups milk gradually maintaining boil and stirring constantly. Cook, uncovered, to 242 to 248 degrees on candy thermometer, hard-ball stage, stirring occasionally. Remove from heat. Beat in vanilla and chocolate. Pour into buttered dish. Cool until firm. Cut into squares. May omit chocolate for plain caramels. Yield: 9 dozen.

Gwen Mills

CARAMELS

1 cup sugar
1 cup corn syrup
1¹/₂ cups whipping cream

Salt to taste
1 teaspoon vanilla extract

Combine sugar, syrup, ¹/₂ cup cream and salt in saucepan; mix well. Bring to a boil. Add ¹/₂ cup cream; mix well. Cook, uncovered, to 234 to 240 degrees on candy thermometer, soft-ball stage. Add remaining ¹/₂ cup cream; mix well. Cook, uncovered, to 242 to 248 degrees, hard-ball stage. Remove from heat. Stir in vanilla. Pour into greased dish. Cool. Cut into squares. Store in airtight container in cool place. May wrap pieces individually in waxed paper. Candy can be cut easily with scissors. Yield: 60 caramels.

Beverly Perkins, Ann Schmitt

BAKED CARAMEL CORN

1 cup butter
2 cups packed brown
  sugar
1/2 cup light corn syrup

1 teaspoon salt
1/2 teaspoon soda
1 teaspoon vanilla extract
6 quarts popped popcorn

Melt butter in saucepan. Add brown sugar, corn syrup and salt. Bring to a boil, stirring constantly. Boil for 5 minutes; do not stir. Remove from heat. Stir in soda and vanilla. Pour over popcorn in large bowl; mix until well coated. Spread into 2 large shallow baking dishes. Bake at 250 degrees for 1 hour, stirring every 15 minutes. Cool completely. Break into pieces. Store in airtight containers. Yield: 5 quarts.

Nancy Winstead

OVEN CARAMEL CORN

3 3/4 quarts popped
  popcorn
1/2 cup margarine
1 cup packed brown sugar

1/4 cup light corn syrup
1/2 teaspoon salt
1/2 teaspoon soda

Place popcorn in two 9x13-inch baking dishes. Combine margarine, sugar, corn syrup and salt in saucepan. Bring to a boil, stirring constantly. Cook over medium heat for 5 minutes. Remove from heat. Add soda; mix well. Pour over popcorn; mix until well coated. Bake at 200 degrees for 1 hour, stirring every 15 minutes. Yield: 4 quarts.

Laverne Hollingsworth

CHOCOLATE CATHEDRAL CANDY

1 cup margarine
4 cups semisweet
  chocolate chips
2 cups finely chopped
  pecans

2 packages multicolored
  miniature marshmallows
1 teaspoon vanilla extract
2 packages coconut

Melt margarine in saucepan over low heat. Add chocolate chips, stirring until melted. Remove from heat. Cool slightly. Add pecans, marshmallows and vanilla; mix well. Divide mixture into

3 portions. Shape into logs. Roll in coconut. Chill until firm. Cut into slices. Store in airtight container. Yield: 60 slices.

Betty Schweinhart

CHOCOLATE-COVERED CHERRIES

2 pounds confectioners'
  sugar
1/2 cup melted butter
1 14-ounce can
  sweetened condensed
  milk

2 10-ounce jars
  maraschino cherries
2 cups semisweet
  chocolate chips
1 3-inch square paraffin
6 tablespoons butter

Sift confectioners' sugar into bowl. Add 1/2 cup butter and condensed milk; mix well. Chill overnight. Drain cherries. Dust hands with confectioners' sugar. Pinch off a small amount of chilled mixture. Flatten with palm of hand. Press 1 cherry into flattened mixture; press around cherry to enclose. Place on waxed paper-lined tray. Repeat with remaining cherries and sugar mixture. Chill until firm. Melt chocolate, paraffin and remaining 6 tablespoons butter in double boiler over hot water. Dip cherries into chocolate mixture. Place on waxed paper-lined tray. Chill until firm. Store in airtight containers between layers of waxed paper. Yield: 4 dozen.

Mary Beeler

CHOCOLATE PEANUT BUTTER RITZ

1 cup semisweet
  chocolate chips
1/2 stick paraffin
1 16-ounce box Ritz
  crackers

1 12-ounce jar peanut
  butter

Melt chocolate chips and paraffin in double boiler over hot water. Spread half the crackers with peanut butter. Top with remaining crackers. Dip peanut butter crackers into chocolate. Place on waxed paper. Let stand until firm. Yield: 4 dozen.

Patsy Dumont

CHOCOLATE FUDGE

3 cups sugar
1/2 cup baking cocoa
1/8 teaspoon salt

1 1/2 cups milk
5 1/2 tablespoons butter
1 teaspoon vanilla extract

Combine sugar, cocoa and salt in saucepan. Stir in milk. Bring to a boil over medium heat, stirring frequently. Cook, uncovered, to 234 to 240 degrees on candy thermometer, soft-ball stage. Remove from heat. Add butter. Cool to lukewarm. Add vanilla. Beat until thick and creamy. Pour into buttered dish. Let stand until firm. Cut into squares. Yield: 3 pounds.

Martha E. Stokes

COURTNEY'S CHOCOLATE FUDGE

2 cups sugar
2 tablespoons light corn
  syrup
3 tablespoons baking
  cocoa

1 cup whipping cream
1/8 teaspoon salt
1 tablespoon butter
1 teaspoon vanilla extract
1 cup chopped walnuts

Combine sugar, corn syrup, cocoa, whipping cream and salt in buttered heavy saucepan; mix well. Cook over low heat until sugar dissolves completely, stirring constantly. Cook to 234 to 240 degrees on candy thermometer, soft-ball stage; do not stir. Remove from heat. Add butter and vanilla; do not stir. Cool to lukewarm. Beat until thick and creamy. Stir in walnuts. Pour into buttered dish. Let stand until firm. Cut into squares.
Yield: 2 pounds.

Helen Courtney

MARSHMALLOW FUDGE

4 1/2 cups sugar
1/2 pound whipped
  margarine
1   14-ounce can Milnot
1   16-ounce milk
  chocolate bar, chopped

2 cups semisweet
  chocolate chips
1   10-ounce package
  miniature marshmallows

Combine sugar, margarine and Milnot in heavy saucepan. Cook over medium heat for 8 to 10 minutes or until mixture comes to a full rolling boil, stirring constantly; remove from heat. Stir in remaining ingredients until well blended. Pour into buttered dish. Let stand until firm. Cut into squares. Yield: 5 pounds.

Shirley Smith

MILLION DOLLAR FUDGE

5 cups sugar
1 12-ounce can
   evaporated milk
1/2 cup butter
3 bars German's
   chocolate, chopped

2 cups semisweet
   chocolate chips
2 cups marshmallow
   creme
1 pound chopped pecans

Combine sugar, evaporated milk and butter in saucepan; mix well. Bring to a boil over medium heat, stirring constantly. Boil for 5 minutes. Pour mixture over German's chocolate in bowl. Add chocolate chips and marshmallow creme; stir until chocolate is melted and marshmallow creme is well blended. Fold in pecans. Pour into greased dish. Let stand until firm. Cut into squares. Yield: 5 pounds.

Patricia R. Henson

MICROWAVE FUDGE

1 pound confectioners'
   sugar
1/2 cup baking cocoa
1/4 cup milk

1/2 cup butter
1 teaspoon vanilla extract
1/2 cup chopped nuts

Combine confectioners' sugar and cocoa in medium glass bowl; mix well. Add milk and butter; do not stir. Microwave on High for 2 minutes; stir until mixed. Add vanilla and nuts; mix well. Pour into lightly greased 8x8-inch dish. Chill for 1 hour. Cut into squares. Yield: 2 to 3 dozen.

Theresa Bennett

CHOCOLATE WHISKEY BALLS

1/2 cup butter, softened
2 pounds confectioners'
  sugar
1 14-ounce can
  sweetened condensed
  milk

6 tablespoons whiskey
4 cups ground pecans
1 1/2 pounds Westchester
  milk chocolate wafers

Cream butter and confectioners' sugar in bowl until light and fluffy. Add condensed milk and whiskey; mix well. Stir in pecans. Shape into 1-inch balls. Place on waxed paper. Let stand for several hours to overnight. Melt chocolate wafers in double boiler over hot water. Do not boil. Dip whiskey balls into chocolate. Place on waxed paper. Let stand until firm. Store in airtight container. Chocolate may be thinned with Paramount Crystals or corn oil if necessary. Yield: 12 dozen.

Helen Courtney

FIJI COCONUT CANDY

3 cups sugar
1 1/2 cups water
1/4 teaspoon salt

1/2 teaspoon vanilla extract
Meat of 1 coconut, grated

Combine sugar, water and salt in saucepan; mix well. Bring to a boil, stirring constantly. Add vanilla and coconut; mix well. Cook for 15 minutes longer or until thickened. Remove from heat. Beat for 15 minutes or until creamy. Drop by spoonfuls onto waxed paper. May add food coloring with vanilla and coconut if desired. Yield: 3 pounds.

Patti Roby

DIVINITY

4 cups sugar
1 cup light corn syrup
3/4 cup water

3 egg whites, stiffly beaten
1 teaspoon vanilla extract
1 cup chopped nuts

Combine sugar, corn syrup and water in saucepan. Cook over low heat until sugar dissolves, stirring constantly. Cook to 255 degrees on candy thermometer, hard-ball stage; do not stir. Remove from heat. Pour into egg whites gradually, beating constantly until mixture has thickened. Stir in vanilla and nuts. Drop by spoonfuls onto waxed paper. Cool. Store in airtight container in cool place. Yield: 4 pounds.

Patsy Dumont

FOREVER AMBER

1 pound orange slice
  candy, finely chopped
2 4-ounce cans coconut
1 tablespoon orange
  flavoring
1 cup chopped pecans

2 14-ounce cans
  sweetened condensed
  milk
1 teaspoon vanilla extract
1/8 teaspoon salt
Confectioners' sugar

Combine candy, coconut, orange flavoring, pecans, condensed milk, vanilla and salt in bowl; mix well. Spread in greased 10x15-inch baking dish. Bake at 275 degrees for 30 minutes; do not brown. Shape into 1-inch balls; roll in confectioners' sugar. Place on waxed paper. Yield: 3 pounds.

Jayne Roberts

KOREAN CANDIED GINGER (Sang Juhn Kiva)

1 cup sliced, peeled
  fresh gingerroot
1/4 cup sugar

1/4 cup light corn syrup
1/4 cup water

Pour boiling water over gingerroot in bowl. Let stand for 5 minutes; drain. Dry on paper towels. Combine sugar, corn syrup and water in saucepan. Bring to a boil. Cook until sugar has dissolved and mixture thickens. Add gingerroot. Cook over low heat until syrup is absorbed and ginger is crystalized. Remove to wire rack to dry. Store in airtight container. Yield: 6 servings.

Gwen Mills

MOCHA RUM BALLS

1/4 cup instant coffee
  powder
1/4 cup rum
1 tablespoon water
2 cups vanilla wafer crumbs
1 cup confectioners' sugar

1 cup chopped nuts
3 tablespoons light corn
  syrup
2 tablespoons baking
  cocoa
Confectioners' sugar

Dissolve coffee in rum and water in bowl. Add vanilla wafer crumbs, 1 cup confectioners' sugar, nuts, corn syrup and cocoa; mix well. Shape by rounded teaspoonfuls into balls. Store in airtight container for several days. Roll in additional confectioners' sugar. Yield: 4 dozen.

Patricia J. Tudor

PEANUT BRITTLE

3 cups sugar
1 cup light corn syrup
1/2 cup water

3 cups Spanish peanuts
2 teaspoons soda

Combine sugar, corn syrup and water in saucepan. Cook to 280 degrees on candy thermometer, soft-crack stage, stirring constantly. Add peanuts gradually. Cook to 300 degrees, hard-crack stage, stirring constantly. Remove from heat. Add soda; mix quickly. Pour onto greased baking sheet. Do not spread. Let stand until cool. Crack into pieces. Yield: 3 pounds.

Barbara Struck

COATED PEANUTS

3 cups peanuts
1 cup sugar
1/2 cup water

1/2 teaspoon vanilla extract
3 or 4 drops of red food
  coloring

Combine peanuts, sugar and water in saucepan; mix well. Bring to a boil. Cook until sugar dissolves, stirring constantly. Add vanilla and food coloring; mix well. Cook until peanuts are coated. Spread on baking sheet. Bake at 250 to 300 degrees for 10 to 15 minutes, stirring twice. Yield: 2 pounds.

Mary Beeler

PEANUT CLUSTERS

1 cup semisweet
  chocolate chips

2 cups butterscotch chips
1¹/₂ cups peanuts

Melt chocolate and butterscotch chips in double boiler over hot water. Add peanuts; mix well. Drop by spoonfuls onto waxed paper-lined tray. Chill for 30 minutes. Store in airtight container. May add coconut, raisins, crispy rice cereal or other favorite ingredients. May substitute peanut butter chips for butterscotch chips. Yield: 1 pound.

Margaret Taylor

TOASTED PEANUTS

2 pounds raw peanuts
Melted butter to taste

Salt to taste

Place peanuts in single layer in shallow baking pan. Bake at 300 degrees for 1 hour and 15 minutes, stirring several times. Season with butter and salt. Yield: 16 servings.

Mary Beeler

PECAN PEANUT BUTTER BALLS

2 cups margarine
2 pounds peanut butter
3 pounds confectioners'
  sugar

1 cup chopped pecans
2 pounds semisweet
  chocolate

Combine margarine and peanut butter in saucepan. Heat until margarine is melted and mixture is well blended. Add confectioners' sugar; mix well. Fold in pecans. Shape into 1-inch balls. Place on waxed paper. Melt chocolate in double boiler over hot water. Dip peanut butter balls into chocolate; place on waxed paper. Let stand for 3 hours or until chocolate is firm. Yield: 17 dozen.

South Central Bell Notes, April, 1981

PEANUT BUTTER CANDY

2 cups sugar
1/2 cup butter
1 5-ounce can
   evaporated milk

1 1/4 cups (or more) peanut
   butter

Combine sugar, butter and evaporated milk in heavy saucepan. Cook, uncovered, to 234 to 240 degrees on candy thermometer, soft-ball stage. Remove from heat. Stir in peanut butter. Beat until thick and creamy. Pour into buttered dishes. Let stand until firm. Cut into pieces. Yield: 3 pounds.

Tammy Brasher

CHOCOLATE AND PEANUT BUTTER SWIRLS

1 cup peanut butter
1/2 cup confectioners'
   sugar
1/4 cup coconut

1/2 cup light corn syrup
2 cups Cheerios cereal
1 cup milk chocolate chips
2 tablespoons water

Combine peanut butter, confectioners' sugar, coconut and corn syrup in bowl; mix well. Add cereal; mix well. Shape into 1 1/2-inch balls. Place on waxed paper; flatten balls slightly. Melt chocolate chips with water in saucepan over medium heat, stirring constantly. Dip tops of balls into chocolate mixture. Place on waxed paper-lined tray. Chill for 30 minutes or until firm. Store in airtight container in refrigerator. Yield: 24 pieces.

Nancy Winstead

COATED PECANS

3 cups pecan halves
1/2 cup water

1 cup sugar
Cinnamon to taste

Combine pecans, water, sugar and cinnamon in saucepan. Bring to a boil. Cook over medium heat until pecans are coated. Spread in single layer on baking sheets. Bake at 250 to 300 degrees for 10 to 15 minutes, stirring several times. Yield: 16 servings.

Mary Beeler

GLAZED PECANS

3 cups pecan halves
3/4 cup sugar
1/4 cup light corn syrup

1 tablespoon oil
1/8 teaspoon salt
1/4 cup butter

Place pecan halves in 9x13-inch pan. Bake at 250 degrees for 5 minutes. Combine 1/2 cup sugar, corn syrup, oil and salt in saucepan; mix well. Bring to a boil, stirring constantly. Boil for 5 minutes; do not stir. Remove from heat. Stir in butter until melted. Pour over pecans; toss to coat well. Bake at 250 degrees for 50 to 60 minutes, tossing several times. Sprinkle with remaining 1/4 cup sugar; toss well. Spread on ungreased baking sheet. Let stand until cool. Separate pecan halves. Store in airtight container in refrigerator. Yield: 24 servings.

Juyne Bushart

GEORGIA'S GOLDEN PECAN BRITTLE

1 tablespoon butter, softened
1 1/2 cups large pecan halves
1 cup sugar
1/2 cup light corn syrup

1/8 teaspoon cream of tartar
2 tablespoons cold water
Salt to taste
2 tablespoons unsalted butter
2 teaspoons vanilla extract

Grease bottom of 9x13-inch baking dish with 1 tablespoon butter. Place pecan halves in single layer in dish. Combine sugar, corn syrup, cream of tartar, water and salt in heavy saucepan; mix well. Bring to a boil. Cook, uncovered, to 300 to 310 degrees on candy thermometer, hard-crack stage; do not stir. Stir in 2 tablespoons unsalted butter. Remove from heat. Cool slightly. Add vanilla; mix well. Pour syrup over pecan halves quickly; toss quickly with wooden spoon until coated. Spread brittle as thinly as possible. Let stand until cool. Break into pieces. Store in airtight container. Yield: 3/4 pound.

Patricia J. Tudor

COOKIES

APRICOT BARS

²/₃ cup dried apricots
¹/₂ cup margarine
¹/₄ cup sugar
1 cup flour
2 eggs
1 cup packed brown sugar
¹/₃ cup flour

¹/₂ teaspoon baking powder
¹/₄ teaspoon salt
¹/₂ teaspoon vanilla extract
¹/₂ cup chopped pecans
Confectioners' sugar

Cook apricots in water to cover in saucepan for 10 minutes. Drain, cool and chop apricots. Mix margarine, sugar and 1 cup flour in bowl until crumbly. Press into greased 8x8-inch baking pan. Bake at 350 degrees for 25 minutes. Beat eggs in mixer bowl. Add brown sugar; beat until smooth. Sift in ¹/₃ cup flour, baking powder and salt; mix well. Mix in vanilla, pecans and apricots. Spread over baked layer. Bake for 30 minutes longer. Cool on wire rack. Cut into 1x2-inch bars. Roll in confectioners' sugar. Yield: 32 bars.

Gwen Mills

BOHEMIAN SLICES

1¹/₄ cups margarine, softened
1¹/₂ cups sugar
4 egg yolks

1 teaspoon vanilla extract
2 cups flour
4 egg whites, stiffly beaten
1 can pie filling

Cream margarine and sugar in mixer bowl until light and fluffy. Beat in egg yolks and vanilla. Add flour; mix well. Fold in stiffly beaten egg whites gently. Spread evenly on cookie sheet. Drop pie filling by teaspoonfuls ¹/₂ inch apart on cookie layer. Bake at 350 degrees for 30 minutes. Garnish with sprinkle of confectioners' sugar while warm. Cool on wire rack. Cut into pieces. Yield: 30 servings.

Pat Cole

CARAMEL CRISPY TREATS

1/4 cup margarine
4 cups miniature
  marshmallows

5 cups crisp rice cereal
2 wrapped caramel sheets

Melt margarine in saucepan over low heat. Add marshmallows and cereal; mix well. Press half the mixture into 9x9-inch pan. Top with caramel sheets, pressing lightly to cover well. Top with remaining cereal mixture, pressing lightly. Cool completely. Cut into squares. Yield: 16 servings.

Beverly Sowders

EDITH'S CHESS SQUARES

1/2 cup melted butter
1 2-layer package yellow
  cake mix
1 egg
2 eggs, beaten

1 pound confectioners'
  sugar
8 ounces cream cheese,
  softened

Combine butter, cake mix and 1 egg in mixer bowl; mix well. Press into 9x13-inch glass dish. Combine 2 eggs, confectioners' sugar and cream cheese in mixer bowl; mix until smooth. Spread over cake mix layer. Bake at 325 degrees for 40 minutes. Cool on wire rack. Cut into squares. Yield: 32 servings.

Ivory S. Henry

BROWNIES

1/2 cup margarine, softened
1/2 cup shortening
2 cups sugar
4 eggs
1/2 cup baking cocoa

11/2 cups flour
1 teaspoon salt
2 teaspoons vanilla extract
1 cup chopped nuts

Cream margarine, shortening and sugar in mixer bowl until light and fluffy. Beat in eggs. Add cocoa, flour and salt; mix well. Mix in vanilla and nuts. Spoon into greased baking pan. Bake at 325 degrees for 30 to 35 minutes or until brownies test done. Cool on wire rack. Cut into squares. Yield: 32 servings.

Erma S. Messer

CHOCO-MALLOW BROWNIES

1/2 cup butter, softened
1 cup sugar
2 eggs
3/4 cup flour
1/2 teaspoon baking
  powder
Pinch of salt

3 tablespoons baking
  cocoa
1 teaspoon vanilla extract
1/2 cup chopped pecans
2 cups miniature
  marshmallows

Cream butter in mixer bowl until light. Add sugar gradually, beating until fluffy. Beat in eggs 1 at a time at medium speed. Combine flour, baking powder, salt and cocoa in bowl. Add to creamed mixture; mix well. Stir in vanilla and pecans. Spoon into greased 9x9-inch baking pan. Bake at 350 degrees for 18 to 20 minutes or until brownies test done. Sprinkle with marshmallows; cover with foil. Let stand for 5 minutes or until marshmallows are melted. Cool, uncovered, on wire rack. Frost with chocolate frosting. Cut into squares. Yield: 16 servings.

Marty Hill

MARBLED BROWNIES

5 tablespoons butter,
  softened
6 ounces cream cheese,
  softened
1/3 cup sugar
2 eggs
2 tablespoons flour
3/4 teaspoon vanilla extract
1 family-size package
  brownie mix

2 tablespoons water
3 eggs
3 tablespoons butter
2 tablespoons baking
  cocoa
1 1/2 cups confectioners'
  sugar
1 teaspoon vanilla extract
2 tablespoons (about) milk

Cream 5 tablespoons butter and cream cheese in mixer bowl until light. Add sugar, 2 eggs, flour and 3/4 teaspoon vanilla; mix well. Combine brownie mix, water and 3 eggs in large bowl; beat 50 strokes by hand. Pour half the batter into greased 9x13-inch baking pan. Spread cream cheese mixture over brownie layer. Drop remaining brownie batter over cream cheese layer. Cut through all layers with knife to marblelize. Bake at 350 degrees for 35 to 40 minutes or until brownies test done. Cool on wire rack. Melt 3 tablespoons butter in medium saucepan. Stir in cocoa. Add confectioners' sugar, 1 teaspoon vanilla and enough milk to make of spreading consistency; mix until smooth. Spread on brownies. Let stand until frosting is firm. Cut into squares. Yield: 24 to 50 servings.

Betty Jo Daniel

MINT SWIRL BROWNIES

1/4 **cup butter, softened**
3 **ounces cream cheese,**
  softened
3/4 **cup sugar**
2 **eggs**
2/3 **cup flour**
1/2 **teaspoon baking**
  powder
1/4 **teaspoon salt**
1/3 **cup chopped nuts**
1 **ounce unsweetened**
  chocolate, melted, cooled

1/2 **teaspoon peppermint**
  extract
Several drops of green
  food coloring
1 **ounce unsweetened**
  chocolate
1 **tablespoon butter**
1 **cup sifted confectioners'**
  sugar
1/2 **teaspoon vanilla extract**
2 **tablespoons (about)**
  boiling water

Cream 1/4 cup butter, cream cheese and sugar in mixer bowl until light and fluffy. Add eggs; beat until smooth. Sift in flour, baking powder and salt; mix well. Divide into 2 equal portions in bowls. Add nuts and melted chocolate to 1 portion; mix well. Drop by tablespoonfuls in checkerboard design into greased 9x9-inch baking pan. Add peppermint extract and food coloring to remaining batter. Spoon into remaining spaces. Swirl lightly with spatula; do not overmix. Bake at 350 degrees for 15 to 20 minutes or until brownies test done. Cool on wire rack. Melt 1 ounce chocolate and 1 tablespoon butter in saucepan over low heat, stirring constantly; remove from heat. Add confectioners' sugar and vanilla, stirring until crumbly. Add enough boiling water to make of spreading consistency; mix well. Spread on brownies. Cool. Cut into squares. Yield: 16 squares.

Tina Fields

OATMEAL BROWNIES

1/2 cup melted butter
1/2 cup sugar
1/3 cup packed brown
  sugar
1 teaspoon vanilla extract
2 eggs, slightly beaten
2/3 cup flour

1/2 teaspoon baking
  powder
1/4 cup baking cocoa
1/3 cup chopped pecans
3 tablespoons quick-
  cooking oats

Combine butter, sugar, brown sugar and vanilla in mixer bowl; mix well. Beat in eggs. Add mixture of flour, baking powder and cocoa; mix well. Stir in pecans and oats. Spoon into greased 8x8-inch baking pan lined with waxed paper. Bake at 350 degrees for 18 minutes; center will be soft. Cool in pan for 10 minutes. Invert onto plate; remove waxed paper. Cut into squares. Yield: 24 servings.

Marty Hill

ROCKY ROAD BROWNIES

1/2 cup butter, softened
1 cup sugar
1 ounce unsweetened
  chocolate, melted
2 eggs, beaten
1/2 cup flour
1/2 cup chopped pecans
1/4 cup butter, softened
6 ounces cream cheese,
  softened
1/4 cup sugar
1 egg
1 tablespoon flour
1/4 cup chopped pecans

1/4 teaspoon vanilla extract
1/2 cup miniature
  semisweet chocolate
  chips
2 cups miniature
  marshmallows
2 ounces unsweetened
  chocolate
1/2 cup butter
1/2 cup milk
1/4 teaspoon vanilla extract
4 cups sifted
  confectioners' sugar

Cream 1/2 cup butter and 1 cup sugar in mixer bowl until light and fluffy. Add chocolate, 2 eggs, 1/2 cup flour and 1/2 cup pecans; mix well. Spoon into greased and floured 9x13-inch baking pan. Cream 1/4 cup butter, cream cheese and 1/4 cup sugar in mixer bowl until light. Add 1 egg, 1 tablespoon flour, 1/4 cup pecans and 1/4 teaspoon vanilla; mix well. Spoon carefully over chocolate layer; do not mix. Sprinkle with chocolate chips. Bake at 350 degrees for 35 to 45 minutes or until brownies test done. Cool slightly. Sprinkle with marshmallows. Melt 2 ounces chocolate and 1/2 cup butter in milk in double boiler. Stir in 1/4 teaspoon vanilla and confectioners' sugar. Spread over brownies. Cool. Cut into squares. Store in refrigerator. Yield: 42 servings.

Patricia J. Tudor

CHOCOLATE CHERRY BARS

1   2-layer package devil's
    food cake mix
1 can cherry pie filling
2 eggs, beaten
1 teaspoon almond extract

1 cup sugar
5 tablespoons margarine
1/3 cup milk
1 cup semisweet
    chocolate chips

Combine first 4 ingredients in large bowl; mix well by hand. Spoon into greased and floured 10x15-inch baking pan. Bake at 350 degrees for 20 to 30 minutes or until layer tests done. Combine sugar, margarine and milk in saucepan. Bring to a boil, stirring constantly. Remove from heat. Stir in chocolate chips. Pour over warm baked layer. Cool. Cut into bars. Yield: 36 servings.

Paula Goodlett

CHOCO-CHEWY BARS

12 ounces semisweet
    chocolate
2 tablespoons butter
1   15-ounce can
    sweetened condensed
    milk
1 cup melted butter

1 pound brown sugar
2 eggs
2 cups flour
1 teaspoon salt
1 teaspoon vanilla extract
1/2 cup chopped pecans
1/2 cup flaked coconut

Heat first 3 ingredients in double boiler over boiling water; blend well. Combine melted butter, brown sugar and eggs in bowl; beat until smooth. Mix in flour and salt. Stir in vanilla, pecans and coconut. Spread half the mixture in greased 10x15-inch baking pan. Drizzle with chocolate mixture. Dot with remaining batter; swirl lightly with knife. Bake at 350 degrees for 30 to 35 minutes. Cool on wire rack. Cut into bars. Yield: 48 servings.

Terri Bailey

FUDGE NUT THINS

1/2 cup margarine
2 ounces premelted
   unsweetened chocolate
3/4 cup flour
1 teaspoon baking powder
1 cup sugar

2 eggs
1/4 teaspoon salt
1/2 teaspoon vanilla extract
1/2 cup chopped walnuts
1 can chocolate frosting
1/2 cup chopped walnuts

Melt margarine with chocolate in double boiler over low heat, stirring constantly. Remove from heat. Add flour, baking powder, sugar, eggs, salt and vanilla; mix well. Stir in 1/2 cup walnuts. Spoon into greased 10x15-inch baking pan. Bake at 350 degrees for 12 to 15 minutes or until layer tests done. Cool on wire rack. Spread with frosting. Sprinkle with 1/2 cup walnuts. Cut into bars. Yield: 36 servings.

Jean Geary

CRUNCHY FUDGE SANDWICHES

12 ounces butterscotch
   chips
1 cup peanut butter
8 cups crisp rice cereal
3 tablespoons water

12 ounces semisweet
   chocolate chips
1 cup confectioners' sugar
1/4 cup margarine

Melt butterscotch chips with peanut butter in heavy saucepan over low heat, stirring constantly. Remove from heat. Stir in cereal. Press half the mixture into buttered 9x13-inch pan. Chill in refrigerator. Combine water, chocolate chips, confectioners' sugar and margarine in saucepan. Cook over low heat until well blended, stirring constantly. Spread over chilled layer. Top with remaining cereal mixture, pressing gently. Chill in refrigerator. Let stand at room temperature for 10 minutes before cutting into squares. Yield: 24 squares.

Denise Stottmann

MOCHA CREME BARS

1 cup unsalted sweet
  butter
2 cups sugar
4 eggs
1 tablespoon vanilla
  extract
1/2 teaspoon salt
1 3/4 cups flour
1 cup chopped pecans
2 ounces unsweetened
  chocolate, melted

1/2 teaspoon instant coffee
  granules
1 tablespoon hot water
1/2 cup unsalted sweet
  butter
1 tablespoon baking cocoa
2 cups confectioners'
  sugar
1/2 teaspoon vanilla extract
1 egg yolk
Pinch of salt

Cream 1 cup butter and sugar in mixer bowl until light and fluffy. Add eggs, 1 tablespoon vanilla and 1/2 teaspoon salt; mix well. Mix in flour. Divide into 2 equal portions in bowls. Stir pecans into 1 portion. Spread in greased 9x13-inch baking pan. Blend melted chocolate into remaining portion. Spread evenly over pecan layer. Bake at 350 degrees for 30 minutes. Cool on wire rack. Dissolve coffee in hot water. Combine 1/2 cup butter, cocoa, confectioners' sugar and coffee mixture in bowl; mix until smooth. Add 1/2 teaspoon vanilla, egg yolk and pinch of salt; mix well. Spread over cooled bars. Yield: 48 servings.

Patricia J. Tudor

TOLL HOUSE PAN COOKIES

1 cup butter, softened
3/4 cup sugar
3/4 cup packed brown
  sugar
1 teaspoon vanilla extract
2 eggs

2 1/4 cups flour
1 teaspoon soda
1 teaspoon salt
2 cups semisweet
  chocolate chips
1 cup chopped nuts

Cream butter, sugar, brown sugar and vanilla in mixer bowl until light and fluffy. Beat in eggs. Add mixture of flour, soda and salt gradually; mix well. Stir in chocolate chips and nuts. Spread into greased 10x15-inch baking pan. Bake at 375 degrees for 20 minutes. Cool on wire rack. Cut into 2-inch squares. Yield: 35 servings.

Judy Wallis

WOW BARS

4 cups flaked coconut
1 14-ounce can
  sweetened condensed
  milk
2 teaspoons vanilla extract

1/2 teaspoon almond extract
1 4-ounce package
  German's sweet
  chocolate, broken

Combine coconut, sweetened condensed milk and flavorings in bowl; mix well. Spread into greased 9x13-inch baking pan. Bake at 350 degrees for 25 minutes or until golden brown. Sprinkle chocolate on top; cover lightly with foil. Let stand for 3 minutes. Spread chocolate evenly over top. Cool on wire rack. Cut into bars. Yield: 48 servings.

Patricia J. Tudor

FROSTY WINTER BARS

1 cup butter
1 cup sugar
1 egg, beaten
1/2 cup milk
1 1/2 cups flaked coconut
1 cup chopped pecans
1 cup graham cracker
  crumbs

Whole graham crackers
1/2 cup butter, softened
5 tablespoons light cream
2 cups confectioners'
  sugar
1 teaspoon vanilla extract
1/4 cup chopped pecans

Melt 1 cup butter in saucepan. Stir in sugar, egg and milk. Bring to a boil over low heat, stirring constantly. Remove from heat. Stir in coconut, 1 cup pecans and cracker crumbs. Arrange 1 layer graham crackers in 9x13-inch pan. Spread with coconut mixture. Top with a second layer of graham crackers. Cream 1/2 cup butter in mixer bowl until light. Add cream, confectioners' sugar and vanilla; beat until fluffy. Spread over crackers. Sprinkle with remaining 1/4 cup pecans. Chill for several hours to overnight. Cut into bars. Yield: 32 servings.

Donna Browning

GOOEY BARS

1 2-layer package lemon
   cake mix
1 egg
1/2 cup melted butter
2 eggs

1 pound confectioners'
   sugar
8 ounces cream cheese,
   softened
Confectioners' sugar

Combine cake mix, 1 egg and butter in bowl; mix by hand for 5 minutes. Press into 9x13-inch baking pan. Combine 2 eggs, confectioners' sugar and cream cheese in mixer bowl; beat until smooth. Spread over cake mix layer. Bake at 350 degrees for 30 to 40 minutes or until layer tests done. Cool on wire rack. Sprinkle with additional confectioners' sugar. Cut into bars. May substitute other flavors of cake mix for variety. Yield: 32 servings.

Brenda Collins

LEMON DELIGHT BARS

1/2 cup margarine, softened
1 cup flour
1/4 cup sugar
2 eggs
1 cup sugar

3 tablespoons lemon juice
2 tablespoons flour
1/2 teaspoon baking
   powder
Confectioners' sugar

Combine margarine, 1 cup flour and 1/4 cup sugar in bowl; mix well. Press into 9x9-inch baking pan. Bake at 350 degrees for 10 minutes. Combine eggs, 1 cup sugar, lemon juice, 2 tablespoons flour and baking powder in bowl; mix well. Spread over baked layer. Bake for 20 minutes longer. Sprinkle with confectioners' sugar. Cool on wire rack. Cut into squares. Yield: 16 servings.

Betty Krueger

★ Decorate cookies with frosting and colored sugar or candy sprinkles.

LEMON MARCUS BARS

1 2-layer package lemon
cake mix
2 eggs
1/2 cup margarine, softened
2 eggs

8 ounces cream cheese,
softened
1 pound confectioners'
sugar

Combine cake mix, 2 eggs and margarine in mixer bowl; mix well. Press into 9x13-inch baking pan. Combine remaining 2 eggs, cream cheese and confectioners' sugar in mixer bowl; mix well. Spread over cake mix layer. Bake at 350 degrees for 35 to 40 minutes or until golden brown. Cool on wire rack. Cut into bars. Yield: 32 servings.

Johnnie Harper

LEMON SQUARES

1 cup butter, softened
3/4 cup confectioners'
sugar
2 cups sifted flour
4 eggs

2 cups sugar
1/4 cup flour
Juice and grated rind of 1
lemon

Combine butter, confectioners' sugar and 2 cups flour in bowl; mix well. Press into 10x15-inch baking pan. Bake at 350 degrees for 20 minutes. Beat eggs in bowl. Add sugar, 1/4 cup flour, lemon juice and lemon rind; mix well. Pour over baked layer. Bake for 20 minutes longer. Sprinkle with additional confectioners' sugar. Cool on wire rack. Cut into squares. Yield: 48 servings.

OATMEAL AND COCONUT TOFFEE BARS

1 cup flour
2/3 cup quick-cooking oats
1/3 cup sugar
1/2 cup unsalted butter,
softened
3/4 cup packed brown
sugar
2 eggs

2 tablespoons flour
1/2 teaspoon baking
powder
1 tablespoon vanilla
extract
1/4 teaspoon salt
1 cup flaked coconut

Combine 1 cup flour, oats, sugar and butter in mixer bowl; mix for 2 minutes or until crumbly, scraping bowl frequently. Reserve 3/4 cup mixture. Press remaining mixture into ungreased 9x9-inch baking pan. Bake at 350 degrees for 15 to 20 minutes or until light brown. Combine brown sugar and next 5 ingredients in mixer bowl. Beat at low speed for 1 to 2 minutes or until smooth. Stir in coconut. Spread over baked layer. Sprinkle with reserved crumb mixture. Bake for 15 to 20 minutes or until set in center. Cool on wire rack. Cut into bars. Yield: 24 servings.

Patricia J. Tudor

PEANUT BUTTER SQUARES

1 1/3 cups melted butter
1 wrapped package
   graham crackers, crushed
1 1/2 cups peanut butter

3 cups confectioners'
   sugar
12 ounces semisweet
   chocolate chips, melted

Combine first 4 ingredients in bowl; mix well. Press into 9x13-inch dish. Spread melted chocolate on top. Cool until chocolate begins to set. Cut into squares before chocolate sets completely. Store in refrigerator. Yield: 32 servings.

Judy Seitz

SOUTHERN PECAN BARS

1 1/3 cups flour
1/2 cup packed brown
   sugar
1/2 teaspoon baking powder
1/3 cup margarine, softened
1/4 cup chopped pecans
3/4 cup corn syrup

1/4 cup packed brown
   sugar
3 tablespoons flour
2 eggs
1 teaspoon vanilla extract
1/2 teaspoon salt
3/4 cup chopped pecans

Combine first 4 ingredients in mixer bowl; mix until crumbly. Mix in 1/4 cup pecans. Press into greased 9x13-inch baking pan. Combine corn syrup and next 5 ingredients in mixer bowl; mix well. Pour over first layer. Sprinkle with 3/4 cup pecans. Bake at 350 degrees for 25 to 30 minutes or until brown. Cool on wire rack. Cut into bars. Yield: 36 servings.

Jean Geary

CHINESE ALMOND COOKIES

1½ cups butter, softened
1 cup sugar
3 cups flour, sifted
¼ teaspoon baking
   powder
½ teaspoon salt

1 egg, beaten
1 teaspoon almond
   extract
½ cup finely chopped
   walnuts
Red food coloring

Cream butter and sugar in mixer bowl until light and fluffy. Add flour, baking powder and salt; mix well. Add egg, almond extract and walnuts; mix well. Shape into walnut-sized balls; place on cookie sheet and flatten slightly. Dip end of small cork in food coloring. Stamp center of each cookie with cork. Bake at 350 degrees on center rack of oven for 10 minutes or just until light brown. Cool on cookie sheet for several minutes. Remove to wire rack to cool completely. Yield: 5 dozen.

Gary Lee Figg

ALMOND HORNS

1 cup butter, softened
5 tablespoons sugar
2 cups flour
1 teaspoon vanilla extract

Pinch of salt
1 cup finely chopped
   blanched almonds
Confectioners' sugar

Cream butter in mixer bowl until light. Add sugar, flour, vanilla and salt; mix well. Mix in almonds. Chill in refrigerator. Shape into finger-sized crescents. Place on cookie sheet. Bake at 350 degrees for 15 to 20 minutes or until light brown. Roll in confectioners' sugar. Cool on wire rack. Yield: 5 dozen.

Alice Arterburn

APRICOT BALLS

1 cup dried apricots
1 cup coconut
½ cup pecans
1 teaspoon grated lemon
   rind
2 teaspoons grated orange
   rind

⅛ teaspoon salt
4 teaspoons lemon juice
4 teaspoons (about)
   orange juice
Sugar

Put apricots, coconut and pecans through fine food chopper or chop in food processor. Combine with salt, rinds, lemon juice and enough orange juice to make of desired consistency in bowl; mix well by hand. Shape into 3/4-inch balls. Roll in sugar. Yield: 3 dozen.

Gwen Mills

BONBON COOKIES

3½ cups vanilla wafer
  crumbs
2 tablespoons baking
  cocoa
½ cup confectioners'
  sugar

¼ cup light corn syrup
⅓ cup Southern Comfort
1 cup chopped walnuts
1 cup chocolate chips
1 tablespoon shortening

Combine crumbs, cocoa, confectioners' sugar, corn syrup, Southern Comfort and walnuts in bowl; mix well. Shape into balls. Melt chocolate chips with shortening in saucepan over low heat. Dip balls into chocolate mixture; place on waxed paper. Chill overnight. Serve cold. Yield: 4 dozen.

Nellie Leitner

BUTTER COOKIES

1 cup butter, softened
½ cup sugar
1 egg

½ teaspoon almond
  extract
2½ cups flour

Cream butter in large mixer bowl until light. Add sugar gradually, beating until fluffy. Beat in egg and almond extract. Add flour gradually, mixing well after each addition. Chill in refrigerator. Roll ⅛ inch thick on floured surface. Cut into desired shapes with floured cutters. Place on ungreased cookie sheet. Bake at 350 degrees for 8 to 12 minutes or until golden brown. Remove to wire rack to cool. May press unchilled dough through cookie press onto cookie sheet into desired shapes if preferred. May add 1 cup chopped gumdrops (omit licorice) and 1 cup coconut; drop unchilled dough by rounded teaspoonfuls onto cookie sheet. Yield: 7 to 8 dozen.

Clara Nance, Nancy Winstead

AWARD-WINNING CHOCOLATE CHIP COOKIES

1 cup butter, softened
3/4 cup sugar
3/4 cup packed brown
  sugar
1 teaspoon vanilla extract
2 eggs

2 1/4 cups flour
1 teaspoon soda
1 teaspoon salt
2 cups chocolate chips
1 1/2 cups chopped pecans

Cream butter, sugar, brown sugar and vanilla in mixer bowl until light and fluffy. Beat in eggs. Add mixture of flour, soda and salt gradually, mixing well after each addition. Mix in chocolate chips and pecans. Drop by rounded teaspoonfuls onto ungreased cookie sheet. Bake in convection oven at 375 degrees for 8 to 10 minutes or until light brown. Remove to wire rack to cool. This recipe took third prize at the 1987 Kentucky State Fair. The secret is the convection oven. Yield: 6 dozen.

Dana Fendley

CHOCOLATE CRINKLES

1/2 cup oil
4 ounces unsweetened
  chocolate, melted
2 cups sugar
4 eggs
2 teaspoons vanilla extract

2 cups flour
2 teaspoons baking
  powder
1/2 teaspoon salt
1 cup confectioners' sugar

Combine oil, melted chocolate and sugar in mixer bowl; mix until smooth. Beat in eggs 1 at a time. Add vanilla, flour, baking powder and salt; mix well. Chill for several hours to overnight. Drop by teaspoonfuls into confectioners' sugar, shaping into balls. Place on greased cookie sheet. Bake at 350 degrees for 10 to 12 minutes or until light brown. Yield: 6 to 8 dozen.

Gale Marcum

CHOCOLATE OATMEAL COOKIES

1/4 to 1/2 cup milk
1/2 cup margarine
2 to 4 tablespoons baking
  cocoa

1 1/2 to 2 cups sugar
1/4 to 1/2 cup peanut butter
1 1/2 to 3 cups oats
1 teaspoon vanilla extract

Bring first 4 ingredients to a boil in saucepan. Cook for 1 minutes; remove from heat. Add peanut butter, oats and vanilla; beat until of desired consistency. Drop by teaspoonfuls onto waxed paper. Let stand until firm. Yield: 2 to 3 dozen.

Paula Goodlett, Betty Hunter
Melinda Miller, Celesta Wilson

CHOCOLATE SNOWBALLS

3/4 cup margarine, softened
1/2 cup sugar
2 teaspoons vanilla extract
1 egg
2 cups sifted flour

1/2 teaspoon salt
1 cup chopped walnuts
1 cup chocolate chips
Confectioners' sugar

Cream first 3 ingredients in mixer bowl until light and fluffy. Beat in egg. Stir in mixture of sifted flour and salt. Mix in walnuts and chocolate chips. Shape into 1-inch balls; place on ungreased cookie sheet. Bake at 350 degrees for 15 to 20 minutes. Roll in confectioners' sugar. Cool on wire rack. Yield: 6 dozen.

Jean Geary

CHOCOLATE CHIP COOKIES

1 cup butter, softened
3/4 cup sugar
3/4 cup packed brown
  sugar

1 tablespoon vanilla extract
2 1/2 to 3 cups flour
1 cup chocolate chips
1/2 cup chopped pecans

Cream butter, sugar, brown sugar and vanilla in mixer bowl until light and fluffy. Add enough flour to make stiff but not dry dough. Mix in chocolate chips and pecans. Shape into balls; place on cookie sheet. Bake at 350 degrees for 12 to 13 minutes or until light brown. Remove to wire rack to cool. Yield: 4 dozen.

Nancy Winstead

COWBOY COOKIES

1 cup margarine, softened
1 cup sugar
1 cup packed brown sugar
2 eggs, beaten
1 teaspoon vanilla extract
2 cups flour
1 teaspoon soda
1 teaspoon baking powder
1/2 teaspoon salt
1/2 cup chopped nuts
1 cup chocolate chips
2 cups quick-cooking oats

Cream margarine, sugar and brown sugar in mixer bowl until light and fluffy. Stir in eggs and vanilla. Sift in mixture of flour, soda, baking powder and salt; mix well. Stir in nuts, chocolate chips and oats. Drop by tablespoonfuls onto greased cookie sheet. Bake at 350 degrees for 15 minutes. Remove to wire rack to cool. Yield: 5 dozen.

Jeanne McReynolds

CHRISTMAS ROCKS

1 cup butter, softened
1 1/2 cups sugar
3 eggs, beaten
1 teaspoon soda
2 tablespoons hot water
3 cups flour
1 teaspoon cinnamon
1 teaspoon cloves
1 pound raisins
1 pound dates, chopped
1/2 cup chopped
    maraschino cherries
1 pound pecans, chopped

Cream butter and sugar in mixer bowl until light and fluffy. Beat in eggs and soda dissolved in hot water. Add flour and spices; mix well. Mix in fruits and pecans. Drop by teaspoonfuls onto cookie sheet. Bake at 350 degrees for 8 to 12 minutes, depending upon degree of chewiness desired. Remove to wire rack to cool. For Sugar-Free Christmas Rocks, use low-fat butter and substitute 2 cups Sugar Twin and 4 egg whites for sugar and whole eggs. Omit raisins and cherries and substitute 1/2 pound walnuts for pecans. Yield: 6 to 8 dozen.

Patsy Akers, Ella (Babe) Young

COCO-NOT COOKIES

1/2 cup butter, softened
1 cup sugar
1 tablespoon coconut
  flavoring
1 egg, beaten

1 small package
  buttermilk baking mix
1 small package instant
  potato flakes

Cream butter, sugar and flavoring in mixer bowl until light and fluffy. Beat in egg. Add baking mix and potato flakes; mix well. Shape into small balls; place 2 inches apart on ungreased cookie sheet. Bake at 375 degrees for 10 to 12 minutes or until light brown. Remove to wire rack to cool. Yield: 4 dozen.

Grace Dabney

CREAM CHEESE COOKIES

1/4 cup butter, softened
8 ounces cream cheese
1 egg yolk

1 teaspoon vanilla extract
1   2-layer package yellow
  or devil's food cake mix

Cream butter and softened cream cheese in mixer bowl until light and fluffy. Beat in egg yolk and vanilla. Add cake mix 1/3 at a time, mixing well after each addition; mix last 1/3 by hand. Chill, covered, for 30 minutes. Drop by level teaspoonfuls onto ungreased cookie sheet. Bake at 350 degrees for 8 to 10 minutes or until light brown. Cool on cookie sheet for several minutes. Remove to wire rack to cool completely. Yield: 5 dozen.

Bernidea Fort

DATE DAINTIES

1 cup chopped dates
1/2 cup margarine
1 cup sugar
1 egg

1 cup chopped pecans
3 to 4 cups crisp rice cereal
Confectioners' sugar
Coconut

Combine dates, margarine, sugar and egg in saucepan. Cook for 8 minutes. Remove from heat. Stir in pecans and cereal. Shape as desired. Roll in confectioners' sugar or coconut. Let stand until, cool. Store in airtight container. Yield: 5 dozen.

Nancy Winstead

DATE KISSES

2 egg whites
1 cup confectioners' sugar
1 tablespoon baking cocoa

¹/₈ teaspoon salt
1 cup chopped pecans
1 cup chopped dates

Beat egg whites with confectioners' sugar in mixer bowl until stiff peaks form. Fold in cocoa, salt, pecans and dates. Drop by teaspoonfuls onto greased cookie sheet. Bake at 300 degrees for 12 to 15 minutes or until light brown. Remove to wire rack to cool. Yield: 5¹/₂ dozen.

Cindy Jones

FORGOTTEN COOKIES

2 egg whites, at room
  temperature
²/₃ to ³/₄ cup sugar
1 teaspoon vanilla extract

Pinch of salt
1 cup chocolate chips
1 cup chopped nuts

Beat egg whites in mixer bowl until foamy. Add sugar gradually, beating until stiff peaks form. Fold in vanilla, salt, chocolate chips and nuts. Drop by teaspoonfuls onto foiled-lined cookie sheet. Place in 350-degree oven. Turn off oven. Let stand in closed oven overnight. May reduce amounts of chocolate chips and nuts to ¹/₂ cup and add ¹/₂ cup chopped dates if desired. Yield: 3¹/₂ dozen.

Aggie Burks, Peggy Graviss

CANDIED FRUIT COOKIES

2 cups graham cracker
  crumbs
1 cup chopped candied
  fruit

1 cup chopped nuts
1   14-ounce can
    sweetened condensed
    milk

Combine cracker crumbs, candied fruit, nuts and sweetened condensed milk in bowl; mix well. Drop by teaspoonfuls 1 inch apart onto greased and floured cookie sheet. Bake at 325 degrees for 12 minutes. Remove immediately to wire rack to cool. Yield: 5 dozen.

Cindy Jones

PURE FRUIT COOKIES

1½ cups mashed banana
⅓ cup peanut or safflower
 oil
1 teaspoon vanilla extract
⅛ teaspoon salt

1½ cups oats
½ cup oat bran
1½ cups coarsely
 chopped, mixed dried fruit
½ cup chopped walnuts

Combine first 4 ingredients in bowl; mix well. Stir in oats and remaining ingredients. Drop by tablespoonfuls 1 inch apart onto greased cookie sheet; flatten slightly. Bake at 350 degrees for 20 to 25 minutes or until edges are light brown. Remove to wire rack to cool. Store in refrigerator. Yield: 2 dozen.

Shirley Bott

FUSS COOKIES

1 cup butter, softened
6 tablespoons sugar
3½ cups flour

2 teaspoons vanilla extract
Crabapple or plum jelly
Pecan halves

Cream butter and sugar in mixer bowl until light and fluffy. Add flour and vanilla; mix well. Shape into balls; place on cookie sheet. Press indentation in each cookie. Fill with jelly; top with pecan half. Bake at 325 degrees for 25 minutes. Garnish hot cookies with sprinkle of confectioners' sugar. Remove to wire rack to cool. Yield: 5 dozen.

GINGER CRINKLES

⅔ cup oil
1 cup sugar
1 egg
¼ cup molasses
2 cups sifted flour

2 teaspoons soda
½ teaspoon salt
1 teaspoon cinnamon
1 teaspoon ginger
¼ cup sugar

Combine oil and 1 cup sugar in mixer bowl; beat until smooth. Beat in egg. Stir in molasses. Add sifted mixture of flour, soda, salt and spices. Drop by teaspoonfuls into ¼ cup sugar, turning to coat well and shape into balls. Place 3 inches apart on ungreased cookie sheet. Bake at 350 degrees for 10 minutes. Remove to wire rack to cool. Yield: 4 dozen.

Joyce Alexander

BLENDER GINGER CRINKLES

2¼ cups sifted flour
1½ teaspoons soda
¼ teaspoon salt
1 teaspoon cinnamon
½ teaspoon ginger
⅛ teaspoon cloves
1 egg
½ cup molasses
¾ cup shortening
¾ cup sugar

Sift flour, soda, salt, cinnamon, ginger and cloves into bowl. Combine egg, molasses, shortening and sugar in blender container. Process at high speed until smooth. Add to dry ingredients; mix well. Chill in freezer for 1 hour or in refrigerator for 2 hours. Shape into walnut-sized balls. Roll in additional sugar. Place 2 inches apart on greased cookie sheet. Bake at 375 degrees for 12 to 15 minutes or until light brown. Remove to wire rack to cool. Yield: 4 dozen.

Pearl Hodges

KING-SIZE GINGERSNAPS

2 cups sifted flour
1 tablespoon soda
½ teaspoon salt
1 teaspoon cinnamon
1 teaspoon ginger
1 teaspoon cloves
¾ cup shortening
1 cup sugar
1 egg, beaten
¼ cup molasses

Sift flour, soda, salt and spices into bowl. Cream shortening and sugar in mixer bowl until light and fluffy. Beat in egg and molasses. Add dry ingredients; mix well. Shape into 1-inch balls. Roll in additional sugar. Place on greased cookie sheet. Bake at 350 degrees for 10 minutes for moist cookies. May bake longer for crisp cookies. Remove to wire rack to cool. Yield: 3 dozen.

Judy Damron

HAYSTACKS

1 cup chocolate chips
1 cup butterscotch chips
Peanut butter to taste
1 3-ounce can chow mein noodles

Melt chocolate chips and butterscotch chips in double boiler. Stir in peanut butter until blended. Add noodles; mix well.

Drop by teaspoonfuls onto waxed paper. Let stand until firm. Yield: 2 dozen.

Judy Seitz

JAM DIAGONALS

1/2 **cup margarine, softened**
1/4 **cup sugar**
1 **teaspoon vanilla extract**
1/8 **teaspoon salt**
1 1/4 **cups flour**

1/4 **cup raspberry jam**
3/4 **cup confectioners'**
  sugar
4 **teaspoons lemon juice**

Cream margarine, sugar, vanilla and salt in mixer bowl until light and fluffy. Add flour gradually, mixing well. Divide into 3 portions. Roll each portion into 9-inch rope on floured surface. Place 3 inches apart on lightly greased cookie sheet. Make 1/2-inch deep depression with finger down center of each rope. Fill with jam. Bake at 350 degrees for 12 to 15 minutes or until light brown. Cool on cookie sheet. Blend confectioners' sugar and lemon juice in small bowl. Drizzle over jam. Let stand until glaze is firm. Slice diagonally into 1-inch cookies. Yield: 2 dozen.

Jean Geary

HEATH BAR COOKIES

1/2 **cup butter, softened**
6 **tablespoons sugar**
6 **tablespoons light brown**
  sugar
1/2 **teaspoon vanilla extract**
1 **egg**
1/2 **teaspoon soda**

1/2 **teaspoon salt**
1 1/4 **cups plus 2**
  tablespoons flour
1   **9-ounce package Heath**
  bars, crushed
1/2 **cup chopped nuts**

Cream butter, sugar and brown sugar in mixer bowl until light and fluffy. Add vanilla, egg, soda and salt; mix well. Stir in flour. Mix in candy and nuts. Drop by teaspoonfuls onto greased cookie sheet. Bake at 350 degrees for 8 to 10 minutes or until light brown. Crush candy bars easily by freezing and crushing in wrappers. Yield: 3 dozen.

Patricia J. Tudor

NEW ZEALAND KIWI CRISPS

1 1/2 cups flour
1 tablespoon baking
  powder
Pinch of salt
3/4 cup chocolate chips

1/2 cup butter, softened
2 tablespoons sugar
2 tablespoons sweetened
  condensed milk

Mix flour, baking powder, salt and chocolate chips in bowl. Cream butter and sugar in mixer bowl until light and fluffy. Add chocolate chip mixture; mix well. Stir in sweetened condensed milk. Drop by tablespoonfuls onto greased cookie sheet; press lightly with fork to flatten. Bake at 350 degrees for 20 minutes. Remove to wire rack to cool. Yield: 2 dozen.

Beverly Both

THE ORIGINAL LITTLE DEBBIE COOKIES

3/4 cup shortening
1/2 cup sugar
1 cup packed brown sugar
1 egg, beaten
1/4 cup water
1 teaspoon vanilla extract
1 cup flour, sifted
1/2 teaspoon soda

1 teaspoon salt
3 cups oats
3/4 cup shortening
1 1/2 cups confectioners'
  sugar
1   7-ounce jar
  marshmallow creme
1/2 teaspoon vanilla extract

Cream 3/4 cup shortening, sugar and brown sugar in mixer bowl until light and fluffy. Add egg, water and 1 teaspoon vanilla; mix well. Add flour, soda, salt and oats; mix well. Drop by teaspoonfuls onto ungreased cookie sheet. Bake at 350 degrees for 8 to 10 minutes or just until light brown; do not overbake. Remove to wire rack to cool. Cream remaining 3/4 cup shortening, confectioners' sugar, marshmallow creme and remaining 1/2 teaspoon vanilla in mixer bowl until light. Spread between cookies. Yield: 1 1/2 dozen.

Debbie Windhorst

NO-BAKE COOKIES

2 cups oats
2 teaspoons flour
2 tablespoons peanut
  butter
2 cups sugar

1/2 cup butter
2 tablespoons baking
  cocoa
1/4 cup milk
1 teaspoon vanilla extract

    Mix oats, flour and peanut butter in bowl. Combine sugar, butter, cocoa, milk, and vanilla in saucepan. Bring to a boil. Cook for 3 minutes. Remove from heat. Add oats mixture; mix well. Drop by spoonfuls onto waxed paper. Let stand until cool. Yield: 3 dozen.

Karen Hill

OATMEAL COOKIES

1 1/4 cups margarine
1/2 cup sugar
3/4 cup packed brown
  sugar
1 egg
1 teaspoon vanilla extract

1 1/2 cups flour
1 teaspoon soda
1 teaspoon salt
1 teaspoon cinnamon
1/4 teaspoon nutmeg
3 cups oats

    Cream margarine, sugar and brown sugar in mixer bowl until light and fluffy. Beat in egg and vanilla. Add mixture of flour, soda, salt and spices; mix well. Stir in oats. Drop by rounded teaspoonfuls onto ungreased cookie sheet. Bake at 375 degrees for 8 to 9 minutes for chewy cookies and for 10 to 11 minutes for crisp cookies. Cool on cookie sheet for 1 minute. Remove to wire rack to cool completely. Store in airtight container. Yield: 4 1/2 dozen.

Cletus and Mildred Bittel

★ Spread drop cookie batter in greased baking pan, bake and cut into bars — it is quicker.

COCONUT OATMEAL COOKIES

1 cup sifted flour
1/2 teaspoon baking
  powder
1/2 teaspoon soda
1/2 teaspoon salt
1/2 cup butter, softened
1/2 cup packed brown
  sugar

1/2 cup sugar
1 egg
1 teaspoon vanilla extract
1/2 cup quick-cooking oats
1 cup coconut
1 cup chocolate chips
Coconut

Sift flour, baking powder, soda and salt into bowl. Cream butter in mixer bowl until light. Add brown sugar and sugar gradually, beating until fluffy. Beat in egg and vanilla. Add dry ingredients 1/4 at a time, mixing well after each addition. Mix in oats, 1 cup coconut and chocolate chips. Drop by teaspoonfuls onto ungreased cookie sheet. Sprinkle with additional coconut. Bake at 375 degrees for 9 to 12 minutes or until golden brown. Remove to wire rack to cool. Yield: 4 dozen.

Patricia J. Tudor

CHOCOLATE CHIP OATMEAL COOKIES

1 cup shortening
1 1/2 cups sugar
2 eggs
1 teaspoon vanilla extract
1 teaspoon soda
1 teaspoon hot water

1 1/2 cups sifted flour
1 teaspoon salt
2 to 2 1/2 cups oats
1 cup chocolate chips
1 cup chopped nuts

Cream shortening and sugar in mixer bowl until light and fluffy. Beat in eggs 1 at a time. Mix in vanilla and soda dissolved in hot water. Add flour and salt; mix well. Stir in oats, chocolate chips and nuts. Drop by spoonfuls onto cookie sheet. Bake at 350 degrees for 15 minutes. Remove to wire rack to cool.
Yield: 4 dozen.

Ladonna Darnell

504

OATMEAL DROP COOKIES

1 cup shortening
1 cup sugar
1 cup packed brown sugar
2 eggs
1 teaspoon vanilla extract
2 cups flour
1 teaspoon soda
1/2 teaspoon baking powder
2 cups quick-cooking oats
2 cups Wheaties
1 cup coconut or chopped nuts

Cream shortening, sugar and brown sugar in bowl until light and fluffy. Beat in eggs. Add vanilla; mix well. Combine flour, soda, baking powder, oats, Wheaties and coconut in large bowl; mix well. Add to creamed mixture; mix well. Drop by teaspoonfuls onto lightly greased cookie sheet. Bake at 350 degrees for 15 minutes. Remove to wire rack to cool. Yield: 4 to 5 dozen.

Cora A. Hoover

OATMEAL RAISIN COOKIES

1 cup sifted whole wheat flour
1/2 teaspoon soda
1/2 teaspoon salt
1/4 teaspoon cinnamon
1/8 teaspoon cloves
1/8 teaspoon nutmeg
1 1/2 cups quick-cooking oats
1/4 cup chopped dates
2 egg whites, slightly beaten
1/2 cup packed brown sugar
1/3 cup oil
1/2 cup skim milk
1 teaspoon vanilla extract
1 cup raisins

Sift flour, soda, salt, cinnamon, cloves and nutmeg into large bowl. Stir in oats. Combine dates, egg whites, brown sugar, oil, milk, vanilla and raisins in bowl; mix well. Add to flour mixture; mix well. Drop by teaspoonfuls onto oiled cookie sheet. Bake at 375 degrees for 15 minutes. Shorter baking time results in a chewy cookie; longer baking time results in a crisp cookie. Remove to wire rack to cool. Yield: 2 dozen.

Betty Jo Daniel

NO-BAKE OATMEAL COOKIES

2 cups sugar
1/2 cup milk
1/4 cup Nestles Quik
1/2 teaspoon vanilla extract
6 tablespoons butter, softened
1/4 cup peanut butter
1 1/2 cups oats

Combine sugar, milk and Nestles Quik in large saucepan; mix well. Bring to a boil, stirring constantly. Cook for 2 to 3 minutes, stirring constantly. Remove from heat. Add vanilla, butter, peanut butter and oats; mix well. Drop by spoonfuls onto waxed paper. Let stand until cool. Yield: 1 1/2 dozen.

Jeannie Wynn

SOUTHERN OATMEAL COOKIES

1 cup shortening
1 cup sugar
2 eggs
2 cups flour
2 cups quick-cooking oats
Pinch of salt
1 teaspoon (scant) soda
1 tablespoon buttermilk
1 teaspoon vanilla extract
1 cup raisins
1 cup chopped nuts

Cream shortening and sugar in bowl until light and fluffy. Add eggs; mix well. Combine flour, oats, salt and soda in bowl; mix well. Add to creamed mixture; mix well. Stir in buttermilk and vanilla. Fold in raisins and nuts. Drop by teaspoonfuls onto cookie sheet. Bake at 350 degrees for 10 to 12 minutes. Remove to wire rack to cool. Yield: 4 to 5 dozen.

Della Mundy

OATMEAL WHITE CHIPPERS

1 cup flour
1 teaspoon soda
3/4 cup margarine, softened
1/2 cup sugar
1/2 cup packed brown sugar
1 egg
2 1/2 cups oats
1 1/2 cups coarsely chopped white chocolate
1/2 cup finely chopped almonds

Combine flour and soda in small bowl; mix well. Beat margarine in large mixer bowl at medium speed for 30 seconds. Add sugar and brown sugar. Beat until fluffy. Add egg; beat well.

Add flour mixture; mix well. Stir in oats, chocolate and almonds. Drop by rounded tablespoonfuls 3 inches apart onto cookie sheet. Flatten slightly. Bake at 375 degrees for 10 minutes or until light brown. Cool on cookie sheet for 1 minute. Remove to wire rack to cool. Yield: 3 dozen.

Patricia J. Tudor

ORANGE NO-BAKE COOKIES

12 ounces confectioners'
   sugar
1 16-ounce package
   vanilla wafers, crumbled
1/2 cup butter, softened

1 cup chopped nuts
1 6-ounce can frozen
   orange juice concentrate,
   thawed
Coconut

Combine confectioners' sugar, vanilla wafers, butter, nuts and orange juice in bowl; mix well. Shape into balls. Roll in coconut. Yield: 3 dozen.

Wanda Wiegand

PAINTED COOKIES

1/2 cup shortening
1/2 cup margarine, softened
1 1/2 cups sugar
1 egg
1 tablespoon vanilla
   extract
3 cups flour

1/2 teaspoon salt
1 teaspoon baking powder
1 teaspoon cinnamon
2 egg yolks
2 teaspoons water
Food coloring

Cream shortening and margarine in bowl until light. Beat in sugar until fluffy. Add egg and vanilla; beat well. Sift flour, salt, baking powder and cinnamon into large bowl; mix well. Fold into creamed mixture. Roll 1/8-inch thick on floured surface; cut with cookie cutters. Mix eggs yolks and water in bowl. Pour into several dishes. Tint with food coloring. Paint cookies as desired. Place on cookie sheet. Bake at 375 degrees for 10 minutes. Remove to wire rack to cool. Yield: 3 dozen.

Jean Geary

PEANUT BLOSSOMS

1¾ cups sifted flour
1 teaspoon soda
½ teaspoon salt
½ cup shortening
½ cup peanut butter
½ cup sugar

½ cup packed brown
   sugar
1 egg
2 tablespoons milk
1 teaspoon vanilla extract
36 milk chocolate kisses

Sift flour, soda and salt into bowl. Cream shortening and peanut butter in mixer bowl until light and fluffy. Add sugars gradually; mixing well. Beat in egg, milk and vanilla. Add flour mixture; mix well. Shape by teaspoonfuls into balls. Roll in additional sugar; place on cookie sheet. Bake at 375 degrees for 8 minutes. Press chocolate kiss into each cookie. Bake 2 to 5 minutes longer. Remove to wire rack to cool. Yield: 2 dozen.

Martha Hooper, Grace Murphy

PEANUT COOKIES

2 cups flour
Pinch of salt
1 teaspoon baking powder
1 cup chopped peanuts
½ cup sugar

2 tablespoons butter,
   softened
1 egg
½ cup milk
Oil for frying

Sift first 3 ingredients into bowl. Add peanuts and sugar; mix well. Add butter; mix well. Add egg and milk; mix well. Roll ¼-inch thick on floured surface. Cut into bars. Fry in hot oil in skillet until golden brown. Drain. Yield: 3 dozen.

Freddie Clinton

PEANUT BUTTER COOKIES

1 cup peanut butter
1 cup sugar

1 egg

Combine peanut butter, sugar and egg in bowl; mix well. Shape into 1-inch balls. Place on cookie sheet. Bake at 350 degrees for 8 to 10 minutes. Remove to wire rack to cool. Yield: 1½ dozen.

Nancy Winstead

PEANUT BUTTER BALLS

1/2 cup melted butter
1 pound confectioners'
  sugar
1 18-ounce jar extra
  crunchy peanut butter

1 teaspoon vanilla extract
2 cups crisp rice cereal
1 1/3 cups semisweet
  chocolate chips

Mix butter, confectioners' sugar and peanut butter in bowl. Stir in vanilla. Fold in cereal. Shape into 1-inch balls. Place on waxed paper. Chill for several minutes. Melt chocolate in double boiler. Dip balls in chocolate with toothpicks. Place on waxed paper to cool. Chill in refrigerator. May be rolled in additional confectioners' sugar. Yield: 3 to 4 dozen.

Naomi Simpson

PEANUT BUTTER CUPS

1 3/4 cups flour
1 1/4 cups packed brown
  sugar
1 tablespoon baking
  powder
1 teaspoon salt
1 cup milk

1/3 cup shortening
1/3 cup peanut butter
1 teaspoon vanilla extract
2 eggs
24 miniature milk
  chocolate covered peanut
  butter cups

Mix flour, brown sugar, baking powder, salt, milk, shortening, peanut butter, vanilla and eggs in large bowl at low speed until moistened. Beat for 2 minutes at medium speed. Fill paper-lined muffin cups 2/3 full. Remove paper from peanut butter cups. Press peanut butter cup into batter until top edge is even with batter. Bake at 350 degrees for 18 to 28 minutes or until peanut butter cups test done. Yield: 2 dozen.

Margaret Taylor

★ Try whole wheat flour in cookies for more body and nutrition — just use a bit less than all-purpose.

PEANUT BUTTER KISSES

1 cup peanut butter
1 cup shortening
1 cup packed light brown
 sugar
1 cup sugar
1/4 cup milk
2 teaspoons vanilla extract

2 eggs
31/2 cups flour
2 teaspoons soda
1 teaspoon salt
1/3 cup sugar
1 11-ounce package
 Hershey's kisses

Combine peanut butter, shortening, brown sugar and 1 cup sugar in large bowl; mix well. Stir in milk, vanilla and eggs. Combine flour, soda and salt in bowl; mix well. Add to peanut butter mixture; mix well. Shape into 1-inch balls; roll in remaining 1/3 cup sugar. Place on ungreased cookie sheet. Bake at 375 degrees for 8 minutes. Press chocolate kiss into each cookie. Bake for 3 minutes longer. Remove to wire rack to cool. Yield: 6 to 7 dozen.

Patricia J. Tudor

RITZ PEANUT BUTTER COOKIES

1 package vanilla almond
 bark

Ritz Crackers
Peanut butter

Melt almond bark in saucepan over medium heat, stirring constantly. Spread half of crackers with peanut butter. Top with remaining crackers. Dip peanut butter crackers in melted almond bark to coat. Place on waxed paper. Let stand until cooled and firm. Yield: 3 dozen.

Dorothy Luckett

PECAN CRUNCHERS

2 tablespoons margarine,
 softened
1/2 cup packed brown sugar
1 cup chopped pecans
1/2 cup margarine, softened
11/4 cups packed brown
 sugar

2 cups flour
1/2 teaspoon baking
 powder
1 egg
1 teaspoon rum extract
1/2 teaspoon vanilla extract

Mix 2 tablespoons margarine, 1/2 cup brown sugar and pecans in bowl. Combine remaining 1/2 cup margarine, remaining 1 1/4 cups brown sugar, flour, baking powder, egg, rum extract and vanilla in large bowl; mix well. Stir in pecan mixture. Shape by teaspoonfuls into balls. Place on cookie sheet. Flatten with glass dipped in flour. Bake at 375 degrees for 10 to 12 minutes. Remove to wire rack to cool. Yield: 4 dozen.

Jean Geary

BUTTER PECAN COOKIES

2 cups flour
1/4 teaspoon salt
1 cup butter, softened
1 1/2 teaspoons vanilla
  extract
1/2 teaspoon almond extract
1 cup confectioners' sugar
2 egg yolks
1 tablespoon cream
1/2 cup pecan halves

Sift flour and salt into bowl. Cream butter, vanilla and almond extract in mixer bowl until light. Add confectioners' sugar gradually, creaming until fluffy. Add flour mixture 1/4 at a time, mixing well after each addition. Shape into 1-inch balls. Place 2 inches apart on cookie sheet. Flatten with spoon. Mix egg yolks and cream in small bowl. Brush tops of cookies with egg mixture. Press pecan half into center of each cookie. Bake at 400 degrees for 10 to 12 minutes or until light brown. Remove to wire rack to cool. Yield: 3 1/2 dozen.

Dana Fendley

SOUTHERN PECAN BALLS

1 cup butter, softened
1 cup confectioners' sugar
2 1/4 cups flour
2 teaspoons vanilla extract
2 cups chopped pecans
Confectioners' sugar

Cream butter and confectioners' sugar in bowl until light and fluffy. Add flour; mix well. Stir in vanilla and pecans. Shape into 1-inch balls. Place on cookie sheets. Bake at 300 degrees for 30 minutes. Roll warm cookies in additional confectioners' sugar. Store in airtight container. Yield: 5 dozen.

Patricia J. Tudor

PECAN COOKIES

1 cup butter
2 cups sifted flour
1/2 teaspoon salt
2 cups packed brown
  sugar
4 eggs

2 teaspoons baking
  powder
1 cup flaked coconut
1 cup chopped pecans
Confectioners' sugar
  frosting

Mix butter, flour and salt in bowl until crumbly. Press into 9x13-inch baking dish. Bake at 375 degrees for 10 minutes oruntil lightly browned. Combine brown sugar, eggs, baking powder, coconut and pecans in bowl; mix well. Spread over baked layer. Bake for 15 minutes longer. Spread confectioners' sugar frosting over top. Cut into bars. Yield: 54 bars.

Yocianne Everett

PIZZA COOKIE

1/2 cup margarine, softened
3/4 cup packed brown
  sugar
1 egg
1 teaspoon vanilla extract
3/4 cup flour
Pinch of salt
1/2 teaspoon baking
  powder

1/2 teaspoon soda
1 cup oats
1/2 cup coconut
1 cup semisweet
  chocolate chips
1/2 cup chopped walnuts
1/2 cup coconut
1/2 cup "M&M's" Chocolate
  Candies

Cream margarine, brown sugar, egg and vanilla in mixer bowl until light and fluffy. Add flour, salt, baking powder, soda and oats; mix well. Stir in 1/2 cup coconut. Spread dough in greased 12-inch pizza pan. Sprinkle with chocolate chips, walnuts, remaining 1/2 cup coconut and chocolate candies. Bake at 350 degrees for 13 to 15 minutes or until golden brown. Cool. Cut into wedges. Yield: 12 servings.

Jean Geary

PRALINE STRIPS

24 graham crackers
1 cup butter

1 cup packed brown sugar
1 cup chopped pecans

Place crackers in 9x13-inch baking dish. Combine butter and brown sugar in saucepan. Bring to a boil. Reduce heat. Cook for 2 minutes, stirring constantly. Stir in pecans. Spoon over cracker layer. Bake at 400 degrees for 6 to 7 minutes. Cut into strips while still warm. May soften praline strips in oven for several seconds if they harden. Yield: 2 dozen.

Dorothy O'Neal

PUMPKIN COOKIES

2 cups sugar
2 cups shortening
1   16-ounce can pumpkin
2 eggs
2 teaspoons vanilla extract
4 cups flour
2 teaspoons baking
** powder**

2 teaspoons soda
1 teaspoon salt
2 teaspoons cinnamon
1 teaspoon nutmeg
1/2 teaspoon allspice
2 cups raisins
1 cup chopped nuts
Cream cheese frosting

Combine sugar, shortening, pumpkin, eggs, vanilla, flour, baking powder, soda, salt, cinnamon, nutmeg, allspice, raisins and nuts in bowl; mix well. Drop by teaspoonfuls onto cookie sheet. Bake at 350 degrees for 10 to 15 minutes. Remove to wire rack to cool. Store in airtight container. Spread cream cheese frosting over cookies. Yield: 4 dozen.

Margaret Taylor

★ Substitute broken or chopped candy bars for chocolate chips in drop or bar cookies.

RAISIN BRAN COOKIES

2 cups shortening
2 cups sugar
4 eggs
4 cups flour
1 teaspoon salt

1/2 teaspoon soda
4 cups Raisin Bran
1 to 2 cups chopped nuts
2 tablespoons grated
  orange rind

Cream shortening and sugar in mixer bowl until light and fluffy. Add eggs; mix well. Sift flour, salt and soda into bowl. Add to creamed mixture. Fold in Raisin Bran, nuts and orange rind. Drop by teaspoonfuls onto cookie sheet. Bake at 325 degrees for 10 to 12 minutes or until brown. Remove to wire rack to cool. May substitute 1 cup butter for 1 cup of shortening.
Yield: 4 dozen.

Chrissy Robey

SAND TARTS

1 cup butter, softened
6 tablespoons
  confectioners' sugar

2 cups flour
1 teaspoon vanilla extract
1 1/2 cups crushed pecans

Cream butter and confectioners' sugar in mixer bowl until light and fluffy. Add flour and vanilla; mix well. Stir in pecans. Shape into 1-inch balls. Place on cookie sheet. Bake at 350 degrees for 15 minutes. Remove to wire rack to cool. Roll in additional confectioners' sugar. Yield: 2 dozen.

Patsy Akers

MRS. PEDDY'S SNICKERDOODLES

1/2 cup butter, softened
1/2 cup shortening
1 1/2 cups sugar
2 eggs
2 3/4 cups sifted flour
1 teaspoon soda

2 teaspoons cream of
  tartar
1/2 teaspoon salt
2 tablespoons sugar
2 teaspoons cinnamon

Cream butter, shortening and sugar in mixer bowl until light and fluffy. Add eggs; mix well. Sift flour, soda, cream of tartar and salt in bowl. Add to creamed mixture; mix well. Chill in refrigerator.

Combine remaining 2 tablespoons sugar and cinnamon in small bowl. Shape into 1-inch balls. Roll in cinnamon-sugar. Place 2 inches apart on cookie sheet. Bake at 400 degrees for 8 to 10 minutes or until light brown but still soft. Remove to wire rack to cool. Yield: 5 dozen.

Henry Bennett, Marty Hill

SPRINGERLES

4 eggs
1 pound confectioners'
  sugar, sifted
4 cups flour

1/2 teaspoon baking
  powder
1/2 teaspoon (or less) anise
  oil

Beat eggs in mixer bowl for 10 minutes until yellow and thick. Add confectioners' sugar gradually, beating well. Sift flour and baking powder into bowl. Fold into egg mixture. Add anise oil; mix well. Roll 1/2 inch thick on lightly floured surface. Roll with springerle rolling pin or press springerle mold onto dough. Cut into squares. Let stand for 12 to 14 hours to dry. Place on lightly greased cookie sheet. Bake at 300 degrees for 20 minutes or until faint yellow but not brown. Remove to wire rack to cool. Store in airtight container. Yield: 4 to 5 dozen.

Sally Trent

SPRITZ COOKIES

1 cup shortening
3/4 cup sugar
1 egg, beaten
1 teaspoon almond extract

2 3/4 cups cake flour
1/4 teaspoon salt
1/2 teaspoon baking
  powder

Cream shortening and sugar in mixer bowl until light and fluffy. Add egg and almond extract; mix well. Sift flour, salt and baking powder into bowl. Fold into creamed mixture. Spoon dough into cookie press. Press onto cookie sheet. Bake at 375 degrees for 12 to 15 minutes. Remove to wire rack to cool. Yield: 4 dozen.

Pearl Hodges

SUGAR COOKIES

1 cup margarine, softened
1 cup sugar
1 egg
1 tablespoon vanilla
 extract
2¹/₂ cups flour
2 teaspoons baking
 powder
¹/₄ teaspoon soda
Pinch of salt

Cream margarine and sugar in mixer bowl until light and fluffy. Add egg and vanilla; mix well. Sift flour, baking powder, soda and salt in bowl. Add to creamed mixture; mix well. Chill for 1 hour. Drop by teaspoonfuls onto greased cookie sheet. Bake at 350 degrees for 10 to 12 minutes. Sprinkle with additional sugar. Remove to wire rack to cool. Yield: 2 to 3 dozen.

Chrissy Robey

DELICIOUS SUGAR COOKIES

1 cup margarine, softened
1 cup oil
1 cup sugar
1 cup confectioners' sugar
2 eggs, well beaten
1 teaspoon vanilla extract
4 cups flour
1 teaspoon salt
1 teaspoon soda
1 teaspoon cream of tartar

Mix margarine, oil, sugar and confectioners' sugar in large bowl. Add eggs and vanilla; mix well. Sift flour, salt, soda and cream of tartar in bowl; mix well. Add to sugar mixture; mix well. Shape by teaspoonfuls into balls. Roll in additional sugar. Place on lightly greased cookie sheet. Flatten with glass dipped in sugar. Bake at 350 degrees for 6 to 8 minutes. Remove to wire rack to cool. Dough may be stored in refrigerator if desired. Yield: 4 dozen.

Annette W. Becker, Jean Freshley,
Peggy Noel

SUGAR AND PECAN COOKIES

¼ cup butter, softened
¼ cup shortening
½ cup sugar
1 egg
¼ teaspoon vanilla extract

1¼ cups flour
¼ teaspoon soda
Dash of salt
¼ cup finely chopped
  pecans

Beat butter and shortening in mixer bowl for 30 seconds. Add sugar; beat until fluffy. Add egg and vanilla, beat well. Combine flour, soda and salt in bowl; mix well. Add to butter mixture gradually; mix well. Stir in pecans. Chill, covered, in refrigerator. Divide dough in half. Roll each half ⅛-inch thick on lightly floured surface. Cut into ten 3-inch circles. Place on cookie sheet. Repeat with remaining dough. Bake at 375 degrees for 8 to 10 minutes. Remove to wire rack to cool. Yield: 20 cookies.

Shirley Smith

"S" COOKIES

1 cup butter, softened
1 cup sugar
4 cups flour
Juice of ½ lemon

5 egg yolks
1 whole egg
Grated rind of ½ lemon

Cream butter and sugar in mixer bowl until light and fluffy. Add flour and lemon juice; mix well. Add egg yolks, egg and lemon rind; mix well. Roll small portions into pencil-sized ropes. Cut into 3-inch pieces. Shape into "S" shapes. Place on cookie sheet. Bake at 350 degrees for 12 minutes. Cool on wire rack. This is a Christmas cookie. Yield: 6 dozen.

Pearl Hodges

★ Try baking your chocolate brownies or other cookie dough in your waffle iron for 3 minutes, they are crisp and crunchy.

FUDGE CIRCLES

1 1/2 cups flour
1/2 cup unsweetened
  baking cocoa
1/4 teaspoon soda
1/4 teaspoon baking powder

1/2 cup butter, softened
1 cup sugar
1 egg
1 teaspoon vanilla extract

Sift flour, cocoa, soda and baking powder into bowl. Beat butter in mixer bowl for 30 seconds. Add sugar; beat until fluffy. Add egg and vanilla; beat well. Add flour mixture gradually, mixing well. Roll 1/8-inch thick on lightly floured surface. Cut dough into 3-inch circles. Place on cookie sheet. Bake at 375 degrees for 8 minutes. Remove to wire rack to cool.
Yield: 2 1/2 dozen.

Shirley Smith

TEA FINGERS

1/2 cup butter, softened
5 tablespoons
  confectioners' sugar
2 cups flour

2 tablespoons water
2 teaspoons vanilla extract
1 cup finely chopped
  pecans

Cream butter and confectioners' sugar in mixer bowl until light and fluffy. Cut in flour until crumbly. Add water, vanilla and pecans; mix well. Add additional water if necessary. Roll into finger shapes. Place on cookie sheet. Bake at 350 degrees for 20 to 25 minutes or until light brown. Remove to wire rack to cool. Roll in additional confectioners' sugar. Yield: 2 dozen.

Gwen Mills

THUMBPRINT COOKIES

1/2 cup sugar
1/2 cup butter, softened
1 teaspoon vanilla extract
2 eggs
21/2 cups sifted flour

2 teaspoons baking powder
1/2 teaspoon salt
1 egg white, slightly beaten
1 cup finely chopped nuts
Jelly

Cream sugar and butter in mixer bowl until light and fluffy. Add vanilla and eggs; beat well. Combine flour, baking powder and salt in bowl; mix well. Add to creamed mixture; mix well. Shape into 1-inch balls. Dip in egg white; roll in nuts to coat. Place on lightly greased cookie sheet. Make indentation in each cookie with thumb. Bake at 375 degrees for 12 minutes. Remove to wire rack to cool. Fill indentations with jelly. Yield: 2 to 3 dozen.

Cindy Jones

WORLD'S BEST COOKIES

1 cup butter, softened
1 cup sugar
1 cup packed brown sugar
1 egg, beaten
1 cup oil
1 cup oats

1 cup crushed cornflakes
1/2 cup coconut
1/2 cup chopped nuts
31/2 cups flour
1 teaspoon vanilla extract

Cream butter, sugar and brown sugar in mixer bowl until light and fluffy. Add egg, oil, oats, cornflakes, coconut and nuts; mix well. Stir in flour and vanilla. Shape by teaspoonfuls into balls. Place on cookie sheet. Flatten with glass. Bake at 325 degrees for 8 to 12 minutes. Remove to wire rack to cool. Yield: 8 dozen.

Bernidea Fort

★ Line your cookie sheets with foil. There will be no greasing required between batches.

PIES

APPLE PIE WITH OAT TOPPING

5 cups sliced peeled
  apples
1 baked 9-inch deep-dish
  pie shell

1/2 cup margarine
1/2 cup sugar
1/2 cup oats

Layer apples in pie shell. Combine margarine, sugar and oats in bowl; mix until crumbly. Sprinkle over apples. Bake at 350 degrees for 1 hour. Yield: 8 servings.

Patsy Ford

APPLE CRUMB PIE

5 to 7 tart apples, peeled,
  sliced
1 unbaked 9-inch pie shell
1/2 cup sugar

1 teaspoon cinnamon
1/2 cup sugar
3/4 cup flour
1/3 cup butter

Arrange apples in pie shell. Sprinkle mixture of 1/2 cup sugar and cinnamon over apples. Combine remaining 1/2 cup sugar and flour in bowl. Cut in butter until crumbly. Sprinkle crumb mixture over apples. Bake at 400 degrees for 40 minutes or until apples are tender. Granny Smith apples are very good for this pie. Yield: 6 servings.

Ella (Babe) Young

GRATED APPLE PIE

2 cups grated apples
1 cup sugar
2 tablespoons flour
1 teaspoon cinnamon

1/2 cup melted margarine
1 egg, beaten
1 unbaked 9-inch pie shell

Combine apples, sugar, flour, cinnamon, margarine and egg in bowl; mix well. Pour into pie shell. Bake at 350 degrees for 1 hour. Top with whipped cream or ice cream.
Yield: 6 servings.

Jenny Corp

MOCK APPLE PIE

1½ cups sugar
2 teaspoons cream of
  tartar
2 cups water
28 Ritz crackers

1 recipe 2-crust pie pastry
¼ cup margarine
1½ tablespoons lemon
  juice
Cinnamon to taste

Combine sugar and cream of tartar in saucepan; mix well. Stir in water. Bring to a boil; remove from heat. Add crackers; do not stir. Bring to a boil. Pour mixture into pastry-lined 9-inch pie plate. Dot with margarine. Drizzle lemon juice over filling. Sprinkle with cinnamon. Cut remaining pastry into strips; arrange lattice-fashion on pie. Seal ends; flute edges. Bake at 425 degrees until brown. This pie will be thin and watery until baked. Yield: 8 servings.

Norma Hamilton

BANANA SPLIT PIES

2 cups confectioners'
  sugar
½ cup butter, softened
1 cup sour cream
8 ounces cream cheese,
  softened
2 9-inch graham cracker
  pie shells

1 16-ounce can crushed
  pineapple, drained
4 bananas, sliced
½ cup chopped pecans
16 ounces whipped
  topping

Combine confectioners' sugar, butter, sour cream and cream cheese in bowl; mix until smooth. Pour mixture into pie shells. Cover with pineapple, bananas and pecans. Spread whipped topping over top. Sprinkle with additional chopped pecans. Chill until firm. Yield: 12 servings.

Shirley Smith

BLACKBERRY JAM PIE

4 eggs
1 cup sugar
1/2 cup melted butter
1 cup blackberry jam

2 tablespoons flour
1 tablespoon cornmeal
1 teaspoon lemon extract
1 unbaked 9-inch pie shell

Combine eggs, sugar, butter and jam in bowl; mix well. Add mixture of flour and cornmeal; mix well. Stir in lemon extract. Pour into pie shell. Bake at 350 degrees for 45 minutes. Serve with whipped cream. Yield: 8 servings.

Sandi Tipton Clark

BROWN SUGAR PIE

2 cups packed brown
  sugar
1/4 cup (heaping) flour
4 egg yolks
2 tablespoons butter
1 teaspoon vanilla extract
2 cups boiling water

1 baked 9-inch graham
  cracker pie shell
4 egg whites
1/2 teaspoon vanilla extract
1/4 teaspoon cream of
  tartar
6 tablespoons sugar

Combine brown sugar and flour in saucepan. Add egg yolks, butter and vanilla; mix well. Stir in boiling water gradually. Cook over medium heat until thickened, stirring constantly. Pour into pie shell. Beat egg whites, vanilla and cream of tartar in mixer bowl until soft peaks form. Add 6 tablespoons sugar gradually, beating until stiff peaks form. Spread over filling, sealing to edge. Bake at 350 degrees until brown. Yield: 8 servings.

Ethel C. Thompson

★ For a crisp top crust, brush with milk and sprinkle with
  a little sugar. Bake as usual.

BUTTERMILK PIE

2 cups sugar
1 tablespoon self-rising
  flour
1/2 cup melted butter

4 eggs
2/3 cup buttermilk
1 unbaked 9-inch deep-
  dish pie shell

Combine sugar, flour and butter in bowl; mix well. Add eggs 1 at a time, beating well after each addition. Add buttermilk; mix well. Pour into pie shell. Bake at 350 degrees for 45 minutes. Yield: 8 servings.

Peggy Posante

BUTTERSCOTCH PIE

2 tablespoons (heaping)
  cornstarch
1 cup packed light brown
  sugar
Dash of salt
1 small can evaporated
  milk
1 cup milk

4 egg yolks, beaten
1/2 cup butter, softened
1 teaspoon vanilla extract
1 baked 9-inch pie shell
4 egg whites
1/4 cup sugar
1/8 teaspoon cream of
  tartar

Combine cornstarch, brown sugar and salt in double boiler. Scald evaporated milk with milk in saucepan. Stir 1/4 cup hot milk into beaten egg yolks; stir egg yolks into hot milk. Pour into brown sugar mixture; mix well. Add butter. Cook until thickened, stirring constantly; remove from heat. Stir in vanilla. Pour into pie shell. Beat egg whites in mixer bowl until soft peaks form. Add sugar and cream of tartar gradually, beating constantly until stiff peaks form. Spread over filling, sealing to edge. Bake at 350 degrees until brown. Yield: 6 servings.

Ladonna Darnell

JOHN Y. BROWN PIE

1 cup sugar
1/2 cup flour
1/2 cup melted butter
2 eggs, slightly beaten

1 cup pecan pieces
1 cup butterscotch chips
1 teaspoon vanilla extract
1 unbaked 9-inch pie shell

Combine sugar and flour in bowl. Blend in butter. Stir in eggs, pecans, butterscotch chips and vanilla. Pour into pie shell. Bake at 325 degrees for 1 hour or until golden brown. Pie will set as it cools. Yield: 8 servings.

Ladonna Darnell

CHEESECAKE PIE

8 ounces cream cheese, softened
1/3 cup sugar
2 teaspoons vanilla extract

8 ounces whipped topping
9-inch graham cracker pie shell
Strawberries

Beat cream cheese, sugar and vanilla in mixer bowl until smooth. Fold in whipped topping gently. Spoon into pie shell. Chill for 4 hours or until set. Arrange strawberries over filling just before serving. Yield: 8 servings.

JoAnn Lamb

CHERRY CREAM PIES

2 envelopes whipped topping mix
1 cup cold milk
1 teaspoon vanilla extract
Pinch of salt
8 ounces cream cheese

2 cups confectioners' sugar
2 tablespoons milk
2 9-inch graham cracker pie shells
1 can cherry pie filling

Combine topping mix, 1 cup milk, vanilla and salt in mixer bowl; beat until soft peaks form. Blend softened cream cheese, confectioners' sugar and 2 tablespoons milk in bowl until creamy. Fold gently into whipped topping mixture. Pour into pie shells. Spoon cherry pie filling into center of cream cheese filling. Yield: 12 servings.

Phyllis L. Allen

CHERRY ICEBOX PIE

1 3-ounce package
   cherry gelatin
1 cup boiling water
1 pint vanilla ice cream

1 can Michigan Bing
   cherries, drained
1 baked pie shell

Dissolve gelatin in boiling water in bowl; Chill until partially set. Beat ice cream in mixer bowl until soft. Add gelatin; beat well. Fold in cherries. Spoon into pie shell. Chill until serving time. Yield: 6 servings.

Dot Berry

FAST CHERRY PIE

1 can cherry pie filling
1 tablespoon butter
3/4 cup flour
1/2 cup sugar

2 teaspoons baking
   powder
1/2 cup milk

Pour pie filling into buttered 2-quart baking dish. Combine flour, sugar and baking powder in bowl; mix well. Stir in milk. Pour batter over pie filling. Bake at 350 degrees for 20 minutes or until crust is brown. May substitute other cooked fruits or pie fillings for cherry. Yield: 8 servings.

Evalena England

TV CHERRY PIE

1 can sweetened
   condensed milk
Juice of 2 lemons
1 can pie cherries, well-
   drained

8 ounces whipping cream,
   whipped
1 cup chopped pecans
1 9-inch graham cracker
   pie shell

Combine sweetened condensed milk and lemon juice in bowl; blend well. Add cherries. Fold in whipped cream and pecans gently. Pour into pie shell. Chill for 6 to 8 hours. May add 2 beaten egg yolks and/or 1 small container whipped topping for whipped cream and substitute Bing cherries for pie cherries. Yield: 8 servings.

Laverne Hollingsworth, Betty Schweinhart

CHESS PIE

1½ cups sugar
1 teaspoon white vinegar
1 tablespoon self-rising
  cornmeal
½ cup melted butter

3 eggs
¼ teaspoon vanilla extract
⅓ teaspoon nutmeg
1 unbaked 9-inch deep-
  dish pie shell

Combine sugar, vinegar, cornmeal, butter, eggs, vanilla and nutmeg in bowl; stir just until mixed. Pour into pie shell. Bake at 350 degrees for 50 minutes. Yield: 8 servings.

Molly Hisel, Peggy Posante

MRS. HALE'S CHESS PIES

2 cups sugar
½ cup melted butter
6 egg yolks, beaten
1 large can evaporated
  milk

1 tablespoon flour
1 tablespoon cornmeal
1 tablespoon vanilla
  extract
2 unbaked 9-inch pie shells

Cream sugar and butter in mixer bowl until light. Add egg yolks; beat until fluffy. Add evaporated milk; beat until sugar is dissolved. Add flour, cornmeal and vanilla; mix well. Pour into pie shells. Bake at 350 degrees for 45 minutes. May top with meringue if desired. Mrs. Hale was noted for her delicious meals, served family-style at her hotel/restaurant in Smithland, Kentucky. Yield: 12 servings.

Della Mundy

CHOCOLATE PIE

1 cup sugar
3 tablespoons baking
  cocoa
3 tablespoons flour
2 egg yolks

2 cups milk
2 tablespoons margarine
1 teaspoon vanilla extract
1 baked 9-inch pie shell
1 recipe meringue

Combine sugar, cocoa and flour in saucepan. Beat egg yolks in small bowl; stir into cocoa mixture. Add milk and margarine; mix well. Cook over medium heat until thickened, stirring constantly; remove from heat. Add vanilla. Pour into pie shell. Top with meringue, sealing to edge. Bake at 350 degrees until brown. Yield: 6 servings.

Patsy Ford

FRENCH MINT PIE

1¼ cups vanilla wafer
  crumbs
2 tablespoons sugar
⅓ cup melted margarine
1½ cups sifted
  confectioners' sugar
½ cup margarine, softened

2 ounces unsweetened
  chocolate, melted
2 eggs, well beaten
½ teaspoon vanilla extract
6 drops of oil of
  peppermint

Combine crumbs, 2 tablespoons sugar and ⅓ cup margarine in bowl; mix well. Press firmly over bottom and side of 8-inch pie plate. Bake at 350 degrees for 10 minutes. Cool. Cream confectioners' sugar and margarine in mixer bowl until light and fluffy. Add chocolate, eggs, vanilla and oil of peppermint; beat until light in color. Pour into pie shell. Chill overnight. Garnish with whipped cream. Yield: 6 servings.

Gwen Mills

FUDGE BROWNIE NUT PIE

1 14-ounce can
  sweetened condensed
  milk
¼ cup margarine
½ cup baking cocoa
3 eggs, beaten

3 tablespoons flour
1 teaspoon vanilla extract
1½ cups chopped pecans
1 unbaked 9-inch pie shell
Whipped cream
¼ cup chopped pecans

Combine condensed milk, margarine and cocoa in saucepan. Cook over low heat until margarine melts, stirring constantly; remove from heat. Add eggs, flour, vanilla and 1½ cups pecans; mix well. Pour into pie shell. Bake at 350 degrees for 50 minutes or until center is firm. Garnish with whipped cream and remaining ¼ cup pecans. Serve warm or cold. Yield: 10 servings.

Juyne Bushart

KENTUCKY FUDGE PIE

1 1/2 cups chopped pecans
1/2 cup butter, softened
1 cup sugar
2 eggs
1 tablespoon vanilla extract
2/3 cup sifted flour
1/2 cup baking cocoa
1/4 teaspoon salt

Spread pecans in shallow pan. Toast in 350-degree oven for 10 minutes, stirring frequently. Cool. Beat butter, sugar, eggs and vanilla in medium mixer bowl until light and fluffy. Add mixture of flour, cocoa and salt; mix until well blended. Stir in pecans. Spoon into greased 8-inch round pan. Bake at 350 degrees for 30 minutes or until toothpick inserted in center comes out with moist crumbs; do not overbake. Cool in pan on wire rack. Remove from pan; place on serving plate. Spoon ice cream onto center of pie. Cut into wedges. Yield: 8 servings.

Patricia J. Tudor

CHOCOLATE ICE CREAM PIE

1 cup evaporated milk
1 cup semisweet
  chocolate chips
1 cup miniature
  marshmallows
1/4 teaspoon salt
1 12-ounce package
  vanilla wafers
1/2 gallon vanilla ice cream

Combine evaporated milk, chocolate chips, marshmallows and salt in heavy saucepan. Cook over low heat until chips and marshmallows melt completely and mixture thickens, stirring constantly; remove from heat. Cool. Line 9-inch pie plate with vanilla wafers. Alternate layers of ice cream and chocolate mixture over wafers. Freeze for 3 to 5 hours before serving. Garnish with pecans. Yield: 10 servings.

Mary B. Mason

LUCY'S CHOCOLATE PIE

2/3 cup sugar
1 1/2 tablespoons baking
  cocoa
2 tablespoons flour
1 1/2 cups milk
3 egg yolks
1 1/2 tablespoons butter
1 baked 9-inch pie shell
1 recipe meringue

Combine sugar, cocoa and flour in saucepan. Add milk and egg yolks; mix well. Cook over medium heat until thickened, stirring constantly. Add butter; mix well. Pour into pie shell. Spread meringue over filling, sealing to edge. Bake at 350 degrees until light brown. Yield: 6 servings.

Chrissy Robey

THOROUGHBRED PIE

1 cup sugar
1/2 cup flour
2 eggs, beaten
1/2 to 1 cup melted
    margarine

1 teaspoon vanilla extract
1/2 to 1 cup chocolate chips
1 cup chopped pecans
1 unbaked 9-inch pie shell

Combine sugar and flour in mixing bowl. Add eggs and margarine; mix well. Stir in vanilla. Add chocolate chips and pecans. Pour into pie shell. Bake at 350 degrees for 30 to 50 minutes or until set. Serve warm. Yield: 8 servings.

Vickie Florence, Lloyd Hall

VICTORIAN WHITE CHOCOLATE PIE

1/2 cup flour
1/4 cup unsalted butter,
    softened
3 tablespoons light brown
    sugar
1/2 cup chopped pecans,
    toasted

3/4 cup unsalted butter,
    softened
3/4 cup sugar
3 ounces white chocolate,
    melted
1 egg
1 teaspoon vanilla extract

Combine flour, 1/4 cup butter, brown sugar and pecans in food processor container fitted with steel blade. Process until crumbly. Press evenly over bottom and side of 8-inch pie plate. Bake at 350 degrees for 10 minutes or until golden brown. Cool. Cream 3/4 cup butter and sugar in mixer bowl until light and fluffy. Add white chocolate; beat well. Add egg and vanilla; blend well. Pour into pie shell. Refrigerate for 4 hours or longer. Garnish with dollops of whipped cream. Yield: 8 servings.

Patricia J. Tudor

CALLY'S COCONUT CREAM PIE

3/4 cup sugar
3 tablespoons cornstarch
Dash of salt
2 cups milk
3 egg yolks, beaten
1 teaspoon vanilla extract

2 tablespoons butter
1 1/2 cups coconut
1 baked 9-inch pie shell
1 cup whipping cream
2 tablespoons
   confectioners' sugar

Combine sugar, cornstarch and salt in double boiler. Stir in milk. Cook over boiling water until thickened, stirring constantly. Cook for 15 minutes longer. Stir 1/2 cup hot mixture into egg yolks; stir egg yolks into hot mixture. Cook for 2 minutes; remove from heat. Stir in vanilla, butter and 1 1/2 cups coconut. Cool. Pour into pie shell. Whip cream with confectioners' sugar in mixer bowl. Spread over filling. Sprinkle with additional coconut.
Yield: 6 servings.

Alice Ritchey

COCONUT CREAM PIE

1 cup sugar
2 tablespoons flour
Dash of salt
1 small can evaporated
   milk
1 1/3 cups milk
2 egg yolks, beaten

1 teaspoon vanilla extract
1 cup flaked coconut
1 baked 8-inch pie shell
2 egg whites
1/2 teaspoon vanilla extract
1/4 teaspoon cream of tartar
1/4 cup sugar

Combine sugar, flour and salt in heavy saucepan. Stir in evaporated milk and milk. Blend in egg yolks and vanilla. Cook over low heat until mixture thickens, stirring constantly. Add 1 cup coconut. Cook for 3 minutes, stirring constantly. Spoon into pie shell. Beat egg whites, vanilla and cream of tartar in mixer bowl until soft peaks form. Add sugar gradually, beating until stiff glossy peaks form. Spread meringue over hot filling, sealing to edge. Sprinkle additional coconut over meringue. Bake at 350 degrees for 12 minutes or until golden. Cool. Dip knife into water before cutting meringue-topped pie. This is my mother's recipe. When I make it everyone says, "It's the best!" Yield: 6 servings.

Billie Y. Weatherington

COCONUT CRUNCH PIE

4 egg whites
1 cup sugar
1/2 cup coconut
1 cup graham cracker
  crumbs

Dash of salt
1 teaspoon vanilla extract
1/2 cup chopped pecans

Beat egg whites in mixer bowl until stiff peaks form. Fold in sugar, coconut, crumbs, salt, vanilla and pecans gently. Pour into greased 9-inch pie plate. Bake at 350 degrees for 30 minutes. Yield: 8 servings.

Dot Berry

COCONUT PIE WITH MILE-HIGH MERINGUE

3/4 cup sugar
3 tablespoons cornstarch
1/4 teaspoon salt
3 egg yolks, slightly beaten
2 cups milk
2 tablespoons butter
1 teaspoon vanilla extract

1 cup coconut
1 baked 9-inch pie shell
4 egg whites
1/2 teaspoon baking
  powder
1/2 cup sugar

Combine 3/4 cup sugar, cornstarch and salt in saucepan; mix well. Stir in egg yolks. Blend in milk. Cook over low heat until thickened, stirring constantly; remove from heat. Add butter and vanilla; mix well. Stir in coconut. Pour into pie shell. Beat egg whites with baking powder in mixer bowl until stiff peaks form. Add 1/2 cup sugar gradually, beating until very stiff. Spread over pie, sealing to edge. Bake at 350 degrees for 10 minutes or until brown. May substitute 1 cup well-drained crushed pineapple for coconut. Yield: 8 servings.

Ladonna Darnell

MOTHER'S COCONUT CREAM PIE

3 eggs, separated
3/4 cup sugar
Dash of salt
1/4 cup flour
3 cups milk
1 teaspoon vanilla extract

1 cup shredded coconut
1 baked 9-inch pie shell
1/4 teaspoon cream of tartar
1/8 teaspoon salt
6 tablespoons sugar
1/2 teaspoon vanilla extract

Beat egg yolks in mixer bowl. Add mixture of 3/4 cup sugar, dash of salt and flour gradually. Pour in milk 1 cup at a time, mixing well after each addition. Stir in 1 teaspoon vanilla. Pour into heavy saucepan. Cook over medium-low heat until thickened, stirring constantly. Cool. Add 1 cup coconut. Pour into pie shell. Beat egg whites with cream of tartar and 1/8 teaspoon salt in mixer bowl until foamy. Add 6 tablespoons sugar gradually, beating until stiff peaks form. Fold in 1/2 teaspoon vanilla. Spread over filling, sealing to edge. Sprinkle additional coconut over meringue. Bake at 350 degrees for 10 minutes or until golden brown. Yield: 6 servings.

Joyce Alexander

THREE-MINUTE COCONUT PIE

1/4 cup melted margarine
1 cup sugar
3 eggs
1/4 cup buttermilk

1 teaspoon vanilla extract
1 cup coconut
1 unbaked 8-inch pie shell

Combine cooled margarine, sugar, eggs, buttermilk and vanilla in bowl; mix well. Stir in coconut. Pour into pie shell. Bake at 325 degrees for 35 to 45 minutes or until set. Yield: 8 servings.

Virginia McQuigg

SAWDUST PIE

1 1/2 cups sugar
1 1/2 cups coconut
1 1/2 cups graham cracker
  crumbs
1 1/2 cups coarsely chopped
  pecans

7 egg whites, unbeaten
1 unbaked 9-inch pie shell
Whipped cream
Bananas, sliced

Combine sugar, coconut, crumbs, pecans and egg whites in large bowl; stir until well mixed. Pour into pie shell. Bake at 350 degrees for 30 to 35 minutes or until set; do not overbake. Top with whipped cream and sliced bananas. Serve warm. Yield: 8 servings.

Ladonna Darnell, Bernidea Fort

VANILLA CREAM PIE with Variations

1/3 **cup flour**	1/2 **teaspoon vanilla extract**
2/3 **cup sugar**	**1 baked 9-inch deep-dish**
1/4 **teaspoon salt**	**pie shell**
2 cups milk, scalded	**3 egg whites**
3 egg yolks, slightly beaten	**6 tablespoons sugar**
2 tablespoons butter	

Combine flour, sugar and salt in saucepan. Stir in milk gradually. Bring to a boil over medium heat, stirring constantly. Cook until thickened, stirring constantly. Cook for 2 minutes longer; remove from heat. Stir a small amount of hot mixture into egg yolks; stir egg yolks into hot mixture. Cook for 1 minute, stirring constantly. Add butter and vanilla. Cool slightly. Pour into pie shell. Beat egg whites in mixer bowl until soft peaks form. Add 6 tablespoons sugar gradually, beating until stiff peaks form. Spread over filling, sealing to edge. Bake at 350 degrees until brown. Yield: 8 servings.

Banana Cream Pie—Slice 3 bananas into pie shell; top with Vanilla Cream Pie filling and meringue.

Butterscotch Pie—Substitute brown sugar for granulated sugar in Vanilla Cream Pie filling and increase the butter to 3 tablespoons.

Chocolate Cream Pie—Increase sugar to 1 cup in Vanilla Cream Pie filling and add 2 ounces chopped unsweetened chocolate with milk.

Coconut Cream Pie—Add 1 cup flaked coconut to Vanilla Cream Pie filling and sprinkle 1/3 cup coconut over the meringue before baking.

Evalena England

EGGNOG CHIFFON PIE

1 envelope unflavored
 gelatin
1/4 cup milk
1 1/2 cups commercial
 eggnog
3 egg yolks, beaten
1/4 cup sugar
3 tablespoons Brandy

1/2 teaspoon vanilla extract
3 egg whites, at room
 temperature
1/4 cup sugar
1 baked 9-inch pie shell
1/2 cup whipping cream
1 tablespoon sugar
Chocolate curls

Soften gelatin in milk in small bowl for 5 to 10 minutes. Heat eggnog in double boiler over boiling water. Beat egg yolks with 1/4 cup sugar in small mixer bowl until thick. Stir 1/2 cup hot eggnog into yolk mixture; stir yolks into hot eggnog. Cook for 10 minutes or until thickened, stirring frequently. Remove from heat. Add gelatin mixture; stir until dissolved. Stir in Brandy and vanilla. Chill until consistency of unbeaten egg whites. Beat egg whites in mixer bowl until foamy. Add remaining 1/4 cup sugar 1 tablespoon at a time, beating until stiff peaks form. Fold egg whites gently into eggnog mixture. Pour into pie shell. Chill until set. Beat whipping cream with 1 tablespoon sugar in mixer bowl until stiff peaks form. Garnish with whipped cream and chocolate curls. This is a good way to use leftover eggnog. Yield: 8 servings.

Patricia Tudor

FAVORITE FRUIT PIE

1 11-ounce can mandarin
 oranges, drained
1 16-ounce can pitted red
 cherries, drained
1/4 cup flaked coconut

1 ripe banana, peeled,
 chopped
16 ounces vanilla yogurt
1 8-inch graham cracker
 pie shell

Combine oranges, cherries, coconut, banana and yogurt in large bowl; fold together gently. Pour into pie shell. Freeze for 8 hours to overnight. Remove from freezer 1 hour before serving. Yield: 6 servings.

Monica Kayse

FROZEN LEMONADE PIE

1 6-ounce can frozen
  lemonade concentrate
1 pint vanilla ice cream,
  softened

3¹/₂ cups whipped topping
1 9-inch graham cracker
  pie shell

Place lemonade concentrate in large mixer bowl. Beat for 30 seconds. Spoon in ice cream gradually; blending well. Fold in whipped topping. Add yellow food coloring if desired. Beat until smooth. Freeze until mixture will mound when dropped from spoon. Spoon into pie shell. Freeze for 4 hours or until firm. Store in freezer. Yield: 8 servings.

Kay Owen, Wanda Wiegand

GRASSHOPPER PIE

24 cream-filled chocolate
  cookies, finely crushed
¹/₄ cup melted butter
¹/₄ cup Crème de Menthe

1 13-ounce jar
  marshmallow creme
2 cups whipping cream,
  whipped

Combine cookie crumbs and butter in bowl; mix well. Reserve ¹/₂ cup mixture. Press remaining crumbs into 9-inch springform pan. Blend Crème de Menthe and marshmallow creme in bowl. Fold in whipped cream gently. Pour into prepared springform pan; sprinkle with reserved crumbs. Freeze overnight. May substitute ¹/₄ cup milk and several drops each of green food coloring and peppermint extract for Crème de Menthe. Yield: 8 servings.

Donna Hearn

ICE CREAM PIE

¹/₂ gallon Cookies-n-
  Cream ice cream,
  softened

1 9-inch chocolate crumb
  pie shell
4 or 5 Oreo cookies

Press ice cream into pie shell. Garnish with cookies. Store in freezer. Yield: 8 servings.

Terri Arnold

KEY LIME PIE

6 egg yolks, slightly beaten
1   15-ounce can
      sweetened condensed
      milk
1/2 cup lime juice

1 baked 9-inch graham
   cracker pie shell
6 egg whites
1/4 cup sugar

Combine egg yolks and condensed milk in bowl; mix well. Add lime juice; blend well. Pour into pie shell. Beat egg whites in mixer bowl until soft peaks form. Add sugar gradually, beating until stiff peaks form. Spread meringue over pie, sealing to edge. Bake at 300 degrees until color of pale honey. Yield: 8 servings.

Sandi Tipton Clark

LEMON PIE

Pulp, juice and grated rind
   of 1 lemon
1 cup sugar
3 tablespoons flour
2 egg yolks, well beaten

3/4 cup milk
2 tablespoons melted
   butter
2 egg whites, stiffly beaten
1 unbaked 9-inch pie shell

Combine lemon pulp, juice, rind, sugar, flour, egg yolks and milk in bowl; mix well. Stir in butter. Fold in stiffly beaten egg whites gently. Pour into pie shell. Bake at 350 degrees for 40 minutes. Yield: 8 servings.

Lila Mae White

LEMON SPONGE PIE

1 cup sugar
3 tablespoons flour
1/3 cup lemon juice
2 egg yolks, slightly beaten

1 cup milk
2 egg whites, stiffly beaten
Pinch of salt
1 unbaked 9-inch pie shell

Combine sugar and flour in bowl. Add lemon juice, egg yolks and milk; mix well. Fold in egg whites and salt gently. Pour into pie shell. Bake at 375 degrees for 45 minutes.
Yield: 8 servings.

Clara Nance

LEMON ICEBOX PIE

4 egg yolks
Juice of 2 lemons
1/2 cup sugar
4 egg whites, at room
   temperature

1/4 cup sugar
1 cup whipping cream,
   whipped
1 teaspoon vanilla extract
Vanilla wafer crumbs

Combine egg yolks, lemon juice and sugar in saucepan. Cook over medium heat until thickened, stirring constantly. Beat egg whites in mixer bowl until soft peaks form. Add 1/4 cup sugar gradually, beating until stiff peaks form. Fold hot cooked mixture into egg whites gently. Cool. Whip cream in small mixer bowl. Fold gently into cooled egg mixture. Sprinkle vanilla wafer crumbs over bottom of 9-inch pie plate. Pour in filling. Cover with additional vanilla wafer crumbs. Serve with whipped cream. Yield: 8 servings.

Gwen Mills

LEMONADE PIE

1 cup flour
1/2 cup margarine
1 cup chopped pecans
1 6-ounce can frozen
   lemonade concentrate,
   thawed

1 medium container
   whipped topping
1 14-ounce can
   sweetened condensed
   milk

Combine flour, margarine and pecans in bowl; mix until crumbly. Press into 9-inch pie plate. Bake at 350 degrees for 13 minutes. Blend lemonade concentrate, whipped topping and condensed milk in bowl. Pour into pie shell. Chill overnight. May substitute pink lemonade for lemonade and/or vanilla wafer crumbs for flour in pie shell or use graham cracker pie shell. Yield: 6 servings.

Laverne Hollingsworth, Clara Nance
Barbara Swank

MACAROON PIE

12 dates, chopped
1/2 cup chopped pecans
12 saltine crackers, finely
 crushed
1/4 teaspoon baking powder
1 cup sugar
3 egg whites
1 teaspoon almond extract

Combine dates, pecans, cracker crumbs, baking powder and sugar in bowl; mix well. Beat egg whites in mixer bowl until soft peaks form. Add almond extract, beating until stiff peaks form. Fold egg whites into date mixture gently. Spoon into 9-inch pie plate. Bake at 350 degrees for 20 minutes. Serve with whipped cream or ice cream. This pie forms its own shell. Yield: 8 servings.

Gladys Glanz

MINCEMEAT PIE

1 1/3 cups sugar
1/2 teaspoon salt
1/2 teaspoon cinnamon
1/4 teaspoon cloves
1/4 teaspoon ginger
1 1/2 cups chopped peeled
 apples
1 cup raisins
1/2 cup canned jellied
 cranberry sauce
1/2 cup coarsely chopped
 walnuts
1 teaspoon grated orange
 rind
1/2 teaspoon grated lemon
 rind
1/4 cup lemon juice
1 recipe 2-crust pie pastry
Butter

Combine sugar, salt, cinnamon, cloves and ginger in large bowl; mix well. Add apples, raisins, cranberry sauce, walnuts, orange rind, lemon rind and lemon juice; mix well. Spoon into pastry-lined pie plate. Dot with butter. Top with remaining pastry. Seal edge and cut vents. Bake at 400 degrees for 30 minutes or until brown. Yield: 8 servings.

Mary Cook

PEACH PIE ALASKA

1   3-ounce package
  peach gelatin
2/3 cup boiling water
1 cup vanilla ice cream
3¹/2 cups whipped topping

1 cup chopped fresh
  peaches
1 baked 9-inch deep-dish
  pie shell

Dissolve gelatin in boiling water in bowl. Add ice cream by spoonfuls; mix until smooth. Add whipped topping and peaches; mix well. Chill until partially set. Spoon into pie shell. Chill or freeze for 3 hours or until firm. Yield: 6 servings.

Betty Krueger

PEANUT BUTTER PIE

1 cup crunchy peanut
  butter
1 cup confectioners' sugar
3 ounces cream cheese,
  softened

16 ounces whipped
  topping
1   9-inch graham cracker
  pie shell

Combine first 4 ingredients in large bowl; mix well. Spoon into pie shell. Chill before serving. Yield: 8 servings.

Virginia Emmitt

PEANUT PECAN PIE

1 cup butter, melted
¹/2 cup flour
³/4 cup sugar
¹/2 to ³/4 cup packed brown
  sugar
2 eggs, beaten
1 teaspoon vanilla extract

¹/2 teaspoon cinnamon
1¹/2 cups chopped pecans
1¹/2 cups chocolate chips
1¹/2 cups peanut butter
  chips
1   9-inch graham cracker
  pie shell

Combine cooled melted butter with next 6 ingredients in large bowl; mix well. Stir in pecans, chocolate and peanut butter chips. Spoon into pie shell. Bake at 325 degrees for 1 hour. May reduce chips to 1 cup each and add 1 cup coconut. Yield: 8 servings.

Johnnie Harper

ORANGE AND PECAN PIE

3 eggs, beaten
1/2 cup sugar
1 cup dark corn syrup
1 tablespoon grated
   orange rind
1/3 cup orange juice

1 tablespoon flour
1/4 teaspoon salt
1 cup chopped pecans
1 unbaked 9-inch pie shell
3/4 cup pecan halves

Combine eggs, sugar, corn syrup, orange rind, orange juice, flour and salt in mixer bowl; beat at medium speed until well mixed. Stir in chopped pecans. Pour mixture into pie shell. Arrange pecan halves over top. Bake at 350 degrees for 55 to 60 minutes or until set. Yield: 8 servings.

Wilma Allen

SOUTHERN PECAN PIE

3 eggs
1 cup packed brown sugar
1 cup dark corn syrup
1 teaspoon vanilla extract

1 1/2 cups pecan halves
Pinch of salt
1 unbaked 9-inch deep-
   dish pie shell

Combine eggs, brown sugar, corn syrup, vanilla, pecans and salt in bowl; stir just until mixed. Pour into pie shell. Bake at 350 degrees for 45 minutes. May add 1/3 cup melted butter to filling. Yield: 8 servings.

Nancy Lockard, Peggy Posante

PECAN PIE VARIATION

Using your favorite Pecan Pie recipe, reduce pecans to 1/2 cup and add 1/2 cup semisweet chocolate chips, 1/2 cup raisins and 1 tablespoon Bourbon. Bake using recipe directions. This is a delicious change from ordinary pecan pie.

Rebecca Ray

PINTO BEAN PIE

1/2 cup cooked pinto
  beans, mashed
3 eggs
1 teaspoon vanilla extract
1/2 cup margarine, softened

1 1/2 cups packed brown
  sugar
1/2 cup sugar
1 cup coconut
1 unbaked 9-inch pie shell

Combine beans, eggs, vanilla, margarine, brown sugar, sugar and coconut in mixing bowl; mix well. Pour into pie shell. Bake at 350 degrees for 1 hour. Yield: 8 servings.

Nancy Winstead

PUMPKIN CHIFFON PIE

1 cup mashed cooked
  pumpkin
3 cups miniature
  marshmallows
1 teaspoon allspice

1/4 teaspoon salt
1 envelope whipped
  topping mix
1 baked 9-inch pie shell

Combine pumpkin, marshmallows, allspice and salt in saucepan; mix well. Cook over low heat until marshmallows are melted, stirring constantly. Cool. Prepare whipped topping mix using package directions; fold into pumpkin mixture gently. Pour into pie shell. Chill until firm. Yield: 8 servings.

Helen Lovan

PUMPKIN CUSTARD PIE

1/2 cup sugar
1 tablespoon cornstarch
2 eggs
2 cups milk
2 tablespoons butter,
  chopped

1/2 teaspoon allspice
3 tablespoons (heaping)
  pumpkin
1 unbaked 8-inch pie shell

Combine sugar and cornstarch in bowl; mix well. Add eggs; beat until light. Add milk, butter and allspice; mix well. Stir in pumpkin. Pour into pie shell. Bake at 425 degrees for 25 minutes or until set. Yield: 6 servings.

Ida L. Omer

PUMPKIN PRALINE PIE

1 unbaked 10-inch pie shell
5 tablespoons unsalted
  butter, softened
1/2 cup packed light brown
  sugar
3/4 cup chopped walnuts
1/2 cup sugar
1 tablespoon unflavored
  gelatin
1 teaspoon cinnamon
1/2 teaspoon ginger
1/2 teaspoon nutmeg
11/2 cups eggnog
3 egg yolks
1 16-ounce can mashed
  pumpkin
3 egg whites
1/4 teaspoon cream of tartar
1/4 cup sugar
1 cup whipping cream

Bake pie shell at 450 degrees for 10 minutes. Cream butter and brown sugar in mixer bowl until light and fluffy. Stir in walnuts. Spread mixture in bottom of pie shell. Bake for 5 minutes or until sugar bubbles. Cool on wire rack. Combine 1/2 cup sugar, gelatin, cinnamon, ginger and nutmeg in saucepan. Add eggnog and egg yolks; mix well. Cook over medium heat until thickened, stirring constantly; do not boil. Remove from heat. Stir in pumpkin. Cool until thick enough to mound. Beat egg whites in large bowl until foamy. Add cream of tartar. Beat until soft peaks form. Add 1/4 cup sugar gradually, beating until stiff peaks form. Spoon over pumpkin mixture. Beat whipping cream in large bowl until stiff peaks form. Fold pumpkin with egg whites into whipped cream gently. Spoon into pie shell. Chill for several hours. Garnish with additional whipped cream and pecan halves. Yield: 8 servings.

Patricia J. Tudor

RAISIN PIE

1 cup cold water
1 cup raisins
1 cup packed brown sugar
2 tablespoons flour
1 tablespoon butter
1 baked 9-inch pie shell

Combine water and raisins in saucepan. Add mixture of brown sugar and flour. Cook over medium heat until thickened, stirring constantly. Cool. Stir in butter. Pour into pie shell. Bake at 400 degrees for 40 minutes. Yield: 6 servings.

Gwen Mills

RITZ CRACKER PIE

3 egg whites
1 cup sugar
20 Ritz crackers, coarsely
  broken

1 cup chopped pecans
Strawberries
Whipped cream

Beat egg whites in mixer bowl until soft peaks form. Add sugar gradually, beating until stiff peaks form. Fold in crackers and pecans gently. Pour into well-greased 9-inch pie plate. Bake at 275 degrees for 25 minutes; do not overbrown. Cool. Top with strawberries and whipped cream. Pie should be made the day before serving. Store in refrigerator. Yield: 8 servings.

Ethel C. Thompson

PENNSYLVANIA DUTCH SHOO-FLY PIE

$1/2$ teaspoon soda
$3/4$ cup boiling water
$1/2$ cup molasses
1 egg yolk, beaten
$1/4$ cup (or less) brown
  sugar
1 unbaked 9-inch pie shell

$3/4$ cup flour
$1/2$ cup brown sugar
$1/4$ teaspoon salt
$1/8$ teaspoon nutmeg
$1/8$ teaspoon ginger
$1/8$ teaspoon cloves
2 tablespoons butter

Dissolve soda in boiling water in bowl; cool slightly. Stir in molasses, egg yolk and $1/4$ cup brown sugar. Pour into pie shell. Combine flour, $1/2$ cup brown sugar, salt, nutmeg, ginger and cloves in bowl. Cut in butter until crumbly. Sprinkle evenly over liquid. Bake at 400 degrees for 15 minutes. Reduce temperature to 350 degrees. Bake for 25 minutes longer. Do not pack brown sugar while measuring; the less brown sugar used in the filling, the drier the bottom of the pie. Yield: 8 servings.

Nancy A. Thiry

BLACK BOTTOM STRAWBERRY PIE

1/4 cup butter
20 Oreo cookies, finely
   crushed
14 whole Oreo cookies
1 quart strawberry ice
   cream, slightly softened

1 pint fresh strawberries
1/2 cup whipping cream,
   whipped

Melt butter over low heat in medium saucepan; remove from heat. Reserve 2 tablespoons cookie crumbs for topping; stir remaining crumbs into butter. Press into bottom of 9-inch pie plate. Stand whole cookies around side of pie plate. Freeze for 15 minutes. Spread strawberry ice cream evenly into cookie crust. Sprinkle with reserved crumbs. Freeze for 2 to 3 hours or until firm. Arrange whole strawberries stem end down in center of pie. Pipe whipped cream border between strawberries and cookies. Yield: 8 servings.

Juyne Bushart

FRESH STRAWBERRY PIE

1 cup sugar
1/4 cup cornstarch
2 cups water
1/8 teaspoon salt
1 tablespoon butter

Red food coloring
2 cups fresh strawberry
   halves
1 baked 10-inch pie shell
Whipped cream

Combine sugar and cornstarch in saucepan; mix well. Stir in water and salt. Cook over low heat until thickened, stirring slowly. Remove from heat. Add butter and desired amount of red food coloring; mix well. Let stand at room temperature for several hours. Alternate layers of sauce and strawberries in pie shell. Top with whipped cream. Serve pie immediately while pie shell is crisp. Yield: 8 servings.

Mary J. Abell

BETTY'S STRAWBERRY PIE

3 tablespoons strawberry
  gelatin
3 tablespoons flour
1 cup sugar

1 cup water
1 pint (or more)
  strawberries
1 baked 9-inch pie shell

Combine gelatin, flour and sugar in saucepan. Stir in water. Bring to a boil, stirring constantly. Remove from heat. Arrange whole strawberries in pie shell. Pour gelatin mixture over berries. Chill until firm. Garnish with whipped topping. Yield: 6 servings.

Betty Hunter

UPSIDE-DOWN STRAWBERRY MERINGUE PIE

3 egg whites
1/2 teaspoon vinegar
1/4 teaspoon salt
1/2 cup sugar
1/2 teaspoon vanilla extract
1 baked 9-inch pie shell
1/3 cup sugar

2 tablespoons cornstarch
1/2 cup water
2 cups strawberries,
  mashed
1 cup whipping cream,
  whipped
Whole fresh strawberries

Beat egg whites with vinegar and salt in mixer bowl until soft peaks form. Add 1/2 cup sugar and vanilla gradually, beating until stiff peaks form. Spread over bottom and side of pie shell. Bake at 325 degrees for 12 minutes. Cool. Combine 1/3 cup sugar and cornstarch in saucepan; mix well. Stir in water and mashed strawberries. Cook until mixture thickens and comes to a boil, stirring constantly. Cook for 2 minutes longer, stirring constantly. Tint with red food coloring if desired; cool slightly. Spread over meringue. Chill for several hours. Garnish with whipped cream and whole strawberries. Yield: 8 servings.

Ladonna Darnell

MOTHER'S SYRUP PIE

2 tablespoons flour
1/2 cup sugar
1 cup light corn syrup

3 eggs, beaten
1 teaspoon vanilla extract
1 unbaked 9-inch pie shell

Combine flour and sugar in bowl; mix well. Stir in corn syrup, eggs and vanilla. Pour into pie shell. Bake at 300 degrees for 1 hour or until light brown and firm. Yield: 8 servings.

Patsy Ford

TRANSPARENT PIE

Pastry for 10 pie shells
2 1/2 cups sugar
9 or 10 egg yolks

1/2 cup melted margarine
1 teaspoon vanilla extract

Divide pastry into 10 equal portions. Roll very thin on floured surface; handle as little as possible. Place on baking sheets; pierce with fork. Bake at 400 degrees; do not overbake. Combine sugar, egg yolks and margarine in double boiler. Cook over medium heat until thickened, stirring constantly. Remove from heat. Stir in vanilla. Layer pastry and filling alternately on serving plate, ending with filling. Yield: 10 to 12 servings.

Pat Gosnell

WHITE MOUNTAIN PIES

1   14-ounce can
    sweetened condensed
    milk
1   20-ounce can crushed
    pineapple, drained
1/2 cup coconut

1/2 cup chopped pecans
2 tablespoons lemon juice
16 ounces whipped
   topping
2 baked 9-inch pie shells

Combine condensed milk, pineapple, coconut, pecans and lemon juice in bowl; mix well. Fold in whipped topping gently. Spoon into pie shells. Chill until serving time. Yield: 16 servings.

Patsy Dumont

BUTTER TARTS

1 tablespoon (rounded) butter
1 cup slightly packed brown sugar
1 egg

1/2 cup (scant) raisins
1/4 cup chopped pecans
1/2 teaspoon vanilla extract
6 tart shells

Cream butter and brown sugar in mixer bowl until light and fluffy. Add egg; beat well. Stir in raisins, pecans and vanilla. Fill tart shells 3/4 full. Bake at 350 degrees for 6 to 8 minutes. Reduce oven temperature to 300 degrees. Bake for 6 to 8 minutes longer. May substitute currants for raisins. Yield: 6 tarts.

Trudie Gadjen

CHEESECAKE TARTS

24 ounces cream cheese, softened
3/4 cup sugar
3 eggs

1 tablespoon vanilla extract
24 vanilla wafers
1 can fruit pie filling

Combine cream cheese, sugar, eggs and vanilla in mixer bowl. Beat for 5 minutes. Place 1 vanilla wafer in bottom of each of 24 paper-lined muffin cups. Fill 3/4 full with batter. Bake at 350 degrees for 25 minutes. Tarts do not brown, but tops crack when done. Cool. Spoon favorite pie filling onto tarts. Store in refrigerator. Yield: 24 tarts.

Leona Fulkerson

★ Ready made pie crusts come as refrigerated, frozen and quick mixes. Regular pie pastry, graham cracker, chocolate crumb and vanilla wafer pie shells are all available at the supermarket.

PECAN TARTS

1/2 cup margarine,
  softened
3 ounces cream cheese,
  softened
1 cup sifted flour
1 egg
Dash of salt

3/4 cup packed brown sugar
1 tablespoon margarine,
  softened
2 tablespoons corn syrup
1 teaspoon vanilla extract
3/4 cup chopped pecans

Cream margarine and cream cheese in mixer bowl until light and fluffy. Add flour; mix well. Shape into 1-inch balls. Press over bottom and side of miniature muffin cups. Combine egg, salt, brown sugar, margarine, corn syrup and vanilla in mixer bowl; beat well. Stir in pecans. Fill pastry-lined cups 3/4 full. Bake at 350 degrees for 25 minutes. Store in refrigerator. Yield: 24 tarts.

Donna Barrett, Joan Butler

FLAKY PIE PASTRY

6 cups flour, sifted
1 tablespoon salt
1 pound lard

1 egg, beaten
Water

Combine flour and salt in bowl; cut in lard until crumbly. Beat egg with enough water to measure 1 cup. Add to flour; mix until smooth. Wrap in waxed paper. Store in refrigerator for up to 3 weeks. Yield: 6 pie shells.

HIGH SOFT MERINGUE

3 egg whites
1 tablespoon water

1/4 teaspoon cream of tartar
6 tablespoons sugar

Beat 3 egg whites with water in bowl until fluffy. Add cream of tartar, beating until soft peaks form. Add sugar gradually, beating until stiff peaks form. Spread over pie, sealing to edge. Bake at 400 degrees for 7 minutes. Yield: 1 meringue.

Sarah Hopson

Craftsmen are still at work in Eastern Kentucky, making Kentucky crafts sought after all over the world. This is an example of the detailed work that goes into making a dulcimer. (A stringed musical instrument.)

Special Helps

GLOSSARY OF COOKING TECHNIQUES

Bake: To cook by dry heat in an oven or under hot coals.

Bard: To cover lean meats with bacon or pork fat before cooking to prevent dryness.

Baste: To moisten, especially meats, with melted butter, pan drippings, sauce, etc. during cooking time.

Beat: To mix ingredients by vigorous stirring or with electric mixer.

Blanch: To immerse, usually vegetables or fruit, briefly into boiling water to inactivate enzymes, loosen skin, or soak away excess salt.

Blend: To combine two or more ingredients, at least 1 of which is liquid or soft, to produce a mixture that has a smooth uniform consistency quickly.

Boil: To heat any liquid until bubbly; the boiling point for water is 212 degrees, depending on altitude and atmospheric pressure.

Braise: To cook, especially meats, covered, in a small amount of liquid.

Brew: To prepare a beverage by allowing boiling water to extract flavor and/or color from certain substances such as coffee, tea, herbs or spices.

Broil: To cook by direct exposure to intense heat such as a flame or an electric heating unit.

Caramelize: To melt sugar in heavy pan over low heat until golden or light brown, stirring constantly.

Chill: To cool in refrigerator or in cracked ice.

Clarify: To remove impurities from melted butter by allowing the sediment to settle, then pouring off the clear yellow liquid. Other fats may be clarified by straining.

Cream: To blend butter, margarine, shortening, usually softened, or sometimes oil, with a granulated or crushed ingredient until the mixture is soft and creamy. It is usually described in the method as light and fluffy.

Curdle: To congeal milk with rennet or heat until solid lumps or curds are formed.

Cut in: To disperse solid shortening into dry ingredients with a knife or pastry blender. Texture of the mixture should resemble coarse cracker meal. Described in method as crumbly.

Decant: To pour a liquid such as wine or melted butter carefully from 1 container into another leaving the sediment in the original container.

Deep-fry: To cook in a deep pan or skillet containing hot cooking oil. Deep-fried foods are generally completely immersed in the hot oil and will rise to the surface when almost cooked through.

Deglaze: To heat stock, wine or other liquid in the pan in which meat has been cooked, mixing liquid with pan juices, sediment and browned bits to form a gravy or sauce base.

Degorger: To remove strong flavors or impurities before cooking, i.e. soaking ham in cold water or sprinkling vegetables with salt, then letting stand for a period of time and pressing out excess fluid.

Degrease: To remove accumulated fat from surface of hot liquids.

Dice: To cut into small cubes about 1/4-inch in size. Do not use dice unless ingredient can truly be cut into cubes.

Dissolve: To create a solution by thoroughly mixing a solid or granular substance with a liquid until no sediment remains.

Dredge: To coat completely with flour, bread crumbs, etc, usually before frying.

Fillet: To remove bones from meat or fish. (Boneless piece of fish is called a fillet. Boneless meat or chicken piece is called a filet.)

Flambé: To pour warmed Brandy or other spirits over food in a pan, then ignite and continue cooking briefly to allow alcoholic content to burn off.

Fold in: To blend a delicate frothy mixture into a heavier one so that none of the lightness or volume is lost. Using a rubber spatula, turn under and bring up and over, rotating bowl 1/4 turn after each folding motion.

Fry: To cook in a pan or skillet containing hot cooking oil. The oil should not totally cover the food.

Garnish: To decorate food before serving.

Glaze: To cover or coat with sauce, syrup, egg white, or a jellied substance. After applying, it becomes firm, adding color and flavor.

Grate: To rub food against a rough, perforated utensil to produce slivers, crumbs, curls, etc.

Gratiné: To top a sauced dish with crumbs, cheese or butter and broil until brown.

Grill: To broil, usually over hot coals or charcoal.

Grind: To cut, crush, or force through a chopper to produce small bits.

Infuse: To steep herbs or other flavorings in a liquid until liquid absorbs flavor.

Julienne: To cut vegetables or meat into long thin strips.

Knead: To press, fold, and stretch dough until smooth and elastic. Method usually notes time frame or result.

Lard: To insert strips of fat or bacon into lean meat to keep the meat moist and juicy during cooking. Larding is an internal basting technique.

Leaven: To cause batters and doughs to rise, usually by means of a chemical leavening agent. This process may occur before or during baking.

Marinate: To soak, usually in a highly seasoned oil-acid solution, to flavor and/or tenderize food.

Melt: To liquify solid foods by the action of heat.

Mince: To cut or chop into very small pieces.

Mix: To combine ingredients to distribute uniformly.

Mold: To shape into a particular form.

Panbroil: To cook in a skillet or pan using a very small amount of fat to prevent sticking.

Panfry: To cook in a skillet or pan containing only a small amount of fat.

Parboil: To partially cook in boiling water. Most parboiled foods require additional cooking with or without other ingredients.

Parch: To dry or roast slightly through exposure to intense heat.

Pit: To remove the hard inedible seed from peaches, plums, etc.

Plank: To broil and serve on a board or wooden platter.

Plump: To soak fruits, usually dried, in liquid until puffy and softened.

Poach: To cook in a small amount of gently simmering liquid.

Preserve: To prevent food spoilage by pickling, salting, dehydrating, smoking, boiling in syrup, etc. Preserved foods have excellent keeping qualities when properly prepared and then properly stored.

Purée: To reduce the pulp of cooked fruit and vegetables to a smooth and thick liquid by straining or blending.

Reduce: To boil stock, gravy or other liquid until volume is reduced, liquid is thickened and flavor is intensified.

Refresh: To place blanched drained vegetables or other food in cold water to halt cooking process.

Render: To cook meat or meat trimmings at low temperature until fat melts and can be drained and strained.

Roast: (1) To cook by dry heat either in an oven or over hot coals. (2) To dry or parch by intense heat.

Sauté: To cook in a skillet containing a small amount of hot cooking oil. Sautéed foods should never be immersed in the oil and should be stirred frequently.

Scald: (1) To heat a liquid almost to the boiling point. (2) To soak, usually vegetables or fruit, in boiling water until the skins are loosened; see blanch, which is our preferred term.

Scallop: To bake with a sauce in a casserole. The food may either be mixed or layered with the sauce.

Score: To make shallow cuts diagonally in parallel lines, especially meat.

Scramble: To cook and stir simultaneously, usually eggs.

Shirr: To crack eggs into individual buttered baking dishes, then bake or broil until whites are set. Chopped meats or vegetables, cheese, cream, or bread crumbs may also be added.

Shred: To cut or shave food into slivers.

Shuck: To remove the husk from corn or the shell from oysters, clams, etc.

Sieve: To press a mixture through a closely meshed metal utensil to make it homogeneous.

Sift: To pass, usually dry ingredients such as flour, through a fine wire mesh in order to produce a uniform consistency.

Simmer: To cook in or with a liquid at or just below the boiling point.

Skewer: (1) To thread, usually meat and vegetables, onto a sharpened rod (as in shish kabob). (2) To fasten the opening of stuffed fowl closed with small pins.

Skim: To ladle or spoon off excess fat or scum from the surface of a liquid.

Smoke: To preserve or cook through continuous exposure to wood smoke.

Steam: To cook with water vapor in a closed container, usually in a steamer.

Stew: To simmer, usually meats and vegetables, for a long period of time. Also used to tenderize meats.

Stir-fry: To cook small pieces of vegetables and/or meat in a small amount of oil in a wok or skillet over high heat, stirring constantly, until tender-crisp.

Strain: To pass through a strainer, cheesecloth or sieve in order to break down or remove the solids or impurities.

Stuff: To fill or pack cavities especially those of meats, vegetables and poultry.

Toast: To brown and crisp, usually by means of direct heat or to bake until brown.

Toss: To mix lightly with lifting motion using 2 forks or spoons.

Truss: To bind poultry legs and wings close to the body before cooking.

Whip: To beat a mixture until air has been thoroughly incorporated and the mixture is light and fluffy, the volume of mixture is greatly increased, and the mixture holds its shape.

Wilt: To apply heat causing dehydration, color change and a limp appearance.

SUBSTITUTION CHART

	Instead of:	Use:
Baking	1 teaspoon baking powder	1/4 teaspoon soda plus 1/2 teaspoon cream of tartar
	1 tablespoon cornstarch (for thickening)	2 tablespoons flour or 1 tablespoon tapioca
	1 cup sifted all-purpose flour	1 cup plus 2 tablespoons sifted cake flour
	1 cup sifted cake flour	1 cup minus 2 tablespoons sifted all-purpose flour
	1 cup fine dry bread crumbs	3/4 cup fine cracker crumbs
Dairy	1 cup buttermilk	1 cup sour milk or 1 cup yogurt
	1 cup heavy cream	3/4 cup skim milk plus 1/3 cup butter
	1 cup light cream	7/8 cup skim milk plus 3 tablespoons butter
	1 cup sour cream	7/8 cup sour milk plus 3 tablespoons butter
	1 cup sour milk	1 cup milk plus 1 tablespoon vinegar or lemon juice or 1 cup buttermilk
Seasoning	1 teaspoon allspice	1/2 teaspoon cinnamon plus 1/8 teaspoon cloves
	1 cup catsup	1 cup tomato sauce plus 1/2 cup sugar plus 2 tablespoons vinegar
	1 clove of garlic	1/8 teaspoon garlic powder or 1/8 teaspoon instant minced garlic or 3/4 teaspoon garlic salt
	1 teaspoon Italian spice	1/4 teaspoon each oregano, basil, thyme, rosemary plus dash of cayenne
	1 teaspoon lemon juice	1/2 teaspoon vinegar
	1 tablespoon mustard	1 teaspoon dry mustard
	1 medium onion	1 tablespoon dried minced onion or 1 teaspoon onion powder
Sweet	1 1-ounce square chocolate	1/4 cup cocoa plus 1 teaspoon shortening
	1 2/3 ounces semisweet chocolate	1 ounce unsweetened chocolate plus 4 teaspoons granulated sugar
	1 cup honey	1 to 1 1/4 cups sugar plus 1/4 cup liquid or 1 cup corn syrup or molasses
	1 cup granulated sugar	1 cup packed brown sugar or 1 cup corn syrup, molasses or honey minus 1/4 cup liquid

EQUIVALENT CHART

	When the recipe calls for:	Use:
Baking	½ cup butter	4 ounces
	2 cups butter	1 pound
	4 cups all-purpose flour	1 pound
	2½ to 5 cups sifted cake flour	1 pound
	1 square chocolate	1 ounce
	1 cup semisweet chocolate pieces	6 ounces
	4 cups marshmallows	1 pound
	2¼ cups packed brown sugar	1 pound
	4 cups confectioners' sugar	1 pound
	2 cups granulated sugar	1 pound
Cereal–Bread	1 cup fine dry bread crumbs	4 to 5 slices
	1 cup soft bread crumbs	2 slices
	1 cup small bread cubes	2 slices
	1 cup fine cracker crumbs	28 saltines
	1 cup fine graham cracker crumbs	15 crackers
	1 cup vanilla wafer crumbs	22 wafers
	1 cup crushed corn flakes	3 cups uncrushed
	4 cups cooked macaroni	8 ounces uncooked
	3½ cups cooked rice	1 cup uncooked
Dairy	1 cup shredded cheese	4 ounces
	1 cup cottage cheese	8 ounces
	1 cup sour cream	8 ounces
	1 cup whipped cream	½ cup heavy cream
	⅔ cup evaporated milk	1 small can
	1⅔ cups evaporated milk	1 13-ounce can
Fruit	4 cups sliced or chopped apples	4 medium
	1 cup mashed banana	3 medium
	2 cups pitted cherries	4 cups unpitted
	3 cups shredded coconut	½ pound
	4 cups cranberries	1 pound
	1 cup pitted dates	1 8-ounce package
	1 cup candied fruit	1 8-ounce package
	3 to 4 tablespoons lemon juice plus 1 tablespoon grated lemon rind	1 lemon
	⅓ cup orange juice plus 2 teaspoons grated orange rind	1 orange
	4 cups sliced peaches	8 medium
	2 cups pitted prunes	1 12-ounce package
	3 cups raisins	1 15-ounce package

	When the recipe calls for:	Use:
Meat	4 cups chopped cooked chicken 3 cups chopped cooked meat 2 cups cooked ground meat	1 5-pound chicken 1 pound, cooked 1 pound, cooked
Nuts	1 cup chopped nuts	4 ounces shelled 1 pound unshelled
Vegetables	2 cups cooked green beans 2½ cups lima beans or red beans 4 cups shredded cabbage 1 cup grated carrot 8 ounces fresh mushrooms 1 cup chopped onion 4 cups sliced or chopped potatoes 2 cups canned tomatoes	½ pound fresh or 1 16-ounce can 1 cup dried, cooked 1 pound 1 large 1 4-ounce can 1 large 4 medium 1 16-ounce can

Measurement Equivalents

1 tablespoon = 3 teaspoons 2 tablespoons = 1 ounce 4 tablespoons = ¼ cup 5⅓ teaspoons = ⅓ cup 8 tablespoons = ½ cup 12 tablespoons = ¾ cup 16 tablespoons = 1 cup 1 cup = 8 ounces or ½ pint 4 cups = 1 quart 4 quarts = 1 gallon	1 6½ to 8-ounce can = 1 cup 1 10½ to 12-ounce can = 1¼ cups 1 14 to 16-ounce can = 1¾ cups 1 16 to 17-ounce can = 2 cups 1 18 to 20-ounce can = 2½ cups 1 20-ounce can = 3½ cups 1 46 to 51-ounce can = 5¼ cups 1 6½ to 7½-pound can or Number 10 = 12 or 13 cups

Metric Equivalents

The metric measures are approximate benchmarks for purposes of home food preparation.

Liquid	Dry
1 teaspoon = 5 milliliters 1 tablespoon = 15 milliliters 1 fluid ounce = 30 milliliters 1 cup = 250 milliliters 1 pint = 500 milliliters	1 quart = 1 liter 1 ounce = 30 grams 1 pound = 450 grams 2.2 pounds = 1 kilogram

MICROWAVE TIPS

- Always choose the minimum cooking time. Remember, food continues to cook after it is removed from the microwave.
- Keep your microwave clean. Built-up grease or food spatters can slow cooking times.
- When poaching or frying an egg in a browning dish, always prick the center of the yolk with a fork to keep the egg from exploding.
- Do not try to hard-cook eggs in a shell in a microwave. They will build up pressure and burst.
- Do not use metal dishes or aluminum foil except as specifically recommended by the manufacturer of your microwave.
- Never use a foil tray over ¾ inch deep in your microwave.
- When heating TV-style dinners, remove the foil cover, then place tray back in carton. Food will heat only from the top.
- Be sure to prick potatoes before baking to allow steam to escape.
- Cut a small slit in pouch-packed frozen foods before heating in microwave to allow steam to escape.
- When placing more than one food item in microwave, arrange foods in a circle near edges of oven.
- Cover foods that need to be steamed or tenderized.
- Do not try to pop popcorn without a microwave-approved corn popper.

DID YOU KNOW YOU CAN...?
- (Use High setting for the following unless otherwise indicated.)
- Use your microwave oven to melt chocolate, to soften cream cheese and to soften or melt butter.
- Roast shelled nuts for 6 to 10 minutes, stirring frequently.
- Peel fruit or tomatoes. Place in 1 cup hot water. Microwave for 30 to 45 seconds; remove skins easily.
- Plump dried fruit by placing in a dish with 1 to 2 teaspoons water. Cover tightly with plastic wrap. Heat for ½ to 1½ minutes.
- Precook barbecued ribs or chicken until almost done, then place on the grill to sear and add a charcoal flavor.
- Soften brown sugar by placing in a dish with a slice of bread or apple. Heat for 30 to 45 seconds, stirring once.
- Dry bread for crumbs or croutons. Place cubed or crumbled bread on paper towels. Heat for 6 to 7 minutes, stirring occasionally.
- Warm baby food or baby bottles by removing metal lid and heating for 10 to 20 seconds.
- Freshen chips and crackers by heating for 15 to 30 seconds. Let stand for 2 to 3 minutes.
- Dry herbs by placing on paper towels and heating for 2 to 3 minutes or until herbs are dry.
- Ripen an avocado by heating on Low for 2 to 4 minutes.

INDEX

564

572

The cover of our cookbook is an original work by artist Jan Anderson. Jan is a native of Western Kentucky, and has been a professional artist for eleven years. Personally signed reproduction prints are available for sale by the Purchase Council (size 17¹/₂x22 inches).

You may order as many prints as you wish for the price of $20.00 per print plus $5.00 postage and handling per order. Mail to:

Kentucky Chapter 32
Telephone Pioneers of America
P.O. Box 32410
534 Armory Place B-9
Louisville, Kentucky 40232

Number of prints ordered _____

Amount enclosed_____

Please make checks payable to:
Kentucky Chapter 32 Purchase Council, TPA

Please Print:

Name _____

Street Address_____

City, State, Zip_____

Your Tele. No. _____
(in case we have questions)

You may order as many of our cookbooks as you wish for the price of $7.00 each plus $1.50 postage and handling per book ordered. Mail to:

Kentucky Chapter 32
Telephone Pioneers of America
P.O. Box 32410
534 Armory Place B-9
Louisville, Kentucky 40232

Save postage and handling by picking up your books at the Chapter Pioneer office located in:
Room B-9, 534 Armory Place
Louisville, Kentucky
Tele. No. (502) 582-8319

Number of books ordered _____

Amount enclosed _____

Please make checks payable to:
Kentucky Chapter 32, TPA

Please Print:

Name _____

Street Address _____

City, State, Zip _____

Your Tele. No. _____
(in case we have questions)